O9-BUC-320

WITHDRAWN

Where Law Ends

RANDOM HOUSE

NEW YORK

Where Law Ends

INSIDE THE MUELLER INVESTIGATION

Andrew Weissmann

Quotations are not verbatim and are based on my memory, as the Department of Justice prohibited my keeping any notes or other documents upon leaving the Special Counsel's Office.

Copyright © 2020 by Andrew Weissmann LLC

All rights reserved.

Published in the United States by Random House, an imprint and division of Penguin Random House LLC, New York.

RANDOM HOUSE and the HOUSE colophon are registered trademarks of Penguin Random House LLC.

Hardback ISBN 978-0-593-13857-1
Ebook ISBN 978-0-593-13858-8

Printed in the United States of America on acid-free paper

randomhousebooks.com

9 8 7 6 5 4 3 2 1

First Edition

Book design by Debbie Glasserman

To Mom and Dad, with love and admiration

Wherever law ends, tyranny begins.

—JOHN LOCKE

■ CONTENTS

■ INTRODUCTION

IT WAS SUNDAY AFTERNOON, March 24, 2019. I was passing through the Lincoln Tunnel in my old gray Subaru, heading toward the soulless thruways that stretch between New York City and Washington, D.C. On the passenger side floor was Innis, my English cocker spaniel, curled up and dozing. His breeder had promised me he was a great travel dog who would easily be lulled to sleep in a moving vehicle, a quality that had come in handy, given my peripatetic lifestyle over the years, ping-ponging between my home in New York and my job at the Department of Justice. The trips had grown increasingly rare, though, as I found myself working around the clock in Washington.

As numbing as this drive usually was, this particular trip was wistful. I had spent the past twenty-two months working as a prosecutor for Robert S. Mueller III, leading one of the three main teams in the Special Counsel's Office charged with investigating Russian interference in the 2016 presidential election and coordination between the Russians and the presidential campaign of Donald J. Trump. Two days before, on Friday, March 22, we had finally delivered our report, all 448 pages of it, to the new attorney general, William Barr. We were feeling a note of finality to our collective mission. The Special Counsel's Office had already largely dissolved. We'd said our goodbyes. I was driving back to Washington, one last time, to polish a couple of last "memos to file" and organize the documents in my office for the government archivists who would preserve our papers for posterity. At age sixty-one, after more than twenty years as a federal prosecutor, I would be returning to teach at NYU School of Law as a private citizen in my hometown.

After months of speculation, the press now had written confirmation from Barr himself that our report had been submitted and that he would soon be issuing a public statement about it. All weekend, the drumbeat in the media grew louder, as the press and many other Americans who felt invested in our work awaited the attorney general's announcement. Internally, of course, we already knew what the report contained and had not breathed a word of it, true to our no-leak reputation.

The special counsel's report was a devastating recitation of how Russian government operatives had infiltrated our electoral process, a conclusion that we all believed to be our most important long-term finding and one that required immediate and decisive action by our political leaders. As to whether any member of the Trump campaign, or anyone else, conspired with the Russians, our report was mixed. We had found insufficient evidence to criminally charge a conspiracy with the Russians beyond a reasonable doubt—the high standard of proof required for any criminal charge and conviction. But the frequency and seriousness of interactions we uncovered between the campaign and the Russians were nevertheless chilling, with Trump campaign officials both receptive to, and soliciting, Russian assistance throughout the summer and fall of 2016.

The final question our investigation pursued was whether the president had obstructed justice before or after our office was up and running. The facts here were no less appalling, although we had not indicted the president or, frustratingly, even taken the final leap of putting a label on what the facts added up to. Instead, our report set out numerous episodes that provided clear evidence against the president. However, we were forbidden from indicting him for these crimes, as we were employees of the Department of Justice and bound to follow an internal Department policy that no president could be indicted while in office—whether we agreed with that rule or not.

Given this idiosyncratic circumstance, Mueller had decided it would be unfair to say that we found the president had committed a crime, as Trump would not be able to challenge our conclusion in court, at least until he left office. Thus our report laid out the proof of his criminal conduct in detail, but did not give our legal assessment of it—we never said outright that he'd committed a crime. Instead, we had left it to Congress to make its own assessment of our evidence, or to another prosecutor in the future, who would be free to indict the president once he'd left office.

We were well aware that this approach would read awkwardly and, frankly, as a transparent attempt to hide our true thoughts. Anyone reading the report as a whole would see that when the evidence did not rise to such a level, we had explicitly said so, including when the conduct was that of the president. By contrast, our silence on whether Trump had obstructed justice—whether the president of the United States had broken the law—would be deafening. When he was not guilty of certain crimes, we said so; and when he was, we were silent. But we had found no other way of dealing with Mueller's decision to abide by the principle of protecting anyone who could not have his or her day in court.

I spent most of the five-hour drive to Washington awaiting news of Barr's announcement on the radio. I was listening on my iPhone, as the radio in my car had been on the fritz ever since a mechanic had jump-started my battery improperly around the time I'd joined the Special Counsel's Office, and I'd never found a moment to get it fixed. For hours, there was only endless blather and speculation on air, filling the time. But, late that afternoon, as I drove along the New Jersey Turnpike, that changed: There was real news to report.

My ears perked up. The CNN announcers reported that they had their hands on a four-page letter from the attorney general, summarizing the conclusions of our report. This immediately struck me as odd. We knew that only diehards would read the entire report, which was written by lawyers and filled with dense legalese, so we had prepared summaries of our findings, highlighting key conclusions and evidence in both volumes of the report. When Barr announced he would be issuing something public shortly after receiving our report, I had assumed it would be these summaries. That would be the easiest way to get information to the public quickly, as Barr professed he wanted to do, and would not carry any risk of skewing one way or the other what the special counsel had determined. After all, the whole point of appointing a special counsel was to ensure an investigation of the president would be conducted independently, rather than led by the attorney general, a presidentially appointed cabinet member who might, therefore, be beholden to the subject of the probe. But from what I was now hearing, Barr had clearly not taken this approach, as our summaries were much longer than four pages.

The voices on the radio then began breathlessly announcing key takeaways from Barr's letter: Mueller had concluded that the Russians had meddled in the 2016 presidential election. Mueller had concluded that there was no evidence of collusion. Mueller had not found that the president obstructed justice, but neither did he find that the president had not obstructed justice. Instead, they explained, the letter claimed that the special counsel had left the obstruction determination to the attorney general—and that Barr, along with his deputy Rod Rosenstein, had concluded that there'd been no obstruction by the president. That was that: Trump was cleared.

I stiffened up behind the wheel. Something was very wrong. That was not, in fact, what our report said. I figured that in its initial, quick reading of the letter, CNN had screwed up. I kept listening, expecting clarifications, but none came. How could Barr and Rosenstein have weighed in at all? The whole reason Mueller had been appointed by Rosenstein was because the Department of Justice had determined that it could not objectively investigate the president—a classic fox guarding the henhouse issue. That Barr had recently replaced Jeff Sessions as the attorney general did not change that legal issue one whit; and how could Rosenstein now do an about-face and say the country didn't need an independent assessment? And their assessment of the facts in our report showed why they should not be making this call.

Knowing the evidence inside and out, I found it inconceivable that Barr and Rosenstein had digested our voluminous discussion of the facts and come away believing that the president had not obstructed justice. Barr could not have written what they said, I thought. But when our report would become public, it was obvious that Barr had spun our findings for political gain, at best, and lied for the president, at worst. Because the media did not yet know what our investigation had actually found, no one was raising that possibility. No one had reason to be skeptical that Barr's letter accurately reflected our report, and no one was noting that it barely quoted from the document itself—that Barr had

not even relayed a single full sentence we'd written. By now, I was closing in on Washington, D.C., and stepped on the gas. I needed to read
this letter for myself.

When I had learned, a few months earlier, that Barr had been nominated to replace the much-beleaguered Jeff Sessions as attorney general,
the news had brought a sense of relief. All my colleagues in the Special
Counsel's Office believed, as I did, that Barr would likely be an institutionalist. He had already run the Department of Justice earlier in his
career—in fact, he had signed my framed certificate appointing me as a
federal prosecutor in 1991. Barr, I thought, would be like Sessions, who
understood the attorney general's unique place in the firmament of cabinet members: a political appointee on whom it was incumbent to keep
his arm of the government independent of politics.

Sessions had many flaws and held many views that I found antithetical to the ideals of the Department of Justice, but he understood the
need for the Department to be independent. During his tenure, at the
outset of the Trump era, he had thrown his body in front of efforts by
the administration to make law enforcement just another arm of the
political machine they were running out of the White House, resisting
the president's remarkable call for the Department to prosecute Democrats, for example—something more in keeping with a tin-pot dictator
than the leader of the free world. And he had paid a significant price for
doing his job and upholding the principles of his office: He was publicly
humiliated by the president and ultimately fired. We were counting on
Barr, with his prior experience and intellectual heft, to hold that line and
maintain the separation of power that is so vital to a democracy.

Sheltering the Department from the political winds in Washington
is always important, but it seemed particularly crucial now. The Trump
presidency was revealing how much our system of checks and balances
drew its power and stability from historical norms, rather than hard-
and-fast legal rules—and those norms were shattering. With the president seeking to use the Department of Justice as a political weapon, the
attorney general's independence would be needed to prevent us turning
into a banana republic.

Which is not to say that all of us in the Special Counsel's Office fully
trusted Barr; I'd read the long, unsolicited memo he had sent to the president's lawyers months before his nomination, arguing that our investi-

gation was illegal, ill-advised, and unwarranted. But I also knew that Barr and his wife were friends with Mueller and his family, and I had watched Barr at his confirmation hearing go out of his way to praise Mueller, saying that he did not believe Mueller would ever engage in a politically motivated witch hunt and thus undercutting Trump's long-standing line of attack on our boss. I expected to disagree, personally, with some of Barr's law enforcement priorities, but having a smart and principled leader overseeing the Department was all I was entitled to ask for.

My drive to Washington had gone from wistful to filled with disbelief and alarm. My mind was racing, but everything else was proceeding in slow motion. It seemed to take days to finally reach D.C. I pulled into my condo's underground garage and ran upstairs, dog in tow; Innis's usual post-trip walk would have to wait until after I read the attorney general's letter. I unlocked the door to my apartment and, dropping everything on the floor, pulled out my iPad and found Barr's letter online.

The letter indeed purported "to summarize the principal conclusions reached by the Special Counsel and the results of his investigation," but it contained so many deceptions, it was hard to take them all in. Some were delicately worded obfuscations. Some were unbridled lies.

Barr's letter claimed that we "did not find that the Trump campaign or anyone associated with it conspired or coordinated with Russia in its efforts to influence the 2016 U.S. presidential election." In fact, we had found a lot of evidence of the campaign coordinating with Russians; what our report actually said was that this evidence was not sufficient to charge the president or any of his campaign staff with a criminal conspiracy. Any lawyer would know that the two are vastly different—and the attorney general surely understood the distinction. Yet Barr did not acknowledge that. Instead, he chose to say we did not "find" a conspiracy or coordination—which slyly presented our report in laymen's terms as a complete exoneration.

The letter was just as pernicious for what it omitted. On the issue of obstruction of justice—which comprised the entirety of the second volume of our report—not one word was said about the facts we'd documented, including the president's many egregious acts that we'd uncovered through interviews with his own staff. There was nothing about the president's maneuvering to fire the special counsel and rid himself of our investigation, and then covering up his attempts to fire us, even going so far as instructing his White House counsel to concoct a bogus memo for the White House files. Instead, Barr's letter merely explained that we looked at "a number of actions by the President"; it then minimized our findings by noting that most of the evidence we recounted was already public—again, a statement that was literally true but hid the damning nonpublic facts that were documented in our report for the first time. Why would one write that particular statement other than to purposely distort our report's factual findings? There was no reason, I thought, other than to mislead the American people.

Moreover, Barr took it upon himself to make the ultimate conclusion about what all of this obstruction evidence meant, announcing his own finding that the president had not broken the law. He wrote barely a word about the procedural dilemma Mueller faced on the obstruction question, or the reasoning that had led Mueller to withhold his judgment in the report. Barr omitted all that, explaining only that Mueller ran up against "difficult issues of law and fact" and ultimately "did not draw a conclusion."

This had the effect of portraying Mueller's principled refusal to answer the obstruction question as an inability to answer it because it was too hard a call. And by implying there'd been such an unexplained hole at the center of our report, Barr cleared the way to step in and fill it, deciding for himself that the president's conduct did not warrant a criminal charge.

Something I knew, and which Barr did not divulge in his letter, made this sleight of hand especially chilling: Mueller had informed Barr weeks before that our report would take this approach with respect to the obstruction determination—he had run our entire plan by Barr, and Barr had not raised a single concern or objection. It now seemed clear that Barr had seen his opportunity to defuse the incriminating facts uncovered by our investigation, undermining the very reason for an independent special counsel.

Barr had been unmasked. His public face as an institutionalist hid a political soul. But this was apparent for now only to us, in the Special Counsel's Office. It would be weeks before everyone else knew—which, it is now clear, was precisely the strategy. Barr had just dramatically shaped the public narrative of our findings. Even after our report was released, it would have to compete with this alternate and counter-factual perception of it, which Barr would go on driving home in press conferences, understanding correctly that his televised summary would be more penetrating than a turgid legal document the size of a very large brick.

I stood inside the doorway of my apartment, holding my iPad, in a state of disbelief. I could not fathom that our work over the past twenty-two months was ending like this. We had gone out of our way to be fair and impartial, to conduct ourselves with professionalism, and to pressure test our investigation and its conclusions. We had given the subjects of the investigation the benefit of the doubt in our report, over and over, and had not leaked a single bit of embarrassing or damning information—only to now be blindsided by a political actor's efforts to twist our investigation. We had just been played by the attorney general.

Before Mueller was appointed as special counsel, there was a general malaise in Washington, a feeling that our constitutional structures and the checks and balances of our system were deteriorating. Trump's fury about the appointment of Mueller and the very existence of our office could largely be explained as rage against any check on his power, of a piece with his war on the press and anyone else who challenges his views. The attorney general is supposed to be a key institutional watchdog to uphold that rule of law from attacks—indeed, if not the head of the Department of Justice, then who? But Barr had cast himself as a partisan.

I had seen an analogous dereliction of duty time and again during my prosecutorial career, most notably in the failure of numerous financial watchdogs to prevent or at least blow the whistle on the corrupt leaders of the Enron Corporation as they pulled off one of the world's most lucrative and destructive corporate frauds. But Barr's complicity was far worse, as it struck at America's core democratic architecture. That Barr and his wife were personal friends of Mueller and his family struck an especially painful chord. Barr had betrayed both friend and country.

. . .

At home in Washington that night, I made the decision to write this book. It was something several of us in the Special Counsel's Office had been discussing for months. Some thought an insider's account of our investigation had to be written, but I was torn. Didn't we speak with one voice through our final report, like a jury delivering a verdict? Wouldn't that be what Mueller, a man whom I revere, wanted?

I thought I knew the answer to that latter question, having worked for Mueller for years prior to our time together in the Special Counsel's Office, serving as his special counsel, and then general counsel, when he was the director of the Federal Bureau of Investigation. I knew he abhorred the limelight and wished only to do his job as quietly as possible; paradoxically, this was part of what made him a hero to every federal prosecutor I'd ever known. Mueller would not be writing a book about this experience—or any other facet of his career. I knew his view of the press: "If you live by the press, you die by the press."

But I also knew another side of Mueller, one that supported transparency and candor. As government lawyers, we both believed our work carried with it a special obligation to the public. I had worked as a public servant for twenty years, under Democrats and Republicans, and had served under every president of the United States since 1991. I had prosecuted small cases that received no press attention, and high-profile ones against the bosses of New York organized crime families and the leaders of the Enron Corporation. Drilled into every federal prosecutor worth her salt is a conviction that, no matter how prominent or peripheral the case, and whether speaking in court or publicly, you must never lie, mislead, or spin. Government lawyers are not private defense counsels, who are ethically entitled to present the facts of a case in a light most favorable to their clients. Instead, we are paid by the American taxpayers, and owe them the unvarnished truth, even when the truth is unfavorable or embarrassing.

Mueller embodied this principle, and I'd seen him adhere to it faithfully under literal life-or-death circumstances while working at the FBI in the spring of 2013. A bomb had gone off at the finish line of the Boston Marathon, killing three people and injuring scores of others. The perpetrators were still at large, and we had no idea how many conspirators were involved or if other attacks were planned. We'd assembled at the Bureau's main headquarters in Washington, in a windowless, secure facility known as the Strategic Information and Operations Center, which had been created after the 9/11 attacks as a kind of situation room for coordinating a response to a terrorist event. We'd identified two potential perpetrators on video surveillance footage of the finish line: "White Hat" and "Black Hat," as we called them based on their caps. White Hat would soon be killed in a shootout in Watertown, Massachusetts, after killing an MIT security officer, but the whereabouts of his Black Hat accomplice were still unknown, and the governor had just put the area on lockdown. The atmosphere was stressful and unnerving, and I had a personal connection to the attacks: My sister lived nearby and my nephew was then attending MIT.

Even in the wee hours of the morning, SIOC was a beehive of agents and analysts, busily running down lead after lead. Still, there was no feeling of chaos or crisis within those walls. Everything was business as usual under Mueller's sangfroid, a steadiness he managed to project simply by standing at the center of a room: tall and slender, soft-spoken but austere. The old trope I'd always heard in war movies or expressed by actual veterans—"He's someone you want to be in a foxhole with"—had never really resonated with me until that moment. I felt both calmer and safer knowing he was at the helm.

Mueller had been up all night. Countless urgent questions and decision points were being thrown at him, which he dispatched with his trademark speed. In the midst of this turbulence, he saw me out of the corner of his eye and beckoned me over. "I need you to pull all the information in our files on Black Hat and White Hat," he said. "Whatever we have: Gather it together, sanitize it for PII"—personal identifying information, such as social security numbers or addresses, which the Bureau is not permitted to publicly release—"and make copies that we can distribute to the press first thing in the morning."

We'd already discovered that, years earlier, the FBI had received a tip of questionable reliability from the Russian government about one of the alleged perpetrators. The FBI had followed up appropriately, only to wind up empty-handed, though we did not yet know that at the time. Mueller knew there'd be a tremendous amount of second-guessing by the press and the public; questions about whether the Bureau had an opportunity to prevent the marathon bombing would be understandable.

But he did not want to wait until we could answer that question our-selves to release this underlying information that would prompt it. "Nothing good comes from not disclosing it," he instructed. "Get it out." Even at that moment, with a terrorist still at large and the threat of more attacks uncertain, he made sure the American people had the facts to which they were entitled.

The example set by Mueller in the days after the Boston bombing informs both why and how this book was written. What we did and how we did it, and what we did not do, are important to record. I was a history major in college and knew how many stories had been lost to history because they were rarely written down. Historians try valiantly to resurrect these voices through scraps of evidence, particularly those of women, African Americans, and the poor—but many others as well. I knew from this experience that if the Special Counsel's Office did not write our own story, it would be written for us by outsiders who did not know what had occurred. The facts would be lost forever.

I had read numerous books on the Watergate investigations and prosecutions, and even further back in history, on the Nuremberg trials of German war criminals after World War II. Archibald Cox and Leon Jaworski, Robert Jackson and Telford Taylor, all had written illuminat-ing accounts of these historic investigations and trials. We have the ben-efit of these and many other firsthand accounts to understand those events. The special counsel's investigation is also an important story to be told, I believe, and one we must add to the historical record. And the historical precedents for this book point the way toward this procedural account that explains our investigative process. That we are in an era in which conspiracy theories and wild speculation masquerade as truth makes it all the more important to have a factual record for the future. Reasoned argument has been replaced by personal taunts. This book will permit the reader to replace invective with fact.

This account is meant to provide the public with the transparency and candor necessary to assess our actions, as well as to understand the failings in the system our nation has in place to undertake an investiga-tion of a sitting president, for good or bad. There is one caveat, however. I am limited by law, not desire, in certain things I can discuss in this book. I cannot address what happened inside the grand jury, unless it has been released already by court order. It is illegal to speak about grand jury matters, except if you are a witness who was called to the grand jury. I also cannot reveal any information that is classified, as it is illegal to do so unless and until it is unclassified. And this entire book had to go through a legal process called prepublication review, which permits the government to read the manuscript and delete material that it deems to violate a legitimate government privilege. Such a privilege would include keeping secret certain sensitive law enforcement techniques that are not generally known, which if made public would diminish their effectiveness by alerting the targets to their use.

Other than these restrictions, this book records our work in the Special Counsel's Office and how it culminated in our end product, the final report issued on March 22, 2019, to the attorney general of the United States.

The principal challenge to our investigation was not the public glare, or the Fox News diatribes, or the president's ad hominem attacks. It was the threat posed by the unique powers of the president that were continually wielded against us: the power to fire us and to pardon wrongdoers who might otherwise cooperate with our investigation. Within weeks of commencing our work, our team's very existence was in doubt, and though the threat of our firing ebbed and flowed throughout, it never entirely abated. This sword of Damocles affected our investigative decisions, leading us at certain times to act less forcefully and more defensively than we might have. It led us to delay or ultimately forgo entire lines of inquiry, particularly regarding the president's financial ties to Russia. Such decisions were not made lightly, nor were they supported unanimously in our office—far from it, in fact. But as Mueller had oft told his staff at the FBI, paraphrasing a famous quote, "We are here to defend democracy, not practice it."

For some, it may be easy to interpret these choices as evidence of a lack of courage or tenacity. But for me the picture is more complex. Everyone in our office, and Mueller especially, understood that Russian interference in our democratic process is an existential threat to our country. It could not be more serious, even though we as a nation have largely ignored it. Russia's attack on our elections was a key issue that the special counsel was tasked with investigating and reporting on, and we did not want anything to limit our ability to uncover and disclose this overriding peril to the American public. Mueller had the task of assessing whether any given investigative step that risked inflaming Trump, and provoking our firing, was important enough to warrant the risk.

But there was yet another kind of disruptive interference that no normal criminal investigation faces. The president's dangling of pardons to those who were considering cooperating with our investigation served, by design, to thwart our uncovering the true facts. Thus, when within days of receiving our report, Barr told Congress that President Trump had fully cooperated with our investigation—in fact, Trump had hampered our ability to get to the ground truth by discouraging cooperation by witnesses—it was merely one more deception that rewrote the reality we in the office had personally experienced every day. (That Trump never agreed to be interviewed made Barr's claim that the president had fully cooperated with us a particularly blatant lie.)

This book should be understood as a record of my reckoning with the successes and failures of our investigation as I watched its afterlife unfold in real time. I began writing it not long after reading Barr's letter on March 24, 2019, and in the intervening year, I have seen the president's unmoored behavior, enabled by the Department of Justice and unchecked by the U.S. Senate. With the upcoming 2020 election, I have recognized the continued saliency of the information documented in our report while also witnessing the vehement distortions of it, a concerted refusal to deal with the fact that we were attacked by a foreign adversary and will continue to be unless we take decisive action. It has been hard not to be dispirited and to question key decisions: Should we have subpoenaed the president to testify in the grand jury, when he continued to refuse a voluntary interview? Should we have conducted a more expansive investigation? Should we have reached a conclusion as to the president's obstruction of justice?

These questions, among many others that have received less attention, are the focus of this book, and a focus that has undeniably sharpened as I've watched the actions by the president, Barr, and other administration and congressional enablers in the days, weeks, and months after our report was finalized. The president, encouraged by a team of sycophants, has disregarded the law again and again, and even duplicated some of the very crimes we discussed in our report: soliciting foreign aid to cheat in the upcoming election during his infamous call with the Ukrainian president, then intimidating witnesses who dared to speak truth to power during the impeachment hearings that were provoked by that misconduct.

The president is unchastened by the past; he seems liberated by no longer having to worry about the rule of law that had been embodied in Robert Mueller. The president's behavior immediately after our report was submitted was of course not within the scope of our investigation, but I find it hard not to wonder: If right after our investigation concluded, he is soliciting foreign leaders to gain a tactical advantage in his presidential bid, had he done it beforehand, and we missed it?

And thus the question arises: Had we given it our all—had we used all available tools to uncover the truth, undeterred by the onslaught of the president's unique powers to undermine our efforts? As proud as I am of the work our team did—the unprecedented number of people we indicted and convicted and in record speed for any similar investigation—I know the hard answer to that simple question: We could have done more. This is the story of our investigation and the choices we made, for all to see and judge and learn from.

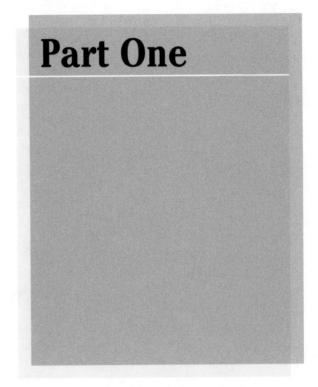

Part One

■ CHAPTER 1

The Beginning: Spring 2017

I SHOWED UP FOR my first full day of work at the Special Counsel's Office in Washington on the morning of June 5, 2017. The offices that the government had initially assigned us were cavernous and windowless, an unused basement of the Justice Department's Patrick Henry Building, two blocks north of the Mall. The space was located behind two steel doors off the lobby and down a long hall into the bowels of the building; it felt hollow and almost forgotten, like a back-office mail room. We were told that, until recently, it had housed attorneys in the Justice Department's Civil Rights Division, which is responsible for upholding some of our nation's most precious ideals. The Trump administration was gutting the division. Walking in that morning, I could not help but appreciate the irony that our team was now moving in.

Robert Mueller had been appointed as special counsel three weeks earlier. His small staff so far consisted largely of people, like myself, who had worked with Mueller previously, though some were strangers to me. This reflected Mueller's strong preference for surrounding himself with colleagues he knew and trusted to work with enough tenacity to meet his exacting expectations. The director, as I still referred to him, had little patience for incompetence or listlessness. If he thought you were hand-wringing unnecessarily, or puttering around on a case without a sufficient sense of urgency or purpose, he'd subject you to a favorite direction: "Stop playing with your food!"

Mueller had already established a structure for our investigation. The Special Counsel's probe would be carried out by three principal teams—Team R, Team M, and Team 600—each with its own complement of attorneys, FBI agents, and analysts, and a small shared squad of paralegals. Team R would cover everything related to Russian interference in the 2016 election—unless it involved Trump's campaign manager, Paul Manafort, and his cohorts. Team M would probe Manafort's activities and those with whom he worked. Team 600, meanwhile, would examine obstructions of justice—either before the special counsel had been appointed or after. (Team 600 was named after the number in the Department's special counsel internal regulations that gave us the mandate to examine obstruction.) Mueller assigned me to lead Team M— the Manafort team—but other than me, Team M did not yet exist. I had no other prosecutors, investigators, or analysts.

The woman who stepped forward to greet me as I walked in was a prototypical Mueller employee. Beth A. McGarry had worked as an assistant U.S. attorney under Mueller decades ago, when he was the U.S. attorney in San Francisco. Now, he'd coaxed her out of retirement and tasked her with overseeing the office's operational functions—everything from the bureaucratic maneuvering required to bring over personnel from other divisions of the Justice Department, to outfitting our office with all the supplies we'd need to do our work. The job amounted to building an aircraft for us while we were already up in the air trying to fly it. But Mueller knew McGarry was up to the challenge. She was immaculately organized, adept, and as blunt as a firecracker. Before long, we would all start calling her by her initials: "BAM."

After exchanging information about all the different people we knew in common—a cherished ritual among longtime career Justice Department attorneys—BAM cut off our chitchat to get to work. "What do you need?" she asked.

"I could use a team," I said.

BAM laughed and walked me to my office, which contained only a desk and a chair—the same inexpensive UNICOR furniture, built by prisoners, that many government offices use. It would be a few days before I had luxuries like a bookcase, whiteboard, and a chair for visitors—

much less a working computer. The entire workplace had the same spare, institutional feel as my office—it clearly had been completely empty before we got there.

We knew these cavernous digs were temporary; the Special Counsel's Office would be moving into another building shortly. And this gave us—a squad of single-minded workaholics to begin with—even less incentive to spruce the place up. I'd brought over some boxes from my office as the head of the Criminal Division's Fraud Section, but I didn't even bother moving in.

The first order of business for Team M—that is, for me—was to learn everything possible about what had already been done within the Department of Justice to investigate Manafort and then report back to Mueller. Manafort was not unknown to law enforcement. Before Mueller's appointment, in fact, various federal agents and prosecutors had opened investigations into his finances and lobbying in the United States. There were four investigations in total. This fact alone was remarkable. Being investigated by the government does not mean you've committed a crime, of course. But there was something jarring about the fact that a man who'd served as the campaign chairman for the current president of the United States had attracted scrutiny from law enforcement for so many different reasons.

It was a testament to Mueller's instincts as an investigator that he homed in immediately on Manafort. Mueller was playing a hunch. Our job was to examine Russian interference in the 2016 election and any potential coordination with the Trump campaign, and Manafort struck Mueller as an obvious place to look closely. Not only had Manafort spent considerable time on the Trump campaign, he had entered that position with close and well-documented ties to Ukraine allies of the Russian president, Vladimir Putin. If there'd been coordination between Russia and the campaign, it would make sense for it to have been conducted through Manafort.

The pending investigations of Manafort might offer us a toehold to get started. None was directly about Russian interference or cooperation between any Americans and Russia, but they presented a slew of potential opportunities to make a merited criminal case against Manafort. The goal would be to charge Manafort, using a criminal charge as leverage, and then convince him to flip, that is to cooperate with our own investigation in exchange for the possibility of a more lenient sentence. From the get-go, this was one of our key goals: We wanted to flip witnesses, including Manafort, to find out what they knew.

Flipping witnesses is an indispensable tool in complex cases, and one I had employed many times while prosecuting organized crime as a federal prosecutor in the Eastern District of New York in the 1990s. I stressed this in my conversations with Mueller from the outset: No matter how many documents you collected and reviewed, it was the rare case that could be made solely on such evidence. And cooperating witnesses could help with another Mueller imperative: speed.

A witness can tell you where the bodies are buried and save you from having to look under every rock. In the age of Big Data, with the proliferation of electronic documents, having such an insider to serve as a guide was necessary if you were going to maximize your ability to make quick headway. The catch-22 is that to flip someone you usually first need damning documents to confront the witness with to show him that you have the goods. So the key is to proceed on two fronts: make educated guesses about how to sift through promising documents, without wasting your time boiling the ocean, and interview low-level witnesses to try to uncover the whereabouts of useful documents and other evidence. All in all, not an easy thing to do quickly, but something Mueller demanded.

I also knew that to flip a witness and make your case, you often have to make your way along an indirect route. The first big break in an investigation I'd worked on involving an internal war in the Colombo crime family, for example, came after a low-level associate was arrested on a state court drug charge. This underling and his drug charge were not central to our much larger murder and murder-conspiracy case against his bosses in the mob, but he agreed to provide useful information in exchange for a possible reduction in his sentence. The same strategy had gotten the Enron investigation off the ground, as well, when we flipped CFO Andy Fastow's right-hand man, based on crimes he had committed unrelated to the core Enron fraud. Similarly, uncovering a crime that Manafort or an underling of his had committed, even if unrelated to the 2016 election, might eventually induce him to provide important information relevant to our Russia investigation.

I began by reaching out to the prosecutors and FBI agents with open cases on Manafort, eager to see what information law enforcement had already gathered and asking for whatever documents would get me up to speed. The special counsel had the authority to take over these existing investigations, or any pieces of them, and it was my job to make an assessment and report back to Mueller about anything that seemed particularly promising that we'd want to bring on board. Within days, thick packs of documents started arriving on my desk—and then, once I had a computer, in digital form, too.

As I dug in, a picture quickly emerged of Manafort as a complicated and dispiriting figure. He was clearly savvy, with an outsized share of intelligence, street smarts, and charm. He was also exceptionally good at his job; he seemed to have superb political instincts and had established himself as a first-rate lobbyist and consultant at an early age. He might have had a long and lucrative legitimate career. But that was not to be.

I learned from the FBI backgrounder—a summary of basic information the Bureau collects about a person under investigation—that Manafort had grown up in New Britain, Connecticut, in an Italian-American family. His father was a businessman who'd risen to become the mayor of that city, only to have his career upended by charges of corruption. Manafort was a diligent student, determined to find his way out. He propelled himself into college at Georgetown, moved on from there to Georgetown Law School, and then, having gravitated toward politics, cofounded a lobbying firm in Washington, D.C., in the 1980s. One of the firm's partners, Charlie Black, went on to become an elder statesman of the Republican lobbying and political consultant class. He would work for, and become a close confidant of, major Republican politicians such as Ronald Reagan and John McCain.

Manafort did not follow that path. He was drawn, instead, to the style of two young colleagues at the firm, Roger Stone and Lee Atwater—two mischievous peas in a pod who were capable of resorting to all manner of dirty tricks to score their clients a win. Atwater had brought us the racist Willie Horton attack ads during the 1988 presidential election, which not so subtly suggested that Michael Dukakis would unleash incarcerated black criminals on white America; Stone had a similar disregard for the truth, which came in handy during his work for Richard Nixon. Both men were comfortable operating in a realm untethered from facts, twisting the smallest kernels of truth to fit ginned-up con-

spiracy theories. These were Manafort's role models as he matured professionally.

Manafort also acquired a taste for the high life and sought work that
could keep him living in style. He was not interested in low-paying
work for Republican clients. He solicited clients who paid loads of
money—and that meant foreign clients with unlimited expense accounts, backed by their own corrupt political regimes. By the end of the
nineties, Manafort was making millions working for leaders in some of
the most corrupt governments in the world: the Philippines, Angola,
Ukraine, and Russia. He became known as a lobbyist and consultant to
the worst of the worst foreign dictators and oligarchs. And along the
way, Stone and Manafort began jointly representing an up-and-coming
real estate mogul in New York named Donald Trump.

These lucrative gigs provided Manafort the lavish quality of life he
craved. He used his ballooning wealth to lease a fleet of Range Rovers
and Mercedes, and purchase garish antiques and silk rugs to furnish
Manhattan lofts and posh estates up and down the East Coast. He spent
millions on clothes. (One store owner reported that it was considered a
failure if Manafort could not be persuaded to spend tens of thousands of
dollars on any given visit to his shop.) The annual gardening bill for his
estate in the Hamptons—which included a pool house, putting green,
home theater, and tennis court—was $100,000, and this excluded extras,
such as preparing the grounds for parties by planting a giant "M" in red
flowers at the center of the circular driveway. Flipping through photos
of Manafort's homes, I thought of the overdone facade and "jungle
room" in Elvis Presley's Graceland.

The man's vanity appeared to consume him. He poured money into
haircuts, dye jobs, and procedures to maintain a wrinkle-free face.
Manafort had even given up a presidential appointment in the Reagan
administration when he could not convince the White House counsel to
grant him an exemption from a law that forbade anyone from representing foreign clients while holding a presidentially appointed position.
Manafort couldn't have gone further in the opposite direction from
Charlie Black, a man who might have once been his mentor. Black was
the quintessential upstanding conservative white man of the Bush 41
era, who looked as though he'd stepped out of the pages of a Brooks
Brothers catalogue—not that dissimilar to Mueller, in fact.

The FBI backgrounder explained that Manafort was suspected to have two principal benefactors, both of whom had ties to the Russian government. The first was Oleg Deripaska, for whom Manafort started working in 2005. Deripaska is a Russian oligarch who heads up one of that country's largest conglomerates, which controls massive aluminum and power resources. I was informed that, like all such Russian oligarchs, Deripaska coordinated his activities with the Kremlin. The FBI report indicated that the extent of Deripaska's relationship with Manafort was unknown.

Manafort's other main source of income was the political party of Viktor Yanukovych, who was a failed Ukrainian politician when he and Manafort first met in Ukraine around 2006. Yanukovych was a pro-Russian thug, whose presidential rival in 2004 mysteriously was poisoned and disfigured during the election (Yanukovych has denied responsibility). When Yanukovych won the first presidential vote, it was thrown out for corrupt electoral practices—which is saying a lot, given endemic corruption in Ukraine. Yanukovych lost the subsequent revote. But in 2010, he mounted an improbable comeback. He ran for president again, against the former prime minister Yulia Tymoshenko, and this time hired Manafort as his campaign manager. Yanukovych was the Russian candidate of choice; Tymoshenko, the American and European. Ukraine had for years been caught between these forces, but Russia had a trump card: It had the oil that Ukraine needed to survive.

Manafort injected the race with his well-honed U.S. tactics of negative campaigning, slick advertising, and extensive polling. He also gave Yanukovych a makeover, making him appear less thuggish and—it seemed clear—more like Manafort himself, outfitting the candidate with a new hairdo and expensive tailored clothes. The strategy worked. Yanukovych was victorious. After the election, there was a show trial against Tymoshenko, after which Yanukovych promptly locked up his opponent, to the consternation of Western democracies. Here, in the United States, Secretary of State Hillary Clinton was joined by many prominent Republicans in strongly condemning Yanukovych's action.

Reading all of this at the Special Counsel's Office, I found it eerie to think back on Trump's rallying cries of "Lock her up" during our own 2016 presidential race—at the same time his campaign was being managed by the man who'd helped Yanukovych rise to power in Ukraine and then imprison his female political rival. Were we now emulating Ukraine's political and legal systems? Surely we are better than that, I hoped. It would be a shock to us two years later, right after our investigation was over, that Trump would be actively seeking a political investigation by Ukraine of his most formidable rival, Joe Biden—precisely the kind of corruption of the rule of law that we had been condemning Ukraine for undertaking.

After Yanukovych's election, Manafort became one of the Ukrainian president's key advisers and reaped huge profits from his new position. Manafort and his staff had unfettered access to Yanukovych, as well as to all top party politicians and government agencies. Manafort was said to be running a shadow government in Ukraine, operating out of a luxury suite at a top hotel, as well as offices in downtown Kiev, staffed by a full team to carry out his secretive work. His right-hand man there was a Russian named Konstantin Kilimnik, who was unknown to any of us in the Special Counsel's Office but would take on significance as our investigation proceeded. Manafort's position of privilege in this autocratic and corrupt regime lasted four years, until the spring of 2014 when a popular uprising forced Yanukovych to flee to Russia, where he remains to this day.

It is not illegal to make a fast buck, of course—nor is it illegal to work for a foreign government. And Lord knows, it is not illegal to have garish taste or to pursue the most outlandish excesses of capitalism. But, as I continued to read up on Manafort, it struck me that his desire for that gold-plated lifestyle might provide a motive to commit financial crimes. The FBI dossier noted that even Manafort's own daughter, in texts that were presumably hacked and then disseminated on the Internet, said that her father had "no moral or legal compass," and that the money he earned was "blood money."

What legal lines might such a man have been willing to cross to obtain his wealth? It seemed possible that, somewhere along the way, Manafort's ambition, greed, and contempt for the rules could have gotten the better of him.

Later that week, at my invitation, about twenty people involved in one of the Manafort investigations came to meet with me at the Special

Counsel's Office. This particular matter was being run out of the Money Laundering and Asset Recovery Section of the Justice Department's Criminal Division, which I knew well and was based just a few floors above my old office in the Department's Fraud Section. This section had recently changed its name, from the Asset Forfeiture and Money Laundering Section. What I'd always known as AFMLS, pronounced "aff-mills," was now MLARS, pronounced "em-lars."

The name change didn't reflect any shift in the section's mission—MLARS still focused on the same kinds of money-laundering cases it always had. The superficial change, instead, reflected the kind of bureaucratic mindset that drove me nuts, and which Mueller had little patience for as well. And it exemplified the ubiquitous government use of acronyms. When I first went to work under Mueller at the FBI, in 2005, as his incoming special counsel, his departing special counsel, Matt Olsen, spent a week schooling me on the dizzying alphabet soup of government acronyms in which I suddenly found myself drowning. On the last day of this training, Matt tested my newfound skills by rattling off something like, "We are going to take a Bu car to meet with the DIRNSA at NSA, where people from GCHQ are meeting with the DNI and CTD and NSD to go over FISA SIGINT issues. But first we have to go to ABP."

I felt very proud of myself: I knew that the first sentence meant we were taking an FBI bureau (Bu) car to go to see the director of the National Security Agency (DIRNSA), where people from Government Communications Headquarters (GCHQ), a British agency, were meeting with the director of national intelligence (DNI), FBI Counterterrorism Division agents (CTD), and Department of Justice National Security Division prosecutors (NSD) to go over signals intelligence (SIGINT) issues that arose on a Foreign Intelligence Security Act (FISA) application. But I couldn't decipher the final acronym. "Wait," I said, "what's ABP?"

"Au Bon Pain," Matt said—the bakery across from the Bureau on Tenth Street. In the FBI, apparently, even a bakery warranted an abbreviation.

The team from MLARS crowded around the table in our sole, makeshift conference room, with various FBI supervisors claiming spots at the table and backbenchers finding seats along the wall. The latter were the analysts and agents whom you usually needed to hear from in order to understand the specifics of an investigation: They were the ones in the trenches, doing the work.

The MLARS team began by explaining that they had opened their case on Manafort several years earlier, and had interviewed him twice, in 2013 and 2014. In those interviews, Manafort had been asked about a number of foreign bank accounts in Cyprus, and offshore companies that he controlled. He admitted that the Cyprus accounts held money that he'd earned from his lobbying and political consulting work in Ukraine and claimed that they were created at the suggestion of the Ukrainian oligarchs who'd paid him. The investigation presumably was launched to examine whether Manafort had used those accounts to launder his income and skirt U.S. tax laws.

But not much happened after those interviews. For more than three years, the MLARS investigation simply stalled—not, as far as I could tell, because of any political interference but because of institutional inertia. Such delay is unacceptable, but unfortunately not unheard of at the Department. Several months prior to Mueller's appointment, the head of MLARS had assigned a new lead prosecutor to the case, and the investigation had perked up, but I got the sense at our June 2017 meeting that these efforts were still very much in their infancy.

Work in the past few months by MLARS suggested that Manafort had other offshore accounts as well—in places like the Seychelles and Saint Vincent and the Grenadines, which, like Cyprus, were known for being illegal tax havens. The investigation uncovered evidence that Manafort was using his offshore accounts to fund his luxurious lifestyle: purchasing clothes at the House of Bijan, an over-the-top tailor in Beverly Hills where an average shirt can cost over $1,000; renting Italian villas for vacations; installing fancy audiovisual equipment in his estates; buying antique rugs; paying his housekeeper and gardener; and the like.

The FBI had started interviewing these vendors, confirming that their business records showed Manafort had made payments from offshore accounts. This sounded promising. I was intrigued by the offshore accounts and how Manafort was using them. A tax charge could be brought if Manafort was intentionally hiding income and not paying taxes on it. It seemed unlikely to me that Manafort would go through the hassle of paying vendors in the United States directly from offshore accounts if this wasn't his intent. It was a way to effectively make that money vanish from detection by the IRS, since the payments never hit a U.S. bank account controlled by Manafort. (A U.S. bank would have an independent obligation to report information to the U.S. tax authorities.)

I asked the MLARS team if they'd sought the bank records for Manafort's offshore accounts—those records could be solid proof of Manafort's control over the accounts, as well as provide clear evidence of his income and how it was spent. Obtaining overseas records is done through a mutual legal assistance treaty—or MLAT—an agreement into which countries all over the world enter with one another, permitting them to obtain documents from each other through a formal legal request. The short answer was no, but one of the attorneys told me it was on their to-do list. I was taken aback. It can take many months, even years, for such a request to be processed and produce any actual documents—you have to contend with the bureaucracy of two countries, not just one—and here the process hadn't even been started! Mueller was going to have a cow.

Though what I was hearing about Manafort was suspicious, it's not a crime to have offshore accounts, or to use the money parked in those tax havens to pay a housekeeper or buy an overpriced shirt. The real question would be whether Manafort was declaring income properly on his tax returns. So I asked the MLARS team what those returns showed.

"We don't know," one of the supervisors told me. "We don't have his tax returns."

I tried not to react, but I was shocked. They'd had this case open for years. How had they not acquired this key piece of evidence? Getting Manafort's tax returns should have been simple: The Tax Division, a separate part of the Department of Justice, is supposed to approve the court application to get those documents if you can meet a minimal standard demonstrating their relevance to your investigation. That standard had clearly been met here. The MLARS supervisor said they had submitted their request a few months before, and it had been rejected. "The Tax Division said that we had not made the necessary factual showing to justify the request," she explained. "We can resubmit if we get more evidence." I knew there was a workaround: Simply subpoena Manafort's tax accountants for their copies of the tax returns. If those unofficial copies showed what we suspected, then you could resubmit the Tax Division application to obtain the official, filed tax returns. But MLARS had not done that, either.

The whole meeting was a series of rude awakenings. It seemed possible that the MLARS team had botched their Tax Division request—that the paperwork failed to demonstrate the obvious relevance of Manafort's tax returns. But the other possibility was more nefarious: Their application had been submitted in 2017, after the Trump administration was in place. Had someone decided it would be unhelpful, politically, to advance a case against the new president's former campaign chairman?

In truth, I thought both explanations could be true: maybe the MLARS application was poorly articulated, and maybe it was rejected by people who were looking for any plausible grounds to bury it. Still, the MLARS team definitely had identified and was pursuing a promising theory. The problem was, they were moving at a pace that Mueller would find intolerable.

It was imperative that we take over this investigation ourselves.

In the days that followed, I had other meetings and conversations like this, as I studied up on each of the four Manafort investigations that were under way. A couple of them were intriguing, and were circling around something that smelled distinctly fishy in Manafort's finances or recent past. I met, for example, with prosecutors and FBI agents from New York who were investigating a series of multimillion-dollar loans made to Manafort just after he resigned from the Trump campaign in August 2016. The loans had been approved by Stephen Calk, the head of the Federal Savings Bank in Chicago. They were the largest the bank had ever made and had required exceptions to its internal lending policies—despite the fact that Manafort had no obvious outside income and had even been sued for defaulting on a bank loan.

After obtaining the loans, Manafort touted Calk to the Trump campaign and got Calk appointed to an advisory committee and interviews for administration positions. Still, any crimes seemed likely to be on the part of the bank, rather than Manafort, so I recommended that investigation be left under control of the agencies already conducting it. The

Special Counsel's Office had to focus on the most promising leads, and not get distracted with tangential cases that might take too long to unravel. I simply asked to be kept in the loop on these less promising matters.

One final investigation I looked into, however, immediately struck me as more vital to our office's work: a probe conducted by the FARA Unit of the Justice Department's National Security Division. I knew virtually nothing about FARA when I started with the Special Counsel's Office. It would be yet another government acronym in my ever-expanding quiver.

FARA stands for Foreign Agents Registration Act, a law that requires anyone who is lobbying our government or doing public relations work in the United States on behalf of a foreigner to register his or her precise activities in a public filing with the Department of Justice. The laudatory purpose of FARA is to make sure Americans are given notice of any actions by foreigners to affect public opinion or influence our elected officials. It is a crime to knowingly violate the FARA law—a person must be aware of the FARA requirements and disregard them intentionally. If a person is unaware, or makes a mistake about what they are required to report, their failure cannot be criminally prosecuted, although the person would still need to file the required registration documents setting out their activities.

It's worth noting that, although the FARA statute is relatively simple and clear, it is rarely followed—a mere fifty to sixty filings were made under the law each year, at most, even though foreign entities spend fortunes on lobbying in America every year. There is little incentive for these lobbyists to register under the law because the law virtually never is criminally enforced or results in even civil penalties. Throughout its history, the FARA Unit has been staffed with only a few lawyers and a paralegal or two, and has focused exclusively on pressuring lobbyists who violated the act to register retroactively, instead of prosecuting them or imposing a fine. In fact, the unit would later tell me that it had never itself brought a single criminal case. Other prosecutors around the country had done so only a handful of times in the past decade.

Manafort, I had learned from the FBI backgrounder, appeared to have a FARA problem stemming from his work in Ukraine under President Yanukovych. Part of Manafort's assignment in Ukraine had been to effect a global makeover and improve the country's image—and, in particular, to change the Western perception that Yanukovych had improperly imprisoned his rival, Tymoshenko. To accomplish this, Manafort retained two Washington, D.C., lobbying firms—one called Mercury, with Republican ties, and another, the Podesta Group, with Democratic affiliations (it is typical, in such lobbying efforts, to cover all bases). These firms orchestrated a massive lobbying campaign in the United States from 2012 until 2014, ending only when Yanukovych was overthrown. Neither firm had filed under FARA. Manafort hadn't filed, either.

Manafort's FARA difficulties came to light in the press after he began working on Trump's campaign in March 2016. It was one of the reasons Manafort ultimately "resigned" in mid-August, at the height of the campaign. (Reports also had emerged that Manafort had been paid millions of dollars under the table for his Ukraine lobbying and consulting work.) After Manafort's resignation, the FARA Unit sent letters to him and the two firms that he'd retained, asking each questions to determine whether they had an obligation to file. Consequently, by the spring of 2017, both Mercury and the Podesta Group had filed under FARA retroactively (though without admitting that they should have done so years earlier, and without paying any penalty). Those new filings—and the documents that the two lobbying firms had voluntarily provided the FARA Unit—revealed that they had been formally hired not by the government of Ukraine, but by a supposedly independent entity in Belgium called the European Centre for a Modern Ukraine. If that organization was truly independent of Ukraine, then the law had a loophole that did not require a FARA filing by Manafort or the two lobbying firms.

By the time Mueller was appointed in May 2017, Manafort still hadn't filed under FARA, and I had questions about how he justified this refusal. Had he not known about the FARA requirements? Was the European Centre for a Modern Ukraine the true client or merely a puppet of the Ukrainian government, with Manafort pulling the strings? Why had the two lobbying firms retroactively filed, but not Manafort?

One afternoon during my second week of work, I found myself, along with two new colleagues on other teams at the Special Counsel's Office, piling into another cramped and windowless Justice Department conference room to meet with the longtime head of the FARA Unit and two of her supervisors. One of these supervisors, David Laufman, explained that the unit was still in the midst of negotiations with Manafort's attorney, trying to convince her to have Manafort file under FARA retroactively.

Manafort, through his counsel, had claimed in a letter to the FARA Unit that it was difficult for him to respond to the unit's inquiries about his work for Ukraine because he did not possess any records from the time period in question. We learned from Laufman, however, that the FARA Unit had done nothing to test this assertion or to investigate Manafort's work for Ukraine themselves. They had not interviewed a single witness or issued a single subpoena in the nine months since the unit opened its case. When we asked why, Laufman explained that they didn't have the authority to issue criminal subpoenas to enforce FARA—a contention that I knew, from a legal perspective, to be wrong: FARA was a criminal statute, so prosecutors could use grand jury subpoenas to investigate a potential violation.

From there, the story only got worse: After taking at face value Manafort's claim that he no longer had any relevant documents, the FARA Unit handed over to Manafort's attorney copies of the tens of thousands of pages of documents they'd received from the lobbying firms in the course of their investigation.

There may be no way for me to sufficiently explain, to an outsider, how flabbergasting this move was. I'd never heard of anything like it before. For one thing, it surrendered a key tool with which to test Manafort's credibility and a means for him to tailor a concocted story to the known evidence: One of the principal ways you test whether people are being candid with you during an investigation is by checking their statements against other evidence. But if you turn over all that evidence to the witnesses in advance, they can tailor their story to fit perfectly in the space between what you're able to prove and disprove, thereby permitting them to lie without being caught.

We refer to this tactic as "puddle jumping." Here, Manafort would be able to sidestep all the potentially messy puddles, because the government had handed over a detailed map of puddles we knew about. Beyond that, it was counterproductive and simply poor form for the FARA Unit to share the documents from one private party with another. The two lobbying firms had supplied documents voluntarily. For the government to then turn the documents over to a third party, without the firms' consent, could discourage them—and any other potential witnesses who heard about it—from cooperating again.

It was clear what my recommendation would be to Mueller. I would be telling Laufman that we were taking over the FARA investigation. He should shut down all communications with Manafort's counsel, and if she called, he should refer her to us. Walking back to my office after the meeting, I could feel myself reeling from what I'd encountered that week. I'd been agitated by the pace of the MLARS investigation, but they had at least developed a solid outline of a potential case. The lack of basic criminal investigative steps or instincts in the FARA case, however, was inexcusable. As Department attorneys, we are paid by the taxpayers to do our job, and to do it efficiently and professionally. In short, this was not the Justice Department's finest hour.

On the merits, however, I could recognize the value of what we now had. The investigations had produced promising leads and some raw materials with which Team M could begin its work. And, although I had issues with the steps various prosecutors had been taking, every senior prosecutor I dealt with could not have been more gracious. "How can we help?" each said. This was not some Deep State conspiracy, but the camaraderie of career law enforcement prosecutors all displaying their commitment to upholding the rule of law. We were trained to look at the facts and follow them where they lead, regardless of political consequences. Thus the appointment of Mueller as the special counsel was a reaffirmation of that principle. And although the internal Department regulations governing the appointment and work of the special counsel explicitly required the other components of the Department to cooperate with us, that was surplusage; we enjoyed enormous cooperation from the career folks steeped in the ethos of the Department's mission.

While I was getting up to speed on Team M, my special counsel colleagues on other teams were doing the same. Team R was meeting with National Security Division lawyers and the FBI and others who had been examining the nature and scope of Russian interference in the 2016 election and interactions with the Trump campaign. They were getting debriefed about George Papadopoulos, Carter Page, and Michael Flynn—who had advised the campaign on national security issues to varying degrees, with the latter being appointed the president's national security adviser, only to be fired a couple of weeks into the job for lying to Vice President Mike Pence.

Team R was also poring over the joint Intelligence Community Assessment about Russian interference and reading the infamous "Steele dossier," which contained various sensational allegations about Trump. Team 600, meanwhile, was focused on two narrow potential obstructions of justice—the firing of FBI director James Comey and Comey's allegation that the president had asked him to go easy on Flynn, who was under investigation for lying to the FBI. It would not be until much later that Team 600 would expand its focus to include White House obstruction of our own investigation.

I understood, full well, that we needed to take the most promising existing investigations on board fast and hit the ground running—sprinting, even. I still had in my head an encounter with Mueller on my first day in the Special Counsel's Office. He and I had crossed paths in the hallway and, in lieu of saying hello, Mueller looked me up and down and greeted me with a question that was clearly a joke, but also a deadly serious expression of his expectations.

"When are you going to indict?" he said.

"That's *my* line," I told him. "That's what I say to all my deputies overseeing cases in the Fraud Section."

But I'd been saying it so long myself that I'd forgotten: "And who do you think you learned that from?" Mueller asked, then kept walking.

CHAPTER 2

Living an Idea

BY THE TIME I joined the Special Counsel's Office, I had spent roughly twenty years in the Department of Justice, almost all of it as a federal prosecutor. I had prosecuted mob bosses and Enron executives, and done two stints under Mueller, including as general counsel of the FBI. That is, even before signing on to investigate the president of the United States, I'd had a lively and gratifying career—one that would have seemed entirely unlikely to my younger self.

In my senior year at Princeton, in 1980, a European cultural studies professor I particularly revered, Carl Schorske, told us—during what, poignantly, was the final lecture of his career—that a person should "live an idea." His words enthralled me, though it would be many years before I figured out exactly how I might begin to apply this advice. I was a nerdy and hyper-meticulous young man, studying European history, but had no real sense of how I might put that admonition, or myself, to use in the world.

I entered law school at Columbia a year after graduating. I found the analytic rigor that education demanded to be invigorating. Law was the opposite of studying history, at least in the way I had been approaching it: No longer was it acceptable to merely critique other people's decisions or identify structural shortcomings of a society from the outside, looking in. Now I was forced to apply my lofty ideals to the gritty particulars of real life. I had to make hard choices, evaluate whom those decisions benefited and whom they harmed, and then defend my choices as forcefully as I could—out loud, in front of the whole class.

After graduation, I went to clerk for a federal judge and quickly realized that federal trial court was where I wanted to be. I couldn't imagine the cloistered life of an appellate attorney for the same reasons I had decided against the life of the mind that the academy entailed. I had already spent too many hours in libraries, reading primary and secondary sources on seventeenth-century history—first at Princeton, then at the University of Geneva on a Fulbright; I was done toiling over old documents in archives. Trial work felt concrete and practical, more engaged with the outside world. It appealed to my deep desire for certainty, my sense that, in every realm of life, a logical and meticulously constructed argument should always prevail. And it was grounded in the rule of law—with the court, the prosecutor, and the defense counsel all playing essential roles in determining whether wrongdoers are held to account.

Trial work had another side to it, though, that appealed to my lifelong love of theater. There is a performance aspect to prosecuting a trial. Although the story a prosecutor tells must be grounded in fact, and not an author's imagination, one needs to frame one's logical arguments persuasively to appeal to the jury. Growing up in New York City, my sister and I often snuck off to see an eclectic mix of shows on Broadway and at the Public Theater—from Edward Albee dramas and Neil Simon comedies to Stephen Sondheim musicals and hippyish hits like *Hair*. On weekends, I performed in a professional children's theater myself. I immediately recognized that there is an inherent dramatic aspect to trials; it made sense that so many plays, movies, and books center around the action in courtrooms: Each trial tells a story of two conflicting sides, with a dramatic denouement when the verdict is reached.

After a stint in "Big Law" as an associate at a large corporate law firm, I was lucky to be hired as a federal prosecutor in the Eastern District of New York in 1991. That particular office was known for its scrappiness; unlike the Southern District of New York, the typical EDNY prosecutor was not an entitled Ivy League–educated nerd (that is, me). EDNY prosecutors largely grew up in the district we oversaw—in Brooklyn, Queens, Staten Island, and Long Island—and ground away at cases with tenacity and street smarts. The newest prosecutors

worked out of the basement of the courthouse in Brooklyn; only supervisors had windows—and even then, the only view those windows afforded was of the legs of a passerby or the occasional vagrant peeing on
the sidewalk.

Like most EDNY prosecutors, I was detailed upon arrival to the
General Crimes Section, where I mainly made cases against low-level
drug mules who smuggled narcotics through JFK Airport, often by
swallowing balloons filled with heroin and cocaine. It was a grueling
boot camp that went a long way toward molding me into a genuine
prosecutor—not just teaching me about criminal process and the law,
but giving me the self-assurance to make difficult decisions. I learned
through making mistakes, and learned from my colleagues to take responsibility for those mistakes with no excuses.

The trials themselves were exhilarating. Before each one, though,
my heart palpitated, my mouth went dry, my hands shook. But gradually, with experience, I learned to manage and overcome my nerves. I
loved the feeling of being switched on at every moment, my adrenaline
pumping—of working a long day in court, then preparing late into the
night for the following day. I learned that there are two types of trial
lawyers: those who eat their way through trials, and those who fast. I
was the latter. By the end of any given trial, my already thin frame would
turn cadaverous, and dark circles would bloom under my eyes. I'd never
been happier.

After my year in General Crimes, I was transferred to the Organized
Crime and Racketeering Section, where I was plunged into prosecuting
the mob. At the time, New York's five crime families—the Genovese,
Gambino, Lucchese, Colombo, and Bonanno families—were the most
powerful crime syndicates in the nation, and my new colleagues brought
me up to speed on their inner workings and unique nomenclature. I
learned that the bosses of the five families together made up the Commission, a kind of intramural council that served to resolve beefs that
arose between the organizations. Internally, each family had the same
structure: a boss, an underboss, and a consigliere—who formed the
upper management known as the Administration. Below the Administration were captains, each with a crew of soldiers and associates.

Every mobster above the associate level was a "made" man. (There
were no women, and only men of at least half-Italian ancestry were eli-

gible to be made.) There was an induction ceremony at which an associate got made; he would swear allegiance to the family, above even the needs of his own wife and children. And he would also take an oath of omertà—silence—meaning he'd never become a "rat" and cooperate with the government. This is what it meant to devote oneself to La Cosa Nostra—literally, "this thing of ours."

This was the inimitable vernacular immortalized in *The Godfather* and *Guys and Dolls* only richer and real. But the true delights of mobspeak, I found, stretched much further. The mobsters we dealt with were adept at casually twisting English into streetwise poetry and hilarious malapropisms. A cooperating witness, Joey Ambrosino, once told me his captain hadn't directly come out and admitted a crime to him—it was more of an "insinuendo," he explained. "Benny Eggs" Mangano—a leader of the Genovese family—described a loan shark victim as being so poor he "didn't have two nickels to rub together."

When Al D'Arco, a leader of the Lucchese crime family, was asked what Vic Orena had done with the body of the murder victim Tommy Ocera, he said they'd given Tommy "luparo bianco"—which he said meant the white rabbit—and made a sinuous gesture with his hand, to suggest putting the body six feet under. (The phrase and arm gesture always went hand in hand, even when D'Arco was on the witness stand telling the jury about the murder.) Patsy Conte, a Gambino family captain, threw himself at the mercy of District Judge I. Leo Glasser at sentencing by telling the court he was so regretful, he was "literally prostate."

My arrival at the Organized Crime Section came at a historic moment in 1992, a turning point in law enforcement's long assault on the mob. Our office had recently signed up a new cooperating witness, Salvatore "Sammy the Bull" Gravano, the underboss of the Gambino family who'd been indicted along with his boss, John Gotti, for a series of murders and other crimes. Gravano had done the unthinkable by flipping, and would offer devastating testimony in numerous trials in the coming years; with his cooperation, the government would convict more than fifty mobsters.

I would put Sammy the Bull on the stand several times myself, including in my prosecution of Vincent "The Chin" Gigante, the boss of the Genovese family, who had feigned mental illness for years by walking around Greenwich Village in pajamas and a cotton bathrobe. An

enterprising squad of FBI agents had caught him acting normally, however, by locating the Upper East Side townhouse of his girlfriend and
conducting surveillance every night to monitor his behavior. (Inside, he
would change out of his shoddy outerwear and don clean clothes, luxu-
riating in a fluffy Brooks Brothers–style bathrobe.)

The most legendary of the EDNY mob cases was the prosecution of
John Gotti, which was in full swing when I came on board. As the head
of the Gambino crime family, Gotti was not your typical mob boss. Most
Commission members tended to lie low, barricading themselves within
fortresses of secrecy and discretion. Gigante, for example, didn't allow
anyone to even use his name, to avoid the risk of being implicated on an
FBI wiretap. But Gotti was a showboat. He regularly hit the town in
flashy clothes and perfectly coiffed hair, then delighted in his coverage in
the tabloids, which called him "Dapper Don." He had another nickname, too: "the Teflon Don," which he'd acquired by earning repeated
acquittals in earlier criminal trials—no charges, it seemed, could stick.

Of course, this was often the result of Gotti's devious obstructions of
justice. In a couple of cases, Gotti had tampered with the jury; in another, a key witness took the stand and testified, out of fear, that he suddenly remembered nothing. I FORGOTTI! one tabloid headline screamed.
The indictment our office was bringing charged Gotti with five murders and a slew of other crimes, including racketeering and obstruction
of justice.

Gravano, who faced the same charges, realized that Gotti's defense
would be that Gravano had committed the crimes behind Gotti's back—
that is, Gravano would be the fall guy—so he decided to flip. He went
privately to the judge and asked for new defense counsel, as he believed
his counsel was "house counsel" for the mob and would report his effort
to cooperate to Gotti, with dire consequences. So in addition to all the
other proof we had, the government now had Gotti's right-hand man as
a star witness.

As lead prosecutor John Gleeson told me—in words that resonate
now in thinking about the facts uncovered during the special counsel
investigation—the case was not about the facts. The proof was incontrovertible that Gotti was the boss of the family and had ordered the murders and other crimes. In the Gotti case the issue was fear: Would the

jury put aside their fear and hold him to account under the rule of law? The jury did, and Gotti spent the rest of his life in prison.

I was soon thrown into another pivotal case, one that would effectively cripple one of New York's five crime families, the Colombos. At the time, the Colombo family was in the middle of a Shakespearean internecine war. The family's boss, Carmine "The Snake" Persico, had been sent away on a life sentence, but rather than relinquish control of the family, he had designated an acting boss to keep the operation running until his son, Alphonse "Allie Boy" Persico, finished a short prison sentence of his own. As the date of Allie Boy's release approached, however, this acting boss, Vic Orena, decided not to step aside. The family split into two factions—one loyal to Orena and the other to the Persicos. These factions—or "fractions," as cooperating witness Joey Ambrosino put it—sent hit teams marauding through New York, looking to take out members and associates on the other side. Multiple murders were committed, and innocent bystanders were wounded and killed as well. One Colombo hit squad killed a woman walking with a baby stroller; another accidentally shot a nun.

John Gleeson, my chief in the Organized Crime Section, paired me with a senior assistant U.S. attorney named George Stamboulidis to investigate the Colombos and bring the violence to an end. George had grown up in Queens. What George lacked in snooty academic pedigree, he made up for by being whip smart, shrewd, aggressive, charming, and a born trial lawyer. He and Gleeson would push me out of my comfort zone as a prosecutor, toughening me up and training me to act with far greater speed and boldness than came naturally to me at the time. They also taught me key lessons about how to build a criminal case from the ground up, lessons that reverberated throughout my career as a prosecutor. George was a talented investigator—you have to think like a criminal, he would say, and put yourself in their shoes to figure out what they were up to.

Our job was to make winnable cases out of the carnage of the Colombo war. But when George and I began, we didn't have remotely enough evidence to charge anyone with any of the murders that had already occurred, or even a conspiracy to commit them. We didn't see a way to get a toehold in the case—no obvious lesser charges for us to bring against those at the bottom of the organization, in order to flip them and work our way up; we couldn't even get a search warrant to stop the hit teams' cars to search them for firearms, since we lacked the necessary evidence to show probable cause. In short, we had to think creatively to find an indirect legal entryway into a larger case—a strategy I'd find myself using repeatedly in my career, including at the Special Counsel's Office.

We started by having the FBI agents work with state law enforcement to tail and pull over the hit teams for any and all traffic violations they observed. This turned out to be easy: The Colombo mobsters were driving around attempting to kill people and avoid being shot themselves; they tended not to focus too hard on the particulars of local traffic laws. They blazed through red lights, changed lanes without signaling, and cruised around town with their taillights out.

We weren't interested in these petty violations in and of themselves, of course, but under New York law, they provided a legal basis to pull the cars over. We knew many of those drivers and passengers would be carrying firearms, and that many had prior felony convictions, and thus would be prohibited from possessing a gun—a federal crime. In short order, we'd charged about a dozen Colombo family members on these felon-in-possession cases and gotten these people off the street at least temporarily. Now we could also start attempting to flip witnesses and gain information, exchanging the prospect of a court reducing a sentence for truthful information, and clawing our way from the fringes toward the heart of the organization.

Our first big break wound up coming from a drug charge brought against a Colombo associate, Carmine Imbriale. Neither Imbriale nor his drug charge were central to the murder and murder-conspiracy case we were seeking to build against his bosses, but he was a way into the case. Imbriale agreed to cooperate, informing on the activities of his immediate boss, Joey Ambrosino. As we gathered more evidence—including vivid conversations captured on a court-approved bug planted in Ambrosino's car as the hit team planned to whack a captain on the Orena side of the war—Ambrosino was persuaded to cooperate.

From there, we were able to make a case against the head of Ambrosino's crew, Colombo captain Michael Sessa, and so on. Within eighteen months, we had numerous cooperating witnesses—and not just lower-level associates. Soldiers and captains turned. Even Carmine Sessa, the family's consigliere, cooperated. One prominent mob defense lawyer wisecracked to me that there was so much flipping going on, the Colombo family was now being referred to among defense attorneys as the House of Pancakes.

Over the next two years, George and I convicted various associates, captains, and even all three members of the Colombo family Administration, including the acting boss, Orena. The hit squads, and the bloodshed they brought to the streets of New York, quickly petered out. Due to the FBI's tenacious work, we had decapitated the organization—but slowly, starting at the very bottom and inching our way up.

Gradually, the grip of organized crime on New York City was loosened. By the end of the nineties, what had once seemed like an unstoppable institution, built on greed, amorality, corruption, and intimidation, would be reduced to a collection of mere street gangs.

It would be too much of a digression to attempt a blow-by-blow recap of all my ups and downs as a federal prosecutor, or to account for every case I investigated and tried. My aim here is merely to give an overview of my experience, highlighting some key lessons I learned, and some prosecutorial tools I acquired and honed, that I'd bring to bear on my work with the special counsel. I was surprised how deeply the lessons I learned in the context of mob families and white-collar cases like Enron would resonate while investigating the president and his campaign.

Ultimately, I would spend a decade at the Eastern District of New York, working my way up to chief of the Criminal Division in 1999, at which point I found myself going from leading significant mob cases to spending my days in interminable management meetings. It all seemed so dull and bureaucratic. Dispirited, I called my mom one evening to vent: It's unfair, I whined. I couldn't pal around with my assistant U.S. attorney friends anymore. Everything I said was now viewed as coming from "the boss," and not from a friend.

There was a pause on the other end of the phone. My mom, who is a psychologist, told me that I had a decision to make. "With power, comes resentment," she said. People don't like being told what to do, so if I wanted only to be liked, I shouldn't be a supervisor. "If this is what you want to do, then you need to learn to live with the resentment." Her advice has stayed with me ever since, through many different leadership positions in government over the years. I've worked to balance openness and friendliness as a supervisor with the authority and distance that is required to be perceived by my employees as fair and impartial. And learned to live with the resentment.

In late 2001, I got a phone call from a former EDNY senior colleague, Leslie Caldwell, asking if I would consider joining the federal government's newly formed Enron Task Force. Enron, a Houston-based energy giant, had just collapsed, filing what was at the time the largest—and maybe most shocking—corporate bankruptcy in American history. It turned out Enron had been engaging in massive fraud, conning its regulators and shareholders by hiding its debts and faking its profits. Enron had used accounting gimmicks, illegal side deals, and outright lies to appear to be financially healthier than it actually was.

The Enron Task Force had been convened by leaders of the Justice Department, including Robert Mueller, the recently appointed director of the FBI. I'd never met Mueller, but knew enough about his career to admire him. He had already accrued legendary status in my world. Known as a real prosecutor's prosecutor, he'd once held the prestigious position in Washington as assistant attorney general in charge of the Justice Department's Criminal Division, and went back to trying murder cases in the local U.S. attorney's office.

I also remembered the unusual email he had sent to every U.S. attorney's office in the country, after taking the helm as the U.S. attorney in San Francisco in the late 1990s, announcing that every supervisory position in his office was now open for applications. Current supervisors could reapply, Mueller explained, but he was committed to choosing the best person for each slot. No one had ever seen a U.S. attorney clean house like that. His boldness was stunning and refreshing. The defense bar in San Francisco was publicly outraged, but privately praised to the hilt his makeover of the office and the new business that would result. Leslie, whom I was working with at EDNY at the time, had been inspired to go off to work for him. Now, Mueller and his colleagues had put her in charge of the Enron Task Force.

I leapt at the opportunity to be Leslie's deputy and headed down to Washington in January 2002, the first of many stints I would do in the nation's capital. Unsure of how long the assignment would be, we lived out of hotels and suitcases—traveling between Washington and Houston almost weekly. An inveterate New Yorker, I found the culture of Washington to be a bit of a shock. It was a company town, overrun with lawyers. In Washington, all the small talk was political, but focused less on substantive issues of policy than on the blood sport of outmaneuvering the other side, or petty gossip about who was in and who was out.

But I soon had more than enough work to put that all aside. If a routine white-collar case was basic algebra, Enron was advanced calculus. The creation of the Enron Task Force was itself a sign of how ill-prepared the Justice Department was to combat large-scale economic crime at the time. There was, theoretically, a section of the Department in place to deal with something like Enron—the Fraud Section, which I would go on to lead a decade later—but it simply didn't have the capacity to detangle such a sweeping, convoluted case.

Moreover, while Leslie and I had been trained to investigate, not just prosecute, this was not the norm for Justice Department lawyers at the time. The traditional distinction—agents investigate and assistant U.S. attorneys prosecute—has eroded over time, but old-school prosecutors still expected FBI agents to show up with a case all wrapped up, which they could then present in court. That approach simply isn't sufficient for teasing out tough, complicated frauds, or tackling other sprawling criminal problems, like terrorism or the mob. The best FBI agents I had worked with told me how to try a case and I told them how to investigate; it was a healthy marriage of give-and-take in all phases of a case.

My first assignment on Enron wasn't looking into the company itself, but the accounting firm Arthur Andersen, which had handled Enron's books. This was my introduction to the importance of effective institutional watchdogs—one that I'd find mirrored, later, in our democracy's ineffective system of checks and balances in reining in an autocratic president. Andersen was one of the country's "Big Five" accounting firms, and it played a key role for publicly traded companies like Enron, auditing the corporation's books to ensure their accuracy before those financials were filed publicly. This diminishes the risk of fraud and provides confidence to the market that a company's books are on the up-and-up.

But accounting firms are not government watchdogs; they are hired and paid by the very companies they are auditing. And Enron was a whale of a client for Andersen, generating an astounding $50 million in fees in 2000; Andersen housed an entire team of its accountants inside Enron's headquarters. All of this made Andersen's independence and integrity as an auditor hard to maintain. When one respected senior auditor, Carl Bass, questioned how Enron was recording its earnings, he was removed from the account altogether by more senior Andersen executives. Others who spoke up were overruled or cowed into silence. Thus the vigilance with which the firm evaluated Enron's financial standing was corrupted by its own pursuit of profits. The watchdog had become an enabler. I would see this phenomenon years later at Attorney General Barr's Department of Justice under Trump.

With respect to Andersen, the facts that we uncovered were not that complicated. Suspicions about the inner workings of Enron had been heightened after the sudden departure of its CEO, Jeffrey Skilling, in August 2001. Then in October, Enron announced, for the first time in its history, that it would not meet its expected earnings target. Until then, Enron's financial health had appeared vigorous and reliable, and this news sent its stock price tumbling. A few days later, the company's chief financial officer, Andrew Fastow, was fired, and Enron disclosed that it was going to restate its earnings. This was an even bigger bombshell than the disappointing earnings report; it was an admission that the financial reports the company had previously filed, and which investors relied on, had contained serious errors, and Fastow's departure suggested there was a troubling backstory yet to come out.

Any responsible Big Five accounting firm would know for sure that civil shareholder litigation and an SEC investigation would promptly ensue—and Andersen was no different, particularly since it was under a form of probation at the time for a previous SEC infraction. But its internal documents clearly showed that, rather than preserve its Enron-related records as evidence in the inevitable government inquiry, Andersen destroyed them. Upon learning privately of the bad news to be revealed publicly, before the SEC could arrive the company started shredding records by the tons and deleting electronic files en masse. Employees were instructed to make this purge look like a routine year-end cleanup.

Ultimately, after Andersen turned down a deferred prosecution agreement (a way to avoid a criminal indictment but be subject to a period of oversight by the Department of Justice), the Department leadership directed us to bring an obstruction of justice charge against the firm, and we won a conviction. Andersen appealed, as was its right, and after it lost the first appeal, in 2004, the Supreme Court reinterpreted the requirements of the obstruction of justice statute and applied them retroactively. This overturned the outcome of our trial, as the jury had not been instructed to find the elements that met these new requirements of the law. This left the Department free to prosecute Andersen under the new legal standard, but by that time, the firm was out of business and the understandable decision was made by senior DOJ leadership not to divert our investigation of Enron to retry the defunct Andersen entity.

Before working on the Andersen trial, I'd been accustomed to a certain kind of obstruction of justice: mobsters intimidating witnesses, tampering with juries, and disposing of bodies so that the evidence of their crimes could never be found. (Once, when I put Gravano on the witness stand, he explained to the jury how he and some associates had dragged one victim's body to the basement of a house and cut it up in a kiddie pool.) I'd even seen the Colombo family successfully race to kill Jack Leale—its own in-house undertaker who was in charge of disposing of bodies—before law enforcement could get ahold of Leale to learn literally where the bodies were buried. But Andersen was the first time I dealt with obstruction of justice in a white-collar and, in comparison, more genteel context. This, of course, was an issue that would resurface prominently in our investigation at the Special Counsel's Office.

Andersen was also my first experience working on a high-profile case, under intense scrutiny from the national press—far more than the local press I'd experienced with mob cases. Leslie Caldwell said we had gone from "B1" to "A1," referring to the local and national sections of *The New York Times.* The media coverage required a thick skin—every flaw I had as a lawyer was laid bare. The *Houston Chronicle,* which covered our court appearances religiously, included a quote in a front-page story that described me as "an East Coast, Ivy League, Evian-swilling carpetbagger." It was the beginning of my education in laughing off this kind of superficial adjectival attack—something that would also come in handy at the Special Counsel's Office with the onslaught of childish but pernicious presidential tweets that relied on attacks by adjective, rather than substance. (Plus I had friends to help do that; as Leslie commented the day that story ran in the *Chronicle,* "That article is so unfair. You don't drink Evian.")

Once the Andersen trial was finished, I was tasked to work on the investigation of Andy Fastow, Enron's former chief financial officer. We proceeded similarly to how the FBI, George Stamboulidis, and I had penetrated the Colombo crime family. We first flipped Fastow's right-hand man—Michael Kopper—by making a case against him for crimes not directly related to the Enron fraud. Then, with Kopper guiding us toward the most corrupt transactions buried in the rubble of the company's accounting, we were able to flip Fastow and a constellation of other cooperators. We were ultimately able to land at the C suite, charging and convicting both Jeffrey Skilling and Enron's founder, Ken Lay.

I would work at the Enron Task Force until 2005, commuting weekly between Washington, Houston, and my home in New York. After Leslie left, I served as its director for a couple of years. In the end, the breadth of dishonesty and complicity that our work uncovered was astonishing, and it raised a profound question to which I'd return, years later, while at the Special Counsel's Office: Why had so many people simply stood by and watched as illegal conduct occurred all around them? Why had no one in a position of power tried to alter the course of that corrupted institution, or say a word in dissent? It wasn't until very shortly before the fraud unraveled—in August 2001—that a single whistleblower, Sherron Watkins, even raised an alarm internally. Weeks later, the firm collapsed.

Was it fear? Self-interest? Is the human conscience so easily silenced by power and money and prestige? Hannah Arendt coined the phrase "the banality of evil" to describe the almost obliviousness with which Adolf Eichmann had seemed to perpetrate evil acts during the Holocaust. Here, we were looking at the banality of the tolerance of evil: the ability of everyone simply to go about their business.

It is easy to think of Enron as a case involving a few amoral fraudsters at the top of an organization, but that would be a mistake. Unfortunately, there will always be people like Lay and Skilling and Fastow. The bigger problem we must confront centers on how and why they were permitted to thrive for so long. The watchdogs and other checks and balances meant to contain their wrongdoing can prove to be more fragile than we assume—and far too easy for those with power to defy, corrupt, or ignore.

After leaving the Enron Task Force, I was recruited to fill a temporary detail to the FBI as Mueller's special counsel—a kind of aide-de-camp to the director. It was only during my interview for this new position that I finally met Mueller face-to-face. After years of hearing about him, and revering him from afar, I was now going to meet the man on the top floor of the Bureau's headquarters in Washington—a heavy, brutalist concrete building that hid an even uglier interior containing miles of linoleum hallways and fluorescent lights. Like the EDNY prosecutor's offices, at the FBI there was a complete mismatch between the importance of its work and the physical surroundings in which it was tirelessly performed.

As I took a seat in his vast office, Mueller slowly surveyed my résumé, then slapped his hand to his forehead.

"Oh no," he said. "Are you another un-supervisable prosecutor from the Eastern District of New York?" I tensed up before realizing this was his way of teasing.

"I have no idea what you mean," I shot back deadpan, and was relieved to have elicited a quick, loud laugh from the man. I learned that he had a particular fondness for the scrappiness of EDNY prosecutors. With that out of the way, we got down to the business of determining when I could start.

I spent the next six months at Mueller's side. I was exposed to the enormous scope of work performed by the Bureau's thirty-six thousand employees: its criminal, cyber, and national security mission; its main headquarters in Washington, D.C., and scores of field offices around the country; and its dozens of international operations around the globe. I got to observe Mueller up close.

He was a seemingly impossible amalgam of everything I'd been led to expect by his austere public persona—though there were also dimensions of his character I hadn't expected at all. He was the cool, analytical, classic WASP we saw in public appearances: a man of few words, who would methodically absorb every part of your presentation to him and ask relentless targeted questions, but then respond only with a terse order as to how you should proceed. He did not feel an obligation to make the ins and outs of his thought process transparent. And yet, he listened carefully and was unafraid to change his views based on what you presented and argued.

You also never doubted that each of his decisions was born out of a commanding sense of duty and patriotism. He rarely opined on these values at length, but he didn't have to. We all knew he'd been raised on Park Avenue and attended an elite boarding school and college, but then volunteered to serve in Vietnam, where he was decorated for his valor. And we all saw, to the left of his massive FBI desk, the many framed pictures of comrades who had died in service—a kind of personal legion of honor, which loomed over all his work.

Mueller was stingy with compliments—with social niceties of any kind. When he did express congratulations, I sensed it was from a tickler in his head that reminded him that such attaboys are good for morale and his role required it. I learned about the time Mueller's family convinced him to host an FBI holiday party at his home for his top staff: At the end of the two-hour window for the event, Mueller flickered the lights to announce the party was over. After 9/11, someone encouraged him to take more of an interest in the emotional well-being of his employees, who were operating under unfathomable stress. Mueller called the first one and said: "Hi. . . . It's Bob. . . . How are you?" The employee said "Fine," and Mueller said "Good" and hung up.

But that impenetrably austere side of Bob Mueller was joined to a very different sort of person. He often surprised you with his thoughtfulness and caring; on numerous occasions, I watched him go out of his way to privately console or encourage a colleague who was struggling.

And to complicate the picture further, Mueller has a good and self-deprecating sense of humor. When he sensed your growing exasperation with his tenacious questioning, he loved telling a joke his former chief of staff once told in the presence of the entire top FBI brass. In the middle of a Mueller unyielding barrage of questions, the chief of staff interrupted to ask him: "What is the difference between the FBI director and a five-year-old?" "What?" Mueller asked sternly. The answer: "Height." Everyone in the room was stunned and silent, waiting to see how this would go over. Mueller roared with laughter.

When my short assignment as his special counsel was over, I departed for a stint in private practice in New York, and then returned to the Bureau in 2011 as Mueller's general counsel. I oversaw the Bureau's sprawling four-hundred-person legal team that provided FBI agents and analysts guidance on how to conduct operations within the bounds of the law. The job necessitated my working around the clock, seven days a week. When early on, Mueller told me to "pace myself," I knew that he meant it sincerely in the moment, but also that his empathy for my predicament didn't at all soften his expectation that I be up to speed on every issue. Nor should it; what we were doing was too important— lives were at stake.

Working so closely with Mueller cemented my admiration for the man. He had been only a week on the job as director of the FBI when 9/11 happened. That Tuesday morning, I had watched the World Trade Center collapse and burn from my office at the Criminal Division in Brooklyn—saw too many people jumping from the buildings to their deaths rather than burn alive. Like a lot of government employees— even those, like me, who did not work directly on counterterrorism—I felt my own vigilant sense of duty to our country intensify. I wanted to help. I wanted us to do better. But Mueller would have the weight of these attacks on his shoulders for another twelve years as FBI director. The prospect of another terror attack occurring in the United States, or harming citizens overseas, weighed on him daily.

I was awed by his work ethic, the rigor with which he digested the president's daily intelligence brief—the PDB—and his almost preter-natural feel for which of the innumerable threats were more imminent and real than others. He was tasked with a seemingly impossible job: Keep every single American safe. And given the massive amounts of data that the FBI and its Intelligence Community partners amassed daily, he considered his ability to sift through it, locking on to the most worrisome threats, to be of paramount importance. It was inspiring to see a human being consumed so completely by duty and mission.

Mueller, however, did not let that sense of mission overwhelm his equal concern for fairness. He was an aggressive prosecutor at heart, but punctilious about due process and rectitude. In 2012, I was made aware that the FBI lab experts had been, for years, testifying erroneously in cases involving hair fiber samples, overstating the level of certainty with which the science could match a sample from a crime scene to a given defendant. Mueller fully supported my view that we needed to implement a top-to-bottom review. Ultimately, we teamed with the Innocence Project to examine thousands of old cases, and briefed Congress, the inspector general, and senior Justice Department officials about what had occurred and what we were doing about it.

When briefing Mueller on the bad news about what we had uncovered, he told me, "There is no such thing as bad news, just news. The key is how we address that news." Instead of vilifying us over our initial failures, the media, to my surprise, held up the FBI as a model for how to confront a problem. This was the by-product of following the classic Mueller approach to problem-solving—a game plan that he inculcated in me and numerous others who worked for him: Admit the problem head-on, devise a solution, and then audit the solution to make sure it worked.

I also learned that Mueller was savvy in the ways of Washington—with its political traps and pitfalls. During one of the first senior staff meetings I attended at the Bureau in 2011, we discussed the arrest of Umar Farouk Abdulmutallab, the so-called Underwear Bomber, who'd carried explosives in the waistband of his underwear onto a flight from Amsterdam to Detroit. (The bomb had not detonated, mercifully, but only due to a malfunction.) Congress was in an uproar, criticizing the FBI for eventually reading Abdulmutallab his Miranda rights and permitting the terrorist to obtain a lawyer—standard FBI procedure, but not required under the case law if there are exigent circumstances, or if you do not intend to use in court the statements elicited from the person. As Mueller and the rest of his staff discussed the controversy, I chimed in and noted that obtaining defense counsel in this situation was not a negative; it could often ultimately play to the government's advantage. A good defense attorney could be our best ally, I noted, as he or she could recognize the severity of the case, and counsel the defendant that it was in his best interest to cooperate.

Mueller looked at me calmly, without a trace of a smile. "If you are going to insist on being logical," he said, "you have no future in this town."

.   .   .

Mueller and I both left the FBI in the fall of 2013, when his statutory term of office expired, but our paths would cross again. I had gone on to be the head of the Justice Department's Fraud Section in 2015. The Fraud Section had changed dramatically from when Leslie and I had headed up the Enron Task Force. Due to the hard work and tough decisions by people like Lanny Breuer and Denis McInerney, it was now spearheading prosecutions of the most important and widespread domestic and international corporate frauds. One illustrative case was our prosecution in 2016 of pervasive environmental fraud by Volkswagen, which had marketed its cars as "clean" but falsified the results of emissions tests. Within one year, our criminal attorneys, along with our good colleagues in the Detroit U.S. attorney's office and the Environmental Division, brought a criminal case against Volkswagen and, importantly, its senior executives. The company ultimately pleaded guilty and had to pay billions of dollars to U.S. victims. Mueller had followed these developments closely; he served as a court-appointed special master in civil litigation that arose from that case and was integral in figuring out the most equitable way to get money back to Volkswagen's victims in the United States.

And so I was not altogether surprised when he called me in for a meeting just before Memorial Day, 2017—about a week after he'd been appointed special counsel. Mueller was beginning to set up shop in his new basement offices at the time, and had brought over a small brain trust of partners from his law firm, WilmerHale. Two of these colleagues, Jim Quarles and Aaron Zebley, attended the meeting as well.

I knew Quarles only by reputation; he spent most of his career in private practice as a seasoned and savvy number two to an eminent patent lawyer. But he'd started out as a junior lawyer on the Watergate investigation in the 1970s, making him one of only a handful of attorneys in America with experience directly relevant to Mueller's new assignment. Quarles would assume the role of elder statesman for the office. He had a bushy Wilford Brimley mustache, projected a kind of avuncular steadiness, and possessed a brilliant and practical mind. He assimilated facts quickly and brought unerring and mature judgment to every dilemma, assets that more than compensated for his lack of experience on criminal cases.

Aaron Zebley I already knew. We'd worked closely together under Mueller at the FBI, where he'd been Mueller's chief of staff. He'd become an FBI agent after law school, and worked on terrorism cases after 9/11. Then, after a short time as a prosecutor, he returned to the Bureau. He was whippet thin, meticulous, and worked long hours with no complaint. While Mueller was decisive, sometimes impulsive, Aaron labored over decisions, carefully assessing pros and cons. His indecisiveness was married to an innate desire to be liked, which led him to instinctively seek compromise. These qualities would cause enormous frustration for the lawyers and agents in the Special Counsel's Office.

In the big picture, Aaron served as a complement, or counterweight, to Mueller's temperament. This was by design. I'd served a similar function for Mueller while I was his general counsel, where my role was to consider the privacy and civil liberties implications of what the Bureau was doing. (I'd heard he referred to my predecessor, who was vigilant on these issues, as "my little Communist.") It was important to Mueller for his own judgments and ideas to bump up against others' and be tested. He valued that friction, kept it close at hand. He wanted his ideas challenged and was unafraid to alter his initial opinions based on a good idea, no matter whom it came from.

It seemed clear in our meeting that Aaron would again perform the function of Mueller's chief of staff in the Special Counsel's Office. Quarles had been put in charge of Team 600, the group focused on obstruction of justice. A third WilmerHale attorney whom I did not know, Jeannie Rhee, would lead Team R, which was charged with investigating Russian election interference.

That left Team M—and the reason Mueller had called me in, although I did not know that at the time. I believed I'd been called in for a kind of informal consultation, to relay relevant leads I'd come across at the Fraud Section. But Mueller had other ideas. For him, I was a natural fit to lead Team M: I had extensive experience with economic crime, both as head of the Fraud Section and the Enron Task Force. Moreover, Mueller was looking for someone who could tackle the Manafort investigation without too much hand-holding. Manafort happened to be represented at the time by other WilmerHale partners as his defense counsel, so it would be ideal for Mueller to supervise Team M, but not have to be directly involved in meetings and communications on this particular front.

Jim, Aaron, and I all sat in chairs in Mueller's temporary, makeshift office. He wanted to know what I thought he needed to do. I told him about possible leads to follow, specific witnesses who might offer information. It would be imperative in a case like this, I said, to obtain an inside cooperating witness, and Mueller nodded in agreement. As one example, I informed him that we currently had a Ukrainian oligarch named Dmitry Firtash under indictment, awaiting extradition in Austria, for FCPA-related crimes. (The Foreign Corrupt Practices Act criminalizes bribing foreign officials to obtain business, and all prosecutions under that statute are overseen by the Fraud Section.) It would be wise for the Special Counsel's Office to reach out to Firtash's defense counsel, I said, to explore if he'd be willing to cooperate—a long shot, perhaps, but with little downside. A couple of months beforehand, I had been prevented from doing so by the new leadership of the Justice Department's Criminal Division, which had my antenna up since it was such an obvious investigative step. It was hard not to conclude that the Department was intentionally refusing to take steps to make the case against Manafort.

It is eerie to reflect back on this initial meeting with Mueller. None of us knew then what we now know about the president's machinations. We had already known that when Trump was a private citizen he had bemoaned the FCPA, noting that the law thwarted his ability to do business overseas because it criminalized making bribes to foreign officials to be awarded contracts. And I knew that shortly after the inauguration, a newly minted Trump appointee had advised me to take a third of my FCPA attorneys—that is a third of the entire nation's prosecutorial FCPA resources—and move them to another unit. I had given all the reasons why that was ill advised and said they would do it over my opposition. What none of us knew at the time was that the president had begun exploring how to get rid of the statute altogether. And that was the statute that Firtash was charged with violating. (We also did not know of reports that Firtash would be scheming with Rudy Giuliani behind the scenes to swap fabricated dirt on Mueller and me in exchange for dropping his criminal case.)

But at the time of our meeting, Firtash represented an obvious lead to pursue to move the case forward rapidly. Mueller got it immediately. When I was finished explaining this, he directed me to reach out to Firtash's defense counsel on behalf of the Special Counsel's Office right away. Classic Bob: decisive and appropriately aggressive. (I spoke with Firtash's counsel, who reported back that his client was interested in cooperating, but purported implausibly to us to have no useful information whatsoever, so the discussions ended abruptly.)

I continued to lay out for Mueller some other leads worth pursuing. There were a few moves he could make, I explained, that might land him cooperating witnesses, including a couple of people like Felix Sater, who had been a cooperating witness during my time at EDNY, and had, after that and in spite of his felony conviction, gone on to work with Trump on various real estate projects. (Corruption and criminality were not rare in the world of New York real estate. Years earlier, a stock short seller I'd prosecuted and flipped had told me that, when he got out of jail, he intended to work in real estate in New York; he'd be barred from the securities markets as a consequence of his guilty plea, he explained, but being that the real estate business was unregulated, he imagined he'd be right at home there.) Mueller again nodded. Finally, we talked about Oleg Deripaska, the powerful Russian oligarch who was close to Vladimir Putin. Deripaska had known ties to Manafort, although the precise nature of their relationship needed investigation. Earlier in the week, Mueller had received various briefings from the components of the Department who had been conducting investigations that he would be taking over, but Mueller told me that Deripaska's name had not come up at all.

In all, our meeting took about an hour. Jim and Aaron largely were in listening mode, but at the end, Quarles noted that I seemed to have more ideas about how the Special Counsel's Office should proceed than people they'd spoken to in the Justice Department who'd been investigating Manafort since 2013. It took me a second to realize that they were, in fact, offering me the job.

I didn't leap at the opportunity, though I find my hesitation mind-boggling now. I loved my role as chief of the Fraud Section. We had made significant progress, bringing important international fraud cases and starting a series of initiatives that I was eager to see through. We were spearheading the use of "Big Data" in detecting and prosecuting healthcare fraud, had made strides in promoting effective corporate compliance programs, and developed DOJ policies that provided greater transparency and fairness. I had the privilege of laboring alongside some of the best prosecutors in the country. It was hard to think of leaving what we were building together.

I told Mueller I needed to think about the offer overnight. Couldn't I just follow up on certain leads for the Special Counsel's Office—moonlight a little—but remain in my post? I asked. In retrospect, the question seems naïve and quaint. That was never going to work. The reality was clear: I had to be all-in or out.

Almost immediately after I left the meeting, however, I realized two things. The first epiphany hit me hard: I couldn't say no to Bob Mueller. It would be unthinkable—simply as a matter of loyalty and duty; if Mueller asked, you answered the call.

As FBI director, serving both Republican and Democratic administrations, Mueller had already achieved the near impossible: remaining apolitical and maintaining a reputation for integrity. At the time, politicians of all stripes were still lauding his selection as special counsel; the political strategy of vilifying Mueller and our investigation had not yet taken hold. My sense was that the American public felt similarly. The day of Mueller's appointment, my sister phoned me and, despite not being a political creature, told me she thought Mueller was a phenomenal choice. "It's an affirmation of the rule of law," she said. "It doesn't matter what he finds." The nation could now be confident, she said, that the facts and the law would be applied. I had precisely the same feeling. I was a career DOJ employee, with a strong conviction that politics should never taint or tread on the law.

My second epiphany was that this was not the time to think about which job I might enjoy personally. The importance of the special counsel's work was sinking in—particularly in that moment, at what appeared to be an inflection point for our democracy. The 2016 election had been dismaying to watch. I found Hillary Clinton's email use to reveal an indefensible imperiousness. She had felt entitled to disregard rules that applied to everyone else. How was it appropriate to keep government work emails on a private server?

Having been the FBI general counsel, I knew that such official correspondence would need to be accessed and available; it often became relevant in government litigation, was requested under the Freedom of Information Act, and was necessary to preserve under the Federal Records Act. At the FBI, we had scrupulously preserved Director Mueller's communications for the National Personnel Records Center; the emails of Secretary Clinton, a political appointee, would have to be preserved this same way, I thought. This dustup reminded me of an incident when Mueller had shown me a new shiny toy—an Apple iPhone—that the FBI tech group had given him to use. The problem was that we had not yet figured out how to deal with the security issues for that device or how to preserve all of its communications, which was required by the federal records laws. Jennifer Love (the head of the FBI Security Division) and I had to break the news to the director, as I physically removed the device from his clutches that very day. As the Clinton debacle snowballed in the run-up to the election, I couldn't help wondering, from my parochial vantage point, how the State Department's legal adviser could have allowed this lapse to occur in the first place.

It was even more destabilizing to watch Clinton's opponent conduct his campaign with a blithe disregard for the rule of law, and in ways that cut deeper than Clinton's irresponsible record keeping. Donald Trump's candidacy seemed antithetical to the core principles of the Department of Justice, which stood for equal justice under the law and against judging people based on immutable traits, such as race and national origin. Trump, for example, had denigrated the federal judge who was presiding over a case involving Trump, claiming that because the judge was Mexican (in fact, he was American, with ancestors from Mexico), he was biased and couldn't fairly oversee the case. In court, this contention would be legally impermissible.

It was equally painful, personally and as an American, to watch the Trump campaign demonize immigrants. I'm the child of an immigrant myself—a first-generation American. My father was born in Vienna and fled at the age of eight, soon after the Nazis invaded Austria, and ultimately settled with his parents on the Upper West Side of Manhattan. Early in my career, as a law clerk, I had watched countless naturalization ceremonies, in which a federal judge swears in new citizens who, like my father and grandparents, had come to this country from all around the globe. The judge for whom I clerked—Eugene Nickerson—

always made a point of reminding those immigrants that they were the glory of America and that it was their diversity that made this country different from many others. He urged them to hold on to their customs and traditions, even as they assimilated to their new home. Those ceremonies were always filled with tears of joy. I even caught the judge welling up occasionally, despite having presided over such ceremonies for decades.

The principles Trump flouted are enshrined in the U.S. Constitution; they are not new and wild-eyed ideals or attributes of one political party. A friend of mine—an appellate lawyer who'd worked in the Department for more than thirty years—astutely pointed out what made the Trump campaign so troublingly unique. As she put it, a candidate to lead the U.S. government was promoting views that the same government tasked her and her colleagues with fighting against.

By the time Mueller called me in for that initial meeting in May 2017, I had seen Trump's anti-immigrant campaign rhetoric morph into policy. In January 2017, the administration's first iteration of the Muslim ban, for example, clearly violated existing Supreme Court precedent by providing no legal process for foreigners who were living in this country legally. Having wrestled with the rights of such people as general counsel of the FBI, in connection with the implementation of the no-fly list and other restrictions after 9/11, I found such cavalier disregard for the law and the dire consequences of such an executive order disturbing. The administration simply moved precipitously to bar such people from returning to the United States. That wasn't just unlawful—it was callous.

I'd started noticing that same corrosion of professionalism and norms spreading elsewhere through the government, as well. At one meeting in the Criminal Division of the Justice Department, I watched a career chief of MLARS tell a new Trump appointee how thrilled he was to have Trump's new attorney general, Jeff Sessions, on board. "The only downside," the chief said, "is that we lost a seat in the Senate." Leaving aside the pandering, his statement violated the spirit if not the letter of the Hatch Act, which prohibits political activity in federal buildings. And yet, he said it so freely, as though such rules no longer applied.

I had seen during the Enron case the importance of watchdogs providing guardrails and how, if we succumb to fear, don't speak truth to power, or simply go along to get along, those with no regard for the law are effectively given permission to subvert it. The Constitution has set up checks and balances and established the ideal that we would be a nation of laws, not men. But already, in that early stage of the Trump era, there appeared to be precious few checks remaining: The press and the law, it seemed to me, were the last two standing, and the press was under constant attack. Soon Mueller would be subject to similar attacks, for the same reasons: because he represented a check on the president's unfettered power.

Thirty-seven years after I'd sat in that lecture hall at Princeton, there was no question in my mind as to what idea I'd chosen to live by when I became a career prosecutor at the Department of Justice: that the rule of law that binds us together as a society must remain inviolable; that no person is above it—not mobsters, not corporate executives, not politicians—and that those who undermine it must be held to account. This adherence to the rule of law is what separates us from Russia or Ukraine—what makes us a democracy instead of a banana republic.

I realized that joining the Special Counsel's Office would be the opportunity of a lifetime: a chance to preserve the ideals of the Department of Justice and those embedded in the Constitution. Along the way, I'd be accused of being anti-Trump. But I was not anti anyone. I was, rather, pro the rule of law. If I was fighting against anything, it was the quiet corrosion I saw undoing it—and the prospect of that order giving way. "Wherever law ends, tyranny begins," John Locke wrote, a sentiment that is carved indelibly into the limestone walls of the Department of Justice in Washington.

I was on board.

CHAPTER 3

Getting Traction

IT TOOK SEVERAL WEEKS, but we eventually hired enough staff at the Special Counsel's Office for Mueller to call an all-hands introductory meeting. By this point, we had moved into our new space, on the third floor of another, less dreary but equally bland, government building—one in a cluster of such buildings that was named (aptly, I like to think) Patriots Plaza. We now had windows along the perimeter of our space, but due to security concerns, the blinds were adjusted to an angle that prevented peering eyes from seeing in—and had the effect of keeping the entry of natural light into our space to a bare minimum. Now, a table in our largest conference room was pulled to one end for the speakers. Well in advance of the appointed time, the entire staff huddled in front of it and lined the walls, waiting for our boss to arrive.

There were by then maybe forty of us working in the office, and everyone was gathered: not just attorneys, but FBI analysts and agents, administrative assistants, paralegals, back-office staff. This being a government operation, there was no budget for platters of Danish or wraps, sparkling water or coffee. A lot of the faces in the room were familiar to me by now, though I'd not yet had occasion to meet most of the staff. There was no group dynamic yet, or anything approaching esprit de corps. The Special Counsel's Office wasn't the kind of place where you did team-building exercises.

Although the press heralded us as a "dream team," we all knew better. The hiring process had unfolded more haphazardly than one would expect. Aaron Zebley lacked any supervisory experience, and staffing decisions turned out to involve a fair amount of randomness and disorganization. Early on, for example, Jim Quarles impulsively hired a junior attorney straight out of a Supreme Court clerkship, with no true work experience, let alone any as a prosecutor. Jim simply liked the young man and, touchingly, saw a lot of himself in the guy. But then, when it came time to assign this neophyte to one of our three teams, Jim insisted that he couldn't take him on Team 600—the kid had no experience!

The hiring process was also subject to Mueller's own peccadillos. As was his penchant, Mueller had three EDNY prosecutors join the office, the largest contingent from any one district. Jeannie Rhee, our Team R leader, and I spent weeks interviewing other experienced white-collar prosecutors, mainly from the U.S. attorney's office for the Southern District of New York, only to have Mueller reject our recommendations, one after another. He did not know these people, which was a strike against them, and, though he generally regarded the prosecutors that SDNY produced as smart and effective, he also felt they had a reputation for hand-wringing—a mortal weakness in Mueller's book—and being a little too cocky for Mueller's understated manner. Still, Mueller's reticence ran deeper than that, and was hard for Jeannie and me to decipher or appease. Various candidates seemed to lack something ineffable, but absolutely indispensable in Mueller's mind. Finally, one day, we pressed him for an explanation: What exactly were all these applicants missing?

"Pizazz," Mueller responded, with steely-eyed seriousness. Then, as it became clear we had no idea what concrete, prosecutorial strengths or qualifications that word could possibly communicate, he pointed at Jeannie and, said: "Like you. You have pizazz."

I'd gotten to know Jeannie fairly well by then, and Mueller's meaning was suddenly crystal clear. Jeannie is a diminutive Asian American woman with a quick and raucous laugh whose blindingly big personality draws you in immediately. She is also hyper-stylish, and stood out in our office: a bolt of Prada clothes, Jimmy Choo shoes, and Céline bags. (I and nearly everyone else typically dressed in the same sort of drab blue suit and white shirt; as a stylish friend, Katya Jestin, once warned me, I'd be in trouble if "fashion crimes" ever got included in the federal code.) Whereas the only personal item I'd bothered to bring into our first, temporary basement offices was a water bottle, Jeannie had tricked out her workspace with rugs, lamps, and numerous framed pictures of her smiling children and husband, until it resembled a Bloomingdale's showroom.

And yet, none of this was pizazz as Mueller was defining it. Pizazz had nothing to do with flashiness or physical appearance; instead, it was a mindset—a kind of can-do, combustible energy with which Jeannie addressed herself to the world. I'd come to see her as a paragon of pizazz, a type A prosecutor with an inventive and meticulous legal mind. She had gone to Yale, for both undergrad and law school; her mother, she said, would have had it no other way. (If she got a 99 on a test, her mother would ask her what went wrong.)

Jeannie had served as a federal prosecutor in the Washington, D.C., U.S. attorney's office and in the esteemed Office of Legal Counsel at the Department of Justice, and then joined WilmerHale, where Mueller had latched on to her as soon as he arrived. Aaron, in one of our first conversations, told me that Jeannie and I were going to love each other. Much later, after Jeannie and I grew closer—forging a tight friendship as we rejoiced, commiserated, and gossiped together multiple times a day for the next two years—we'd joke that this was one of the few things we agreed Aaron had predicted correctly.

At the precise appointed time, Mueller arrived for the orientation meeting in our conference room, along with Andrew McCabe, then the acting director of the FBI. At the Bureau I had adapted to this same punctuality, an attribute I quickly learned when I sauntered into a meeting with senior agents a few minutes after the start time, only to see everyone in place, eyes glaring at me. At the FBI, if you were not early for a meeting, you were late.

It was nice to see Andy McCabe. I'd known him for years, but given his new responsibilities at the FBI I had not connected with him in a while. I considered him a good work colleague, if not exactly a personal friend, though in the nomenclature of Washington, I'd found, the latter often substituted for the former. Andy had been the head of the FBI's Counterterrorism Division when I was the agency's general counsel, and we'd spent many long, hectic days together following the Boston Marathon bombing, and toiling through the many legal and policy issues in the aftermath of Edward Snowden's leaks. Andy was calm, smart, and hyper-articulate, widely known as the best briefer in the Bureau for his ability to cogently synthesize and distill sweeping amounts of information for whichever particular director, attorney general, president, or congressional committee had asked to be brought up to speed on an issue. He also had a law degree—we spoke the same language.

At that point, Andy had been acting director for a couple of months, thrust into the role after the president fired Jim Comey. I was happy Andy was leading the Bureau, though I was troubled by the circumstances under which he'd been handed the job. Comey's firing was one of the first areas Team 600 would be investigating, determining whether it was proof of the president's obstruction of justice. And since the firing, the president had ramped up his childish attacks on Andy on Twitter, suggesting that he be removed from his position for some invented conflict of interest having to do with his wife's campaign for state senate in Virginia almost two years earlier. It was all so much blather—yet another sign of our institutional systems of oversight being undermined and attacked for personal and political reasons.

I understood that Andy had cleared the issues arising from his wife's decision to run for office with the Bureau's meticulous ethics officer, Patrick Kelley, who had signed off on it. I also knew that, like all good agents, he was more than capable of remaining staunchly apolitical in his work. That ethos of objective detachment was part of the Bureau's fabric. One followed the facts and the law; personal views were irrelevant and could be easily set aside.

Mueller invited Andy to kick the meeting off, and Andy—essentially a guest in Mueller's house—kept his comments brief. He assured us that the Special Counsel's Office had the full support of FBI headquarters— what we called "Big Bu." We would get whatever help we needed, Andy said, and he stressed that all FBI personnel detailed to our investigation would, as always, act apolitically and in sole service of the facts.

With that, Andy turned the floor back over to Mueller. Looking around at the assembled staff, I imagined that some of those people, particularly the younger hires, would be expecting a big, inspiring St. Crispin's Day speech. I'd given—or, more accurately, aspired to give—many such pep talks myself at the Fraud Section, though it never came naturally. I'd forced myself to do it, for the sake of morale. It seemed reasonable for the uninitiated to expect Mueller to lay out our mission at length, to thank us for signing on and acknowledge the sacrifices we'd be making: the long nights and weekends, the burdens on our families, the stress.

But I'd been around Mueller long enough to know that this was going to be a meeting run by someone who detested meetings. Those in his inner circle at the FBI knew that if you wanted to provoke Mueller's ire, expressed through a long hard glare, all you need do was suggest the formation of a "working group" to meet on an issue. Mueller wanted action and decisiveness. And Mueller didn't feel an obligation to encourage his employees with superficial bromides. This wasn't halftime at a high school basketball game. It was the Special Counsel's Office, and Mueller simply took it for granted that everyone felt as privileged as he did to be in this job, representing the United States and working for the betterment of our country. Any external validation or motivation he could offer would be superfluous.

Mueller began by reminding us to conduct ourselves professionally and never speak a word about the investigation outside the Special Counsel's Office. There would be no leaks, because leaks would only undermine our credibility and work. It was vitally important, Mueller explained, that our office speak through our actions: any arrests made, complaints sworn out, indictments issued, briefs filed. This was an outgrowth of a Department of Justice tenet that had been driven into all of us from day one: "Put up or shut up"—you don't get to malign people who have not been charged by a grand jury. He then gave his cursory thanks for the sacrifice our families were making to support the long days and nights ahead.

And that was it. The meeting was over. In the end, we'd spent more time waiting for him and Andy to show up than we did listening to them. We all headed back to our desks.

CHAPTER 4

The Start of the Obstruction Investigation

IT WAS ONLY A few weeks into our investigation in June 2017 when Jim Quarles walked into my office one morning and placed a document on my desk.

"Read this," he told me. "It's tinfoil helmet material."

Jim meant the document resembled the kind of paranoid, unstructured ravings you'd expect to hear from unhinged "pro se" litigants representing themselves in court—the sort of people who wear tinfoil hats to keep aliens from intercepting their thoughts. This document, however, was written by the president of the United States.

As part of Team 600's investigation into the Comey firing—its first order of business—Quarles had obtained Trump's original draft statement, setting out his reasons for dispensing with the FBI director. (A significantly revamped version of the document became Comey's actual termination letter.) After the firing, the White House had conspicuously touted another memo, this one written by Deputy Attorney General Rod Rosenstein—as the purported justification for Comey's dismissal. But here, it seemed, was a direct window into Trump's thinking, preserved in a revealing and alarmingly raw form.

Comey was fired by the president on May 9, 2017. I was still working in the Fraud Section of the Justice Department when the firing was announced, and remember reading at my desk the Rosenstein memo immediately. The memo's subject line was "Restoring Public Confidence in the FBI." In it, Rosenstein offered a sharp critique of Comey's public pronouncements during the Clinton email investigation, specifically the press conference he'd held the previous July, in which he'd rebuked Clinton for her extreme carelessness but then announced that, ultimately, the Bureau did not recommend any criminal charges.

"The way the Director handled the conclusion of the email investigation was wrong," Rosenstein wrote. Comey violated basic Department of Justice norms, he said, by publicly disparaging someone who had not been charged with a crime. "As a result, the FBI is unlikely to regain public and congressional trust until it has a Director who understands the gravity of the mistakes and pledges never to repeat them."

I remember, at the time, telling a colleague in the Criminal Division that Rosenstein's reasoning was spot-on. And yet, I also knew it would be naïve to accept that memo as reflecting the president's true reasons for firing Comey. It was impossible to believe that a man who'd spent much of the summer and fall of 2016 fomenting chants of "Lock her up!" at campaign rallies was suddenly offended that Comey had unfairly maligned Hillary Clinton. In context, the effort to use the Rosenstein memo as the basis for the firing smelled distinctly fishy, and warranted investigation as to what the true reasons were for his firing and whether it constituted an obstruction of justice.

Still, as a career Justice Department prosecutor, I found the situation more nuanced than the black-and-white terms on which it was frequently discussed, and feel it's worth laying out those complexities. Full disclosure: I'm no fan of Jim Comey. I disapproved of much of his conduct in the run-up to the 2016 election for precisely the reasons Rosenstein articulated, and I certainly didn't feel any great personal outrage on Comey's behalf when I heard he'd been terminated. A bedrock principle for every prosecutor and agent in the Department of Justice is that, prior to conviction, you do not publicly announce your opinion of a person's guilt or innocence. Your views are irrelevant; it is up to a grand jury to determine whether to bring charges, and then it is up to a trial jury to decide on that person's guilt. Disclosing a personal opinion treads on the accused's presumption of innocence.

In the past, other prosecutors and agents—including some people who Comey knew well—had gotten into serious trouble for crossing this line when publicly unveiling new charges against a defendant. This is why, in keeping with Department protocol, many of our indictments at the Special Counsel's Office would contain references to "Person A" or "Company B" or "Vendor C." We did not publicly identify any entities that weren't being charged, to keep them from suffering any opprobrium. We were not doing anything unique; this is what federal prosecutors do every day when announcing charges.

But the implications of Comey's press conference about Clinton were even worse because Clinton was not being charged with a crime at all. The FBI was recommending declination; it hadn't found sufficient evidence of criminal wrongdoing. For Comey nevertheless to condemn her behavior, and hold forth about her culpability, was, therefore, even more improper, as he had to know as a longtime federal prosecutor. The conclusion of the email investigation could have been a teachable moment; the Department and the FBI could have used the opportunity to explain to the American public why the government does not ever publicly air the evidence it's gathered on someone who has not been charged with breaking any laws, and certainly why it must not editorialize or disparage that person—why, in short, it's critical for the Department to always take the high road.

To those of us steeped in these principles, Comey's performance was outlandish. He apparently perceived himself to be above the rules of the bureau he led and department of which he was a part. Comey's conduct violated another precept of the Department—a more inside-baseball issue, but one that I knew was dear to Mueller: Stay in your lane. Do not overstep your role in the structure of the larger institution.

The FBI gathers evidence; it is not the agency that decides whether to move forward with a case. That decision may be based on the work and private recommendation of the FBI, but it is a decision made, solely, by the lawyers at the Department of Justice. At his press conference, Comey was purporting to give the Department the Bureau's recommendation. But that was the thinnest of false veneers for what he was doing. Since when does the Bureau give its recommendations publicly, let alone with all the accoutrements of a high-profile press conference?

What if the Department lawyers had disagreed with Comey's recommendation—how would this discrepancy, unfurled in full view of the public, shape the Department's criminal case as it went forward? Comey's announcement was no recommendation; it was intended to give the appearance that the Clinton matter was now settled—that he, himself, had settled it. This is not a unique view on my part. When asked much later about Comey's press conference, Attorney General Loretta Lynch noted, with her characteristic understatement, "That was certainly an unusual way to receive an FBI recommendation."

Comey's actions three months later, in October 2016, were even less warranted—and even more dangerous. At the time, the FBI was conducting a separate investigation into Anthony Weiner, the husband of Clinton aide Huma Abedin, and the Bureau had found some of Abedin's emails on Weiner's laptop—correspondence that it had not collected during the original Clinton email investigation, which was now closed.

As we all know, Comey reported this development to Congress in a letter during the last week of October, explaining that this discovery compelled him to reopen the FBI's Clinton investigation, so that these additional emails could be examined. It was a mere eleven days before the presidential election. That afternoon, I got a phone call from a senior supervisory special agent I knew at the FBI, a man who'd investigated political corruption cases for years. He was choking back tears. "Comey just threw the reputation of the Bureau under the bus," he said. "It will take years before we recover."

There is a rule, drilled into every FBI agent, that no public actions must be taken before an election that might, in any way, tilt its result. The Bureau recognizes it must not arrogate to itself the enormous power to influence an election by casting criminal aspersions that can't be promptly tested by the accused in our legal system. Anyone impugned by the Bureau right before votes are cast will not have the opportunity to defend him- or herself in court, or even sufficiently clear their name in the public square. And, moreover, there is simply no reason to short-circuit the standard process for adjudicating and resolving such problems—again, no need to swerve outside one's lane. If a criminal case eventually needs to be brought, and is meritorious, the public will learn the facts and be able to assess them soon enough. Even if the target has been elected to office at that point, he or she can still be impeached, re-

sign, or get voted out. This is not a decision like those involving imposi-
tion of the death penalty, where there is no chance to go back and correct
a mistake.

Comey would defend his actions by claiming that the discovery of
the additional emails presented a hard case with only two options, both
of them bad: He could either keep this new evidence secret or reveal it
publicly. He is partly correct: It was a hard case. But in no way does that
justify throwing out the Bureau's rule book, which is made for the hard
cases, not the easy ones. The history of the FBI under J. Edgar Hoover is
a testament to the serious threat to our democracy posed by a director
who feels licensed to privilege his own judgment over the rules of the
institution. Rules are established, with great forethought, to give us
guardrails in difficult times—to guide us toward ethical and responsible
solutions and away from mistakes and personal recklessness. You don't
simply start winging it when thorny dilemmas arise.

Moreover, Comey's characterization of his predicament as binary—
his description of himself as stuck between a rock and a hard place—is
overly simplistic. There were many more nuanced, better ways in which
he might have proceeded than publicly disclosing to eight Republican
chairmen in Congress that the FBI had found more emails. According
to the inspector general's report issued later about this conduct, at the
time Comey wrote his letter to Congress, the Bureau had already decided not to pursue looking at more of Abedin's emails because the likelihood of them containing any pertinent information appeared to be
exceptionally low. Why not include this context in your letter to Congress, thus blunting any ginned-up air of scandal when the letter inevitably leaked?

I suspect Comey feared such a disclosure would reflect poorly on the
Bureau for not pursuing these emails previously. (A thorough investigation would have checked Abedin's husband's computer for additional
emails from her in the first place.) By omitting this information in the
letter, Comey misled the American electorate, and dangled the possibility that some new trove of incriminating evidence had just been unearthed. Another option: Simply conduct the Weiner laptop review
promptly and then report the findings, if there were any. (This, in fact,
was the option that Attorney General Lynch ordered, immediately after

Comey unilaterally disclosed the renewed criminal investigation. And that investigation revealed no new information, as the FBI had suspected all along, but did not reveal publicly.) There were myriad other options.

This is all to say, I found Rosenstein's criticisms of Comey's conduct sound. By smearing Clinton, twice, before the election, Comey had not only violated core Department of Justice precepts but also violated both Clinton's rights and those of the American electorate. I never discussed this with Mueller, but I knew he would concur. His entire twelve-year career as FBI director was a testament to rectitude and restraint. He would never have taken such action, period.

And yet, that was hardly the whole story. It was obvious to me, as it was to many Americans, that the White House was merely using the Rosenstein arguments to mask Trump's desire to dispense with Comey. It seemed distinctly possible that Trump had fired Comey to stifle the FBI's investigation into Russian election interference, and—we would soon learn—because Comey had refused to bow to the president's request that he drop the investigation of Trump's new national security adviser, Michael Flynn. If true, this would support a finding that it constituted obstruction of justice. To make that legal determination, the pertinent question was not whether there was a legitimate reason that Trump could now articulate to fire Comey. The question was why he actually fired him.

Puzzling this out was one of our office's first and most pressing tasks after Mueller was appointed special counsel, and the director set up Team 600 expressly to tackle it. At the outset, it seemed like the most discrete and straightforward arm of our overall investigation. Little did we know that the issue of obstruction would slowly sprawl and destabilize nearly every dimension of our work.

The draft statement on Comey's firing that Jim Quarles had plunked on my desk—the tinfoil hat document—was our first key evidence of the president's true motivation in firing Comey. Trump had written this draft with the help of his adviser Stephen Miller, while the two were holed up at the president's golf course in New Jersey, the week before

Comey was fired. This preceded the Rosenstein memo; in fact, we eventually learned, Trump and Miller had written this document before Rosenstein was even aware that the president planned to fire Comey.

I read the document immediately, while Jim stood over my desk. It was excruciatingly juvenile, disorganized, and brimming with spite—incoherent and narcissistic. You could almost feel the spittle coming off the paper. The draft was prepared shortly after Comey had testified to Congress, where he'd confirmed that the FBI had opened an investigation into Russian interference and links to the Trump campaign but refused to answer questions about whether the president himself was a target of that investigation.

In the memo, Trump went out of his way to mention, repeatedly, that Comey had assured him "on three separate occasions" that he was not under investigation. From there, it devolved into a stream-of-consciousness tirade against Comey, his investigation into Russian interference in the election, his handling of the Clinton investigation, his mishandling of the FBI, and other grievances, both real and imagined. You might expect the leader of the free world to praise an attempt by the FBI to safeguard the integrity of our elections from foreign interference. Instead, Trump dismissed the entire issue of Russian meddling as fabricated and politically motivated.

Jim Quarles and I both knew we were looking at perhaps the rawest, most authentic record of the president's thought process—a distillation of his state of mind as he set Comey's firing in motion. There were legitimate reasons to dismiss Comey, but this letter was merely a rambling collection of slights and invective. It's a big deal to fire an FBI director; only one, William Sessions, had ever been dismissed, and that was under very different circumstances involving clear ethical impropriety. (The FBI director has a statutory ten-year term, to remove the director from the political cycle of presidential elections, although the president can override that and fire the director at will.) The Trump-Miller diatribe did not rise to the seriousness this occasion warranted.

Moreover, this document served to corroborate a depiction of the president set forth in another set of documents that Team 600 had obtained. These were the personal memos that Comey wrote shortly after his conversations with the president in 2017—some of which Comey would later describe in his congressional testimony after being fired. I did not take the accuracy of these memos as a given, and they certainly did not purport to be verbatim transcriptions. The inspector general's report into the Clinton investigation is replete with evidence that Comey's recollections of other key meetings differed significantly from those of other credible people and contemporaneous documents. But in this instance—with Comey's memos about Trump in hand—we knew that Comey's stories about the president were not being retroactively colored by his firing. He'd written these memos beforehand.

The Comey memos illustrated a lot about the president and about Comey. They evidenced the president's obsession with personal loyalty and his deep desire for Comey to declare publicly that Trump was not under investigation in the Russia probe. As to the latter, I felt the president had good reason to be perturbed. I found it curious that Comey both refused to make such an announcement and failed to explain why he refused to do so to the president, given that Comey did not deny that he had already repeatedly assured Trump in private that he was not under investigation. Had Comey not been willing to divulge this information to the president—either publicly or privately—his reticence to accede to the president's demand that he make such a public statement would have been understandable. But here Comey was simply refusing to say publicly what he had said privately, which was far less defensible.

I also found it unusual that, according to his memos, Comey made so much about not being left alone with the president of the United States. There is nothing wrong with the FBI director meeting alone with a president—other directors have done so. Comey made it sound improper for Attorney General Sessions to have left Comey alone with the president. Then again, I intuited that Comey was not bristling against the theoretical prospect of an FBI director being left alone with a president; he was reluctant to be left alone with this particular president, as he suspected that might leave him vulnerable to improper requests or attempts at coercion.

In fact, Comey's memoranda contained a damning recitation of the president's doing just that, broaching with him in the Oval Office the fate of his national security adviser, Michael Flynn. Flynn had got caught up in the Russia investigation as a result of two calls he'd had with the Russian ambassador, Sergey Kislyak. The first phone call occurred in December 2016, right after the Obama administration had imposed sanctions on Russia for its election interference. Flynn asked Kislyak to keep Russia from reacting with countermeasures, which would have been a normal response to such sanctions. The Flynn call worked; Putin did not retaliate.

In January 2017, when the call was revealed by the press, Flynn lied about it to Vice President Mike Pence and others, including FBI agents, denying that he'd discussed sanctions with Kislyak. As a result, the vice president went on national TV and denied that such a call had occurred. There is no question that a conversation happened between Flynn and Kislyak. (The government in the spring of 2020 released transcripts of some of these, and the Special Counsel's Office report makes clear that the vice president and other White House officials viewed FBI evidence and concluded, for themselves, that Flynn had lied about the matter.) In retrospect, one oddity of the Flynn story is that, despite being a newly minted national security adviser, he was apparently not sophisticated enough to think that his conversations with Kislyak might be monitored by both the United States and Russia, and that lying about them could therefore be futile and perilous. If he lied to the American government, he could be easily found out and charged with a felony. And even if he somehow got away with lying, the Russians could use the call to black-mail him. (Ultimately, our office brought a false statement charge against Flynn, and he pleaded guilty in December 2017 and said he would coop-erate with our investigation. His commitment to that cooperation would prove tenuous, but Barr nevertheless orchestrated a spurious motion to dismiss his criminal case.)

The troubling discussion with Trump that Comey described in his memos occurred long before Flynn's plea, however—in February 2017, a month into the new administration. Comey leaked the substance of it to the media after he was fired, then recounted it in his book—published, unhelpfully, while our investigation was ongoing. According to the memo Comey wrote immediately after the meeting, the president told him: "I hope you can see your way to letting this go, to letting Flynn go. He is a good guy. I hope you can let this go."

I always believed that the reason the president made this request was in part because he felt some responsibility for Flynn; he knew that Flynn had merely been carrying out his wishes when he spoke with Kislyak. It was inconceivable that Flynn would take this step without

Trump's knowledge and approval. And it was in keeping with Trump's stated position during the campaign that our country should have better relations with Russia. If that was your goal, preventing an escalating exchange of sanctions would make sense, especially if the sanctions were for election interference that the president was refusing to accept as fact.

There was also substantial evidence that several of the president-elect's advisers, including Steve Bannon and foreign policy adviser K. T. McFarland, had advance knowledge of Flynn's call to Kislyak and approved of it. It thus seemed impossible that Flynn, Bannon, and McFarland would make such a significant strategic move without permission from the incoming president. What would possibly be gained by not alerting him? The president clearly would know immediately that Russia had not taken normal and expected retaliation in response to the Obama administration's sanctions. (In fact, the next day, Trump praised Putin's inaction.)

Flynn couldn't just admit the Kislyak calls, however, because of the Logan Act, an arcane criminal law. That statute mandated that there would be only one presidential administration acting at a time in foreign affairs and made it illegal for private citizens to communicate with foreign governments without U.S. approval. The statute, however, had never resulted in a prosecution—but Flynn and others could hardly start the transition of the new administration by admitting it violated the law, particularly since the communications were with the Russian government. Trump's hands were tied when Flynn stupidly lied about the phone call to Vice President Pence, who then repeated the falsehood publicly. For Trump, it wasn't the phone call that did Flynn in, but the exposed lie to Pence. So he had to fire Flynn, but that did not mean he wanted Flynn to be prosecuted when he repeated the same lies to the FBI. (This all would explain Trump's ongoing championing Flynn, which would otherwise seem completely unjustified, given his lying to his own vice president. Barr would end up doing the dirty work of getting Flynn out of his legal predicament, without Trump having to pay the political cost of pardoning Flynn.)

When the president of the United States asks the director of the FBI to go easy on somebody, it's hard to view that as a mere suggestion. And so, understandably, Comey took the president's words about Flynn to be an order. The president claimed in the press that he did not "order" Comey to be lenient to Flynn, nor require him to do anything improper. But the president was never willing to testify under oath or, ultimately, even sit for an interview with our office to explain his behavior. He did not even agree to answer written questions on this topic. Comey, on the other hand, not only had this interaction recorded in contemporaneous notes, but was also willing to let us interview him about it, knowing that any deliberately false statement to us was a felony. Thus, this was not simply a question of one man's word against another's—since, when push came to shove, one of those men was not willing to tell his side of the story.

Over the next six months, Team 600's interviews with White House staff, including Stephen Miller, Don McGahn, Hope Hicks, and Sarah Huckabee Sanders, as well as interviews of Department of Justice senior staff, brought the true story into clearer focus: The president had first announced his determination to fire Comey over dinner with advisers on May 3, a full five days before Rosenstein was ever asked his opinion or told by the president to write a memorandum evaluating whether such action was justified. Numerous witnesses told us that there was no room for discussion; the president had made the decision to fire Comey. Indeed, one senior national security staffer who worked for Rosenstein recorded in her notes that, rather than simply laying out arguments that supported his firing, the Rosenstein memo initially included a more explicit recommendation that Comey be removed, but it was taken out because he knew "the decision had already been made."

Thus, what so many Americans had immediately suspected became definitively clear to Team 600: The White House's effort to pass off the Comey firing as Rosenstein's idea was a fabrication. The Rosenstein memo merely offered a more legitimate justification for a decision that had already been made for different reasons. The Office of White House Counsel wanted the public announcement to rely on the Rosenstein memo as the sole rationale for the firing. They advised that the Trump draft never see the "light of day" and privately worried that the handling of the Comey firing might be the beginning of the end of the presidency. And, as detailed in our report, the White House's attempt to pin the Comey firing on Rosenstein had unraveled only when Rosenstein refused to be the fall guy. When, on the night of Comey's firing, the president wanted Rosenstein to hold a press conference about the matter, Rosenstein explained to Trump that this would be unwise, as he intended to answer all questions about the firing honestly, and explain to the media that it was not, in fact, his idea, as the White House had claimed publicly.

The president then had to admit the ruse—ironically first to a pair of Russian government officials, in a meeting from which the U.S. media was barred. On the morning of May 10, 2017, Trump met privately with Russian foreign minister Sergey Lavrov and Russian ambassador Sergey Kislyak in the Oval Office. The media later reported that Trump brought up the Comey firing with the two men, explaining, "I just fired the head of the FBI. He was crazy, a real nut job. I faced great pressure because of Russia. That's taken off."

White House Counsel Don McGahn told our office that the president told him much the same thing shortly after the Lavrov-Kislyak meeting. (Notably, the White House never disputed this story.) Eventually, in 2019, the press would learn from a memo prepared about the meeting that Trump had also assured the Russians that he was unconcerned about the election interference their country had just perpetrated on the United States. (Astoundingly, we at the Special Counsel's Office had not known this; no memo of this meeting was turned over by the White House in response to our numerous requests for pertinent documents. Thus, in addition to all the other evidence of obstruction that we would set out in our report, one can add a new and important fact: hiding this evidence. What is unclear is who knew about that memo and made the decision not to disclose it.)

The evening after the Lavrov-Kislyak meeting, Trump further fessed up to his thinking on national television, during an interview with NBC's Lester Holt. "I was going to fire regardless of [the] recommendation," Trump said. "He [Rosenstein] made a recommendation. . . . But regardless of [the] recommendation, I was going to fire Comey.

"And in fact," the president added, "when I decided to just do it, I said to myself—I said, you know, this Russia thing with Trump is a made-up story."

It was as though Trump had nothing to lose; by then, it was clear that the initial cover story—that the whole thing was Rosenstein's idea—was never going to fly.

.   .   .

This was the real story of the Comey firing, as Team 600 reconstructed it. It seemed clear that the firing was meant to stifle the power of the justice system for Trump's personal benefit. But, as occasionally happens, a situation that seems straightforward on a gut level is more complicated in the view of the law. For the purposes of our investigation, there was an additional layer of uncertainty: To determine whether the firing was an obstruction of justice, we didn't merely have to uncover the facts of what happened, but also settle on an appropriate interpretation of the law against which to evaluate those facts. It was possible that the president's actions would be drawn into a legal gray area.

The legal issue at play was new, and hinged on a question that has never been decided by the Supreme Court: Is it possible for a president to commit obstruction of justice in the course of exercising his constitutional powers?

No one disputes that it is within a president's constitutional powers to fire his FBI director; like all agency heads and cabinet officers, the director serves at the president's pleasure. Therefore, one side of this argument goes, it does not matter why the president is firing the director. As president, he is permitted to wield that particular power for any reason he wishes, or even for no reason at all. This view adheres to the preeminence of executive authority—what some term a so-called imperial presidency, but to my mind, it carries an uncomfortable resonance with Louis XIV's famous quip "L'état, c'est moi" ("I am the state"). This belief was espoused by none other than William Barr in a lengthy, unsolicited missive he sent to President Trump while Barr was a private citizen in January 2018—a move many interpreted as Barr's audition for the role of attorney general, for which Trump promptly nominated him several months later. Still, Barr's stance by no means reflects a consensus view of the presidency.

The opposing view insists on limits to what a president, or any other government official, is permitted to do while exercising his powers. This view was supported by Michael Dreeben, who as director of our legal team at the Special Counsel's Office, was responsible for guiding our legal analysis.

We all recognize, for example, that if a particular firing was motivated by the employee's race, sex, or religion, it would be a clear case of illegal discrimination. The same holds with respect to obstruction of justice, which has been defined by statute and the Supreme Court as encompassing an intentional act that has a natural tendency to interfere with an investigation, with a purpose of thwarting it. That is, a federal official who fires a subordinate in order to extinguish that employee's investigation into wrongdoing by the official, or the official's family, is committing obstruction. That official may ordinarily have the authority to fire that subordinate, but the power to fire for legitimate reasons does not place the official wholly beyond the reach of the law.

Frankly, I find it difficult to imagine the functioning of a world in which a president is given license to obstruct justice with total immunity. Accepting the imperial presidency view could lead you to argue, for example, that Nixon could have simply disregarded the subpoena for his White House tapes during Watergate and, instead, destroyed them. Even Barr had to concede there must be limits. When pressed during his confirmation hearing, he agreed that a president could not, for example, instruct a witness to lie; such an overt instance of obstruction apparently crossed some indistinct line in Barr's mind. (Still, I was shocked, in October 2019, to discover an even more ludicrous example unfolding in real life. During a proceeding in the U.S. Court of Appeals for the Second Circuit, in which the president's attorneys challenged a subpoena for Trump's tax returns by insisting that the president was exempt from such legal demands, the judge asked Trump's counsel how far this line of argument might go: If the president shot someone in the middle of Fifth Avenue, as he had once offhandedly joked about doing, the government wouldn't be able to arrest or prosecute him? "That is correct," the president's attorney replied.)

Acting attorney general Rod Rosenstein clearly disagreed with Barr's view of the law—at least, he did at the time he wrote Mueller's appointment order in May 2017. Under Barr's view of the obstruction question, it would make little sense for the special counsel to investigate whether the president had obstructed justice by firing Comey, or even to care whether Trump had disguised his reasons for firing Comey after the fact. Rosenstein, though, had indeed authorized Mueller to examine these questions—to investigate all prior and future obstruction of the Russia investigation, including the president's firing of Comey and his importuning regarding the investigation of Flynn. Rosenstein then oversaw our investigation for its full run of twenty-two months. At no point did he tell us to stop the factual investigation into obstruction by the president because of a legal impossibility, and he testified before Congress that he saw nothing improper about our conduct.

To me, the facts of the Comey firing appeared to satisfy all the elements of the crime of obstruction of justice; there was simply no other credible conclusion one could reach, particularly given the president's shifting, after-the-fact stories as to why he acted. And those post hoc fabrications could be used to show Trump's criminal mental state—that is, that he knew what he was doing was wrong, which the law would require the government to prove. I did not yet know, however, how Mueller would settle on conveying that in our report.

The whole affair reminded me of the John Gotti case, which was ongoing when I arrived in the Organized Crime Section of the U.S. attorney's office in 1992. I distinctly remember the lead prosecutor, my boss John Gleeson, explaining to me that the outcome of this case would not hinge on the proof—the proof was overwhelming. The verdict hinged, instead, on the degree to which the proceedings would be corrupted or undone by interference—whether witnesses would be coerced out of testifying, the jury would be tampered with, or the jury would simply be too intimidated to render the proper decision.

As the special counsel's investigation wore on, I realized we'd been thrust into a similar position. There were already numerous issues, such as the Comey firing, where the facts we turned up were glaring. But the norms and institutions responsible for adjudicating them were being corroded and delegitimized more severely than we understood.

CHAPTER 5

Team M Ramps Up

I WAS AT MY desk one afternoon in June 2017, reading up on Manafort, when I heard a knock on my open door. "Can I come in?" It was Jim Quarles, but this time I knew something was up—none of us ever knocked and announced; we just moved right in and out of one another's offices and carrels all day long. I motioned him in, and he closed the door behind him. He had a clean yellow pad in his hands.

"I just came back from a meeting with the White House," he said. As the head of Team 600, Jim had the unenviable task of being our liaison with the administration, though he was perfectly suited to it: calm, professional, savvy. "They raised a number of questions I need to ask you about."

I was perplexed, but said, "Go ahead, shoot."

"The White House is still tracking this down, but they believe you gave public speeches while at the Department of Justice critical of President Trump."

"That's absurd," I said. "A, that would be a violation of the Hatch Act," I said, referring to the statute that would prohibit such conduct. "And B, that is simply untrue. I have never done that. Period."

Jim was satisfied and moved on to a second issue. "Well, Jared Kushner raised an issue of whether you have a conflict of interest, because he used to be the owner of a newspaper in New York that ran an article years ago that was critical of you. He does not want you to work on any investigation of him. It seems far afield, but I wanted to raise it."

What Jim was referring to was that Kushner had owned *The New York Observer,* a little-known paper in New York. The article he was referring to was one I had only recently been made aware had run in that newspaper—a screed by Sidney Powell, a lawyer for a convicted Enron executive who had made a name for herself solely by attacking members of the Enron Task Force. I had long ago written off anything she claimed, as all of her attacks had been rejected by the courts and bar associations to which she'd filed repetitious meritless complaints. It had not occurred to me to connect her diatribes with Kushner until Jim raised the connection. I explained all of this to him.

"I suspected as much," Jim said.

Still, Kushner's objection bothered me on principle. "Since when do people we may be investigating get to dictate who will investigate them?" I asked. "Especially based on such a thin reed?"

"They don't," Jim said. "And we won't let them." This was the first time I learned of Kushner's fear of the investigation, and of me in particular. Later on, Steve Bannon—no fan of Kushner's—would stoke this fear by lauding me publicly. (It occurred to me that he may have been doing this to get under Kushner's skin.) Bannon referred to me as a master prosecutor, the "LeBron James" of money-laundering investigations, able to ferret out crimes. The day that Bannon statement came out, Jeannie taped a picture of the famed basketball player on my door, with my tiny head pasted atop his towering, muscular body.

"Don't worry about any of this," Jim said. And with that, he walked out of my office, and the issues ended there.

It was late June, a month into our investigation. Our work on Manafort was barreling ahead at an impressive pace, powered now by the core group of dogged FBI agents and analysts we had assembled on Team M.

Right away, I'd known I would need a lead FBI agent for the team, an investigator whom I could depend on and deploy for a wide array of problems, a kind of human Swiss Army knife. And for this job, I had only one candidate in mind: my old friend Special Agent Omer Meisel.

Omer and I had met during the Enron investigation, where we

worked side by side for the better part of two years, and had stayed in touch since. He was an unimposing figure—with a tall, gangly frame topped by mussed and thinning hair—but as an investigator he couldn't have been more formidable. Omer had exactly the right background for a sprawling, complex case. He had worked many complicated economic investigations before, but also had deep experience with national security cases. (For a time, he was assigned as the primary FBI officer, or "legat," in Israel.) He knew how to obtain foreign assistance and review classified and foreign intelligence.

In short, there was seemingly no element of Team M's overall project that Omer wouldn't know how to handle. And, frankly, he brought something to the table that I needed: He was adept at handling me. He was a genuine partner with whom I could strategize and was so attuned to my weaknesses—my tendencies toward micromanaging and perfectionism, which often lead me to get uptight and easily annoyed—that he could see problems coming a mile away and neutralize them. Omer knew, for example, that if a task I'd assigned was not done thoroughly, or if I asked a question and got a half-assed answer back, I would wait until he and I were alone, in private, and vent until I'd played my irritation out. Omer knew exactly what to say to calm me down. "I'm handling it," he'd say, and I'd have perfect faith that he was.

Mueller was just as much a fan of Omer as I was. The two men knew each other from their time together in San Francisco, when Mueller had been the U.S. attorney and Omer was a young, intrepid FBI agent with the requisite pizazz, and Mueller swiftly gave me the green light to bring him on board. The problem was Omer was currently assigned to an FBI field office in California, where he and his wife lived with their two young children. But after I let him know of Mueller's job offer, he and his wife answered the call. (Omer would spend the next year and a half commuting home to the West Coast every other weekend to see his family.)

From the moment Omer joined Team M, I could feel my blood pressure dropping. He occupied the office next to mine and became one of the few people in the Special Counsel's Office with whom I'd regularly socialize—one of the few people I socialized with at all, actually, since it became increasingly complicated and awkward, while sealed in the confidential bubble of our investigation, to spend time with friends on the outside. At least once a week, Omer and I would go out for pizza and beer. I'm not typically an enthusiastic or knowledgeable beer drinker, but even here, Omer had a way of smoothing the rocky path in front of me. Having tracked my likes and dislikes, he'd survey the taps and tell the bartender "He'll try that one" or "Give him one of those." Omer was my beer whisperer. When Omer was not around, I was at a loss—whether at a bar or in the office.

After roping in Omer, I poached a trio of impressive women from the Justice Department's MLARS unit and the Bureau. Two were FBI forensic accountants—Renee Michael and Morgan Magionos—who had dazzled me during my otherwise dispiriting meeting about Manafort with their team, and the third was a smart and meticulous young attorney named Kyle Freeny, who brought expertise in tracing money. In the first weeks of our investigation, the lead FBI agent initially assigned to the Special Counsel's Office, Pete Strzok, had told me that, if we decided to absorb any existing investigations, he'd assign whatever FBI personnel I wanted from those matters, as well. However, if there was someone I did not think was up to the task, I was under no obligation to take them: "Don't feel like they have sweat equity in the case," Strzok said. "This is the time to prune them."

And so, when my initial meeting with MLARS concluded, I pulled aside the acting head of the section and asked her if the forensic accountants sitting in the back of the conference room were really as good as they seemed—it was clear they'd done some tenacious work sussing out Manafort's foreign accounts. The supervisor confirmed my impression: They were best in class, she said. I made a mental note at the time: It would be important to have these two on Team M.

Before long, all three of them were holed up together in a cluster of carrels right outside my office, burrowing into Manafort's finances from different directions. The key question was whether Manafort was reporting as income on his tax returns the vast sums of money he spent from his offshore accounts. They had gone ahead and prepared for my review several mutual legal assistance treaty—MLAT—requests, which I approved and we got out the door, in an attempt to secure Manafort's bank records from Cyprus and other tax havens. We also had one of the heads of the Department of Justice's Office of International Affairs, Randy Toledo, assigned to review our MLAT requests. To keep our investigation independent of the normal DOJ chain of command, Randy was assigned to assist us, but she did not report on such matters to her normal supervisor. She would prove tenacious in pushing our MLATs forward, one more hidden gem of a career DOJ lawyer.

Still, I knew we could not hold our breath for these MLAT requests to be fulfilled, no matter how hard we pushed. I told Mueller we had to assume we were not going to get evidence from Ukraine, Cyprus, or other countries, and had to build our case independent of that. If the MLATs bore fruit, so much the better, but we needed to develop a sustainable case without them. To do this, our team reverse engineered some of that foreign information by subpoenaing the records from "correspondent banks" in the United States, through which those foreign banks had conducted some of Manafort's transactions. Those U.S. institutions were within our reach and subject to our subpoena power.

In short order, we were swimming in gigabytes of data, coming in from banks as well as stores where Manafort shopped. It was up to Renee and Morgan, as the forensic accountants, to parse this data first, and I stopped by Renee's carrel to make sure that they weren't feeling overwhelmed. "We've already scheduled out all the bank records," she told me, barely looking up from her work. Those records pointed to still more accounts, she explained, and yielded more names of shops and businesses that Manafort had paid. So they'd now need additional subpoenas to see what those records revealed. They'd been keeping a detailed list as they went, Renee explained. "Kyle has it and is working on drafting the subpoenas now," she told me. "You should have them shortly for review."

I don't remember exactly what I told her in response, but I remember what I thought: *Holy crap.* The life of an FBI analyst might seem less glamorous than that of an agent. Analysts don't carry guns or get shipped off to Quantico to learn to make arrests or conduct searches. Still, they have the specialized knowledge required to carry out investigations in our increasingly opaque and digital world. Team M's two forensic accountants would be a perfect example. From that day on, Renee and Morgan would update their findings every day, so we could see, in real time, the facts of our investigation unfolding. Along with Kyle, they were a money-tracing juggernaut.

We also subpoenaed documents from Manafort's tax preparer in Virginia and the bill-paying service in California that Manafort used to pay some of his vendors. It took some time to jump over a hurdle the firms raised, as to whether those documents were covered by attorney-client privilege. An accountant can claim this privilege if they've done the work for a defense attorney, in connection with a criminal case. But the records we wanted pertained to Manafort's heyday in Ukraine, from 2010 to 2014, well before he even knew he was under criminal investigation. Before long, this second tranche of data arrived. The documents from the bill-paying firm were terrific largely because of what they did not contain: Manafort was using them to pay vendors, but the records made clear that he did not have the firm pay anything from his offshore accounts. Who would go to the trouble of hiring a company to pay all your bills, except omit making payments from offshore accounts, which you handle yourself? Answer: a person who wants to keep those offshore accounts secret.

When the third tranche of documents came in from Manafort's tax preparer, we all pounced, knowing they should contain Manafort's tax returns and give us a clear look at what he was, and wasn't, reporting to the IRS. I was so eager to get a look at these records, in fact, that I started poking through them before the FBI could even upload them onto the Bureau's computer platform, an antiquated program called BIDMAS that allowed us to search and tag documents in a systematic way. We divided up the documents among us, but I was too impatient. After reviewing my share, I tried to speed-read everything else, as well.

I started by searching through Manafort's correspondence with his lead tax preparer, who'd worked on his tax returns for years—clicking through email after email to get a sense of what we had. One popped out at me. It was the kind of dramatic evidence we call a "hot" document—or what I called a "summation" document, meaning it was so compelling that it should be used in our closing argument to a jury. The email included a series of questions that Manafort's tax preparer had emailed him while working on one of his annual tax returns, as well as Manafort's replies. The latter was in a blue script, to helpfully differentiate them from the queries in black. One of the questions the tax preparer asked was whether Manafort had any offshore accounts, as they needed to be reported. The answer Manafort gave in blue was "None."

Bingo. This was false—a critical piece of evidence to prove Manafort's intent. This back-and-forth made it impossible for Manafort to credibly claim that he didn't know he was required to report his foreign bank accounts; here, his accountant was asking him to provide that information for his return, and Manafort was clearly lying and saying he had no foreign accounts to report. (U.S. banks automatically make filings to the IRS about U.S. bank accounts, but that is not true of foreign banks. Federal tax returns thus require us to report any foreign bank accounts.)

In the end, we would find that Manafort never disclosed any of his offshore accounts to his tax preparers in any of their communications, and similarly did not tell his bill payer about the foreign accounts, so that firm could not reveal the accounts to the tax preparer with whom they coordinated. Thus, the foreign accounts were never reported on any of his tax returns: Manafort had hidden the millions of dollars he'd stashed overseas and shortchanged the government on the millions of dollars it was owed in taxes. We saw that Manafort was doing the same thing in his business tax returns, but I brushed those aside: "Let's keep our main case clean and clear for a jury. We can deal with these other things at sentencing, but let's get there first." I could hear Mueller in my head: "Stay focused; move fast."

To ensure a successful criminal prosecution, we would have to do a lot more technical legwork to neutralize the typical defenses that spring up in such cases—to show, for example, that this money Manafort was spending was actual income, and not just funds he'd inherited or been loaned. And we'd have to interview the tax preparers and bill payers, of course, to confirm the accuracy of what we were looking at. But, for the moment, this bit of correspondence was damning and clear. The document was as hot as they come. I taped it up on the large whiteboard in my office—the first exhibit in what would become a collage of incriminating documents.

I ran next door to Omer's office and showed him what I found.

"Motherfucker," Omer said.

Then, together, we hustled over to Renee, Morgan, and Kyle's carrels. "If this holds up," I told them, showing off the document, "he's dead."

I shared it with Jeannie Rhee, the Team R leader, next, who let loose with a freewheeling hoot. And, eventually, I went to report our discovery to Mueller as well, trotting down the hall like a proud hound with a pheasant in its mouth. "Guess what we found," I told him, and began to lay out the story.

When I finished, Mueller gave me a slight, barely perceptible nod. "Good," he said.

"I have an idea," Omer told me. "You ready for it?"

"Yes," I said, with trepidation and excitement; I liked it when Omer Meisel got ideas.

It was only mid-July 2017, and Omer and I had continued to pull the Manafort investigation together, sifting through our flood of subpoenaed documents and chasing down various leads. Now, having mapped out our progress on the whiteboard in his office, we were sitting around, batting around next steps.

"Let's get a search warrant for Manafort's condo in Virginia."

"I love it!" I shot out reflexively. Then I started thinking it through.

We had recently interviewed one of the witnesses we'd inherited from the MLARS investigation—a young man who'd worked for Manafort here in the United States. He was the only one of Manafort's employees who still remained with him, working as a kind of errand boy. He picked up Manafort's relatives at the airport, schlepped boxes to a storage unit, and chauffeured him around at the Republican convention in 2016.

We interviewed him in a tiny spare room in a SCIF, or sensitive compartmented information facility, two floors under our ground floor offices in the Patrick Henry Building, a truly forgotten place. We led him and his attorney down a narrow set of internal stairs into the bowels of the building, past a series of locked doors. It was worth all these logistics. The gopher turned out to be a somewhat awkward millennial; his speech patterns and mannerisms reminded me of my nephew and his friends—lots of "likes," "ums," and "you knows." He was quite likable, and though clearly a bit scared to be called into our office, was willing to open up about what he knew.

For starters, he explained that Manafort had frequently given him his old computers and phones when he upgraded to newer ones. "He sometimes told me to get them wiped, but then I could use them," he said. He still had them all in a drawer at home, he explained, and hadn't always bothered to wipe them, either. He turned them over to us. For us to access them legally, it would take some careful legal strategizing and search warrant applications on our part—made more complicated because we were intent on trying not to reveal unnecessarily this young man's identity in any of our court filings. His help would ultimately lead to our obtaining about a dozen of Manafort's computers and other devices and scouring many of them for more leads and evidence for the investigation.

The young man also described files that had been moved into Manafort's condo after Manafort closed down his Virginia office in 2015. These files appeared to include documents covering Manafort's work in Ukraine. In the fall of 2016, Manafort had falsely told the FARA Unit that he no longer had pertinent Ukraine documents, and clearly he didn't want the government to see them. Omer was thinking that this information, combined with the material he'd seen in Manafort's emails and the items Manafort purchased with the offshore money, constituted probable cause for a search warrant. I ran this by Kyle Freeny—at that point, still the only other lawyer on Team M—and she agreed. We could make an argument to the court that we should be allowed to search Manafort's condo to get those documents ourselves.

A search warrant is a useful tool in an investigation, but not always the appropriate one. A warrant permits the government to enter a particular location and search for particular items, if a federal judge determines that—as laid out in a sworn affidavit from an FBI special agent, like Omer—there is probable cause to believe the premises contain evidence of the crime being investigated. Even if you can meet the legal threshold for a warrant, getting one is often unnecessary, and even counterproductive.

In a white-collar corporate case, for example, you can generally trust that if you subpoena documents from a reputable company—or even just ask for them to be provided voluntarily—the firm's attorneys will comply. Showing up with a search warrant, by contrast, and subjecting a responsible company to the kind of public spectacle that such searches tend to create, could be overly antagonistic, and will likely discourage further cooperation. As chief of the Fraud Section, I only rarely felt compelled to approve proceeding by search warrant.

But, given the peculiarities of our predicament with Manafort, I could see that Omer had a point. "He lied to the government already," Omer explained, and fairly elaborately; not only had Manafort told the FARA Unit he didn't possess any of the documents they were asking for, he even provided them with a supposed "Document Retention Policy" for his company, which claimed that he routinely destroyed all documents and emails after thirty days of receipt. As Omer now pointed out, "There's no way he's going to be producing documents to us now if we subpoena them."

It was true: Manafort had placed himself in a bind. If we issued a subpoena for those documents, he could either repeat his previous lie to us and say he did not have any, or he could produce responsive documents as legally required, but thereby reveal that he had lied to the FARA Unit. Most likely, therefore, his counsel would have him assert what's known as the "act of production privilege." Under the Fifth Amendment to our Constitution, no person has to produce documents if the production would tend to incriminate him or her. And if Manafort suddenly gave all those materials to us, he'd be proving that he had lied to the government the first time—a federal offense. I told Omer his logic here was exactly right—a warrant was the way to go, since a subpoena would not result in our getting any documents.

But we had work to do if we were going to get Mueller to sign off on the idea. Most important, we needed a plan in place to deal with any privileged documents in the condo—that is, communications between Manafort and his attorneys that were likely to be protected by attorney-client privilege and that, therefore, we weren't allowed to see. If we wound up reviewing any such privileged documents as a result of searching the condo, a court could determine we had tainted our investigation. And so, we would recommend to Mueller that we employ a separate team of lawyers and paralegals—a "taint team" of people not in the Special Counsel's Office—to review everything first and set aside any privileged materials before we could see them.

I knew exactly who should oversee this operation, too: Elizabeth Aloi, a terrific attorney at the Justice Department who had worked with me when I was in the Fraud Section, investigating leads from the Panama Papers—a massive trove of documents leaked from a Panamanian law firm. Liz and her team had tackled that project expertly, carefully walking through a minefield of complex privilege issues with exceptional meticulousness and blinding speed. I also decided I would phone Manafort's defense attorney at WilmerHale once the search of the condo was concluded—to be as up front as possible about our process and get their input on what documents they believed were privileged. The lead defense attorney, Howard Shapiro, was also a former FBI general counsel, whom I'd dealt with over the years and respected immensely.

Having worked up this plan for several days, Omer and I tromped down the hall to Mueller's office to get some time on his calendar. I also stepped into Aaron Zebley's office to fill him in on our proposed plan. Aaron, Mueller's deputy, gave a kind of fatalistic smile and told us he appreciated the heads-up. It was in his nature to be overly cautious, and I could tell we were moving faster than he'd have preferred. But Aaron confessed that he knew Mueller was going to love the idea. He must have felt like he was strapped to the back of a raft, watching the rest of us all paddling together, about to shoot some rapids.

Later that same afternoon, we met with Mueller and laid out our plan. After hearing from everyone, asking for all the pros and cons, he signed off on it right there. "Let's do it," he told us. "But no battering ram!" he said with a twinkle in his eye. (A so-called battering ram can be used when there is an exigency to gain access to the search location and the door is locked. This was not that situation.)

A few days later, armed with a search warrant from a Virginia federal court, in the early morning hours of July 27, 2017, a team of taint agents knocked on the door of Manafort's condo in Virginia and said, "FBI." Manafort and his wife were both home, though no one came to the door. Maybe they didn't hear the knock from their bedroom, or maybe they ignored it. Maybe they shot out of bed panicked, then simply froze like deer. After knocking again to no avail, the agents unlocked the door with a key they'd obtained. They found Manafort standing just a short distance from the foyer. (Searches must typically be conducted during daytime hours, and only after knocking on the door; in exigent circumstances, where, for example, there is some substantiated danger posed to the agents conducting the search, you can obtain a "no knock" warrant. We did not get such a warrant, and knocked before entering, but that did not stop Manafort and his allies from later falsely claiming the agents raided the apartment without knocking and after picking his lock. Manafort's publicly playing the victim of an FBI "raid" goaded the president to later disparage our "mob" tactics. And, as a result, the FBI agents enjoyed calling me "No-Knock Weissmann.")

The search would last several hours. I was in our office, but Omer had gone out to Virginia and was waiting nearby, to handle any logistical flare-ups. That afternoon, he called to report that all was going well: The taint team was almost finished sorting through all the documents, computers, thumb drives, and phones, and seizing what was called for by the warrant.

It had been important to me that we not seize any of the luxury goods that Manafort had purchased with money from his offshore accounts, even though our warrant authorized us to do so. Granted, those possessions were evidence: The clothes, silk rugs, and antiques could support the tax charges we were pursuing by showing where Manafort's undeclared income had gone and by serving as overwhelming physical proof of the man's materialism—a motive for his crimes. Still, I decided there were less intrusive means by which to accomplish our goal. Photographing those items would serve our purpose. Further, if we loaded everything up and carted it off, Manafort could gin up stories in the press about government overreach—how he'd been victimized by the Special Counsel's Office. Omer agreed.

But even just photos of the scene inside the condo were staggering. One of our agents would describe them as revealing a "sickness." There were endless rows of shirts and ties, piles of slacks, and rack after rack of suits in blue, pinstripes, checks, and plaids, made from cashmere, wool, silk, and linen. Manafort's $15,000 ostrich-leather bomber jacket, which would eventually become a punch line in the press, was only one in a glut of preposterous ostentations.

The search yielded a trove of other evidence. Sometimes one leaps through all the requisite search warrant hoops—writing up an application, submitting it to the court, executing the search, deploying a taint team, consulting with the defense counsel in the taint review, and so on—only to walk away with nothing of value. In any investigation, you go down a lot of dry holes. That's what makes investigative work exhilarating: hunting for clues and coming up with creative ways to obtain evidence.

Manafort's condo was not a dry hole. Agents uncovered scores of damning documents, showing that Manafort had devised and orchestrated the U.S. lobbying scheme for Ukraine, and had deliberately masked the fact that he and the government of Ukraine were directing it—thus proving, squarely, that he'd both clearly violated FARA by not registering under the law and also deceived the FARA Unit's investigators when he denied having such documentation.

Other evidence detailed Manafort's relationship with Oleg Deripaska, the powerful Russian oligarch close to Vladimir Putin. We had been aware of Manafort's ties to Deripaska, but it was breathtaking to see the extent and nature of their dealings laid out in black and white. Manafort's files clearly revealed his modus operandi in assisting his client, Deripaska, who had paid him millions of dollars to go into various countries in order to help install political regimes that would advance Deripaska's business interests there. Ukraine was one of their targets, Montenegro another—followed by various African countries. One 2005 memorandum written by Manafort's firm for Deripaska referenced the need to brief the Kremlin on the benefits this regime-change work would confer on "the Putin Government." In short, this was all evidence that Manafort was a hired gun, willing to subvert governments at the behest of Deripaska and his Kremlin overseers. In terms of "links" between Russia and the Trump campaign—one of the key topics we were tasked to investigate—this certainly confirmed Manafort was one.

Later that day, Omer again phoned from Virginia, to let me know the search was finished. I relayed this to my Team M colleagues, all waiting nearby for the latest word, and then to Mueller and Aaron.

"Any sign of the press?" Mueller asked.

Keeping things quiet was one of Mueller's top priorities, but it was particularly important to Aaron, who was highly sensitive to how the press could stir up negative reactions to our investigative actions among our superiors at the Department of Justice and inside the White House. "If we do X," Aaron would repeatedly argue, "the White House may stop cooperating with us on Y." Jeannie and I could only privately scoff: So far, we were not getting much cooperation from the White House anyway, beyond what we were entitled to through subpoenas and standard court process. Even Jim Quarles, who was patient and diplomatic, would tell Aaron: "If the White House agreed we would get Y if we didn't do X, then maybe. But they don't want to give us Y at all."

In Virginia, the agents had managed to conduct the entire search

without media attention. "There was one van opposite the condo building that the agents thought might be press," I told Mueller, "but it left
early on, and they didn't see anything else all day." Manafort and his allies on cable news would not be able to claim that we were playing to the
cameras or attempting to publicly demean him.

"Good," Mueller said. "And good work."

Still, a couple of days later, with no peep about the search appearing
in the press, President Trump's personal lawyer, John Dowd, told Jim
that the president knew about the search and was unhappy with our
tactics. Dowd said he was trying to calm Trump down.

CHAPTER 6

The Trump Tower Meeting

IN EARLY JULY, a few weeks before the Manafort condo search and before Jeannie or I had our teams fully up and running, *The New York
Times* published a story with the straightforward yet explosive headline:
"Trump Team Met with Lawyer Linked to Kremlin During Campaign." The article revealed that the president's son Donald Trump, Jr.,
had been approached by a Russian operative in June 2016, four months
before the election, and met with her at the campaign headquarters at
Trump Tower on June 9, 2016. Jared Kushner and Paul Manafort attended the meeting as well. I remember first hearing about the *Times*
reporting on CNN. It was news to me. It was news to all of us at the
Special Counsel's Office.

There are many infuriating downsides to working on an investigation that is constantly in the headlines. The media attention often spooks
people out of telling you everything they know, as those you interview
understand that divulging new incriminating information could eventually land them in the news. "I don't recall" winds up being a frequent
refrain. The disincentive for flipping is even greater. It's hard enough to
admit wrongdoing to yourself and your family and friends. But in the
Enron case, I'd watched each witness we flipped be subject to front-page
headlines and scalding scrutiny, making the path of cooperation that

much less attractive for the next person we homed in on as we moved up the ladder.

Now, however, the Special Counsel's Office was enjoying a rare upside of working a high-profile case: As we began boring into the events of the campaign time period, a swarm of enterprising reporters was churning up their own evidence in parallel. At times, the stories the media published proved to be dead ends, which we, nevertheless, were obliged to spend time running down. These numerous leads would include our spending months debunking reports about Trump's watering down support for Ukraine in the Republican Party platform during the convention—which would have been favorable to Russia's interests in Ukraine and thus raised a red flag—and our running to ground, around the globe, the claim by a Belarusian call girl that she had tapes of Deripaska admitting to Russian election interference in the 2016 election. But there were also genuinely important facts revealed by the press along the way. This story, about the Trump Tower meeting, was the biggest one.

The *Times* published its story on a Saturday and, realizing that the meeting fell into the purviews of both Team R and Team M, Jeannie and I immediately hunkered down together, reading the article side by side, and making a list of leads to pursue.

First, why had the Trump campaign hidden this meeting—why were we learning about it only now? Notably, Jared Kushner had failed to list it, among many other interactions with foreign contacts, on his initial disclosure forms required to receive a security clearance for his new senior position at the White House. And Don Jr. had previously gone out of his way to deny ever attending or setting up any meetings with Russians as part of his role on the campaign. When asked by the press if he'd had such interactions, his answer was, "A hundred percent no."

Both Jeannie and I noted that the story included a written response from Don Jr., meaning the *Times* had clearly called him for comment and held the story long enough for him to prepare a response. His statement described the meeting this way: "It was a short introductory meeting. I asked Jared and Paul to stop by. We primarily discussed a program about the adoption of Russian children that was active and popular with American families years ago and was since ended by the Russian government, but it was not a campaign issue at the time and there was no follow up."

Don Jr.'s statement seemed transparently misleading and raised myriad questions that Jeannie and I bounced off each other excitedly. We first asked the obvious one: If the meeting was inconsequential, why hide it? The next detail that grabbed our attention was Don Jr.'s use of the word "primarily"—a classic tell in our line of work. Words like "primarily" or "generally" are almost always deployed to mask a more fulsome story, the natural follow-up question for any lawyer worth her salt being: "What else was discussed?" More important, it took only a barebones understanding of the larger political context to know that a discussion about adoptions was not as innocent as Don Jr. hoped it would sound. Adoptions, I was learning, are simply the flip side of Russian sanctions.

The principal Russian operative who met with Don Jr., Kushner, and Manafort that day was a lawyer named Natalya Veselnitskaya, who had close links to the Kremlin. Veselnitskaya had worked vigorously to repeal the Magnitsky Act—a law I wasn't then familiar with, but quickly read up on. The act had been passed by Congress in 2012 and imposed financial and other sanctions on Russia in response to human rights abuses. (It was named after Sergei Magnitsky, a Russian tax accountant who'd been investigating government fraud before dying under suspicious circumstances—an all-too-common story in Russia.) The sanctions infuriated Putin, and he retaliated by canceling all American adoptions of Russian babies.

Ever since, there'd been a vehement anti–Magnitsky Act movement in Russia, of which Veselnitskaya was a major voice. She had employed legal and political operatives to lobby for the act's repeal, and even helped produce a film about its purported unfairness. Because Russian adoptions were used as a countermeasure by Russia against the Magnitsky Act, it was inconceivable that a discussion of Russian adoptions—and particularly one with Veselnitskaya, much less between Veselnitskaya and the highest-level staff of a presidential campaign—was not, in reality, a discussion about repealing the Magnitsky Act. For us, this was the first inkling as to what the Russian government wanted out of a Trump administration: an end to Russian sanctions.

Jeannie quickly got on the phone to the defense counsel for the Trump campaign, alerting them that we'd need all documents related to this meeting. We were determined to find out how Veselnitskaya had managed to get an audience with the upper echelon of the campaign, and who else was in attendance. Was there, for instance, a security sign-in book in the lobby of Trump Tower we could obtain? We also put a request for documents and an interview to Don Jr.'s personal criminal defense attorney, Alan Futerfas, whom I'd dealt with extensively in my prior life as an organized crime prosecutor in Brooklyn. The last time I dealt with Alan was at a trial in which he'd represented a soldier in the Colombo crime family who was convicted of murdering the Colombo family consigliere Jimmy Angelina. Now he was representing the son of the president of the United States.

Don Jr. could, of course, refuse our request for an interview and documents. Even if we were to serve him with a grand jury subpoena, he had a constitutional right, under the Fifth Amendment, not to speak with us or to turn over any documents that he believed, in good faith, might incriminate him. But corporate entities, such as the Trump campaign, have no Fifth Amendment rights. This was the reason we approached both Don Jr. and the campaign.

As it turned out, it wasn't difficult to get at least a few of the pertinent documents. No doubt understanding the inevitability of these documents surfacing in light of the explosive news story, Don Jr. took to Twitter and released some of them himself. He tweeted some—but not all—of the emails that went into setting up the Trump Tower meeting. The emails didn't look good and, in short order, the most damning of them were blaring across countless front pages around the country and being dissected endlessly by talking heads on TV.

The email to arrange the meeting was sent to Don Jr. by Rob Goldstone, an events promoter who was well acquainted with both Don Jr. and his father. Goldstone worked for Emin Agalarov, the pop-singer son of Aras Agalarov, a Trump-like Russian real estate baron. Aras Agalarov headed the Crocus Group, a firm with close ties to Putin and other members of the Russian government. That is, Goldstone made sense as a possible indirect go-between—a "cut out" as Jeannie and her agents referred to him—between Putin and the Trumps. His initial approach to Don Jr. read:

Good morning
Emin just called and asked me to contact you with something very interesting.

The Crown prosecutor of Russia met with his father Aras this morning and in their meeting offered to provide the Trump campaign with some official documents and information that would incriminate Hillary and her dealings with Russia and would be very useful to your father. This is obviously very high level and sensitive information but is part of Russia and its government's support for Mr. Trump—helped along by Aras and Emin.

The email said it explicitly: The Russian government was seeking to help Trump and hurt Clinton, and this meeting was being called so that the Russians could give the former "dirt" on the latter. And it was only "part" of the government's support for Trump. To have this all spelled out so clearly, in writing, was a bombshell.

It's worth noting that many of the people orbiting the Trump campaign—many of the characters with whom we were rapidly familiarizing ourselves as our investigation got under way—had a distinct air of grift about them. Manafort was a perfect example. When assessing these people's communications, you couldn't rule out that they might be embellishing the truth, or overpromising, in order to impress their superiors or advance some hidden self-interest. And we always tried to keep that in mind—what is the other side of the story?

But Goldstone's email seemed credible. There was, of course, a possibility that the information he had been given was inaccurate or exaggerated, but he had little motive to be dishonest or oversell any details in his missives to Don Jr.—and he had to know, he'd be easily found out if he did. The Trumps and Agalarovs were friendly, after all. Offering dirt on Clinton, on behalf of the Russians, was a serious move.

Don Jr.'s reply to Goldstone, meanwhile, clearly revealed the campaign's eagerness to accept such assistance. "If it's what you say," he wrote back, "I love it especially later in the summer." Don Jr. wanted the dirt and was already making calculations about the best time to deploy it: later in the summer, once the campaign was in the home stretch.

There it was: The Russians made an offer. The campaign accepted.

• • •

The Special Counsel's Office had been up and running for only six weeks at this point, yet the Trump Tower meeting was actually the second instance we'd found of Russia's approaching the Trump campaign with dirt on Clinton.

The first had also essentially dropped into our laps: One of the earliest leads we'd inherited from the FBI's preexisting investigation into Russian election interference concerned an ambitious but inexperienced young man living in London named George Papadopoulos, who'd managed to get himself hired as a foreign policy adviser to the Trump campaign. Beginning in March 2016, Papadopoulos had a series of interactions with a Maltese academic named Joseph Mifsud, who was the director of something called the London Academy of Diplomacy, and who, we would learn, had suspicious ties to Russian operatives. Mifsud told Papadopoulos that the Russian government possessed thousands of emails that would damage the Clinton campaign.

Papadopoulos was brand-new to the Trump campaign in the early spring of 2016. He was only twenty-eight years old and had been solicited to join a group of foreign affairs and national security advisers that the Trump team was hastily throwing together. The candidate was trying to inoculate himself from criticism about his dearth of foreign policy experience, so he'd done what all candidates do: sought to surround himself with a brain trust of serious and experienced minds, to both buttress his own understanding and burnish his image with voters. The problem was that Trump was not yet the Republican nominee; few people took him seriously as a genuine political force. He, in turn, knew little about policy making and yet expressed suspicion of any expertise beyond his own. This left him scrounging around for respectable-seeming advisers. Papadopoulos, for example, had extremely limited consulting experience in the oil and gas industry; his primary credentials appeared to be that he lived overseas. That this supposed council of sages was helmed by Senator Jeff Sessions—a man hardly known for his experience in international affairs—was a telling indicator of its quality.

The FBI had first interviewed Papadopoulos months before Mueller was appointed, in January 2017, after receiving a tip from a foreign country about his interactions with Mifsud. Even the origin of this tip spoke volumes about Papadopoulos's ineptitude as a political operative: About three weeks after Mifsud first raised the Clinton emails with him in 2016, Papadopoulos had bragged about it to a foreign diplomat during a night of drinking at an upscale London bar. The diplomat would have understood that the potential criminality here was twofold: Not only did Papadopoulos's disclosure signal the possibility of a foreign power influencing a U.S. election, the emails themselves were allegedly hacked, that is, stolen.

That this small bit of information—a neophyte Trump adviser flapping his gums over drinks—would wend its way to the highest levels of the American Intelligence Community, was unsurprising to me. I'd seen from my days working as the general counsel at the FBI in Washington how our Intelligence Community's relationships with its counterparts in other nations have evolved and strengthened since 9/11. Our government has internalized one of that atrocity's key lessons: that sharing intelligence is key to combating an international threat, and that siloing information within the boundaries of old nation-states only assists terrorists, who operate without borders.

The Papadopoulos lead fell squarely into Jeannie's Team R bucket, and she began by reading the FBI's summaries—known as 302s—of its two interviews with Papadopoulos. (302 is the number on the form that the Bureau uses to document the content of its interviews, and the term "302" is widely used in law enforcement and even by courts as a shorthand for any such witness report.) The story that Papadopoulos told the FBI was innocuous. He insisted that his contacts with Mifsud, and a Russian woman Mifsud eventually connected him with, were inconsequential and predated his employment with the Trump campaign. Also, he claimed that Mifsud had merely told him that he had heard the Russians had Clinton's emails. And because Papadopoulos had no idea whether that information was true, he didn't do anything with it. Mifsud struck him as a "nothing," Papadopoulos said. He had exchanged a few insignificant "How are you?" emails with the Russian woman after he joined the campaign, he claimed, but that was all.

Was there something here, or was this one of hundreds of leads that, even then, we expected our office would wind up chasing, only to discover a big load of nothing at the end of the trail? Our job was to find out, not to simply make an educated guess; we couldn't afford to ignore something like this. So Jeannie dug in, issuing subpoenas and obtaining court orders for a variety of documentation, including email, phone, and other communication records, as well as requesting records from the campaign; in other words, Jeannie cut a bunch of process, as we prosecutors say.

This paid solid dividends. The documents made clear that Papadopoulos had lied to the FBI. Moreover, he was a terribly unsophisticated liar; he was lying about matters that any competent investigator would catch. For example, he lied about the timing of his contacts with Mifsud. Records of their communications clearly showed that, while their first contact had been just prior to the campaign's announcing Papadopoulos's appointment, Papadopoulos had already accepted the position. (This, Jeannie posited, was precisely why Mifsud was interested in him.)

More important, Papadopoulos had multiple contacts with Mifsud and various Russian intermediaries after he was working on the campaign advisory committee. Jeannie obtained emails Papadopoulos had written to various people in the campaign about these connections—high-level players, in fact, like Corey Lewandowski and Manafort, which in and of itself indicated that these contacts were far from the trivial communications Papadopoulos had described to the FBI. In fact, Papadopoulos appeared to be working to set up a meeting between Trump and Putin. "Russia has been eager to meet Mr. Trump for quite some time," he wrote to others on the campaign in May 2016.

Jeannie also uncovered substantive evidence of what we call "consciousness of guilt." Having reviewed Papadopoulos's current and former Facebook accounts, Team R noticed that his first account contained various incriminating communications with Mifsud and Russian contacts from the period during which Papadopoulos served on the campaign's advisory committee. But Papadopoulos had deactivated this account the day after his second FBI interview in February 2017. The account he was currently using, which contained no such communications, had been opened the same day in its place.

It was all unmistakably crooked. Jeannie would obviously want to interview Papadopoulos, and she put a border lookout in place to alert her when he reentered the United States. (Team R had learned that he was expected to come into the country over the summer.) She also carefully drafted, and had Mueller sign off on, a criminal complaint establishing probable cause and giving the government legal authority to take Papadopoulos into custody if he materialized back on U.S. soil.

In mid-July, Papadopoulos flew into Dulles International Airport in Washington and was promptly met by two of Team R's FBI agents. He was quietly arrested then and there. After consulting with counsel, he eventually agreed to talk with Team R. Oblivious to the fact that Jeannie's investigators would have done their homework since his February 2017 interview, he proceeded to repeat many of the same lies.

In the months that followed, Jeannie would feel out Papadopoulos as a potential cooperating witness, though she was up front with his defense counsel about her skepticism, being that Papadopoulos had already lied his way through multiple interviews. In the end, flipping him became impossible because he was unwilling to be completely truthful and thus would have no credibility as a witness. While Papadopoulos did reluctantly admit the true timing of his communications with Mifsud and other Russian intermediaries, he remained cagey about much else in his interviews with Team R, giving conflicting accounts of certain events or responding to critical, open questions with thin denials and "I don't recalls." These included the exact content of his conversations with Mifsud and the Russians, and what he might have shared with others in the Trump campaign about them.

On the latter subject, he was particularly squirrelly. He told Jeannie he didn't remember if he'd told anyone in the campaign about these contacts, or whom he told, or how much he might have told them—which struck her as entirely implausible. But it was clear from reading Papadopoulos's emails that he was eager to prove his usefulness to those running the campaign—he was a guy clinging to the lowest rung of the ladder trying to hang on if not move up. It seemed impossible that he would have kept to himself the prospect, however remote, of his delivering thousands of embarrassing Clinton emails to the campaign.

At times, his performance during the interviews turned childish and shameless. In one instance, for example, Jeannie and her agents confronted him with his own handwritten notes, detailing a proposal by his Russian intermediaries to hold a meeting of campaign and Russian officials in London in September 2016. The notes included phrases such as "office of Putin" and "No official letter/no message from Trump" and so forth. But Papadopoulos claimed he couldn't read his own handwriting—not a word of it.

Jeannie determined that he could not be a cooperating witness. In the end, given that Team R had the goods on him—he'd admitted he had intentionally misled us—Papadopoulos agreed to plead guilty to lying to the FBI, the charge he had been arrested for by Team R. But Jeannie walked away from the episode somewhat dejected, even though Team R had brought our first successful criminal case against a member of the Trump campaign and done so in just a couple of months. Papadopoulos represented a promising door that just couldn't be nudged open. And yet, the mere fact that he was so obviously hiding something was significant and tantalizing.

It was possible that Papadopoulos had been a dead end for Russia, as well—that they'd attempted to use him as a conduit to the Trump campaign but, by May 2016, were getting nowhere. With that in mind, it wasn't hard to interpret the emails setting up the Trump Tower meeting, which Don Jr. received just one month later, as a second attempt.

This time, Russia was escalating the matter to a more senior member of the campaign—one who happened to be the candidate's son.

As the summer went on, Jeannie and I continued to gather evidence about the June 2016 Trump Tower meeting, including more emails and texts from the campaign. Eventually, we stepped back to take stock of what we knew.

First, it was clear that the highest levels of the Russian government were trying to help Trump and damage his opponent. Second, the Trump campaign was extremely receptive to this help—Don Jr. had said "I love it"—and apparently felt no qualms about accepting it, even though taking any assistance or contributions of value from a foreign entity is illegal under U.S. campaign finance law. And even if Don Jr. wasn't aware of this law, Manafort—who was an attorney and had been brought on board precisely because of his experience with presidential campaigns—surely was. And yet, Manafort, too, showed up for the meeting to hear the dirt.

Third, the Trump Tower meeting, coupled with the Papadopoulos facts, suggested that the Russian government was approaching the campaign from multiple angles, casting out multiple lines to see where they could get a nibble—either as part of a well-coordinated, sequential strategy, or via an array of self-directed operatives. We had broken out Manafort from our larger investigation assuming he would be the most logical point of contact, but here was an example of the Russians bypassing Manafort and attempting to deal directly with candidate Trump through his son. Indeed, as Goldstone explicitly stated in his email, he wasn't sending the offer of dirt even to Trump's personal assistant, Rhona Graff, because it was "ultra-sensitive."

As valuable as the press is in rooting out criminality and corruption, a hungry press corps can also complicate a high-profile investigation by neutralizing one of your strongest advantages: the element of surprise. By reporting its own investigative stories and talking to witnesses, the press often winds up putting your targets on notice as to problematic evidence, as well as what the investigators may be looking at. Those who would seek to destroy documents or coordinate their stories are given time to circle the wagons before you can pounce.

With its story about the Trump Tower meeting, the *Times* had both delivered us a lead but also limited our ability to act on it. The White House, in fact, had known this story was coming before we did, as the *Times* had called them for a response prior to publication, which is an understandable standard practice. Of course, Don Jr., Manafort, and Kushner had known about the Trump Tower meeting itself for more than a year at that point, but people do not tend to orchestrate a cover story until they believe law enforcement may be on to them.

Jeannie and I both knew that time was of the essence. We quickly discerned one potential means of learning what had happened at that meeting, one that could put us a step ahead of the media and any potential obstruction from the Trump team. The *Times* story mentioned that the Russian lawyer, Veselnitskaya, had brought a translator to the meeting, though it did not report his or her name. This suggested that the reporters hadn't yet been able to speak with the translator. Some fast work by Omer and his colleagues in the FBI identified him as Anatoli Samochornov, a New York State resident. We didn't want to waste even the few hours it would take to dispatch a team of agents there from Washington, so the three of us—Jeannie, Omer, and I—debriefed a team of New York FBI agents over the phone, laying out what we knew and working up a slew of questions for them to pose to Samochornov. We asked the agents to drive out to Samochornov's home that day and try to speak with him right away. Then we all crossed our fingers and waited to hear back.

On the call with the FBI agents in New York, I was struck by Jeannie's flawless facility with all the difficult Russian names: Natalya Veselnitskaya, Anatoli Samochornov, Emin and Aras Agalarov—they all flowed off her tongue. Jeannie later explained that she'd been having trouble sleeping and eventually decided she might as well use that tossing-and-turning time productively, so she propelled herself out of bed in the middle of the night and sat down to master her Russian pronunciations. It was indicative of who Jeannie is: meticulous and committed, with respect to even the tiniest challenges. Omer and I, on the other hand, frankly couldn't be bothered. I tended to describe all the Russians by function—"the lawyer," "the real estate developer"—whereas Omer resorted to nicknames. He took to calling the translator, Samochornov, "Smoochy"—a nickname that stuck.

Still, it was clear to Omer and me that Jeannie was one of us—a third musketeer, who worked with our same no-nonsense style, brainstorming and churning through new information with the same frenetic metabolism. Jeannie and I knew, from the outset, that our investigations were closely aligned: A long-term goal of the Special Counsel's Office would be to trace out where Team M's and Team R's paths might ultimately intersect. We were gratified to be collaborating so closely—and so soon.

Jeannie would be a pillar of friendship and support in the Special Counsel's Office. I knew from my experience on the Enron Task Force that forging such relationships in claustrophobic situations like this was critical, and had explained as much to my new colleagues at the Special Counsel's Office early on. I'd worked on Enron for more than three years, subject to similarly extreme pressure and public scrutiny every step of the way. Sealed in such an environment, with the highly confidential nature of our work, meant there are none of the usual pressure-release valves to open when the work gets too intense. I knew, going into the Special Counsel's Office, that cabin fever would inevitably set in. Having good esprit de corps would be critical to our emotional well-being. I could not have gotten through the Enron case without Leslie Caldwell, Matt Friedrich, Lisa Monaco, and Kathy Ruemmler—a crew Mueller later dubbed the "Enron Mafia." Here, Jeannie joined Omer and me in our new triumvirate—an unwavering confidante.

Our office was generally a sedate place. It was largely an open floor plan, with the lead prosecutor and FBI agent of each team having offices. All other team members clustered in carrels outside their team lead offices, laser-focused on the work in front of them, often wearing noise-canceling headphones to block out whatever ambient sound the others were generating.

Jeannie's squad, however—Team R—could inevitably be heard debating any and all issues of the day while piled on top of one another in a kind of ramshackle lair they'd created by dragging an old couch and some metal chairs into the cramped space between their carrels. Team R called this space the Viking Ship, and had even found some kind of Nordic banner to hang over the couch. (The name originated from the time of our original, temporary digs, where a contingent of FBI agents who'd been made to work in a long, narrow windowless corridor joked that they were like the grunting rowers in the underbelly of a ship, with Mueller—their captain—sending down orders to row harder and faster.) Periodically, out of nowhere, an unmistakable and euphoric yowl would come from their direction. This was, of course, Jeannie, gleefully reacting to some new discovery.

Once, on a Monday morning after I'd managed to briefly escape back home to New York for the weekend, I had procured one of the cardboard signs from the Amtrak "Quiet Car": "Please refrain from loud talking," it read. The morning I returned, before Jeannie got in, I taped the sign over the doorway to Jeannie's office, letting it hang down just as it did on the train. I could tell when Jeannie arrived that morning because I heard an even more raucous laugh than usual. She brought Mueller over to see, knowing it had to be me.

Mueller smiled. "Looks like someone committed a felony by stealing this sign," he said.

Jeannie and I soon heard back from the two intrepid FBI agents who'd trekked up to the home of Veselnitskaya's translator, Smoochy, from their offices in Manhattan. He'd agreed to talk to them and seemed to do so openly.

He'd been hired as an interpreter for the Trump Tower meeting by a sketchy Russian think tank in Washington that was controlled by Veselnitskaya's cohorts. Most notably, in the course of his interview with the agents, Smoochy explained that he had reached out to this think tank after the *Times* story broke, and it offered to pay any legal fees he might incur, but only on condition that he provided information that was consistent with Veselnitskaya's own account of the meeting. Veselnitskaya even had an intermediary send him a transcript of a press statement she had given, so he could line his story up with hers. Her description of the meeting glossed over any offer of damaging information on Clinton, or any connection to the Russian government at all. Smoochy told the FBI agents that he'd refused to go along with this deal; Veselnitskaya wasn't being forthright, and he did not wish to perjure himself. The interview ended with the agents and Smoochy agreeing to talk again the following day.

Smoochy's apparent decision not to take the think tank's deal was commendable, and it was a credit to his character that he told the investigators he'd received such an offer. Zooming out, it now seemed clear that not only had the Trump campaign tried to keep the meeting a secret, originally denying there'd been any such contacts with Russia; now that the meeting had been uncovered, both the campaign and the Russians were moving to obscure what had taken place. Don Jr.'s statement to the *Times* might be dismissed as misleading spin, but the Russian think tank's offer to Smoochy—if we could nail down more evidence than just Smoochy's word to prove it—would be a fairly clear case of obstruction of justice, a federal crime.

I had an idea: What if Smoochy were willing to tape his employer discussing the offer? Jeannie and Omer loved it. It was a chance to quickly crack open this aspect of the case. It would be compelling evidence that something had happened at the meeting that people wanted to hide. And bringing an obstruction case against the think tank and its leader, for attempting to tamper with Smoochy as a witness, would give us leverage to try to flip people and learn more.

We got excited about the prospect and began assessing the various angles: We'd have to convince Smoochy to do it, and place sufficient trust in him to pull it off without alarming the targets. Would Smoochy have to wear a wire and have such a conversation in person, or could we simply place a phone call for the FBI to monitor and record? These are the kind of operational details squarely within the expertise of the FBI—and with Omer we had no one better to think them through.

When the FBI agents reached out to Smoochy the following day, he told them he'd retained an attorney named Larry Krantz, a former EDNY prosecutor I had known for years. In fact, Krantz was the shadow counsel who'd represented Sammy "the Bull" Gravano when he flipped against John Gotti. (Shadow counsel is an attorney approved by the court when a defendant seeks to explore cooperation with the government, but does not want his defense counsel to know, out of concern the attorney will report it back to the mob.) My heart beat a little faster—Krantz was a smart and solid lawyer to deal with and might be receptive to our taping gambit. But our hopes were soon dashed. When Jeannie and I called Krantz, he assured us he would bring the idea to his client, but he was going to recommend against it. He just didn't see an upside for his client.

We tried to convince Krantz. But in truth, we had little leverage at that point, merely pleading for Smoochy's help, rather than holding any knowledge of criminal behavior over him to procure his cooperation. We argued that wearing a wire did stand to benefit Smoochy; it would short-circuit the inevitable accusations that he was lying about the think tank's offer in exchange for testimony. We spelled this out for Larry, who said he'd take it to his client, but we could tell he was not convinced.

He called back the next day. Smoochy's answer was no.

At first, I felt deflated: Without Smoochy's wearing a wire, it became impossible to indict the think tank leader for obstruction of justice—all we'd have was Smoochy's word. Then again, the simple fact that this effort to coordinate stories took place underscored how suspicious the meeting was.

Losing such opportunities happens all the time in criminal investigations, but this one was particularly dispiriting, given its potential and the gravity of the situation. But that opportunity was now behind us, and we had to keep moving forward. Ultimately, for me, the entire episode crystallized a phenomenon of the larger Trump Tower meeting investigation—and, I'd eventually find, of the Mueller report as a whole: The dashed prospect of learning something even more shocking diminished our perception of what we actually had in hand.

In the coming months, Jeannie and I collected accounts of the Trump Tower meeting from as many people who'd attended as possible.

The press was having a field day ferreting out the identities of everyone who'd been in the meeting, but our talks with Smoochy had given us a head start. We knew that Don Jr., Kushner, and Manafort had been on the Trump side of the table; on the Russian side sat four others: Veselnitskaya; another lobbyist; a business associate of Aras Agalarov; and Goldstone, the promoter who had set the whole thing up. We'd also zeroed in on several Russians who might have been briefed about the meeting beforehand and afterward, but as they—like Veselnitskaya—were Russian citizens living in Russia, our chances of interviewing them were slim; once the *Times* story broke, they could assume that if they set foot in the United States, they'd be subpoenaed or even potentially indicted. Indeed, we learned that Aras Agalarov's son, Emin, who had a career as a pop singer in addition to being a businessman, was scheduled later to do a four-city U.S. tour, with a first stop in New York. As we suspected, these plans were scrapped—due to "forces beyond my control," as Emin's announcement cagily put it.

When we reached out to Don Jr. through his counsel Alan Futerfas for a voluntary interview, he begged off, as was his right. But shortly thereafter, he went on Fox News to be "interviewed" by Sean Hannity, and I put aside my general aversion to watching TV reports on our investigation so I could hear what he had to say. Unsurprisingly, Don Jr. offered no compelling or credible defense—not even an answer as to why he hadn't previously disclosed the meeting, or, once it was discovered, why he issued such a misleading statement about its purpose. He did not address that he had refused to be interviewed by us—this was at a time when his father was still publicly saying how he looked forward to being interviewed.

It was alarming, frankly, that no one on Trump's campaign seemed to register that it was a bad idea to accept aid from a foreign adversary during a U.S. election—even as a matter of strategy, if not legality and ethics. The Trump campaign would have been breaking campaign finance law by accepting Russia's help, and Russia would have known it. Wouldn't the campaign then feel indebted to Russia, and wouldn't Russia be in a position to later leverage its illegal assistance in some way? Just by meeting with Veselnitskaya under such circumstances, they were handing Putin powerful blackmail material—kompromat, as Russian intelligence calls it—to hold over Trump if he was elected.

None of this seemed to matter to the Trump team, however. It was as though such considerations had never occurred to them—either due to their terrible judgment and ignorance, or because they were so fixated on winning, or both. If a particular move could help Trump prevail, it was good, no matter what negative consequences might spiral out of that decision down the road. Even Steve Bannon, after he was fired from the administration, would malign his former colleagues for taking the meeting, telling a journalist it was "treasonous," "unpatriotic," and "bad shit"—and also laughing at their stupidity for holding such a meeting in a high-profile place like Trump Tower, and without a single one of their attorneys present. "But that's the brain trust they had," Bannon said.

Ultimately, we would speak with everyone who'd been in the room at Trump Tower except Don Jr. and Veselnitskaya, who remained safely in Russia. We also obtained phone records and emails between Don Jr. and Goldstone and the Agalarovs, as well as other documentary evidence against which to check the stories we were told. All of these witnesses indicated that the meeting had essentially been a bust as to its stated purpose. The campaign came in hoping for dirt on Clinton, the Russians came in hoping for a commitment to undo the Magnitsky Act, and neither side walked away with what it wanted—because the Russians didn't have the goods to barter. Kushner claimed he'd known nothing about the purpose of the meeting ahead of time (even though Don Jr. had forwarded him the Goldstone–Don Jr. emails) and attended merely because Don Jr. had asked him.

Kushner arrived for his interview with Team R with an experienced white-collar defense lawyer, though he himself could have passed for an associate at a white-shoe firm on Wall Street: a tall, clean-cut, and youthful man who, Jeannie later explained to me, answered her questions in a manner that felt extremely well rehearsed. He seemed committed to saying nothing more than necessary—likely as a matter of strategy, though it also appeared to be his natural temperament.

Nevertheless, his description of what had happened at the Trump Tower meeting did not appear to be whitewashed or evasive; it seemed to have genuinely struck him as underwhelming. This was corroborated by text messages Kushner had sent to an assistant during the meeting, asking her to give him an excuse to leave. He'd also shot a text to Manafort, while still in the room: "Waste of time." He insisted that he'd never really thought through the question of whether it was illegal to accept a thing of value from a foreigner like Veselnitskaya. Nothing he heard in the room seemed to rise to that level, he said. And as he did not know what the meeting was going to be about beforehand, he claimed, the foreign assistance issue had not even occurred to him.

It seemed like a stretch to Jeannie that he'd had no idea why he was asked to attend, but without contrary proof, her hunch was irrelevant as proof in a criminal investigation. There were slight differences in people's recollections, all of them understandable. As in the movie *Rashomon,* different participants' vantage points and memories of an incident will often vary. But our interviewees agreed that Veselnitskaya was the first to speak substantively, disclosing the existence of the purportedly damaging information on Clinton.

The much-anticipated dirt concerned money allegedly funneled from two Americans, the Ziff brothers, who Veselnitskaya claimed (but did not establish) had broken Russian laws by engaging in tax evasion and money laundering. Various participants said that Veselnitskaya could not establish that those funds had even gone into the Clinton campaign, knowingly or unknowingly on its part. And perhaps because of this, those at the meeting from the Trump campaign did not offer any commitments once the conversation turned to the Magnitsky Act and Veselnitskaya lobbied for the removal of sanctions. All Don Jr. would tell Veselnitskaya was that they could revisit the issue if Trump was elected; as a private citizen, there was nothing his father could do now.

Still, no one told Jeannie that they had any concern about either providing or accepting foreign assistance to a U.S. presidential campaign—a fact that was, frankly, shocking. No one expressed this concern before or after the meeting. What this whole episode established was that the Trump campaign was open for business and interested in Russian campaign assistance, but it needed more than unsubstantiated factual assertions by the Russians.

The will was there on both sides, but the dirt was lacking. The Papadopoulos foray had not led to the provision of campaign assistance, and
this next attempt to coordinate had also fizzled for lack of concrete useful evidence. Alarmed, Jeannie and I kept our eye open for the next Russian and Trump campaign interactions. We did not have to wait long.

Before we moved on, however, we first had to assess—with our office's
own internal legal team, headed by Michael Dreeben—whether the
proof we'd accumulated about the Trump Tower meeting would support any criminal charges. As with the question of obstruction in the
Comey firing, making the legal assessment, as opposed to a mere gut
response, turned out to be complicated.

I liked and respected Michael immensely. Before joining our office,
he had worked as the deputy solicitor general in the Solicitor General's
Office at the Department of Justice, assigned to oversee all criminal matters for the team that handled Supreme Court litigation for the Department. He and I had known each other since working together on Enron.
When the Special Counsel's Office was forming, and Mueller was hunting for someone with the experience to head our legal team, I'd told him
that I thought Dreeben might be interested in coming aboard. Mueller
told me to give it a shot, and I called Michael on my cellphone, on my
way to interview another applicant in New York. Before I could get all
the words out—"Would you be interested in working . . ."—Michael
cut me off. "Yes," he said. Mueller was elated with the news.

Michael and his team sussed out the pertinent law. The relevant
campaign finance law does not allow foreigners to give, or U.S. campaigns to receive, "a contribution or donation of money or other thing of
value." But what the Russians were offering was dirt; there had never
been a case brought for the provision of opposition research as "a thing
of value." We concluded that such information would clearly be encompassed by the law—campaigns paid small fortunes to dig up dirt on each
other. In order for the crime to be a felony, the value of the foreign contribution had to exceed $25,000, and it was hard to know, precisely, how
to put a monetary value on Veselnitskaya's purported dirt. After all, the
Trump team had ultimately dismissed it as having no value at all.

We'd also need to establish for a jury, beyond a reasonable doubt,

that any defendants we charged had criminal intent when they broke
the law—that they'd known their actions were wrong or illegal. Given
these legal hurdles, it was difficult to imagine charging either Don Jr. or
Jared Kushner. Both were new to political campaigning and there was a
dearth of evidence that they understood the law, much less understood
that it forbade accepting monetary contributions from a foreign source,
and that they knew the law encompassed opposition research. One
would be justified in thinking that Don Jr. and Kushner should have
known all this—that they should have made it their business to know
the rules governing presidential campaigns as soon as they found themselves at the top of one. But that argument isn't sufficient to bring a
criminal case. This may strike people as unfair: Don Jr. and Kushner
were getting a benefit from lack of knowledge, and from having failed
to do their homework. But in order to charge someone with a crime, and
potentially send them to prison, the law requires more than negligent or
reckless conduct. And that is as it should be.

There was another argument both could make as well: If we chose to
prosecute Don Jr. and Kushner, each man could claim that they'd assumed taking the meeting was proper because Paul Manafort—whom
they believed to be well versed in campaign rules—had agreed to join
them. If such a meeting was illegal, wouldn't Manafort have quashed it?
This strain of argument is routinely made by defendants in corporate
cases, when accountants and lawyers are in the loop on an economic
transaction. The business people can rightly argue that they assumed the
accountants or lawyers would have flagged the activity, if it were amiss.
That defense fails when we can show that the criminal conspiracy involved the lawyers or accountants. Bannon was right: The naïveté and
impulsivity of most everyone involved was palpable; ironically, all that
dysfunction could be leveraged effectively in their defense to a criminal
charge.

There was another wrinkle, as well. The emails only indicated, beyond dispute, that one person on the American side definitely knew the
purpose of the meeting in advance: Don Jr. We could not prove that others read these emails in advance. Jeannie was doubtful that Don Jr.
wouldn't have talked up the prospect of Clinton dirt to Manafort, Kushner, his sister, or his father, but absent new evidence—a document or
new witness coming forward with a different account—Jeannie's suspi-

cions were not enough. I kept this question on a list of topics to raise if Manafort ever flipped, and Jeannie placed it on her running list of subjects to discuss if and when the president was interviewed.

That left the question of whether we could charge Manafort. After all, unlike Don Jr. and Kushner, he couldn't credibly claim ignorance of campaign finance law. But the nagging question of the value of Veselnitskaya's dirt still complicated any determination. And by the time our factual investigation of the Trump Tower meeting wound down by the end of 2017, we already had Manafort under indictment for far more solid criminal charges. A maxim I drilled into my budding prosecutors was "Gray is not for the criminal law"—meaning, if the issue isn't black-and-white, don't go forward with a criminal prosecution. The Justice Department standard for bringing a criminal charge is that the evidence is "probably sufficient" to obtain a criminal conviction "beyond a reasonable doubt"; anything less should be left for the civil lawyers to assess.

By the end of 2017, we had come to the end of available evidence about the Trump Tower meeting but did not have enough yet to charge anyone for it. There was one other potential crime, however: Right after reading Don Jr.'s slippery statement in *The New York Times,* Jeannie and I had seen enough to loop in Team 600—Jim Quarles's team investigating obstruction of justice. They would pick up this strand of the Trump Tower investigation and, in time, uncover deep layers of deception.

CHAPTER 7

The Trump Tower Cover-Up

DON JR.'S WRITTEN STATEMENT to the media that the meeting had been "primarily" about adoptions struck us as misleading at best, and more likely as an outright lie. To be clear, it was not the Special Counsel's Office's job to be the morality police and ferret out incidences of someone being untruthful with the press. Lying to the media is not a crime—even though it is, to my mind, more pernicious than lying to investigators. I worry that our society is rapidly becoming inured to it from chronic exposure—even to cynically expect it from our politicians. As a lifelong public servant, I've never stopped being shocked that public servants paid by the taxpayers believe it acceptable to lie to the public. This strikes me as analogous to a lawyer lying to a client, or a doctor lying to a patient—a violation of one's professional duty.

Corey Lewandowski would later proudly boast under oath to Congress that he lied to the press since, he said, the press lies, too. And Deputy Attorney General Rod Rosenstein gave a squirrelly non-denial denial, when reporters pressed him after the firing of FBI Director Comey about whether he was so concerned about the president's mental state that he had discussed the invocation of the Twenty-Fifth Amendment and wearing a wire to the White House. If a corporate executive made such misleading statements, he would land in a mess of trouble with the SEC and, if serious enough, with the Department of Justice as well. It is a federal crime for them to lie to or mislead the press about a public company—Enron's CEO and chairman, Ken Lay, had been convicted of this very thing. But no similar law applies to the routine lies and misleading statements we see from public officials. I had been fortunate to be trained by people like Mueller, who demonstrated that, elected or not, if you as a public servant choose to speak, you must be 100 percent candid and not obfuscate or color the facts.

For us on the special counsel investigation, there was one way a lie to the media could also constitute criminal obstruction of justice. Obstruction could be established if we could prove the speaker intended to mislead or thwart our investigation, either by throwing investigators off the scent, or passing off a sanctioned version of the story to model how others were to testify. We didn't know the backstory to Don Jr.'s statement to *The New York Times;* it seemed possible that it was meant to accomplish either one of these jobs—or both.

Team 600 began by looking into who'd been involved in drafting the statement, and if there'd been even earlier iterations of it that revealed the campaign's mindset before they ultimately settled on the version that was put out. The press had been circling around this same issue, as it, too, could immediately see the difference between Don Jr.'s public description of the meeting and the emails he'd released. The latter clearly centered on the Russians' offer of dirt on Clinton.

Another suspicious dimension of this cover-up was a claim in July 2017 by President Trump that he had not been aware of the meeting before it had surfaced in the news. You didn't have to be a cynical investigator to smell a rat there. The president was a notorious micromanager—even if the meeting ultimately failed to deliver the damaging information on Clinton that the Trump team had hoped for, it seemed unlikely that Don Jr. would not have alerted his father about this promising lead he'd received, if only as a way to impress him. Moreover, the lead came from people close to the Trumps—the Agalarovs—so it would be odd to not keep Trump in the loop and to let him be caught off guard when speaking to his friends in the future.

We did not, however, have the benefit of hearing directly from Trump or Don Jr. on these matters. Neither would ever agree to meet with us voluntarily. And it is now a matter of record that Don Jr. also never appeared before the grand jury, though that fact was initially redacted—blacked out—by Barr in the version of our final report he released publicly. (A federal judge eventually ordered his Justice Department to release this information.) A person can fail to testify before a grand jury for two basic reasons: the government does not issue or enforce a grand jury subpoena for that person, or the person refuses to comply with a subpoena based on a privilege, such as the Fifth Amendment privilege to remain silent if a truthful answer would tend to incriminate you.

Under DOJ internal guidelines, if a person seeks to invoke the Fifth, they should not be compelled to go through the rigmarole of doing so in the grand jury if they submit a written statement to that effect to the government. If the latter had occurred with respect to Don Jr. or anyone else, I could not reveal it as there is a law prohibiting revealing grand jury matters, and such a letter could fall within its ambit. It is worth noting, however, the irony that Don Jr. has widely disparaged the Mueller investigation, given that either he was not subpoenaed by our office or he refused to comply based on his assertion of the Fifth Amendment, and in either case, he can hardly complain about how he was treated.

As to the president, we would ultimately decide not to subpoena him to the grand jury, which would have compelled Trump to either provide his account or assert the Fifth Amendment. (I will detail how we reached that decision—and why I disagreed with it—later on.) The president did provide terse written answers to certain questions from our office, however, and notably backed off his initial, categorical assertion to the public that he hadn't known about the Trump Tower meeting before *The New York Times* reported on it. He altered his claim to assert, instead, that he "had no recollection about knowing about the meeting beforehand." Clearly, although Trump publicly claimed he drafted his written responses, he and his lawyers had watered down his public denial so he would not be prosecutable for lying to us in his written answers—which, unlike his lying to the American public in tweets and on television, is a crime.

Still, we had other avenues to learn about the Trump team's machinations to cover up the Trump Tower meeting, minimizing the impact of the firestorm once the story broke. One was our interview of Rob Goldstone, who'd first made the offer to Don Jr. of dirt from the Agalarovs and the Russian crown prosecutor. Goldstone had responded to

Team R's initial request to appear at our office for an interview with a drawn-out attempt to bilk our office for a first-class round-trip ticket to New York from England. Jeannie countered with an emphatic no, and eventually, in February 2018, Goldstone materialized in our office, a mess of a man whose distinct bottom-feeder aura was hard to square with his affiliation with the fabulously wealthy and powerful Agalarovs.

We also obtained Goldstone's emails with the Agalarovs, Don Jr., and Don Jr.'s attorney. From these, we learned of efforts to have participants in the meeting conform their stories, and of Goldstone's work to keep the Agalarovs out of these accounts. The emails revealed that in the weeks just prior to *The New York Times* breaking its July 2017 story about the Trump Tower meeting, but surely after the newspaper had contacted Don Jr. so he could comment for the article, Goldstone was contacted by lawyers for the Trump Organization and Don Jr. to discuss the meeting. Goldstone sent the attorneys Veselnitskaya's name, confirming that she was the Russian attorney in attendance. Later in June, Goldstone emailed Emin Agalarov, alerting him that he was being asked about the meeting by the Trump Organization lawyers and explaining the problem posed by the meeting becoming public, telling Emin that the attorneys were concerned "because it links Don. Jr. to officials from Russia—which he has always denied meeting." Goldstone groused that he'd always thought the Trump Tower meeting was a bad idea, but that Aras Agalarov would not listen and insisted on it going forward.

This conspiratorial scheming may have reached its peak in July 2017, shortly after *The New York Times* story was published, when Don Jr. had an intermediary reach out to Goldstone, asking him to issue a statement that would gloss over key elements of the meeting, including the central one: the Russians' offer of Clinton dirt. Goldstone, to his credit, declined to do so.

Such circling of the wagons is common in criminal investigations of organizations, whether they be of mobsters or financial institutions like Enron or Volkswagen. And through joint defense agreements, corporate lawyers can at times play a role—usually unwittingly—in alerting witnesses as to what other evidence is in play, and clients may use it nefariously. There is a legitimate role for such joint defense agreements in defending people and entities, and the courts recognize joint defense agreements for this reason—people who have a common interest can speak with each other under the cloak of the attorney-client privilege. But the problem for prosecutors is that this legitimate tool can mask criminality by the clients, who are using the joint defense agreement to get their stories straight. And unless we can prove to a court that that is what is going on, we cannot get permission from the court to pierce the agreement. Here, Team 600 determined that we had insufficient proof to warrant such a step.

Team 600 also interviewed several people who had insight into how Don Jr.'s statement to *The New York Times* had been crafted—including how integral a role the president had played. The president himself had shifting stories about his involvement. In July 2017, Trump announced through his personal attorney that he'd had no hand at all in crafting the message his son put out. Later, he admitted to our office, again through his personal counsel, that he in fact had dictated how the statement would read, meaning that his prior public statement was inaccurate and, in our estimation, intentionally so. This and other such public lies posed a conundrum for us. On the one hand, it spoke to the lack of integrity of the president in general and his penchant for prevarication. On the other hand, if he were lying solely for political gain—to deny or spin inconvenient facts that could hurt him politically, but without an intent to interfere with our investigation—that was not itself criminal. He could be lying about the meeting simply to blunt a bad story, but was he doing it to hide facts from us? That was the question for Team 600.

One key to fleshing out this story was Team 600's interview with Hope Hicks in March 2018, just after she resigned from the administration as communications director. Jeannie and I had both helped Jim Quarles prep for his sit-down with Hicks, pooling questions from all three teams. This was our office's standard game plan before consequential interviews like this—at least in theory. At times, members of more than one team were compelled to be present for a particular interview, though Jeannie and I tried to avoid overwhelming witnesses with crowds of investigators. We believed that the smaller the group, the more honest witnesses tend to be. During one interview, for example, a man who helped orchestrate Manafort's illegal lobbying in the United States by foreigners was questioned by Team M about a particularly damning email. He turned quite pensive, then slowly broke down, choking back tears, confessing that he'd been weak willed and had behaved in ways that he was ashamed of, all in the pursuit of power and money. That kind of introspection, self-recrimination, and then forthrightness is hard to expect of anyone, and far harder to do before a large audience of strangers. There's a reason people go to psychoanalysts alone.

In Hicks's case, Jeannie and Team 600 were slated to conduct the interview, but I was immediately made aware of her arrival. Hicks is a striking woman, who stepped into the drab atmosphere of our office sporting a floral-pattered Victorian buttoned-up shirt with sleeves that billowed copiously.

Hicks explained that Don Jr.'s statement had been written on Air Force One, while the president and his staff were flying back from the G20 summit in Hamburg, Germany. The first statement Hicks had brought to the president during the flight described Don Jr. taking a meeting with "an individual who I was told might have information helpful to the campaign." But the president had told Hicks to cut that part, and simply say the meeting was about adoptions. She did so, but then texted this version to Don Jr., who insisted on including the word "primarily" before it went out. In other words, while Don Jr.'s final version might be defended as literally true, but misleading, the president's initial draft was even more so. It did not leave any wiggle room in its description of what the meeting was about, and thus papered over the discussions of Clinton or getting the Magnitsky Act repealed.

Hicks tried her best to provide the president with a partial alibi for his drafting the statement that way—the statement that Trump originally claimed he had nothing to do with. Her story allowed for the inference that the president was not intentionally lying in the statement, but was simply misinformed. Hicks described being in the room on two previous occasions when Kushner and Ivanka Trump had discussed the meeting with the president. According to her, the first time, the president all but cut Kushner off, insisting he didn't want to know anything about the meeting. The second time, however, Kushner told the president the meeting was about adoptions—and this, Hicks insisted, was still Trump's understanding at the time he dictated the statement on Air Force One.

This story presented obvious issues. Hicks described multiple occasions in which Trump made clear to his staff that he did not want to know what happened at the meeting. He simply wanted it to go away. But Hicks also admitted that she had seen Don Jr.'s emails setting up the meeting well before the final statement was issued to *The New York Times*. She recalled being shocked by them and as a consequence she said she warned Trump that the emails looked "really bad," and that the story would be "massive" when it broke.

This defense that Hicks was spinning for the president was tissue thin. She may have thought she was inoculating him from any accusation that he'd been intentionally lying, but what Hicks described was still potentially criminal. The law permits the government to prove criminal intent through "willful blindness," a legal term of art that describes one's purposeful refusal to learn information solely so that one can later lie about it.

Hicks's story reminded me of a memorable anecdote from the Enron case. Enron's CEO and chairman, Ken Lay, was preparing to give a press conference about the company's 2001 third quarter earnings, when his finance team began briefing him on the company's harrowing financial condition, mapping out the bad news on a whiteboard. Lay quickly closed up the whiteboard, explaining that he didn't want to hear it; he had a press conference to give. He proceeded to paint a rosy and false picture of Enron's financials for the media, just weeks before the company would ultimately file for bankruptcy. The law does not permit as a defense such deliberate avoidance of facts, as it is actually evidence that you knew what was going on but wanted to be able to claim you didn't.

Other aspects of the cover-up Hicks described were equally disturbing. Hicks knew the Trump Tower story would break, and it was obvious that Congress would make a document request and that the emails would have to be turned over. But, Hicks explained, the president insisted to her that Don Jr.'s emails would never get out and told her to make sure that the emails weren't circulated widely within the group of attorneys and staffers handling the issue. The president's personal press agent, Mark Corallo, who we also interviewed, corroborated her story, and had even recorded Hicks relaying the conversation to him in contemporaneous notes.

To me, the president's statement that the emails would not get out clearly indicated that he intended to defy his legal obligation to turn them over to Congress, that he planned to keep them hidden. Hicks described repeatedly urging the president to be more transparent with the media about the meeting—to acknowledge that the Russians had offered dirt on Clinton, and that Don Jr. had been receptive—so that their statement would match what was plainly written in the emails. But the president refused. That is, he was not concerned about making claims that could be baldly disproven by the emails, signaling that he did not believe the latter would ever come to light. (It is quaint now to look back on this in light of Trump's complete stonewalling of Congress in connection with his impeachment. Now it is obvious that he would not have agreed to turn over such damning documents.)

Hicks tried to avoid throwing the president under the bus, suggesting Trump intended to turn the emails over to Congress, but simply didn't believe they would become public. I found this absurd; no one in Washington could earnestly believe that explosive documents turned over to Congress would not leak, particularly since it would not even be illegal for someone from Congress to make them public. (The president has since used such inevitable leaks to justify his not providing required documents to Congress.) Moreover, the various alibis Hicks was offering started to become incompatible—the story, as a whole, just didn't make sense. Why would the president believe that the emails were bad and would not get out, if he also believed the Trump Tower meeting was just about adoptions?

What did all of this evidence tell us?

In one sense, compared to the potential obstruction in the Comey affair, the cover-up of the Trump Tower meeting was simple. It involved far more quotidian forms of obstruction, and ones we were all accustomed to dealing with: witnesses who got together to coordinate a false account of what happened, or hide or destroy documents to keep information from falling into investigators' hands—the old obstructionist standbys, the classics.

Still, it was a lot to digest. First, the evidence showed that the president lied. All other matters aside, it was useful to have this documented so clearly. The maneuvering that went into Don Jr.'s statement revealed how comfortable the president was lying to the media, and therefore to the public. Moreover, he lied recklessly—without regard to the likelihood that he'd later be caught in those lies. Confronted with a problem, the president appeared to turn to lying as a strategy for solving it. It was no wonder that, even as the president claimed publicly that he was willing to do an interview with our office, behind the scenes he and his attorneys were fighting our requests tooth and nail.

The episode also demonstrates Trump's apparent willingness to obstruct Congress, too, by withholding documents, a tactic he's since put into practice during the impeachment inquiry—merely one example of unconstitutional conduct that our investigation showed the president mulling over, or testing out, and that he's gone on to execute shamelessly.

Whether these specific, dismaying attempts at deception about the Trump Tower meeting rose to obstruction of justice ultimately depends on the president's motive. His objective would have to be not merely to deceive *The New York Times,* but to disrupt or mislead Congress or the special counsel's investigation. Team 600 would hedge on this question in our report, which allowed this uncertainty to undermine what any intelligent reader will likely understand: The president had lied in order to protect himself from suffering any consequences for the campaign's actions. Team 600 determined that there was insufficient evidence to claim this was criminal obstruction, however, noting that we'd found no witness or document that delineated the motive of the president—that proved that his goal was to deceive Congress or our investigation—either of which would be necessary to bring a criminal case.

But I disagreed with this timorous conclusion of my earnest and well-meaning colleagues on Team 600. Did anyone really believe that the president distinguished in his mind one objective from another? Lying about the Trump Tower meeting would trigger a suite of benefits, all of them interconnected. Getting a false story out that the meeting was inconsequential (that is, it was just about adoptions) arms the president's defenders, in both the media and in Congress, with a counternarrative they can aggressively amplify. And this obfuscation can, in turn, disincentivize Congress—in theory, one of the most powerful checks on presidential power—from looking into the matter. It is fanciful to think the president was solely focused on deceiving the public and not also on disrupting Congress or us. Moreover, it would be myopic to evaluate the president's conduct here in isolation—we would eventually uncover many other facts that evidenced the president's intent to undermine Congress and our investigation, which makes it easier to conclude he was employing the same tactics here.

This question had been left to Team 600, Aaron, and Mueller to ultimately decide, as it was not for Jeannie or me or our teams to determine. But it was a debate within the office that was emblematic of a perpetual divide among those who gave the benefit of every possible doubt to the president and those who thought that some of those doubts were fanciful and unrealistic. I was in the latter camp, as was Jeannie. Andrew Goldstein, a senior member of Team 600 who sat in a carrel outside Jeannie's office and my office, would chastise himself for not more forcefully opposing his colleagues on Team 600, whom he felt lacked the boldness that had been instilled in him in the SDNY.

The FBI agents—a generally more aggressive investigative group than their prosecutorial colleagues—tended to align with us as well. Michelle Taylor, the dynamic and thorough lead FBI agent on Team 600, would routinely grouse to Omer, Jeannie, and me, believing her team was pulling its punches and shooting down her views. Her position was typical for FBI agents in general in criminal investigations. A common FBI agent complaint is that prosecutors are too timid, refusing to bring difficult cases that they might lose. At times, that complaint has a good deal of merit—there is always a reason not to bring a case, if you don't want to, but that does not mean it is the right thing to do. A good prosecutor needs to temper an agent's enthusiasm for bringing a case with a cold, hard assessment of the facts and the law, and the question of whether a case should be brought, even if it can be brought. But fear of losing should never enter into the picture.

As to the Trump Tower meeting, I felt it was premature to throw up our hands on the question of whether the president and Don Jr.'s coverup was meant to deceive the press or us. The president had not yet sat down with us to explain his intent for himself; the endless dance between our office and the president to negotiate his sitting for an interview was just starting.

On the plus side, the president had said publicly that he wanted to sit for an interview, but on the other hand we knew that his counsel would fight like hell to avoid that. They understood that the president was erratic and could well say something that would incriminate himself. It was one thing to be caught lying to the press, but to lie in an interview with us was proscribed by a federal statute. In the summer and fall of 2017 we were all still hopeful, however, that the president would agree to a voluntary interview, given that he had publicly committed to it. But lurking in the back of our heads was that unless Mueller decided soon what he would do if the president did not agree—that is, issue a grand jury subpoena for his testimony—then the president's team would know that we were not willing to use our only leverage to obtain that interview.

"You know Aaron is never going to do that," Omer said. It was still early in our investigation, and I was holding out hope. But privately I was worried, too.

What, then, is the importance of the Trump Tower meeting in the context of the special counsel's investigation as a whole? I want to address this question clearly, because I worry its significance has been twisted by the president's defenders and misunderstood by the public, even since our report was published.

The initial discovery of the meeting had set off a stampede of speculating pundits online and on cable TV, many of whom discussed the revelation with an—albeit premature—air of vindication. There was a hope, or even a presumption, that this meeting would turn out to be the smoking gun, proof of actual cooperation between Russia and the campaign—the so-called collusion that the president kept denying.

In the end, it was hard, given the lack of substance to the meeting, to regard it alone as evidence of a completed conspiracy with Russia, but it would be wrong to contend that the entire episode amounted to a "big nothing-burger"—which is the phrase the administration used when attempting to dismiss it. The Trump Tower meeting cannot be waved away so cavalierly. In truth, it is damning. The evidence provides compelling proof—explicit proof, typed out in Don Jr.'s emails—of the campaign's willingness to accept illegal foreign assistance. The mindset of senior members of the Trump campaign and of the Russian operatives whom they'd welcomed in was equally clear (even without the advantage of knowing that the president, after our report was issued, would tell George Stephanopoulos that he would still accept foreign assistance): All parties were willing to conspire and coordinate to get candidate Donald Trump elected. They simply didn't have the deliverables on that particular day to get a deal done.

Equally shocking was the ease with which members of the administration, and the president himself, lied to cover it up. As with my own disappointment when Smoochy failed to wear a wire, I fear that the hope of uncovering something even greater distorted the perception of what was actually brought to light. That Don Jr. and Veselnitskaya failed to broker a transaction at the Trump Tower meeting must not distract from the astonishing fact that they'd held such a meeting in the first place.

Understanding the mindset of the campaign officials would shape our interpretation of everything we learned from then on. This particular attempt at Russian cooperation had fizzled, but it had also been initiated by fairly inexperienced people on both sides—higher-ranking campaign operatives than Papadopoulos and Mifsud, who appeared to have attempted a similar transaction one month earlier, but still a junior varsity team. But as Team M would soon discover, a far sharper Russian operative flew to New York two months later to meet with Manafort and try one more time.

Meanwhile, Team R was already busily zooming out to understand the larger context into which these isolated events were woven, building off the revelation that the Trump Tower meeting had been, as Goldstone put it, only "part of Russia and its government's support of Mr. Trump."

CHAPTER 8

Firing Mueller

THE DISCOVERY OF THE Trump Tower meeting had been alarming, as it showed a promise of foreign assistance being welcomed by an American presidential campaign. But the most immediate effect it had on the Special Counsel's Office was also one of relief: We had now locked on to something substantial, an incident that went straight to the heart of our investigation's purpose. And this, we naïvely believed, would offer us some much-needed protection, insulating us from an escalating right-wing onslaught.

Throughout our first months of operation, people were on edge. There was pervasive anxiety that the president or one of his minions would fire Mueller at any moment, and that the entire investigation would be shut down. Our discomfort was bolstered by two obvious precedents: Nixon had ordered his attorney general to fire special prosecutor Archibald Cox, igniting the Saturday Night Massacre when the attorney general and his deputy refused Nixon's command and were themselves fired. Jim Quarles had worked for that special counsel, and so that historical event had a living embodiment in our office.

But there was another precedent that was closer to home: Trump's firing of Comey, which had precipitated Mueller's appointment as special counsel in the first place. In fact, though we did not know it at the time, the president had already ordered his White House counsel, Don

McGahn, to instruct Attorney General Sessions to fire Mueller. But McGahn had refused, explicitly noting his not wanting to provoke another Nixonian crisis. We would not learn about this episode until months later, when Team 600 uncovered it as part of their obstruction of justice investigation.

These worries were particularly acute when Jeannie and I started digging into the Trump Tower meeting. At the time, in July 2017, none of our three teams was fully staffed up. Our office space was still under construction. We'd barely gotten started. And yet, even at that early stage, Aaron had appeared while Jeannie and I were interviewing a job applicant and pulled us both out for a moment. "This is just for you two," he explained. He then told us that the office had gotten information that we might be fired that day.

Jeannie and I both froze momentarily. Despite all the speculation in the media, this was the first time we'd gotten any concrete indication that it might actually happen. We thanked Aaron for letting us know and went back to our interview. All we could do was keep working and act like everything was normal.

The public reports about the Don Jr.–Goldstone emails eased that tension, however. We assumed that having this Trump Tower meeting in our sights would give us some breathing room—that it would be harder to attack our investigation as a "witch hunt" or get rid of us. And for a time, we were right; all the chatter from Republican operatives and Fox News pundits about Rod Rosenstein, and whether he should have appointed a special counsel in the first place, quieted down. The pressure from Rosenstein's office on us to speed up and focus narrowly also diminished, likely in proportion to Rod's assessment of his own vulnerability. It was a short reprieve, however. In August, that scene with Aaron replayed itself. This time, he interrupted an interview Omer and I were conducting to warn us that the hammer might be dropping again.

It kept happening: Time after time, throughout that first summer and fall, Aaron would pull me or one of the other team leads aside to warn us that it appeared that we were about to be fired. The entire Special Counsel's Office would operate in this state of limbo for the duration of our investigation, always understanding, on any given day, that we might not be coming into work the following morning.

Jim Quarles had developed a solid professional relationship with Ty

Cobb, one of Trump's personal attorneys, and Cobb had assured Quarles that he'd be "our canary in the coal mine" and give us a heads-up if we were going to be terminated. We could feel the president's obvious irritation and resentment with our investigation weighing down on us—we, like the press, were a check on his power, and thus were to be destroyed. We kept reading in the press that Trump's lawyers were assuring him that we'd have everything wrapped up by Thanksgiving 2017. When that deadline came and went, they assured him that we'd be done by the end of the year. Both dates were ludicrous for an investigation like ours. (Enron, by way of comparison, took more than four years.) Clearly, Cobb was offering these deadlines to mollify Trump and avoid a debacle like Nixon's Saturday Night Massacre. Cobb's deadlines were mere mirages—false oases he kept pointing to in the distance. It was not surprising when, in May 2018, Cobb finally "resigned," and an undoubtedly exasperated Trump brought on a more belligerent legal team.

In the scraps of spare time I'd had since joining the Special Counsel's Office, I had taken to reading various memoirs by participants in the Watergate investigation. I had lived through Watergate, spending the summer of 1973 indoors, glued to a small black-and-white TV to watch the congressional hearings, but those childhood memories had grown dim.

I found the memoir of Judge John J. Sirica, *To Set the Record Straight,* to be particularly poignant. Judge Sirica was the chief judge in the same Washington, D.C., courthouse in which, more than forty years later, we found ourselves almost daily, bringing applications for court orders or filing other papers with current chief judge Beryl Howell. Sirica described meeting with the Watergate grand jury in the same august courtroom in which Aaron, Jim, and I, along with Chief Judge Howell, had selected the special counsel's grand jurors. But the resonances ran deeper. I was taken by Judge Sirica's regret over having supported Nixon's first campaign—"I hope no political party will ever stoop so low as to the likes of Richard Nixon again," he wrote—and his revelatory, even chilling, summation of the lessons he'd drawn from the entire affair. "Watergate," he wrote, "taught us that our system is not invulnerable to the arrogance of power, to misdeeds by power-hungry individuals, and that we must always be on guard against selecting such people as our leaders. It taught us that our system of law is the most valuable asset in this land and that it must be nurtured, protected, and respected."

The Saturday Night Massacre was, of course, a pivotal moment in many of the histories I was reading, and I took special note of the fact that those working in the Special Prosecutor's Office had immediately scrambled to safeguard their files. By law, the records couldn't be destroyed, but some of the staff had raced to their offices and taken files to their homes to ensure that the material wasn't mysteriously "lost" by the Justice Department once they were gone.

I began to fixate on how we, at the Special Counsel's Office, might similarly ensure that our own work couldn't be erased. No one had put much thought into the question, and when it came up briefly, at one of the first daily meetings Mueller held with me and the other two team leads, there had been only some pro forma talk about the need for each team to carefully document what they'd done, what evidence we'd collected, and what leads we still had outstanding. I'm not exactly known for my poker face, and Mueller clearly picked up on the turmoil I was feeling in that moment. When the meeting concluded, he approached me to ask what was wrong. I didn't hold back.

"That's our plan if we're fired?" I said. "To have kept good notes?"

At that point, each team was independently documenting its work as best it could. But Mueller immediately took my point to heart and, in short order, our office got its act together, creating a centralized system for everything: our applications to the court for search warrants; court orders and warrants; subpoenas we had served; witness interview 302s; documents and other physical items we had obtained—all of it would be recorded in electronic files with uniform criteria, all collated and tracked by our amazing paralegals. The voluminous documentary evidence we obtained from searches, subpoenas, and voluntary productions, meanwhile, was housed on FBI computer systems. This assured that all the discovery would remain intact electronically if our office were to suddenly disappear. And organizing this meticulous operation was Aaron Zebley at his best.

We also realized we could use the courts as a kind of external hard drive to back up our work. The applications for search warrants we filed with the court only had to set out a minimum of facts from which the court could find probable cause—a fairly low standard. But by packing those documents with up-to-date details of our investigation, we could create a separate record of our activities—one that would be deposited securely in the judicial system, beyond the reach of the Department of Justice, the White House, or Congress. (Putting such a substantial record before the court had the added benefit of eliciting quick rulings on our applications and demonstrating that we were not tacking too close to the line in establishing the necessary probable cause.)

We filed more than five hundred applications for search warrants, and hundreds of other applications for records, during our twenty-two months of operation, averaging more than one filing a day. The vast majority of these requests were handled by Chief Judge Howell, who thus wound up reading almost daily updates on the various strands of our investigation—not a complete record, but nonetheless an extremely thorough accounting of our progress, cemented durably in a separate branch of government. All of this was intentional.

A final mechanism for securing our records was to disseminate pertinent ones to prosecutors outside our office. Periodically, our investigation would brush into matters that were either outside the scope of our authority, or that we simply didn't have the bandwidth to tackle properly. And often we would refer those cases to the appropriate U.S. attorney's office. Many of these investigations eventually became public—such as the probes of Michael Cohen, Sam Patten, Greg Craig, Mercury, and the Podesta Group. Others did not. (And of course, after the Special Counsel's Office wrapped up its work in the spring of 2019, we referred out all our pending matters, including a criminal case against Roger Stone that resulted in his conviction on all counts for lying to and obstructing Congress.)

To be clear, we never made a referral solely so we could transfer our records, and this line of defense was far from foolproof; those U.S. attorneys still reported to the attorney general, who reported to Trump. But scattering copies of those records through the U.S. attorneys' offices would, at least, make it harder for the Justice Department or the White House to seal off or destroy our documents if they closed us down.

·   ·   ·

These were some of the shrewder moves our office made in case we were fired. But every day, some unquantifiable portion of our energy was diverted into defending against the possibility. In retrospect, it is impossible to truly understand our investigation—its successes, but also its shortcomings—without understanding the degree to which our work was curtailed by the looming possibility that, at any second, we could be shut down. Trump's threats had clear and detrimental effects on our pursuit of justice.

On the most basic level, we put pressure on ourselves to do our jobs quickly and efficiently, dispensing with less promising matters to avoid getting sidetracked or bogged down. I had streamlined our Manafort investigation—keeping the team focused only on the most promising leads and jettisoning all else. In a few instances, a solid lead—one that may have well flowered into a charge and conviction—was assessed but then determinedly put aside, because either the charge or target were deemed too inconsequential in the larger scheme of our investigation, or because making that case would present a challenge that was not worth the effort, given the need for a speedy resolution. In our minds, we had to go straight for the arteries, and leave the capillaries, to get the job done before we were dead.

And what was that job, exactly? Mueller would come to consider the heart of our work to be investigating Russian interference in the election—thoroughly documenting, for the American people, how our democracy had been tampered with and attacked. The more Team R's work progressed, and the more astonishing its findings became, the more staunchly committed to this position Mueller seemed. He felt this part of our investigation must be allowed to run its course at all costs—even if it meant backing away from other important questions and ultimately leaving them unanswered.

One small but clear example of the effect of the right-wing media and Trump's firing power arose as we began interviewing witnesses to investigate the Trump Tower meeting with Veselnitskaya and the other Russian operatives. Though the president's daughter Ivanka had not been part of the meeting, we learned she chatted with the attendees afterward in the lobby, and was later involved in conversations with the president about how the administration might hide the substance of the meeting from the press. Unlike her father and brother, Ivanka did not refuse our requests for an interview; we simply never asked. There was a sense in our office that Ivanka must remain out-of-bounds—regardless of how many critical questions she might help us answer, or how valuable she might prove to various strands of our work. Team 600 feared that hauling her in for an interview would play badly to the already antagonistic right-wing press—*Look how they're roughing up the president's daughter*—and risk enraging Trump, provoking him to shut down the Special Counsel's Office once and for all.

I found this position to be sexist. In my mind, it was a clear investigative error, and one based on a chauvinistic premise: Ivanka was a key player on both the Trump campaign and inside the administration; her gender or personal relationship to the president should be irrelevant.

On a more significant level, to get to the bottom of the Trump Tower meeting—and whatever else Don Jr. knew—we could have forced the issue with him as well. Don Jr. had refused to submit to a voluntary interview, but we could have compelled him to testify. If he'd refused to testify by pleading the Fifth Amendment, we could have immunized him and forced him to testify. (Immunity cancels the Fifth Amendment, but the person remains criminally liable if he then lies in the grand jury or refuses to testify.)

These would not be the only timid decisions we made because we were wary of getting fired, and I will discuss other particular episodes as they come up in this book. But it is important to understand that, from the outset, the specter of our being shut down exerted a kind of destabilizing pull on our decision-making process. Repeatedly during our twenty-two months in operation, we would reach some critical juncture in our investigation only to have Aaron say that we could not take a particular action because it risked aggravating the president beyond some undefined breaking point: that it might either upset our endless negotiations with the Justice Department and the White House as to whether and under what conditions the president would sit for an interview with our office, or anger him to such an extent that he'd lash out and fire us. That is, we were often forced to evaluate not just whether an investigative step was productive and legal and appropriate—whether it would help us, and the American people, get closer to the truth—but how it might affect Donald Trump's feelings.

At certain times, I was ambivalent about how we chose to balance these concerns. For instance, with respect to our reticence to immunize Don Jr. or request an interview with Ivanka, I believed that we'd wound up making overly defensive decisions. In others, such as the initial decision to step gingerly in our financial investigation of the president, I concurred with Mueller and Aaron, understanding why they viewed pulling our punches to be wise—even if, as an investigator who was trained to get to the truth, I resented having to do so.

The president ultimately possessed a power—the power to fire us— that compelled us to make almost impossible decisions, and at times, backed us into making unforced concessions. This was one of the unique weapons he wielded as president that undermined our work, in ways that simply do not exist in normal criminal investigations. We would be beset by others.

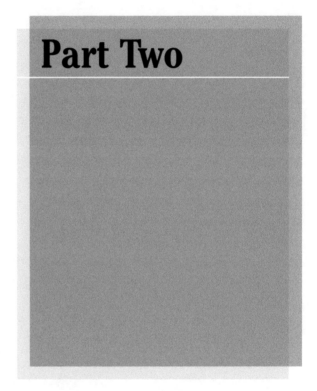

Part Two

CHAPTER 9

Russia's Active Measures

IN THE 1950s, this country was in the grip of the Cold War, seized by the fear that the Soviet Union would seek to expand communism globally and undermine the United States by any means possible. That anxiety metastasized into the so-called Red Scare, fomented by a populist demagogue, Wisconsin Republican senator Joseph McCarthy, and his henchman and chief counsel, Roy Cohn. McCarthy's Senate investigative committee and the House Un-American Activities Committee responded to the Russian threat by whipping the country into a panic against "pinko" elitists and "sleeper" agents—sinister, shadowy figures inside our government and the larger culture, allegedly working to infiltrate and destabilize America. This paranoia led to the blacklisting and firing of academics, government officials, Hollywood directors and screenwriters, and others. People were prosecuted for refusing to "name names" of friends, neighbors, and co-workers suspected of being Communists or sympathetic to the Communist cause.

McCarthy's power was enabled and exacerbated by fear. Large swathes of the mainstream media were too cowed by McCarthy to speak out. (Such silence was akin to the deference I saw among reporters in the run-up to the Iraq War, right after 9/11, at a time when criticizing or scrutinizing the government too aggressively was seen, by many, as akin to siding with terrorists.) But the senator had it exactly backward when he accused these supposed Communist sympathizers of being un-American: McCarthyism, as an ideology and a tactic, violated a basic tenet of the Constitution, most famously articulated by Supreme Court justice Oliver Wendell Holmes, Jr.: that, in the United States, we let the marketplace of ideas winnow out unacceptable views, instead of ordering government crackdowns on those who espouse them.

McCarthy's hold on the country did not last. The demise of McCarthyism was precipitated by courageous people who finally spoke out, like the army chief counsel Joseph Welch, who in 1954 confronted the bullying populist in a public hearing, famously asking, "Have you no sense of decency, sir?" No new laws or constitutional provisions were enacted to thwart the next popular demagogue, but in place of McCarthy's scare tactics and strong-arming, the country devised constitutional means to guard against subversive foreign influence that did not penalize people for their political views.

Those laws effectively addressed the legitimate underlying issue that had fueled the Red Scare and been of concern since our country's founding: protecting our political system from foreign interference. Congress passed a web of laws to prevent foreigners, including foreign governments and their operatives, from undertaking activities that could influence our political process—including foreigners providing "anything of value" to a candidate seeking U.S. office. Another law, FARA, was amended, finally, in 1966 to ensure that any foreign lobbying of American elected officials, or attempts to influence the American public through political advertisements or op-eds, are undertaken only with full transparency.

It is ironic, then, that half a century after McCarthyism, another dangerous demagogue flouted these protections on his way to the presidency, both by seeking assistance for his campaign from Russia, and condoning Russian participation in our electoral process, endangering the integrity of our democracy.

It is easy to forget how atypical Donald Trump's view of Russia was, for a candidate of either party. Trump ran a campaign that included frequent praise for Russia's murderous president, Vladimir Putin, and he was notably unbothered by Russia's 2014 invasion and forced annexation of Crimea—an eastern region of Ukraine—which Americans in both major political parties had strongly condemned. In fact, Republicans had been especially censorious of the invasion of Crimea, correctly viewing Russian expansionism as a threat to our national security interests and the stability of the entire region. As Russia reasserted its territorial ambition, Ukraine was a crucial frontline country, standing in defense of Europe and the Baltic.

Trump's affection for Russia was confounding. Being pro-Russia is not like being pro-life or pro–Second Amendment; there is no tactical political advantage to staking out such a position, no American voter bloc that's clamoring for candidates who are pro-Putin. To be sure, other candidates and even other presidents have sought better relations with Russia, but those politicians still recognized the danger the country posed to us and our allies.

When I joined the Special Counsel's Office in May 2017, I thought that Trump's posture might reflect a willingness to accept a helping hand in the election from any source, even if it was an illegal foreign source, so long as it pushed him closer to victory—Trump's own version of "might makes right," where winning is everything. That would be illegal, but still not as ominous as another possibility: Did Putin have something on the candidate? Was Trump compromised? Was there some unknown explanation for his eagerness to curry favor with the Russians?

It was against this backdrop of befuddlement and suspicion that the American Intelligence Community received the initial report that George Papadopoulos had been approached by a Russian, via Joseph Mifsud, claiming to have dirt on Clinton in the form of thousands of emails. This prompted the FBI to open the original investigation into possible links between Russia and the Trump campaign in July 2016, a year before the appointment of Mueller as special counsel. (And contrary to claims by Trump loyalists, the factual predicate for the investigation had nothing whatsoever to do with the much-maligned Steele dossier.) At around that same time, emails stolen from the Democratic National Committee and Democratic Congressional Campaign Committee computer servers began to be released online. The Intelligence Community determined that Russia was behind those hacks.

And the Russian hacking was known, publicly, well before the election. But instead of accepting the unanimous determination of American intelligence professionals, or even being open to it as a possibility, Trump suggested other theories, seemingly off the top of his head—and with no factual support. He famously ventured on national TV, for example, that the hacks could have been perpetrated by a slovenly adolescent in a bedroom somewhere.

One cannot plausibly deny that Trump was seeking foreign assistance from Russia and was open to accepting it if offered. Trump was—and still is—openly unwilling to accept or even acknowledge clear facts about a major foreign adversary's ongoing efforts to corrupt our democracy. This much is undeniable. And in a fundamental sense, it makes him complicit in those efforts—makes the president of the United States a counterintelligence threat—both soliciting foreign assistance and denying that the solicitation worked. (It is easy now to view what we were confronting in our investigation as the blueprint for the actions that would lead to the impeachment of the president for solicitation of Ukraine dirt on his main political rival.)

But why deny proven Russian election interference? Could there be an innocent explanation? Was it simple insecurity—a fear that acknowledging Russia's interference would put a cloud over his electoral victory in 2016? Was it strategic—an understanding that, if Trump refused to hold Russia to account, Putin would be more likely to help him get elected? Did it stem from Trump's own warped admiration for dictators? All of these are possibilities—and dangerous ones, to be sure, as they leave our country exposed to continued foreign election interference. The remaining explanation—an effort to appease Russia, because of dirt that Putin had on him—is even more dangerous and the one that lurks in all rational minds looking at the situation dispassionately.

These are the hypotheses that I and others had in the front of our minds as we started digging into the facts. And we were well aware that these explanations were not mutually exclusive—multiple could be at play at once to explain the president's bizarre behavior. Three years later, as the 2020 election approaches, these are still crucial questions to which America deserves answers.

As soon as the Special Counsel's Office opened up shop, Team R inherited work produced by other government investigations that had been launched before ours: These included the Papadopoulos lead, the National Security Division's investigation into Russian hacking, and the Intelligence Community's written assessment on Russian interference.

Ingesting this information was the domain of Team R, and Jeannie had quickly gotten to work untangling and synthesizing the facts. A few weeks after I arrived, I asked attorneys in the National Security Division of the Department of Justice to give me the same briefing they had given Jeannie, so I could familiarize myself with the investigation they'd been conducting into Russian hacking.

The meeting was in a SCIF at Justice's imposing art deco headquarters on Pennsylvania Avenue. To avoid eavesdropping, any discussion of classified material needs to take place in a SCIF—a room into which no electronic equipment with Internet or Bluetooth capability can be brought. Given that we, at the Special Counsel's Office, were constantly reviewing classified documents, our entire office space had been designated as a SCIF; every morning, all our phones, laptops, iPads, smart watches, Fitbits, and so on had to be left outside in lockers located in the "man trap"—a small entry space between our SCIF offices and the public hallways, which, much like the air lock on a space station, separated those safe and perilous environments with two sets of highly secure doors. We all found ourselves donning wristwatches again to tell time, often for the first time in years.

Because my debriefing with the National Security Division involved classified information, I cannot discuss its content substantively here. It took a couple of hours, as a team of NSD lawyers graciously walked me through what they had been up to and answered all my questions. As soon as I got back to our offices, however, I made a beeline to Jeannie's office and immediately asked her: "What the fuck?"

"I know," she said. She didn't need me to finish my thought.

We had both been shocked by something we'd heard in our briefings—but it was less the substance of the Justice Department's investigation than its approach. Jeannie knew that she was going to inherit some evidence that Russia had hacked the DNC and DCCC emails, but she was astonished that the National Security Division was not examining what the Russians had done with the emails and other documents they'd stolen from those servers—how the release of that information was weaponized by targeted release, and whether the Russians had any

American accomplices. More alarmingly, the Department was not apparently looking beyond the hacking at all, to examine whether there had been other Russian efforts to disrupt the election.

It was staggering to us that the Justice Department's investigation was so narrowly circumscribed. Election interference by a foreign power was, inarguably, a national security issue; we expected the National Security Division to undertake a comprehensive investigation. Once again, Jeannie and I were left to speculate as to whether this lapse was the result of incompetence, political interference, fear of turning up answers that the Department's political leaders would not like, or all of the above. The Intelligence Community's investigation had assessed that Russia was behind the hacking, but remained seemingly incurious as to everything else. "The rest is going to be up to us," Jeannie explained.

But Mueller's deputy, Aaron Zebley, argued that it was not actually within our remit to look at Russian interference. This defied all logic; the special counsel's appointment order, signed by Rod Rosenstein, had made clear that we had the authority to investigate these matters. Indeed, it was the first responsibility the order assigned us: "to ensure a full and thorough investigation of the Russian government's efforts to interfere in the 2016 presidential election." But Aaron insisted it was out of bounds and instructed Jeannie to focus Team R's investigatory energy only on the question of whether there were "links and coordination" between the Russian government and the Trump campaign—the other central duty spelled out in our appointment order.

Jeannie stormed into my office after this conversation, shut the door, and sat there silently fuming. Only after she had collected herself was she able to tell me what had happened. I shared her outrage. "This is a misreading of the order and nonsensical," she said. "It is impossible to effectively look at this second question without knowing the answer to the first." I agreed: How could we say whether Russia coordinated with the campaign if we didn't even know what they did?

We both were seeing the latest example of Aaron's default instinct to look for the narrowest possible interpretation of what we should do; he was a timorous McClellan to my and Jeannie's Sheridan and Grant. There's a well-worn expression within the FBI that encapsulates this mindset, and Omer and I would often repeat it to each other like a catechism whenever we detected a familiar drag on our investigatory ambitions: "Big cases, big problems. Small cases, small problems. No cases, no problems." Aaron didn't want any problems.

Mueller, meanwhile, signed off on Aaron's directive for his own set of reasons. Even if Aaron's logic did not make sense, walling our office off from that larger inquiry into Russian interference spoke to Mueller's perpetual concern about spreading our resources too thin and his impulse to keep the overall investigation moving quickly. Mueller felt we had too much else to do.

Jeannie was convinced this was wrongheaded: The issue was too important not to undertake ourselves and too central to our remit. She knew that the Department, left to its own devices, was not going to get the job done—with the president publicly expressing antipathy toward substantiating Russian election interference, investigators were not going to get the support for this endeavor—nor would they view digging into this issue as a career enhancer. Mueller and Aaron conceded that if we found Russian links to the campaign, then perhaps Team R could begin to branch out and examine the wider Russian interference effort. Otherwise, Big Bu—the FBI—could handle the interference investigation for now, and simply keep us updated.

Mueller's thinking had logical force only if you believed the Department would run with the ball—something Jeannie, Omer, and I knew was not going to happen. It was hard to think otherwise: The very reason for appointing a special counsel was because of the conflict the Department of Justice had—it was headed by people selected by the White House and had a conflict in investigating whether the White House coordinated with Russians in the 2016 election. That did not mean there was also a conflict in the Justice Department's investigating whether and how Russia interfered with the 2016 election, as that investigation should in normal times be a bipartisan effort. One would think any administration would be incentivized to investigate foreign election interference. Except, it turned out, this one. Jeannie knew that if her team did not do it, it was simply not going to happen.

Nevertheless, Aaron told Jeannie to find an appropriate team at the FBI and ship off this part of the investigation. Though Jeannie and her team of attorneys and agents disagreed, they followed orders. She spent the next six weeks, in the late summer and early fall of 2017, trying to interest various squads at the Bureau in taking up the task. No one there wanted to touch it; it was too hot politically, with zero margin for error. Plus, it would be an arduous investigation, requiring a team with both criminal and cyber expertise to roll up its sleeves. ("No cases, no problems," Omer and I thought.)

In the meantime, she and Lawrence Rush Atkinson, an intrepid young colleague of mine from the Fraud Section who now worked on Team R, and who had cyber expertise, worked late at night, after their other work was done, to keep this part of the investigation moving forward as Jeannie shopped the investigation to people at the Big Bu. She hoped to put herself in a position to reargue Team R's case to Mueller as more facts emerged.

In August 2017, the tide began to turn after Jeannie got a call from lawyers representing Facebook, asking if they could come in and share some information.

For months, Facebook and other Silicon Valley social media companies had been telling Congress and the public that they'd seen minimal evidence of foreign election interference on their platforms, and none of it was paid activity. Now, however, Facebook lawyers who arrived at our office to meet Team R reported that Facebook had performed a closer examination of its data and determined that its initial assessment was "not complete." They saw more Russian activity on their platform than they'd initially believed—namely, posts from Russian-backed accounts, designed to spread or amplify misinformation and exacerbate political divisions. And it included paid activity. They planned to go to the Hill and report this to Congress but wanted to alert us first.

Jeannie and the Team R agents asked for details, rattling off a series of questions: How much more Russian activity were they seeing? What precisely were they doing? Who were they targeting? Which divisive issues were the Russians focusing on? Were their efforts concentrated on any specific geographic regions? And by "Russians," whom exactly did they mean? Had Facebook managed to attribute that activity to the Russian government?

The Facebook lawyers explained the company's process of detection, and how they assessed that the posts had come from Russia in general.

(Although they had not pinpointed the information yet as coming from the government, Jeannie and her team rightly thought it was likely to have emanated from the government, given the country's top-down structure.) But they said that this activity appeared to be more about sowing general discord in America than seeking to advantage one candidate over the other. Moreover, they characterized these efforts as hamhanded; its ultimate effect, paltry. There'd been financial expenditures to promote this misinformation on the platform, but the content had garnered little engagement or impact—not a lot of likes and followers.

Jeannie and her agents had their antennae up. They wondered privately how Facebook had missed this the first time. Was the company being fully transparent now? Team R understood, after all, that Facebook had little incentive to expose the full extent of a problem that would paint the company in a negative light—particularly with respect to a high-profile and contentious issue like election interference. Even if Facebook was being diligent and transparent, it was clear that Team R had an obligation to verify independently whatever information the company had.

Jeannie asked for follow-up meetings. This time, employees from the company attended as well, in order to present more data. Mueller rarely attended meetings like this, but made an exception this time, understanding the potential importance of whatever lay behind the curtain that Facebook would be pulling back. Our largest conference room— the same one in which we just a few weeks earlier had our kick-off meeting with Mueller and McCabe—was brimming with lawyers and FBI agents in somber suits and dresses (there was no "business casual" when attending meetings with the Special Counsel's Office). Our SCO formal attire reminded me of the trip Mueller and I took years earlier to meet various Silicon Valley executives in California, dressed in blue suits, white shirts, and ties; Tim Cook at Apple told us he had dressed up for the event by wearing a polo shirt with a collar, as opposed to his normal T-shirt.

To start, Jeannie asked the company to share Facebook account numbers for the Russian-backed accounts they'd seen disseminating and amplifying disinformation during the campaign. For Team R, this was critical information—leads that would enable them to cut process to obtain more information about those particular accounts and their related

IP addresses. Team R could then do the same with other platforms and uncover any overlap between those IP addresses and other suspicious accounts. Facebook agreed. The company's representatives also walked our investigators through how its platform permitted users to target ads, delivering their messaging to distinct demographic audiences online. This, too, was of use to Team R, allowing them to investigate if and how the Russians had pushed certain content on the platform to certain types of users.

Mueller was fascinated by the mechanics of all of this. He was always captivated by the shiniest and newest gadget even if he, like many of us, did not fully grasp the precise technology that went into creating it. He is an investigator at heart, and clearly enjoyed getting an in-depth look at this digital frontier, enthralled by the leads these social media technologies allowed an investigator to pursue and the new ways criminals would seek to hide their tracks. Mueller left the Facebook meeting having glimpsed the destructive potential of Russian activity on such a platform and knew what needed to be done: He gave Jeannie the green light to dig in, conducting a full investigation into all forms of Russian election interference. Aaron's restriction was overruled.

I remember Mueller announcing Team R's new assignment at our next supervisors' meeting, in the fall of 2017: Jeannie's team, he explained, would now be working to uncover the details of how the Russians had interfered with the election through what appeared to be an "active measures" campaign, as we called this kind of disinformation operation.

Right away, this struck me as an investigatory masterstroke. Election interference was an attack on our country—every bit as much as the Japanese attack on Pearl Harbor was. Except the Russians' assault was more insidious, since it was largely invisible: not a dramatic bombardment, but a slow infection that therefore did not provoke a visceral and immediate patriotic response. It was the etherealness of what Russia had done that allowed the candidate who'd benefited from that interference to dismiss it—to brush it aside as "fake news" in a way that bombing the hell out of our Pacific fleet would never have permitted a sitting president to do. I agreed with Jeannie that if we could uncover and prove what Russia had done, and lay out that story in depth, we'd be doing a vital service to the American public by making that attack feel more visible, galvanizing, and real. This was now Mueller's conviction, too. In time, we would come to see Team R's work as the most important piece of our investigation.

After the second meeting with Facebook, Jeannie and her team huddled together in the Viking Ship to devise a plan. Ascertaining the full extent of Russia's activity online would be a monumental task. They decided to shift from examining the individual posts that Facebook had identified as Russian-backed disinformation to focus more broadly on the political issues that were discussed online during the election and which groups had pressed them. To do this, Jeannie would need to gather mountains of data from Facebook and the other major technology companies: Twitter, Google, LinkedIn, and Yahoo, as well as Microsoft and Apple—so much data that it would threaten to crash our systems once it started coming in.

Jeannie got the approval to enlist as reinforcement a phenomenal lawyer from the Computer Crime and Intellectual Property Section (CCIPS) at the Justice Department's Criminal Division. His expertise was truly invaluable in navigating the numerous technical issues that arose, as well as in helping Team R quickly ferret out a clearer understanding of the story that the data told. With this new expertise, the expanded team worked around the clock—obtaining court orders from Chief Judge Howell for the data, working with the tech companies to get the information in a format that would allow us to ingest it on our systems quickly, and figuring out the best ways to scour the data for salient evidence.

Somehow, in the midst of this beehive of nonstop activity, Jeannie had the foresight to make one other move as well. She smartly anticipated a potential problem in bringing a criminal case against the Russian actors conducting this misinformation campaign, or against any American co-conspirators she might eventually discover. Such a prosecution would require the approval of the Intelligence Community, which weighs in on all criminal matters where public criminal prosecution risks revealing its classified information or otherwise compromising its operations, such as by disclosing intelligence sources or the "methods or means" by which intelligence officers did their jobs. It is important to remember that the Special Counsel's Office needed such approval; we were a part of the Department of Justice, not an independent counsel like Ken Starr. Under the special counsel regulations, we had to comply with internal approval processes just like any other members of the Justice Department. Every indictment we brought would be vetted by senior Justice Department officials. In Jeannie's case, she would also need Intelligence Community sign-off.

I knew, from being integral to this approval process during my time as general counsel at the FBI, that this would be a steep hill for Jeannie to climb. One case I evaluated while I was the general counsel at the FBI involved a technique known as "draft foldering." At the time, there was a useful misconception among bad guys worldwide that if they wrote an email and saved it to the drafts folder, and then had their co-conspirator log in to the same account, read the draft, and write a response, these communications would escape detection, since the email had never actually been sent. But if our investigators gained legal access to that account they could, of course, read everything in it, including the drafts. The technique had been publicized on the front page of *The Washington Post,* in fact, after General David Petraeus, amid the scandal that led to his resignation, had disclosed that he and his paramour had used draft foldering to message each other. We had not been allowed to reference the technique, however.

Jeannie therefore began Team R's active measures investigation with a strategy to minimize any concerns from the IC down the road, even if protecting against them completely would be impossible. She would make sure that Team R built its case using standard criminal legal process—subpoenas, search warrants, and the like—rather than classified national security tools, like FISA and national security letters.

The voluminous criminal process served on Internet service providers quickly began yielding a wealth of material. Because Russians had used American social media platforms to carry out their efforts meant that they'd created, within our borders and thus within our legal jurisdiction, a robust repository of incriminating evidence. Moreover, Team R managed to trace some of this evidence all the way back to the internal email discussions about the operation among the Russians, inside Russia. (I'm limited legally in what I can say about how, precisely, Team R pulled this off.) One day late in the summer, in fact, I heard Jeannie hollering from her office next to mine even more loudly than usual. "Oh. My. God," she kept saying, over and over again. I got up and poked my head in.

"Read this," Jeannie told me, and I came around her desk to find, on one of her computer monitors, an email from a Russian operative named Irina to her family.

"We had a slight crisis here at work," the email read. "The FBI busted our activity (not a joke) so, I got preoccupied with covering tracks together with colleagues. . . . I created all these pictures and posts, and the Americans believed that it was written by their people."

"That's unbelievable," I said.

"Irina is a worker bee," Jeannie explained. Her particular focus, Jeannie told me, was posting material designed to suppress the black vote. Jeannie then pointed to the date of the woman's email: September 13, 2017.

What Jeannie and her team would ultimately uncover was astounding in its overall breadth and details. Although they came across a narrow strain of evidence that Russia sought to sow general discord in America, as Facebook had reported, that characterization was not close to adequately describing the Russian effort to undermine the 2016 election. Russia's work was plainly undertaken to support Trump—who nevertheless has consistently denied, contrary to all of this unassailable evidence, that Russia wanted him to win the presidency, much less helped him win it.

Over the course of the fall and winter of 2017, Team R developed a detailed understanding of a Russian organization that bore the innocuous corporate moniker Internet Research Agency, LLC—a name that struck me as being straight out of George Orwell's *1984*. The Internet Research Agency, or IRA, had hired an army of online foot soldiers to interfere in the American election with the aim of electing Donald Trump. The agency itself aptly described the operation in internal documentation as "information warfare against the United States of America."

What Jeannie and her team uncovered made it abundantly clear that we had been attacked. In fact, we are still being attacked to this day. But neither the White House nor Congress has acted to defend us properly from this new threat. Imagine the United States taking no steps in response to the Japanese attack on Pearl Harbor. That is unthinkable. Yet, this administration has not sought to declare war on Russia, advocate

sanctioning Russia for its attack, or even taken steps to pass strong legis-
lation to protect our electoral system. In fact, the president has chalked
up the attack as just fake news and a hoax. Proving incontrovertibly that
we had been attacked by Russia was imperative. I repeatedly told Jeannie that what her team was uncovering and would soon reveal publicly
in two indictments was of central importance to our democracy and
would be our lasting legacy in service to our nation.

Team R proved the attack, in detail. The IRA had its main hub in an
unremarkable-looking office building at 55 Savushkina Street in St. Petersburg. It employed hundreds of people and spent over a million dollars a month, conducting its work in a highly regimented, systematic
way. The IRA was much like a typical American business, with a management group in place that dealt with operational planning, infrastructure, and personnel; a data analysis department; a graphics department;
an IT group; and a finance department. It masked the Russian origins of
the content it put online by procuring servers and other infrastructure in
the United States, so it all appeared to be generated domestically. Its finances were similarly cloaked in numerous shell companies and more
than a dozen bank accounts. With the help of our forensic accountants
and money-laundering expertise—using the same techniques we had
used on Team M to tunnel through the maze of front companies—
Jeannie's team was able to trace back the IRA's funding to its source: a
Russian oligarch named Yevgeny Prigozhin.

The core work of the IRA was to create fictitious online personas to
target foreign audiences with propaganda and misinformation. With
respect to our 2016 election, this meant conducting a massive public relations campaign to warp voters' perceptions of the candidates and suppress voter turnout among particular demographic groups with the aim
of ultimately tilting the outcome. The operation was well thought out.
In 2014, a two-woman team of Russian operatives had even come to the
United States to do advance work, traveling to nine states. Team R was
able to uncover this activity as they found the report prepared by the
Russian operative upon their return, which set out what they had accomplished in the United States. That is, the women functioned as intelligence gatherers, scouting the IRA's targets, just like the first phase of a
more conventional military or terrorist attack—one carried out on
American soil, rather than in our digital public square.

Team R determined that a core group of approximately eighty so-called specialists at the IRA carried out its election interference online. These specialists were divided into day and night teams, to sustain twenty-four-hour information warfare on social media. Each specialist would create numerous American personas on platforms like Facebook and Twitter, as well as hundreds of fake email and PayPal accounts. These personas—"Alex Anderson," "Andrea Hansen," "Lakisha Richardson"—were created by illegally obtaining social security numbers, dates of birth, and other identifying information of real Americans. Other online accounts were made to look not like individual Americans, but legitimate American political organizations, such as @TEN_GOP (the "Unofficial Twitter of Tennessee Republicans"), or issue-oriented activist groups, such as the Facebook groups "Secured Borders," "LGBT United," or "Tea Party News."

The messages that these accounts posted and spread made their motives clear. One social media post, for example, targeted African Americans and Muslims—groups that traditionally lean Democratic—and sought to discourage them from voting: "We cannot resort to the lesser of two devils. Then we'd surely be better off without voting AT ALL." One phony offshoot of Black Lives Matter that the IRA created to target African Americans was called "Don't Shoot Us." Others aimed to split the Clinton vote: "Choose peace and vote for Jill Stein. Trust me, it's not a wasted vote." And the instructions these operatives were given behind the scenes, gleaned from internal emails that Jeannie's team obtained, were similarly blunt. One February 10, 2016, email instructed the team to "use any opportunity to criticize Hillary and the rest (except Sanders and Trump—we support them)." A September 14, 2016, email chided an employee for her "low number of emails criticizing Hillary Clinton. . . . It is imperative to intensify criticizing Hillary Clinton."

The IRA, meanwhile, amplified these messages by paying for advertisements; according to Facebook, the Internet Research Agency purchased more than 3,500 ads on the platform, which was relatively cheap, costing a hundred thousand dollars. These ads ran throughout the spring, summer, and fall of 2016, touting "Hillary for Prison," or claiming "Hillary Clinton Doesnt Deserve the Black Vote," "We cannot trust Hilary to take care of our veterans!" "Trump is our only hope for a better future!" and so on. So successful was the fake media blitz that Donald Trump Jr., Eric Trump, Kellyanne Conway, and Sean Hannity all retweeted or responded to social media posts that we now know came from IRA-controlled accounts.

But the IRA's active measures were not limited to perpetuating misinformation digitally; its work regularly spilled into the physical, offline world as well. Team R discovered that Russians masquerading online as American activists enlisted unwitting Americans to help stage dozens of pro-Trump or anti-Clinton rallies—actual gatherings, to which crowds of real Americans showed up. The Russians would alert both American journalists and Trump campaign representatives, requesting from the latter the desired Trump campaign paraphernalia for the events. After the Russian-staged rallies, those same Russian accounts would post photos and videos online.

Three such pro-Trump rallies were held in New York, and a series of others took place in Florida and Pennsylvania. At two of these events, the Russian operatives even hired people to build a cage and had an actress playing Hillary Clinton sit inside it. When Team R's FBI agents interviewed the Americans who had been recruited to help orchestrate these rallies, every one of them said they'd had no idea that the online acquaintances who'd hired them were Russian operatives—or foreigners at all. After one IRA account shared photos of a rally it had organized in Miami, the Donald Trump official Facebook account reposted the images with a note: "THANK YOU for your support Miami! My team just shared photos of your TRUMP SIGN WAVING DAY, yesterday! I love you."

But perhaps the most audacious move of the Russian operation—the clearest signal that they were confident they were not being monitored or would ever be caught—came in May 2016, a couple of days before the fifty-fifth birthday of Yevgeny Prigozhin, the oligarch who was funding the IRA's work. An IRA operative, posing online as an American, persuaded an actual American in Washington to go stand in front of the White House for a photo, holding a sign that read, "Happy 55th Birthday Dear Boss."

Which side the IRA had taken in the election was not open to question: The data Jeannie's team gathered clearly demonstrated that the primary goal was to spread negative information about Hillary Clinton and suppress the vote for her, while promoting Trump as well as Clinton's other rivals Bernie Sanders and Jill Stein. Interestingly, during the Republican primaries, the agency targeted Trump rivals Ted Cruz and Marco Rubio. In other words, the IRA did not seek to help any Republican defeat Clinton; from the beginning, it put its muscle behind Trump.

Jeannie knew that when the evidence of such a lopsided Russian effort to help Trump became public it would be attacked as part of a Mueller "witch hunt." That fact-resistant conspiracy theory would be dealt a welcome blow when, after a long investigation, the bipartisan Republican-led Senate Intelligence Committee released its own report on the Russians' active measures campaign. This report came eight months after our own and reached precisely the same conclusion. "The Committee found that the IRA sought to influence the 2016 U.S. presidential election by harming Hillary Clinton's chances of success and supporting Donald Trump at the direction of the Kremlin," the report read.

The committee cited a communication from one IRA worker who described the scene at their headquarters as the American election results came in. When it was clear Trump had prevailed, the worker explained, "We uncorked a tiny bottle of champagne, took one gulp each and looked into each other's eyes. . . . We uttered almost in unison: 'We made America great.'" (Our office had uncovered this same communication, though Aaron had omitted such evidence from our final report, feeling it was too salacious.)

None of this answered the question of whether senior members of the Trump campaign were aware of this precise form of Russian assistance, or condoned or conspired with it. This was an open question for us while Team R conducted its investigation. Omer and I had discussed various possible working theories: One was that Manafort was aware of the Russian efforts but did not share that knowledge with Trump or other senior campaign officials. Another was that the campaign and the Russian government were working in parallel, but never needed to reach any actual agreement—a criminal agreement is necessary to prove a conspiracy—since they were both clearly laboring toward the same goal. There was no need to take the legal risk of formally coordinating efforts.

And, of course, it was theoretically possible that while the Russians were interceding on behalf of the Trump side of the election, the Trump campaign did not condone or coordinate with that effort—that they'd disapproved of it and made a point of keeping their hands clean. The June 2016 Trump Tower meeting made this last possibility moot: The Trump campaign felt no legal compunctions about accepting Russian help. And it made perfect sense to me why the Russians would stake out this pro-Trump position; my work on Ukraine made it easy to surmise their motive. One of the few areas of bipartisan agreement during the Obama administration had been the need to be tough on Russian expansion. After Russia's annexation of Crimea, Secretary Clinton had strongly rebuked Putin and supported kicking Russia out of the G8. She (along with senior Republicans in the Senate) had also been hostile to the pro-Russian Ukrainian regime of Viktor Yanukovych—Manafort's primary patron for his consulting work there. I told Jeannie about the vituperative emails we were seeing in our Team M investigation, common within the Yanukovych regime, condemning Clinton. Manafort's Russian right-hand man in Ukraine, Konstantin Kilimnik, would routinely foment anti-Clinton sentiment. And the Manafort illegal lobbying campaign in the United States on behalf of Ukraine was aimed at undermining the United States' condemnation of Yanukovych, for which Secretary Clinton was a central voice.

Russia would have been likely to favor any candidate for president over Clinton. But Trump was a bonus, almost too good to be true: a candidate who bucked all orthodoxy to stake out a pro-Russian position, while simultaneously attacking our traditional NATO allies; a candidate who went so far as to suggest that the invasion of Crimea was not actually so bad—that Ukraine was really Russian territory, anyway, since most of its residents spoke Russian (a logic that would have him siding with Britain, and against America, in the Revolutionary War).

Week by week, as Jeannie shared whatever new information Team R and its cyber investigators were turning up, this sprawling, coordinated campaign of information warfare came more fully into view. Before long, Jeannie would begin drafting an indictment of thirteen Russian nationals and three Russian companies in connection with this active measures campaign—and all of this information would be laid out in our report. But until Team R dug in, the damning details of this Russian attack had gone undetected. Without Team R's tenacity, and a lucky break Team R had caught with the Facebook attorneys, we as a nation would have never known about it.

For me, it drove home just how vulnerable we are to the new electronic warfare being perpetrated against our democracy. "Jeannie," I told her at one point, as the evidence piled up, "what you are doing is far and away the most important thing we'll accomplish."

Jeannie disagreed, or at least deflected, instead praising Team M's fast work to suss out Manafort's sprawling criminality. But I put my foot down and insisted; we were engaged in a kind of reverse one-upmanship.

"Team M is doing a classic criminal case," I said. "We have a great team, but it's not a difficult case at the end of the day. Your team is uncovering and documenting precisely how we were attacked so we can be ready next time. It's what will have the most long-term, lasting importance."

This time, Jeannie just said thank you. But neither of us knew how the public would react to all this evidence. Jeannie and I were under no illusions that the White House would embrace it, but only as time went on did it dawn on us that a large segment of the population was so inoculated to the truth that even a Russian attack on our democracy could be ignored as a "witch hunt." That U.S. senators would not cry foul at that suggestion was still in the future, and would be yet another shock to the system. In the beginning of our investigation there were still numerous senators, and not just Lisa Murkowski and Mitt Romney, who openly and strongly defended Attorney General Sessions and publicly stated that, under our system of laws, a target of a criminal investigation like Mueller's doesn't get to dictate the scope of that investigation. But even that check on the president would crumble over time, to the point that Senator Romney's sole Republican vote in favor of the obvious guilt of the president during the impeachment trial would be heralded as an act of statesmanship and courage.

CHAPTER 10

Trump's Fixer

IN JUNE 2017, I opened up a new front in the battle to get to the bottom of Manafort's slippery financial history, and started looking at so-called suspicious activity reports, or SARs. Banks are required by law to file SARs with the Treasury Department, informing the government of any questionable financial transactions—large cash transactions from places known for money laundering, for example, such as the Seychelles or Cyprus to name but two of many. (The SAR system was meant to deter drug dealers, money launderers, tax cheats, and the like from using the U.S. financial system to facilitate their frauds.)

I'd asked the FBI to run Manafort's name (and those of several of his associates and companies) through the Treasury Department's Financial Crimes Enforcement ("FinCEN") database, which turned up numerous SARs. I followed up on the more intriguing ones with calls to the outside lawyers for the banks that had filed them. Here, in a roundabout way and entirely by chance, the process would birth a significant break in our investigation—a case that had nothing to do with Manafort but, as it evolved over the following year and eventually produced a cooperating witness, would help shed light on the president's reverential posture toward Russia.

The attorney I'd contacted about one of the Manafort SARs was someone I knew from my Enron investigation days, and whom Jeannie knew from private practice—an avuncular man with a long career in Washington. Soon after our initial contact, the attorney reached out to us, unsolicited, to give us a heads-up about a new, intriguing SAR his client, a foreign bank, would soon be filing. The bank wanted us to see it right away, he said. He emailed us a PDF.

I opened the file and my eyes grew wide. The bank was reporting suspicious activity related to a personal account held by Michael Cohen, the president's longtime attorney and so-called fixer. Cohen had not been of significant interest to our office at the outset of our investigation; we initially worked under the assumption that he was merely one of a cast of unsavory characters lurking inside the Trump Organization. He was not believed to have played a role in the campaign, and as we did not have leeway to go after such satellite figures for crimes unrelated to our mandate of Russian interference, looking into possible unrelated crimes to flip him was not a weapon we had at our disposal. On top of all this, as a lawyer, Cohen would be largely off-limits to our investigation as his communications would be cloaked in attorney-client privilege—unless, of course, we developed solid evidence he was involved in criminality.

The bank was reporting a couple of things. It was reporting that a Cohen business account was receiving, soon after the 2016 election, payments from a source linked to a Russian oligarch. And the bank was also reporting that the same account made a transfer, prior to the 2016 election, of $130,000 to an account associated with an adult film star. I went to Jeannie's office and told her to stop what she was doing. She needed to read this. The second nugget didn't hit me with the same exhilarating jolt as other potential leads. Instead, my stomach sank. My first thought was of the infamous blue dress, the one that provided incontrovertible proof of a sexual encounter between President Bill Clinton and Monica Lewinsky during Ken Starr's independent counsel investigation. Even as Starr's probe uncovered perjury and sexual harassment by the president, it had strayed very far from its original mandate and lasted much too long; for many people, the blue dress was a symbol of overreach and abuse, and the salacious territory into which the investigation had veered.

We at the Special Counsel's Office did not want to be, or be perceived to be, another Ken Starr investigation. In fact, the explicit reason the special counsel regulations, which governed our activities, had been written in 1999 was to place reasonable restraints on future investigations and prevent them from running that same course. The special counsel regulations placed our work within the Department of Justice, with the aim of maintaining an investigation's focus, efficiency, and compliance with DOJ policies and necessary approvals to bring charges. Mueller took that ethos to heart; it suited his personality. He was fixated on acting quickly and steering clear of time-consuming detours so as not to burden the public or the office of the president with our investigation any longer than necessary.

Still, we could not avoid the information staring us in the face. These payments to Cohen appeared to be a Russian link that we were tasked with investigating, and the payments from Cohen also suggested something possibly illegal; the boss needed to see it to decide what to do. Jeannie and I dropped off copies of the email with Mueller, Aaron, and Jim. It took Jim only a few minutes on Google to determine that the adult film star Stephanie Clifford was known by the stage name Stormy Daniels and appeared to be a client of the lawyer to whom Cohen had paid the money. There were some reports in the media of a settlement and the general odor of a "catch and kill" scheme with the *National Enquirer*—paying people for the rights to their stories only to keep that information from ever being published. Jeannie noted that we could be looking at a credible path to flipping Cohen. Paying the woman to keep quiet, in order to keep such a revelation from derailing Trump's chances in the election, would be a possible campaign finance law violation. Or, if Cohen had lied to his bank by, for instance, masking the true purpose of the transaction, there'd be an opportunity to pressure him to come clean and strike a deal.

The only bucket this matter could fit into was Team R, so Mueller tasked Jeannie with looking into the Russian payments and examining the potential for moving forward, understanding that if we were going to take on the payments by Cohen to the porn star, we would need to go back to Rosenstein to make sure this was within our mandate. While prosecutors in a U.S. attorney's office have free rein to examine all potential federal crimes, we had a far narrower remit: In writing our appointment order, Rosenstein had initially cabined our investigation to Russian interference with the election, links to the Trump campaign, and any obstruction of our work. That purview also enabled Team M to investigate Manafort's income and work in Ukraine.

Cohen appeared to have committed a campaign finance crime or bank fraud, but unrelated to Russian interference—and thus, unrelated to the specific contours of our appointment order. The only way to go forward with such an investigation ourselves would be to go back to Rosenstein and ask him to expand our jurisdiction in a new order. Mueller was at times willing to do that, such as when Team M had come across evidence on Sam Patten, a business partner of Konstantin Kilimnik's. But there was always a downside to consider, as asking permission to extend our investigatory purview, even slightly, could be perceived as overreach. Aaron was almost universally against seeking expansions.

And Aaron had a point; his position could not be dismissed out of hand as more McClellan-like behavior. A maxim in the legal world holds that prosecutors should investigate crimes, not people—that is, you don't begin by just targeting a particular individual, simply because of who they are, and see if you can dig something up. And yet, that principle glosses over the reality that once an investigator has uncovered articulable criminal conduct by someone, all of that person's criminality is fair game. As I knew from my mob and Enron investigations, this is particularly true in high-profile cases, where there are significant forces arrayed against cooperation. The ability to look more widely for potential charges, and examine the totality of a person's crimes, could often provide the critical proof needed to flip a witness and get an otherwise impossible break in the case. That had happened time and time again in my prior work. The upshot in the Special Counsel's Office, however, was that if Jeannie wanted to pursue Cohen's potential election fraud or lies to a bank, we would first have to go back to Rosenstein and request his permission to do so.

This specific request could come with a possibly fatal cost to our investigation. I previously discussed that we took certain defensive precautions to temper the omnipresent threat of Mueller being fired. Here, it was obvious to all of us that asking Rosenstein for such an expansion risked upsetting our precarious equilibrium with the White House and could precipitate our firing; the more we appeared to be straying from our initial remit, the more we'd feed into the perception that we were another runaway Ken Starr investigation, if not a modern-day Torquemada. At the time, in the summer of 2017, our investigation was still only getting off the ground; to risk our termination at that point would mean potentially sacrificing our investigation of Russia's incendiary foreign attack on the American election. It was hard to argue that digging into Michael Cohen's payment to a porn star was important enough to justify such a risk—especially since there was another option.

Mueller eventually called a short meeting on the subject, solicited the pros and cons from all aides, and made a characteristically decisive call: We would not approach Rosenstein for an expansion on the film star issue. Instead, we would hand off this aspect of the Cohen investigation to the prosecutors in the Southern District of New York and stay focused on our core mandate; we would dig into Cohen's links to Russia. Meanwhile, we could still use any eventual prosecution by the SDNY as leverage to flip Cohen. The downside of that approach was that we were at the mercy of another office, which reported up the usual chain of command to the attorney general and the president, without the protections of the special counsel rules that—theoretically, at least—kept us more insulated from the administration.

Mueller wanted to keep us working with focus and efficiency; this decision appeared to reflect his genuine desires for our office. And yet, it was also apparent to me that, practically speaking, our options had been unjustly limited. The president, simply by incessantly repeating his witch hunt claim, had found a way to encourage us to contain ourselves. We could not afford to be mistaken for the fictitious villains he said we were.

In this particular instance, I agreed with Mueller's logic and his conclusion that it was best for us to stand down on this part of the Cohen investigation, though, as you'll see, I would find it hard to stomach other, similarly timorous decisions, as time went on—including the following summer, when the Cohen matter reared up, more consequentially, again.

In general, for those of us in the office who'd worked as assistant U.S. attorneys, the limitations of our appointment order, coupled with the reticence of Aaron to test them and antagonize the White House, would come to feel like fighting with one hand tied behind our back. Jeannie and I had arrived at the Special Counsel's Office expecting to conduct a rigorous financial probe, for example. There was no shortage of intriguing threads to pull on when it came to Donald Trump and the Trump Organization: tax fraud, foreign bribery, election fraud, bank fraud.

For instance, if one were trying to determine if any foreign funds had been surreptitiously paid into the Trump campaign coffers or its political action committees, one would start by looking at all the funding records kept by the campaign and the Federal Election Commission to identify leads. (In fact, I came across precisely that kind of secret payment, again by happenstance: A Ukrainian oligarch paid $50,000 to the Trump inaugural committee, surreptitiously using an American "straw donor" to pose as the legitimate contributor. Foreigners cannot lawfully make such contributions.)

But our office was put on notice by the White House, early on, that engaging in such a broad-based financial investigation might lead to our firing. Asked by a reporter about the possibility of us looking into his finances, Trump had characterized such a move as crossing a "red line"—a threat that, ironically, suggested he might have something to hide.

Another admonition came early in the summer of 2017, after our office had issued subpoenas to Deutsche Bank, a large German financial institution that had, over years, loaned enormous sums to Trump. Our subpoenas had nothing to do with these loans; the Team M subpoena, for instance, was merely following up on a SAR filed by Deutsche Bank relating to Paul Manafort's income from Ukraine—part of our efforts to trace Manafort's assets, and merely one of many similar subpoenas we'd filed with numerous banks. Still, the White House learned—presumably through a Deutsche Bank employee—that we were in contact with the bank, but apparently did not learn the details of our subpoenas. The president became anxious, and the White House reached out to our office, demanding to know if we had issued subpoenas and wanting to know why.

Needless to say, that is not how criminal investigations normally proceed. The people being investigated do not get to dictate, or even make valid inquiries about, what steps are being taken. We didn't owe the White House an explanation. We simply could have told the president to pound sand, explaining that we, as prosecutors, are not in the business of informing the subjects of our investigation what we are, and aren't, looking at; it wasn't our concern if Trump was feeling irritated by our work.

But these were not normal circumstances, and the person we were investigating had the power to pull the plug on our investigation at any moment. The White House's request, and Trump's red line statement, impressed upon us that pivoting to such a broad financial investigation would set off—at a minimum—a presidential hissy fit. And Mueller and Aaron were concerned that pursuing the matter now, and needlessly rankling the president, might thwart future White House cooperation and endanger our ability to fully uncover and chronicle Russia's interference in the election.

Aaron then collected the facts about the two subpoenas we'd issued to Deutsche Bank and, with Mueller's blessing, reported back to the White House that we'd not been seeking Trump's financial information. At that point, any financial investigation of Trump was put on hold. That is, we backed down—the issue was simply too incendiary; the risk, too severe. In fact, when the press later reported, incorrectly, that we were seeking Trump's financial records from Deutsche Bank, I and others in the office suspected that the story had been planted, either by someone in the White House or at the Department of Justice, specifically to enrage Trump and precipitate our firing.

Again, I can't claim I took issue with Mueller's decision at this stage: It was not a typical concession, but our investigation was atypical. It struck me—at least for now—as a reasonable approach to attempt to maintain a professional working relationship with the legal team at the White House, which was producing documents and not asserting executive privilege to block access or tie us up in litigation for months. (At that time, Ty Cobb was our main interlocutor there and our rapport was rooted in trust.) There was no reason, at that early stage, to poke the bear unnecessarily, and we told ourselves that we could always move that piece of the investigation forward if we obtained more direct evidence of criminality.

It was hard not to suspect that, in time, such evidence would arrive.

CHAPTER 11

Indicting Manafort and Gates

WE INDICTED PAUL MANAFORT in U.S. District Court in Washington, D.C., on October 27, 2017, three months after Team M conducted the search of his condo in Virginia and five months after Mueller was appointed. The grand jury charged Manafort with violating FARA for his failure to register as a lobbyist for a foreign government, with lying to the Department of Justice, with criminal tax charges for concealing the millions of dollars of income he'd funneled into his undisclosed offshore accounts, and with money laundering. The twelve-count indictment also sought tens of millions of dollars in forfeiture of the properties and financial accounts that Manafort had obtained from his crimes.

Along with Manafort, the indictment charged Rick Gates, Manafort's longtime right-hand man. Gates was forty-five years old and had been working for Manafort, both in Ukraine and the United States, since 2006. When Manafort joined the Trump campaign, he brought Gates along, and Gates soon assumed the role of deputy campaign chairman.

Gates was not on the radar of any of the ongoing investigations I'd surveyed when I first joined the Special Counsel's Office. But after learning that the FARA Unit had turned over the cache of thirty thousand lobbying firm documents to Manafort's attorneys, I'd asked for copies and spent a weekend in July 2017 on my special counsel laptop scrolling, page by page, through them all. They included several years of emails between Manafort and Gates; reading through that correspondence gave me an intimate view of their relationship. It became clear that Gates wasn't just another Manafort lackey, as I had initially thought. He was a trusted deputy in Manafort's political consulting business and a full-fledged partner in his crimes.

The emails mainly opened a window into the period from 2012 to 2014 when Manafort was orchestrating a global lobbying and public relations campaign for Ukraine president Yanukovych. Gates was managing that effort in the United States, and was the day-to-day conduit for Manafort's instructions to Ukraine's Washington lobbyists. Gates relayed daily instructions and held the firms under tight control, demanding specific steps and reports as to what each firm had accomplished each week. His brusque manner and demanding oversight engendered a lot of grousing and resentment. I made a mental note of this; it might be useful in getting people to talk candidly about Gates if the need arose.

When I reported to the folks on Team M what I had learned over the weekend, the agents started taking a look at Gates's bank accounts, tax returns, and other data. We learned that Gates had his own undeclared foreign bank accounts and tax violations, though he did not profit personally from these crimes nearly to the extent that Manafort had. Gates was first and foremost Manafort's employee, making money for his boss. He struck me as a perfect candidate to become a cooperating witness, the kind of person who might flip against his superiors.

I ran this by Mueller, explaining that building the case against Gates would not slow us down, but could prove enormously important: It was a path worth taking. I drew an analogy to the Enron investigation, knowing Mueller had followed it as the FBI director. Our toehold into that case, I reminded him, was Andy Fastow's right-hand man, Michael Kopper. Mueller wondered aloud if Gates was within the scope of our office's appointment order and asked me to run that question by Michael Dreeben. If we needed to go back to Rod Rosenstein to expand the scope of our order, Mueller told me, I should let him know. Dreeben quickly determined that Gates fell within our remit and gave us a green light to go forward.

We spent the rest of the summer gathering a formidable cache of evidence against Manafort and Gates, with help from a new addition to our team in August 2017, an old friend from the Eastern District of New

York named Greg Andres, a senior lawyer capable of shouldering his share of the growing workload. With respect to the tax charges, Kyle, Renee, and Morgan—Team M's money-tracing trio—had established that Manafort had illegally moved nearly $75 million through his offshore accounts. Thirty-two different LLCs or other entities had been set up, in the United States and abroad, to facilitate this money laundering—all with Gates's assistance.

We'd also traced the sprawling contours of Manafort's illegal lobbying operation. For example, Team M established that the front organization known as the European Centre for a Modern Ukraine had been used to enable the Yanukovych regime in Ukraine to hire two Washington lobbying firms. Due to a loophole in the FARA law—one that Congress has still not remedied—a person did not need to register under FARA if they worked for a private foreign entity, as opposed to an arm of a foreign government. Thus, Manafort had devised an easy scheme to make it appear that these lobbyists were working for a private entity and avoid the extensive public FARA registration requirements. On paper, the lobbyists' foreign client looked like an independent NGO, when in fact Ukraine was the actual client.

Smart people at the lobbying firms saw through this ruse: In one of the emails we obtained, a young lawyer at one of the Washington lobbying firms described the European Centre for a Modern Ukraine as a European "hot dog stand," reflecting deep skepticism that the organization was in fact their true client. Another email from the head of the lobbying firm advised the staff to think of the Ukraine president as their actual client. But the firms did not file under FARA, instead using the sham European Centre as a way to maintain plausible deniability that Ukraine was calling the shots. The scheme revealed a seamy side of Washington, having effectively kept Ukraine's lobbying of numerous lawmakers and executive branch employees secret from the American public for years. It also permitted Manafort to place pro-Ukraine op-eds in U.S. newspapers—pieces that appeared to be objective but were actually tracts paid for and approved by Ukraine.

As we amassed more evidence that July and August, I proudly reported each new finding to Mueller, who absorbed my updates with characteristic restraint. At the end of one weekly meeting, he looked up and down our weekly report—a one-page memo each team prepared for him—and said: "You have done everything each week that you said you would do." Kyle beamed; from Mueller, this counted as high praise. The most outwardly enthusiastic response I ever got from the man was a sly "You are having entirely too much fun." Another time, he told me, "I don't think you need any more evidence because it will be unfair to the defense," and I responded with a clear-eyed assessment of our case:

"Frankly, sir," I told him, "while the evidence is far-flung across the globe, if we cannot make this case in the next two months, with the team you put together, you should fire me." Mueller, with a smile, told me he would hold me to that. This was fundamentally a bread-and-butter tax and money-laundering case, but piling up an overabundance of evidence was precisely the point: Only a commanding and indefensible case would create the incentive for Manafort or Gates to cooperate. And if we had to take either person to trial, we needed to make the case bullet-proof.

Following Department policy, once we were ready to go with the proof we had amassed, we'd send our FARA charges to be reviewed and approved by the National Security Division, and submit our tax and money-laundering charges to the Tax Division's own painstaking re-view process. Beginning in early September, senior staff from these two outfits spent weeks double-checking every piece of our evidence. We designated an entire room in our offices for the Tax Division lawyers, and, day after day, fielded their requests for more documents, interview notes, and grand jury testimony.

"Are they done yet?" was Mueller's refrain at each of our daily five P.M. supervisors' meetings. He was increasingly frustrated by the pace of these auditors but controlled his natural impatience, knowing it was beneficial to have them double-check our work. Ultimately, getting both divisions to sign off, in writing, on our charges, imbued our indict-ment with even more legitimacy, shoring it up against the inevitable at-tacks on our office as a rogue gang of partisan prosecutors. By the time we filed our indictment, I felt that all of us—Team M, along with these two other divisions of the Department—had done our jobs thoroughly, and it was gratifying to have the DOJ seal of approval that we had got-ten it right. The fact that we obtained such sign-off has been lost in the media hype generated by the White House—the Manafort case, like our other criminal cases, was blessed by this administration's own Department of Justice, headed by Republicans selected by the president.

In truth, managing Mueller's impatience over the Department approval process was a good distraction from my own. I, too, was restless. For me, the best time in a criminal case is the investigation. My father was a scientist, and I am often struck by the similarities between his work and mine: a prosecutorial investigation, like a research experiment, ideally moves from mystery to clarity, from hypotheses tested by hard factual evidence. I love chasing theories and hunches, venturing into that confusion and ferreting out the facts that narrow and focus the investigation into a single historical truth. Preparing and filing the indictment produced by all that legwork—what might seem like a kind of triumphant climax—I regard merely as paperwork: a long slog of typing up and double-checking your results before publication.

Nothing about the special counsel's investigation, however, was ever straightforward or predictable. And even after our proposed indictment was cleared by the National Security and the Tax divisions, the last phase of the process of bringing a public indictment—a usually somewhat perfunctory court proceeding known as the "hand-up"—presented a dizzying set of logistical issues that had to be creatively cracked. We would have to find a way to present the sealed indictment to a judge without setting off a frenzy of speculation in the press and tipping off our targets.

It's necessary here to pause and give some context: In order to charge anyone in this country with a felony, the law requires that we first submit any proposed charges in a document called an indictment to a grand jury, which then votes on whether to approve it. The grand jury, like a trial jury, is made up of ordinary citizens, although there are twenty-three of them, instead of twelve. If the grand jury approves the indictment, it must then present that document to a judge in open court—that is, the grand jury foreperson literally hands up its indictment to a federal magistrate. The charges therein are then formally brought, and the criminal case commences.

In our case, however, the defendants were potential flight risks—Manafort especially, as he had millions of dollars parked overseas and substantial ties to foreign governments. (We'd also discovered he had three different U.S. passports, all in his name.) Mueller worried that as soon as the hand-up happened, Manafort might learn he'd been indicted and simply abscond before he could be arrested. I thought that scenario unlikely, but neither I nor anyone else could conclude that Mueller's concern was fanciful; it was a real risk we needed to address.

Typically, to neutralize such a flight risk, you'd keep the indictment under seal after the hand-up, until the defendant could be taken into custody. The indictment would still be handed up to the magistrate judge in open court, as required, but the indictment itself would not be publicly filed or known about until the person was in custody. The hand-up itself is a brief transaction between the foreperson, the judge, and one or two prosecutors: Simply conducting such a routine affair in a busy courthouse is not enough to tip off someone watching as to who was being charged or for what. No one could connect that short proceeding to a particular defendant or investigation.

But that was not true in our investigation. Given the extreme scrutiny under which we were operating, it would be impossible to mask the fact that our office was indicting someone if we followed the normal procedure. The press was watching the courthouse carefully and knew well the names and faces of our prosecutors and even some of our agents; they'd seen us in other court proceedings or could recognize us from tweets and press reports documenting our comings and goings. (We made a point of entering the courthouse through a side door, but it was hard to go completely undetected.) The press had even identified some of the members of our grand jury. Making matters worse, our grand jury sat only on Fridays—and was the only grand jury sitting at the courthouse on Fridays. If someone saw a hand-up happening on a Friday, she'd know the indictment almost certainly had to be ours.

This issue was complicated by my insistence that Manafort and Gates not be arrested and paraded before the media in handcuffs, a practice that felt not just unnecessarily degrading, but at odds with the understatement with which Mueller demanded we conduct our work. I understood that law enforcement must handcuff the suspects they arrest for the safety of the agents and that of the suspects. And the courts have ruled that so-called perp walks are entirely legal; it's permissible to use them as deterrents to crime. Still, over the years I had come to find that reasoning flawed: At the time of his or her arrest, the suspect is only that—a suspect; there is no deterrent effect to parading them publicly, as only someone who's guilty would provide that deterrence. We cannot presume he or she is guilty until the criminal justice process has played out. In the Enron investigation, the intense media interest in our indictments had led to many perp walks—if only because the defendants were brought publicly to the courthouse and thus the throng of photographers would capture them in handcuffs. In retrospect, as a defense lawyer and law professor, I had come to regret that. At the Special Counsel's Office, I was committed to doing better.

Therefore, my preference was to allow Manafort and Gates to self-surrender—to turn themselves in to the FBI. But this approach had its complications, too: We couldn't possibly deliver the two men to the courthouse right after the hand-up, late on a Friday afternoon, and expect the court's marshals to process them, and the court to conduct its standard pretrial report and bail assessments, before the end of the workday. That is, if we took them into custody immediately, we'd risk leaving them to languish in a jail cell all weekend until they could post bail on Monday. That was not acceptable; no responsible prosecutor should or frankly would do it. At the same time, Mueller did not want us to simply tell Manafort's attorney to have his client show up at the FBI office on Monday morning, either—it would give Manafort all weekend to flee, if he chose to.

So Omer and I devised a rather elaborate plan, and sat down with Mueller in his office to lay it out: On Sunday, before the charges were unsealed, we would position two FBI agents outside Manafort's condo, and I would phone his attorney and inform him that Manafort had twenty minutes to walk outside and turn over all his passports. Manafort would have to agree to stay in his house until the following morning, then drive himself to the FBI office—with the agents following him. After processing there, the FBI would escort him into the courthouse, through the building's underground garage. We'd put the same plan in place for Gates, as well. Mueller asked if everyone agreed, and with no dissent, he nodded his approval; we promised to keep him and Aaron apprised each step of the way.

At the same time, we sought to keep our indictment from attracting attention when it was handed up on Friday, limiting the likelihood that

Manafort could be tipped off by the media. Working with our legal team, we petitioned the court to adopt a different procedure for the hand-up, one that still complied with the rules and would take place in open court, but that unfolded in a less conspicuous manner. Our request was approved, though the exact logistics were left up to the court. The resulting plan was almost comically elaborate and surreal—a kind of judicial Rube Goldberg machine—that drew us, that Friday morning, through many hidden arteries of the courthouse.

The first step, as usual, was for us to present the Manafort and Gates indictment to our grand jury, which voted that morning to approve it—voting a "true bill," as it is known. After that, my Team M colleagues and I, along with the grand jury foreperson, Magistrate Judge Deborah Robinson, her deputy, and several clerks, all assembled for a preliminary huddle in Judge Robinson's chambers. The judge, an elegant, willowy woman who had the clipped refined speech of Katharine Hepburn, looked over the indictment and other paperwork to make sure every-thing was in order, then graciously did her best to make our grand jury's foreperson feel as comfortable as possible under such daunting circum-stances.

The foreperson of a grand jury is an ordinary citizen, who, in our case, had been thrust into the center of one of the nation's biggest news stories and was aware of the press swarming around the courthouse where the grand jury sat every Friday. The limelight was an uncomfort-able burden for Mueller and the rest of us in the office to bear; even more so, we imagined, for a private citizen. I was pleased to see the judge sense all this, and chat amiably with the foreperson about the foreperson's work, background, and children to lessen the tension and help the foreperson feel more settled in this unfamiliar terrain.

Soon, the marshals arrived, and our entire group shuffled out of the judge's chambers together and set out on our convoluted path. We were escorted toward an inconspicuous elevator that is normally used only by judges as they commute between their courtrooms and their chambers. The elevator was tiny; it could hold only four or five of us at a time, so we descended in groups, and then reassembled in the building's under-ground garage.

It was dingy and slightly foreboding down there. The ceilings were low and run through with exposed pipes, many of which had been shored up with duct tape. As the last of our party arrived and we continued on through the garage, a couple of us noted facetiously that we'd stepped into the famous Deep Throat scene from *All the President's Men*. Except, of course, unlike Deep Throat, we were not doing anything illicit; in fact, we were being led around by a federal judge, elegantly robed in her official black garb, and a complement of armed federal marshals.

Judge Robinson walked us through the garage to another service elevator, roomier and brighter than the first, and up we went, again in small groups, into a warren of private corridors behind the courtrooms in the building's annex. Soon, we were piling into the anteroom of another judge's chambers, which Judge Robinson had arranged to borrow. She asked her clerk to check that the courtroom door was unlocked and the room was empty. The judge turned to me and went over what would happen once we entered the courtroom. "As soon as the hand-up's over, you and the foreperson leave immediately," she said to me. "We'll stay and complete the paperwork. Wait for us back here." Finally, it seemed, we were ready to go.

Everyone knew how momentous this normally routine proceeding would be. It was not just the special counsel's first indictment, but an indictment of the sitting president's campaign chairman and deputy campaign chairman—an unprecedented turn of events in American history.

There was a hiccup, however. The court reporter hadn't shown up yet. No one knew where she was, and we couldn't start the hand-up without her there to transcribe the proceeding. And so, we all stood clustered in the small hallway outside the courtroom, waiting, no one saying a word. I don't know how long we waited before the court reporter finally arrived, but it felt like an eternity.

Once she arrived, Judge Robinson had her clerk double-check the courtroom again and commanded, "Let's go." I walked in with the foreperson and stood by the lectern at the front of the open courtroom. My team sat at the government table behind us. The court deputy called the matter—"We have a hand-up, Your Honor"—the foreperson handed over the indictment, and Judge Robinson proceeded to ask the foreperson all the obligatory questions.

And that was it. Out we went, following the federal marshal once again like ducklings. When we eventually reconvened in the anteroom with the judge and her staff, I thanked them all for their extreme consideration.

It had gone like clockwork.

Only hours later, however, the media reported that our grand jury had returned its first indictment. Someone—we still don't know who—leaked the news, though without disclosing who had been charged. Speculation built up in the press all weekend—Manafort, Flynn, and Kushner were the top candidates. We had breathed our collective sigh of relief too soon; all of our careful planning turned out to be for naught.

Meanwhile, Omer's and my carefully orchestrated arrest plan had hit a major snag as well: We learned late in the game that Manafort wasn't at his condo in Virginia; he was staying at another home he owned, in Florida. We were forced to scramble two FBI agents down there and managed to get them stationed outside his house by the time I called Manafort's counsel on Sunday morning.

I told Manafort's attorney that while I could not reveal the precise charges that had been brought until the indictment had been unsealed, Manafort needed to appear at a specified FBI office in Washington on Monday morning. (Manafort's counsel, of course, already knew from our meetings in August what charges we were contemplating, as he had been given the opportunity to argue against being indicted.) The government would permit him to self-surrender to the FBI, provided that Manafort agreed to the following: He would immediately turn over his passports and travel back to Washington, with an FBI escort, that evening. He would spend the night at his condo in Virginia and, on Monday morning, drive directly to the FBI in Washington for processing.

I told Manafort's counsel that we had agents outside Manafort's home in Florida as we spoke, ready to either take possession of his passports, or—if he did not agree to the conditions—place him under arrest. We would need to hear back in thirty minutes.

Manafort's counsel said he understood and thanked me for not arresting Manafort then and there; he agreed to call me back promptly. But as the deadline came and went, I called counsel and got no answer. I waited five minutes more, conferred with Mueller, Aaron, and Omer by phone, then called Manafort's attorney again. He didn't pick up this time, either, so I left a message explaining that if I did not hear back in another five minutes, the FBI agents outside Manafort's home would be directed to effectuate the arrest. This time our ultimatum worked; Manafort agreed to the conditions. It seemed in keeping with Manafort's character to test us, stretching even these rules as far as they'd go. Gates and his counsel presented no such issues; he had readily agreed to the conditions and we were all set there.

I'd already had qualms about the degree to which I was perhaps over-prioritizing the manner of taking Manafort and Gates into custody. Now I realized there was no way I'd be able to responsibly replicate this same system as more indictments came down the pike and more people were taken into custody; my Platonic ideal of an arrest was not reproducible at scale. The FBI would not be able to implement the same plan with respect to all defendants—flying to their home, watching them for hours on end, and then escorting them to a far-flung FBI office. And treating people equally was an important Aristotelian principle at the heart of our criminal justice system, and the Bureau was not going to be able to do this in every other case. I told Omer, who'd gone along with my idea and helped formulate the arrest plan because he knew it was important to me, that he'd been right all along; I hadn't thought this through. Omer was not used to such rare admissions on my part but did not lord it over me. "No problem," he said, "it was worth a try."

In the end, however, the plan had worked: If Manafort or Gates had ever considered fleeing, the system we put in place thwarted that impulse. When Manafort was finally ushered into the FBI's field office in Washington on Monday morning, he found himself unexpectedly reunited with Gates, his former employee, who'd been escorted in from his home in Virginia. Gates immediately noticed that the agent who'd arrested Manafort, Brock Domin, had cuffed Manafort's hands in front of his body, while Gates had been cuffed—less comfortably, but more typical of FBI practice—with his hands behind his back. Gates turned to the agent who'd arrested him, Sherine Ebadi, and objected to this claimed indignity.

"Next time you get arrested," Sherine shot back, "have Brock arrest you."

Later that morning, about an hour after the Manafort and Gates indictment was unsealed, the court unsealed a second case that Jeannie and Team R had prepared, unveiling the guilty plea of George Papadopoulos for lying to federal investigators, and identifying him as an early link between the Trump campaign and Russian interests. Team R had spent the summer exploring whether Papadopoulos would flip, but he continued to lie or mislead Jeannie and her investigators in ways that had made it impossible to sign him up to a cooperation agreement.

Jeannie and I had convinced Mueller to unseal the Team M and Team R cases on the same day, and we had managed to hold Papadopoulos's criminal case under seal for more than three months, with no leaks from our team. The impact created by this coordination was powerful: All at once, the public now saw three different defendants charged by Mueller within months of his appointment: the president's campaign chairman and deputy campaign chairman, as well as one of his foreign affairs advisers who'd lied about his communications with Russian operatives during the campaign. The press misread, however, language in our Papadopoulos plea agreement—borrowed from the standard District of Columbia U.S. attorney's office plea agreements—that noted if the defendant provided cooperation, we would bring that assistance to the attention of the court at the time of sentencing. That provision does not mean the defendant is in fact cooperating, but there was no way for the press to know that, and thus a flurry of press speculation ensued.

Right away, President Trump railed against our office and our indictments on Twitter, though I found I couldn't make sense of his objections. He claimed that the charges against Manafort were for conduct that had taken place "years ago," though they actually encompassed crimes Manafort had committed as late as 2016 and 2017—in other words, during the time Manafort had served as Trump's campaign chairman.

The president's tweets deflected as well, asking why we were not investigating Hillary Clinton instead. It was a ludicrous question—not least because the Special Counsel's Office couldn't permissibly do so under our appointment order crafted by the president's own administration—but this didn't keep the president from tweeting it with five emphatic question marks, as though an abundance of punctuation might make the point more logical.

Still, tweets like these just rolled off our backs by that point in our investigation. We did what Mueller told us to do: kept our heads down and did our work efficiently—without playing with our food.

Mueller came by our offices and congratulated us, shaking my hand and permitting Jeannie to give him a hug. Jeannie and I repaired to her office, privately beaming, proud of these first shots across the bow.

CHAPTER 12

Vilification

EVERY DAY, IN EVERY courtroom across our country, judges, prosecutors, and defense attorneys—human beings with a full array of opinions, religions, and political beliefs—set their personal views aside and play their prescribed roles, impartially, in the machinery of the American justice system.

The judge, for example, who presides over every phase of a criminal trial and is called on to sentence the defendant upon conviction, will inevitably have developed her own view of that defendant's conduct throughout that process. The judge may find the defendant's crimes to be exceedingly heinous; a defendant who is involved in murder, torture, terrorism, or unspeakable greed or heartlessness can expect as much. (For instance, in one particularly unsettling case I supervised at the Fraud Section, a doctor had falsely told his patients they had cancer, letting both the patients and their families believe the patient was dying, merely so that the doctor could provide expensive but unnecessary pharmaceuticals—including some, like chemotherapy, with debilitating side effects.) Still, the judge applies the same legal rules, just as stringently, to the case of such a defendant as she would to any other.

Defense counsel can feel a similar revulsion to their client's crimes. They are often aware not only that their clients are guilty, but that they've lied to counsel about what, in fact, occurred. And yet, they defend such clients anyway. This does not mean those attorneys are sanctioning the defendant's conduct. They are simply fulfilling their responsibility to help preserve the integrity of the legal process, ensuring that the accused is afforded due process, and that the government is held to its very high burden of proof—beyond a reasonable doubt—before it is permitted to remove an individual from society and place him or her behind bars.

Outside the legal system, we take this precept for granted: No one would expect a heart surgeon to repair an artery less diligently if she disagreed with her patient's politics. And yet, some people are apparently skeptical that those of us working in the justice system can possibly temper our personal views and do our jobs dispassionately and without bias. The truth is, it's not difficult. Such impartiality becomes second nature. We recognize that personal opinions are irrelevant to the facts or law at hand. We simply assess those facts and apply the law. And many of us, like me, have in the course of our careers represented parties on both sides of the "v" (a common phrase we use to refer to the "v" in a criminal case name: *United States v. Defendant*). We know that each side has a vital part to play if the justice system is going to work.

This is not to say, of course, that one's conduct is never affected by one's personal or political views. It can happen and must be guarded against. But to make a claim of prejudice or impropriety, it's not enough to accuse a person of having personal views; every human being has opinions—this is hardly alarming or disqualifying. Instead, you must point to a specific action that the person has taken that's been warped by those views—some instance of him or her acting unfairly as a result of those biases. In the legal world, we understand this logic well. We even have a term of art to differentiate legitimate claims of bias from such meaningless attacks: ad hominem—meaning an attack that's leveled strictly on someone's character, without ever linking it to how it affected his or her actions.

As government prosecutors and investigators, we in the Special Counsel's Office initially took this distinction between thoughts and deeds for granted; it was simply the logic according to which our world had always worked. So it was more than a little disorienting when, less than a month after we'd set up shop, our boss came under precisely this sort of ad hominem assault.

There had been a short-lived honeymoon period following Mueller's appointment. Our work had initially been greeted with the approbation of elected officials and others who ranged widely across the political spectrum—from Orrin Hatch, Rob Portman, and Chuck Grassley to Chuck Schumer and the American Civil Liberties Union. This was a reflection of Mueller's stature in Washington. But the bloom came off the rose rather quickly. Within weeks, the first attacks on Mueller's character had bubbled up, as the White House and its allies in Congress realized they'd need to preserve the ability to undermine the investigation if they did not like the results.

The strategy was obvious: The Trump administration was hedging its bets. They understood that we might uncover wrongdoing and sought to minimize the impact of those findings by sowing doubts about the integrity of our investigation in advance—or discrediting our office altogether. (To be fair, this was a time-honored tradition: Other presidents had engaged in such tactics before, most recently Bill Clinton in connection with his attack on Independent Counsel Starr's investigation, even though he was in fact guilty of lying under oath.)

The president had already tested this tactic on the press and garnered proof of concept. Prior to Mueller's appointment, the press had been the main institutional check on Trump's power. And so, as a candidate, and then as president, Trump had mounted a protracted, withering assault on the media. He undermined journalistic outlets with screeds about "fake news," and taunted and dehumanized individual journalists to such a degree that his supporters had started freely screaming obscenities at reporters at his rallies. Trump decried the press as the "enemy of the people," borrowing a phrase from no less an autocrat than Stalin—whether he knew it or not. It demonstrated a fundamental misunderstanding of the First Amendment and the role of the press in our democracy.

To attack the press as a private businessman might be understandable, but from the leader of the free world it is one step toward autocracy. As intended, it served to corrode public perception of the media's integrity among some significant portion of Americans, and therefore blunt the impact of unfavorable stories about Trump in the press. Every new negative report became clouded with a degree of suspicion. Any fact that reflected badly on the president could be perceived as left-wing propaganda masquerading as fact. That, of course, was precisely the goal. The White House never explained why favorable stories spilling out of Fox News were not subject to the same "fake news" epithet.

The attacks on Mueller were a troubling extension of the same corrosion I'd felt creeping into our system of checks and balances even before I joined the Special Counsel's Office. Now Mueller had been installed as another check on the president's power—a custodian of the rule of law—and he was potentially a far more powerful check than the media could ever be, given the tools he had to work with: the ability to issue subpoenas, obtain search warrants, and seek indictments. So it was inevitable that the administration and its surrogates would scramble to neutralize him as well.

Diminishing Mueller's credibility was not easy. First off, he was conducting the special counsel's investigation with unflagging rectitude. Nothing he or our office was doing could be shown to be remotely biased, meaning the only lines of attack open to his critics were ad hominem. Watching this, I'd wanted to shout out: What specific actions have we taken that you dispute? Are Manafort and Gates innocent? That would be a tough tack to take, given that they both would later admit their guilt. Yet that did not prevent the president from bemoaning what "they" had "done" to Manafort, without ever explaining what was so wrong with what happened to Manafort as a result of his own criminal choices.

But even this kind of assault proved difficult for the administration to mount: Putting aside Mueller's sterling reputation in Washington, the man was a lifelong Republican and a decorated marine. And so, a different tack had to be taken: Stories were leaked, surely from the White House, about Mueller's alleged dispute with Trump over a fee at one of the president's golf courses, insinuating that this constituted some fatal conflict of interest—that Mueller held such a grudge over a golf club fee that he'd attempt to concoct criminal evidence against the president in revenge. There were similar whispers about Mueller's harboring resentment about not being chosen to replace James Comey as FBI director, even though Mueller had never applied for the job. A bogus claim was concocted by the president, which Trump repeats to this day, that Mueller is a close friend of Comey, an attempt to stain Mueller by association. Finally, an outlandish allegation surfaced about Mueller having a one-night affair with a woman at a New York City hotel while he was FBI director. This story collapsed before it could gain any traction when the woman who was supposedly at its center refused to attend the press conference meant to launch the story into the media. Moreover, a check of FBI records showed that Mueller had been serving on jury duty in Washington, D.C., on the day in question.

Any rational human being, open to an honest evaluation of the facts, could see straight through these smears. And because Mueller refused to respond to the allegations and directed our press officer to say nothing at all, there was no back-and-forth for the press to grab hold of. At the same time, this meant there was no direct rebuttal to these falsehoods, making it possible to question the ultimate efficacy of Mueller's rectitude and worry it was perhaps an increasingly quixotic value from a bygone era. But Mueller's motto, which everyone who worked closely with him heard time and again, was "Live by the press, die by the press." He just would not take the bait. I think he was right to some extent, as it could lead to an endless tit for tat, and feed a narrative that he was a partisan. But that did not mean he had to be completely silent.

Although as prosecutors you learn in your bones that, prior to a conviction of a person, you speak about that individual only through public charging documents and court filings, one could adhere to that fundamental precept and still perform a valuable and necessary educational function for the public. There was precedent for such an approach in Archibald Cox, the stalwart initial special prosecutor in Watergate, who'd held a legendary press conference to address the principles he was seeking to uphold in going to court to seek tape recordings made by Nixon. That conference did not denigrate Nixon or accuse him of a crime; but it served to counter a concerted campaign by Nixon and his supporters to spin the public. Cox spelled out what he was seeking to accomplish, that the presidency is not above the rule of law.

In our investigation, a press conference could have served that public educational function by discussing the law and DOJ policy on whether a sitting president could be indicted. It was not until our report was finalized that the issue was fully understood by the media and public, but by then twenty-two months had passed in which the public had thought that such an indictment was possible, whereas we knew internally that we had no such option according to Department policy. Even Mueller seemed to have belatedly realized the value of such public appearances, when he took to the Justice Department press podium after our report was issued to give his own summary of the report, after Attorney General Barr had twisted it beyond recognition. But it was so little and so late in the day.

Still, even without public rebuttals, Mueller's character proved difficult to attack effectively, so much so that even Steve Bannon advised the administration that its mudslinging was starting to look silly. It was clear another tack would have to be taken. Before long, our critics reached beyond Mueller and began to strafe the rest of us with accusations. Within weeks of Mueller's appointment, administration operatives, and the president himself, were accusing Mueller of having hired seventeen "angry Democrats," leveraging the president's uncanny ability to pigeonhole his opponents with schoolyard epithets. It was what I described to Jeannie as "argument by adjective." This particular epithet also happened to be objectively untrue.

Department regulations precluded us at the Special Counsel's Office from asking applicants about their party affiliations during the hiring process, but we learned from the internal chatter that arose when these attacks first surfaced that not everyone who wound up working for Mueller was a Democrat. (We'd suspected that our pool of job applicants itself had been imbalanced because not many Republican prosecutors lined up to apply—working for the special counsel could be viewed as a career killer for them.) And it was surely not true that all the agents and analysts who'd been detailed to the office from the FBI were Democrats. In fact, the Bureau, like every other law enforcement agency, is well understood to be a predominately Republican outfit. Trump's attack on the FBI as a hotbed of Deep State Democrats was viewed internally as plain laughable.

Still, even rebutting this accusation buys into the assumption that party affiliation is relevant to the impartial administration of justice. Was Mueller supposed to violate the Department's regulations against politically biased hiring and select only Republicans to be on the team? Wouldn't they, by the same logic, be biased the other way? Should Mueller have hired only independents, or those who did not vote in the past election? Did we really want to go down the road of making political affiliation a criterion in selection—something we as country have strived to get away from precisely so as to de-politicize the government work-force?

Of course, this is applying logic to illogical attacks. The point of the attacks was to appeal first to people's hearts, not their heads, to reaffirm their suspicions of every perceived opponent of the administration. It did not matter that Trump's "angry Democrat" epithet made no logical sense. Rather than pointing out any actual examples of bias in our work, the attack was meant to trigger knee-jerk suspicion that those working on the investigations couldn't possibly conduct themselves with integrity.

As a career prosecutor who has worked hard and assessed every case on its merits, I found this insulting. We all did. We'd be pelted with such name-calling and criticism for the duration of our investigation, and yet no effort was made to tie that supposed bias to any of the work we did, or the criminal cases we brought.

I am a registered Democrat. Does this make Paul Manafort or any of the other thirty-two people our office charged any less guilty? Did Russia not attack our democracy and disrupt our election with its self-described online information warfare operation? Which facts that we alleged in our various indictments—and to which many of those we indicted, including Manafort, would plead guilty—did our attackers believe were invented as a result of our alleged bias as "angry Democrats"? And in the end, as laid out clearly in our report, our office found there to be insufficient evidence of a criminal conspiracy between Russia and the Trump campaign. How did a team of supposedly devious Democratic operatives, led by an allegedly compromised special counsel nursing a petty vendetta with the president over a golf club fee, manage that if we were biased?

These challenges to our integrity never turned on questions of evidence. It was a game of politics, increasingly decoupled from truth. Mueller's response was to keep his head down and to advise us to do the same. He bore it all in silence, never complaining. The only glimmer that any of this was registering was the question I heard him asking, before extending an offer to an applicant: Is there anything in your background that could be used, legitimately, to undermine the investigation?

Aside from that, he concerned himself with our integrity and the work we did. Naïvely or not, he expected the American people to judge us the same way.

Aside from Mueller, I came in for the greatest volume of personal attacks. I did not know it at the time, but this was largely due to my position as the head of Team M. Hundreds of texts we discovered showed Manafort in close communication with Sean Hannity, the Fox News television personality. Once Manafort learned our investigation was homing in on him, he essentially conspired to wheel Hannity and the Fox News apparatus around like a cannon and pointed them straight at me and my team.

In short order, I was being regularly criticized on that network for a text I'd sent to a former Justice Department colleague, Sally Yates (then the acting attorney general), praising her for refusing to enforce President Trump's first iteration of his Muslim immigration ban. I was attacked for giving campaign contributions to Democrats, and for attending an election night event hosted by the Clinton campaign at the Javits Center in New York.

This last accusation was particularly galling, as I had gone to that party not out of some heightened enthusiasm for Clinton's candidacy, but because an old friend, from my days in the EDNY, happened to be related by marriage to Clinton's vice presidential nominee. When my friend learned I would be in New York that evening, he suggested that I come by. As it turns out, he'd invited another friend of his as well—a man who happened to be one of Paul Manafort's criminal defense counsels. This was presumably how Manafort knew about my attendance at the event and was able to leak it to the press. Manafort left out the fact that his own attorney had been there as well, under the same circumstances.

I would like to report that, throughout these attacks on my character, I remained as stoic and classy as Robert Mueller; but I cannot. I'd grown accustomed, throughout my career, to defense attorneys questioning my conduct and that of my colleagues during a case. It is a common tactic, particularly in organized crime cases, for the integrity of the prosecutor, and the agents working with him, to become the centerpiece of a criminal defense. But in the legal context, there is a process for addressing and resolving such criticism: You simply set out what actually happened in court papers or in front of the jury and trust the system to adjudicate the matter and see through any unfounded or spurious accusations. It takes a little getting used to, having your character or conduct assailed and debated. As a lawyer, you consider yourself an instrument for telling your client's story, or for unearthing a cogent, factual time line of events with an investigation like ours. It is a disquieting sensation when you become part of the story yourself. But you get used to it—mostly because you have faith that, in court, facts still matter.

The attacks on me at the Special Counsel's Office were different, however. Not only were they untethered from the truth, they were also playing out in front of a national audience—and, unlike in court, there was no intelligible system for disproving or neutralizing the lies by presenting the actual facts or pointing out their illogic. That is, there was no path to vindication, aside from simply trusting the good judgment of the public to recognize the truth.

One night, I called my sister for moral support, as I'd frequently done throughout my career. She is an oncologist—she deals, literally, with matters of life and death every day—and has a way of putting my work problems into perspective.

"Andrew," she said, "this is what they have on you? That you voted for Hillary? More than half of America did the same thing. It's absurd." That reality check was similar to a crack from my friend Caroline Clark when she learned about the level of my political contributions: "I learned something about you," she quipped. "You are cheap!"

Eventually, as I came to accept the childish nature of the attacks, their sting lessened and then went away completely. Jeannie and I would even develop an ongoing tension-relieving shtick where we argued over which one of us must be Angry Democrat #1 and which was Angry Democrat #2, each trying to pass off the top honorific on the other. Finally, Jeannie's husband settled the matter by having matching baseball caps made for the two of us: Jeannie's said "Angry Democrat #2"; mine said "Angry Democrat #1" with "Weissmann" on the back to nail down the point.

Achieving that kind of good-humored equanimity took a while, however. I was so concerned about the effect that first wave of attacks might have on our investigation that I made a decision: In the summer of 2017, I went to Mueller's office and said, "Sir, do you have a few minutes to talk?"

The director looked puzzled, but waved me in.

"There is nothing more important to me than the success of this office," I said. I had planned out exactly what I was going to say, but Mueller's look of puzzlement was morphing into a look of impatience. Surely he was wondering when I might be arriving at a point.

"I want to be sure you know that, at any juncture, if you think I am a distraction to the work of the office, or unnecessary baggage, I do not want to be here. I'd want to go. I'd want to do what is necessary for the success of our mission."

Mueller started nodding. He could now see where all my meandering was headed, and he was uninterested in taking the ride. "Are you done?" he said.

I nodded.

"Well," he said, "you needn't worry. If I have to fire you, I won't be considering your feelings on the matter at all."

I nodded again and left. As long as Mueller is teasing you, you know you're in his good graces.

As the criminal case against Manafort progressed and grew stronger, the personal attacks on me did not relent, and this scene repeated itself, with Mueller once again brushing aside an offer from me to resign: "I need you too much," he told me. "I'm stuck with you." From time to time, throughout that first summer and fall, he would stop by my office, or keep me behind a moment as our daily five P.M. supervisors' meeting wound down, to ask how I was holding up. "Keep your head down, do your work, and everything will be okay," he'd say. His sensitivity and concern always left me feeling both touched and beset by guilt: I knew that he was under far more strain, and being pilloried more viciously than I.

I offered Mueller my resignation one final time. It was December 2017, and the press was in a tizzy over newly unearthed texts exchanged by FBI agents Pete Strzok and Lisa Page while they were working on the Clinton email investigation. The texts contained harsh criticisms of candidate Trump and his positions. (Strzok, for example, called Trump "an idiot," and when Page expressed worry that Trump might actually be elected, Strzok replied: "No he won't. We'll stop it"—by which, he later explained, he meant the American people, not the FBI.) Lisa had already left the office, after her brief stint with us, to continue her work at the Bureau. But Pete, who was still working for the special counsel, was promptly reassigned back to the Bureau once Mueller learned of the texts.

Ultimately, though, the texts amounted to a salacious distraction—a fixation on individuals' opinions without discussing what, if any, actual conduct those opinions might have distorted. It was inconceivable to me that Pete (whom I did not know well) and Lisa (whom I knew from when I was the general counsel) had taken any actions as a result of their political beliefs. They certainly hadn't during their time at the special counsel's office. I watched Rod Rosenstein throw them under the bus.

They of course showed poor judgment, but the truth is it had not affected their work one bit: They had been among the strongest advocates for taking more aggressive investigative steps in the Clinton email investigation, only to be overruled by the more timid DOJ lawyers on the case. No effort at all was made to tether their alleged bias to any improper conduct. Later, the inspector general would vindicate them, finding no basis to conclude that they had taken any improper actions based on their personal views. (For what it's worth, the inspector general also noted that the two wrote disparaging emails not only about Trump, but Clinton as well.)

The lack of a sufficient counterpunch appeared to further embolden our critics. Soon after, a right-wing opinion writer published a wily piece in *The Washington Post* arguing that, while I was a gifted lawyer, my attendance at the election night event for Clinton and text to Yates about the first Muslim ban created an undue appearance of partiality, and that I, just like Lisa and Pete, should no longer be allowed to work on the investigation. The piece was skillfully done, and carried a veneer of reason and respectability, but its underlying motive was clear: If those attacking us could get a third person removed from the Special Counsel's Office for apparent conflicts of interest, it would further undermine the credibility of our investigation. This was especially true if it were someone as close to Mueller as I was—Mueller's "pit bull," as I was now being described in the press.

I made a point of never watching Fox or MSNBC, to keep from

being distracted. But I did look at the news in mainstream print news-papers like the *Post* and read this piece the morning it was published, shortly after waking up. I instantly felt a knot deep in my chest, swal-lowed hard, and left for work.

Mueller was waiting for me outside my office when I arrived. I said good morning, went inside, took off my backpack, and sat down. He followed me in, standing on the opposite side of my desk.

I had no speech to deliver this time; I was too rattled. But Mueller didn't allow me a chance to speak first.

"I want you to know that your last day in the office is going to be my last day in the office," he told me. This time, there was no teasing—no wry smile, no glint in his eye. I could feel my throat tighten, my eyes water. I fought the emotion back.

"Sir, I want you to know . . ." I started to say.

"No," Mueller told me. "Stop. Not one day sooner." And he turned and left.

Later that day, our press officer, Peter Carr, stopped by to tell me that Mueller had taken the rare step of authorizing him to respond to an in-quiry from a right-wing publication as to whether, in light of the op-ed in the *Post,* he still had full confidence in me. Pete's statement from our office was simple: "Yes."

That same evening, before heading home, I stopped by Aaron's office to share what had happened and let him know how appreciative I was to have such support from the director. It was comforting, I told him, to hear Mueller assure me that I'd be working alongside him for as long as the investigation lasted.

"So," Aaron shot back, "I guess the two of you will be here till the end of the week?"

It was gallows humor—a sign of how acclimated we were, by that point, to living with the possibility of the president's shutting us down.

CHAPTER 13

Ratcheting Up the Pressure

MUELLER WAS NEVER ONE to waste time savoring yesterday's successes, but at the end of October 2017, on the morning following the Manafort and Gates arraignments and the unsealing of the Papadopoulos plea, he took a moment at the start of his weekly meeting with Team M to commend us for our dogged work.

We were meeting in our largest SCIF conference room, known as Elm. (BAM—Beth A. McGarry—had nicknamed our conference rooms after various trees.) Aaron and Jim sat on either side of the director—their usual formation—and Omer and I were across the table from them. While Mueller spoke, I lost myself momentarily in the huge whiteboard directly behind his head, staring at all the squiggles, arrows, and familiar and unfamiliar names that had been written across it in various colors. I recognized it as a map of leads being pursued by Team R, Jeannie's ongoing investigation into Russia's election interference. She must have been there earlier in the day, briefing Mueller as well.

Ever since her meeting with Facebook, Jeannie had been rapidly pulling together enough evidence to indict specific Russian actors who had been engaged in active measures to undermine the 2016 election. She still had a long way to go, not the least of which would be overcoming the enormous hurdle of convincing the IC to let her go forward with her indictment, if she in fact obtained sufficient proof to bring one.

Team 600 was moving forward as well, slowly piecing together the full story of the president's firing of James Comey—largely through long, scrupulous interviews with all of the key players, including Comey, Andrew McCabe, Sally Yates, Rod Rosenstein, and their senior staffs. A lawyer in our office, Brandon Van Grack—an earnest straight shooter with the classic good looks of a 1950s G-man—had been tasked with pulling together the proof as to whether Flynn had lied to the FBI about the substance of his communications with the Russian ambassador in December 2016. In the course of that investigation, Brandon and his assigned agents had also uncovered another crime: a FARA violation by Flynn involving his lobbying in the United States on behalf of a foreign state, Turkey.

Brandon was working meticulously, and productively, though sometimes suffering the wrath of Mueller, who implored him to move faster. It took even some of our office's most seasoned prosecutors time to adjust to Mueller's demanding pace; one could no longer exhaustively review documents before beginning to interview witnesses—as we are classically trained to do. Within a few weeks, Brandon had caught on and adjusted his tempo, and his work fell in line with the rest of ours, barreling forward fast.

In short, as we went back to work after the Manafort/Gates hand-up and the unsealing of the Papadopoulos plea, it felt as though we were on solid footing: Our office had been fully operational for only a few months, but our entire staff was grinding ahead, feeling the momentum of the recent one-two punch. Now, at our weekly Team M meeting, Mueller was reinforcing that confidence, telling us at that he had been reading the news coverage of our charges and that the press was reacting favorably.

"There seems to be agreement in the media," he said. "Have you read any criticisms as to what we should have done differently?"

I told him I had not.

"I think the indictment laid out so much hard documentary evidence that it would be hard for Manafort and Gates to mount a plausible defense. Now," he said, "all that remains to be seen is whether it would compel one of them to throw in the towel and cooperate."

But that had not happened yet. I explained to him that neither defense counsel had given any signal so far that either was considering flipping. In truth, neither Omer nor I were surprised by this. All along, we'd had doubts that this indictment would put enough pressure on the two men to flip. A good defense counsel would evaluate our charges and assure Manafort and Gates that, even if they had no compelling defense, a conviction was not likely to carry a serious enough risk of significant prison time.

I'd been a criminal defense attorney myself, not that long ago, working for five years at a firm in New York; I probably would have given a client a similar read on the situation. Being able to see the case from the defense point of view was useful now that I was back on this near side of the "v." Our FARA charges, in particular, were admittedly obscure. Even though the principle behind FARA could not be more important, the criminal statute had not historically resulted in many prosecutions. The crime was charged so infrequently that it wasn't even included in the federal sentencing guidelines (an official book that lists recommended sentences for particular offenses, as well as other factors for the court to consider). A judge wasn't likely to throw the book at a defendant for such a crime, or even for our money-laundering charge that was predicated on the FARA offense.

Besides, there was one factor that overwhelmed all others in either defendant flipping—a unique, ineluctable fact of this case that upset all the normal calculations by the government and defense: Manafort and Gates could simply refuse to cooperate and hold out for a presidential pardon. It might not matter what a jury would think. They could play, strictly, to a jury of one.

At that point, though, none of us, other than Jim Quarles, who years ago had been a junior lawyer on Watergate, had ever worked on a case where this issue reared its head; we did not anticipate how much this one extraordinary factor would influence decision-making as the case wore on. I had been focusing on the fact that the president—a subject of our investigation—had the power to fire us, an already staggeringly un-usual power that no mobster or gangster I'd prosecuted in the past had possessed. I had not yet come to fully realize how the power of the pres-ident to pardon anyone thinking of flipping would undermine one of the key tools I'd been brandishing for years to advance an investigation.

That said, outwardly our October 2017 charges were still an objec-tive success. But in Mueller's mind, it had brought Team M to a critical turning point. He, too, had not focused on the gravitational pull exerted by the pardon power, away from cooperation with us. What he saw was that strong charges had been brought, and the defendants had not cooperated. It was time to move the investigation more closely within our mandate.

"Whatever pressure you are going to put on Manafort and Gates to flip is now in place," he told us. "And you haven't been able to get them to cooperate. We need to move on now and focus our investigation on Manafort's activities during the presidential campaign."

Knowing Mueller, I wasn't the least bit surprised by this. His decision-making is often governed by his pragmatism, decisiveness, and at times impatience. He wanted us to steer our investigation back onto a more central path at the core of our mandate—because in his judgment, that was the most productive way at this juncture, absent Manafort or Gates cooperating, to determine whether Manafort had been a conduit with Russia.

He'd already begun to reckon with the tilted playing field on which we increasingly found ourselves: The deeper our investigation went into more tangential matters, like Manafort's crimes unrelated to the campaign, the more we opened ourselves up to political attacks. By then, our critics were hammering the idea that our investigation was a "witch hunt"—a baseless accusation, given that the hunt had just produced an indictment and a guilty plea. Still, the idea was out there, and Mueller had to be wary of taking actions that could be spun as evidence to support that thesis—which, in turn, might trigger the president's petulance and further inflame the probability of our firing.

I agreed with half of what Mueller said. Omer and I believed there was a way to both satisfy Mueller's perfectly valid approach and continue to ratchet up the pressure on Manafort and Gates. There were other charges we thought we could bring—charges that would be viewed by the defense as more severe. Maybe we could still persuade at least one of them to flip—particularly Gates, I thought. He was the one Omer and I had our eyes on. Our experience together on the Enron investigation enabled us to see Gates as a potential Michael Kopper, the first cooperator in Enron who allowed us to move up the chain to Lay and Skilling.

Because Gates had aided Manafort in his crimes, he could be charged identically and face a similar potential sentence. And with respect to our biggest challenge—counteracting the potential for a presidential pardon—bringing still more charges for more serious crimes might reduce that hope; at some point, surely, the volume and severity of charges would make a pardon politically unwise. We had no idea then that Trump would use his pardon power shamelessly to free far worse white-collar criminals and send a message not to cooperate.

The possibility of bringing additional serious charges arose from the work of one of Team M's most tenacious investigators, a woman I'd initially encountered while getting up to speed on pending Manafort investigations during my first days on the job. One of those investigations centered on Manafort's son-in-law, Jeffrey Yohai, a kind of workaday, serial scam artist who'd been perpetrating various bank, wire, and mail frauds around Los Angeles for years. (Among the many victims of Yohai's fraudulent investment schemes was Dustin Hoffman.)

I'd been sent a sheaf of documents from the FBI, in order to read up on the case, and I was tremendously impressed by a batch of 302s prepared by an FBI agent based in Los Angeles named Sherine Ebadi. I'd read thousands of 302s in the course of my career, but I'd never seen any so well written, concise, or thorough. Eventually, I got Special Agent Ebadi on the phone and told her, a bit too effusively, how wonderful I'd found her reports to be. There was a pause on the other end. "Thank you," she said. "How can I help you?" She was all business; I liked her even more. When I dispatched Omer on his first assignment for Team M, to follow up on this investigation, I also instructed him to try to recruit Sherine.

Now Sherine was one of us, and she was a dynamo. It was Sherine who'd put Gates in his place when he'd griped about his handcuffs, and she chased down leads with such imperturbable focus and speed that you could almost see steam rising from her carrel in our office. She had left her family in California to work with us in Washington, commuting back home every four weeks—a sacrifice made out of her sense of duty and mission.

Sherine had kept pulling on various threads of the Yohai investigation—uncovering a particularly damning email Manafort had written to Yohai while Yohai was staying in one of Manafort's apartments, instructing him to deceive a bank appraiser who'd soon be visiting the apartment. She'd identified five promising cases of bank fraud committed by Manafort, with Gates's help, all in the past couple of years, even while he was Trump's campaign chairman.

Applying what George Stamboulidis had taught me while prosecuting the Colombo crime family—that an investigator must think like the criminal he or she is investigating—I realized that these bank fraud charges completed the story of Manafort's greed. While Manafort was in his salad days, with Yanukovych in power in Ukraine, he'd made millions. One part of his stratagem to hide this income from the IRS was to bring a considerable chunk of that money into the United States disguised as "loans" made to him by various sham companies. (Loans are not taxable as income.) Another part of the scheme was to keep the income in foreign accounts and use the accounts to pay U.S. vendors directly, without ever reporting the money to the IRS.

But after Yanukovych fled Ukraine in 2014, Manafort's income all but dried up. To obtain the cash flow he needed to support his extravagant lifestyle, he'd sought to obtain real bank loans using as collateral the U.S. real estate he'd purchased with his Ukraine income: a long list of properties, including his luxury condo in Virginia and another in Trump Tower in New York City. But Manafort's lack of income and his "debt," in the form of the fake loans, disqualified him when it came to obtaining actual loans from real banks. In order to qualify for real bank loans, he would need to wipe out his fictitious debt and inflate his nonexistent yearly income.

Eventually Sherine would uncover misrepresentation after misrepresentation that Manafort and Gates made to banks in order to obtain millions of dollars in loans. On one application, Manafort failed to list millions of dollars of debt on a property he owned in Brooklyn. In another instance, Gates wrote up a fake profit and loss statement for Manafort's consulting firm and submitted it to the bank; the document showed $4.5 million in earnings for the year—a full ten times the real amount. Later, Manafort and Gates collaborated on another doctored P&L statement, not even bothering to use the same font as the original forms they were impersonating. Regardless, the ploy worked: Manafort secured another $16 million in loans. His dishonesty was mind-boggling.

We didn't know all the details of the bank fraud crimes at the time of our meeting in the conference room with Mueller. But Omer and I knew there was enough evidence already, and enough promising leads in the case that Sherine was building, that it would be a mistake to abandon it. Expecting Mueller would think we had enough leverage already on Manafort and Gates, we'd carefully charted out a game plan to make our case. Mueller's open-mindedness is one of his greatest attributes; he's willing to reassess his position if you can present a sensible counterargument. I had seen him change his views repeatedly, whether the argument came from a junior agent or the deputy director of the FBI. It was an attribute that made people like me fiercely loyal to the man; in spite of years of experience and fancy titles, he was neither arrogant nor imperious.

"Omer and I agree that we need to focus on the campaign time frame to look at direct evidence of links between Manafort and Russia," I began, and explained that the two of us were prepared to take on that project and turn 100 percent of our personal attention there. "That way you'll have the two lead members of Team M working on it. But I also think we should continue to pull together the evidence against Manafort and Gates on a series of bank frauds that Sherine's been investigating."

I told Mueller how the bank fraud charges fit into the overall picture of Manafort's criminality and explained the strategic advantage of the substantial new pressure those charges would place on Manafort and Gates. These are not minor FARA charges or tax crimes that might not carry lengthy prison sentences. This was classic bank fraud, committed while Manafort and Gates were on the campaign. I knew Mueller would be rightly concerned about pursuing an endless sideshow and explained that pulling the case together could be done efficiently. I laid out the broad strokes of what the remaining bank fraud investigation would entail and told Mueller we could quickly assemble one-pagers to summarize each of the five likely bank frauds, remembering from my time at the Bureau that this was Mueller's preferred means of assessing a potential case. (Mueller had no problem digging into the details of a proposal with you, but the way to tee up a matter for his review was to boil it down into a one-page summary of key points: the known facts, the proposed plan, and a clear time frame for each step.) I added that

Omer and I would prepare a full prosecution memorandum—a "pros memo" is a thorough accounting of the facts, the law, and anticipated defenses—in four to six weeks.

Mueller looked highly skeptical, but said he was willing to look at our one-pagers. Then he glanced around the room, asking if anyone disagreed or had any other questions. No one did.

As it turned out, the matter was resolved the following morning, far less bureaucratically. I walked over to the Keurig coffee machine located near Mueller's office, fixing what had become my usual: a pod of the strongest coffee and a quick splash of milk from the mini-fridge. Mueller's and my routines were becoming increasingly synchronized; frequently, we required a coffee break at exactly the same time—though, being that he got to the office a full hour before I did every morning, typically around seven-thirty, he was making his second cup while I made my first.

Before long, like clockwork, he appeared beside me, to claim the cup that was already waiting in the machine. I saw and smelled it to be his usual, as well: a pod of hazelnut decaf, to which he proceeded to add a generous glug of nonalcoholic Bailey's flavored creamer. I'd always wince just looking at the thing—a sickeningly sweet concoction, what a child might drink if you put a white shirt and necktie on him and stuck him in a government office. This time, I finally decided to say something to Mueller. I explained that, given his austere and increasingly mythic public persona, Americans would surely be disillusioned by his drink of choice: the Robert S. Mueller III people thought they knew would take his coffee black—no milk, no sugar, no affectations.

Mueller looked at me conspiratorially for a moment. "No one will ever know," he said.

We chatted a moment longer as I finished preparing my coffee. Walking back to his office, he turned to me and said, "You know that I'm going to be giving you a hard time on your bank fraud charges." I said that I understood and expected as much. "But," Mueller added, "you also know you're going to roll me."

That was Mueller-speak for "I've thought it over, and I now agree with your argument."

I thanked him, then went right away to tell Omer and Sherine. We wouldn't need to waste any time writing up one-pagers; we could go

right to preparing the pros memo for Mueller's approval. The boss was
on board.

I had Sherine and Greg Andres, a Team M senior attorney, stay on the
bank fraud charges while Omer and I kept our commitment to Mueller
and began probing Manafort's time on the Trump campaign.

Over the previous couple of months, we'd collected the emails from
all known accounts held by Manafort and Gates. (We'd obtained warrants to search the laptops and other devices seized from Manafort's
condo and from the young man who'd worked as his gopher, and procured court orders that required the email providers—companies such
as Google or Yahoo—to turn over other emails.) We had gone through
those emails rather quickly at first, looking for evidence on the tax and
FARA charges. This inevitably focused our attention mainly on a period
of time before the 2016 election. Now I wanted to go back and scour the
emails from roughly March 2016 to August 2016, the five-month period
during which Manafort served on the Trump campaign. Omer and I
split the emails in half and started reading—every single one.

This kind of page-by-page review used to be the norm for investigators but is not nearly as common now. The volume of digital material, in
our era of Big Data, often makes such fine needlework impossible. Typically, when confronted with terabytes of data, you develop search terms
and attempt, however imperfectly, to sift out any relevant documents.
Here, though, Omer and I were examining emails from a relatively limited time frame; it seemed feasible to pore through them the old-
fashioned way, and I knew from prior investigations that, while such
work is tedious, it can pay big dividends in the end.

One ancillary advantage of page-by-page review is that you wind up
developing a keen sense of the person you are investigating, glimpsing
different facets of his character from how he interacts with various
friends, subordinates, and bosses, and from how those people treat him
in kind. Gradually you become immersed in the person's way of life and
his way of seeing the world. For instance, we saw that Manafort was a
punctilious micromanager; in one telling message, he instructed Gates
to contact American Express to settle a dispute on his account for a credit
of only a few dollars. That would come in handy if Manafort claimed he

was unaware of the details of his finances that Gates was helping to co-ordinate on his behalf.

It took Omer and me the entire workweek and the following week-end to read all the emails. But late in the process, we came across one nugget of pure gold. It was a series of messages about a meeting that Manafort took with a former colleague on August 2, at the height of the presidential campaign. The Republican convention had taken place in mid-July, and the Democratic convention had just wrapped up only a few days earlier. The campaign was entering the final stretch. Still, on the evening of August 2, Manafort had stepped away for what, superfi-cially at least, appeared to be an appointment that was completely unre-lated to the election, with a man who had no role on the campaign. The two men had met for dinner at an exclusive cigar bar and restaurant in New York City called the Grand Havana Room, on the top floor of a building whose address, almost too perfectly, was 666 Fifth Avenue. (By odd coincidence, the building is owned by the Kushner family, and was in deep debt.)

The colleague Manafort met was the Russian named Konstantin Kilimnik. Kilimnik was essentially Manafort's Rick Gates in Ukraine—a deputy who had run his day-to-day operation there and enjoyed full ac-cess to President Yanukovych and his senior leaders. Kilimnik's emails displayed a witty, snarky cynicism, but were filled with misdirection, half-truths, and lies to advance his agenda. The FBI had advised us that it assessed Kilimnik to be associated with Russian intelligence.

This assessment was based on a variety of sources, which Omer re-viewed and confirmed and briefed Mueller on. One of the ways we gath-ered information was to ask agencies in the Intelligence Community to provide us relevant information in their holdings. Omer and I made trips to campuses in suburbs of Washington, D.C., and went page by page through their holdings pertinent to this part of our investigation. Many of us thought that our final report should include a classified sup-plement, so Congress and others with a security clearance could review the information that helped support our factual conclusions. Aaron overruled that; he wanted nothing that was not public or that compli-cated our conclusions. Omer was livid. The upshot was we got an oblique reference in just a single part of the report that noted there was additional classified information about Kilimnik.

Aspects of the Manafort-Kilimnik emails had been reported earlier in the summer of 2017 by *The Washington Post*. At the time, Team M had taken note of it as something worth digging into, but in retrospect it should have raised more urgent alarms; we'd been focused on wrapping up the Manafort and Gates indictment quickly.

But since then, we'd turned back to it, identified numerous email accounts used by Kilimnik, and obtained court orders for Kilimnik's emails from U.S. providers. Those documents, in turn, led us to an American living in the Washington, D.C., suburbs, Sam Patten, who'd opened up a lobbying shop with Kilimnik—so we, of course, scoured the earth for everything we could learn about that business and cut process for more email addresses and phone numbers that Kilimnik had used in connection with it.

In the resulting trove of documents we uncovered multiple criminal acts by Patten and Kilimnik; they had, for example, funneled money from a Ukrainian oligarch into Trump's inaugural committee, and then Patten lied to Congress about that and other matters. In the face of such evidence, Patten would flip, in the winter of 2018, and give us additional evidence about Kilimnik, his crimes, and the work he did in Ukraine in 2016 and 2017 for various politicians. (That evidence is not public, and I cannot talk about it here.)

We added all the new documentary evidence to our page-by-page review. The story Omer and I saw emerging raised alarms, even if the picture was still in soft focus—it did not answer all the questions we had. Emails revealed that the August 2 meeting had originated with a message from Kilimnik to Manafort at the end of July 2016. Kilimnik was writing from Moscow—he'd flown there from Kiev earlier that week—and told Manafort: "I met today with the guy who gave you your biggest black caviar jar several years ago. We spent 5 hours talking about his story, and I have several important messages from him to you."

Kilimnik insisted that he and Manafort meet in person, and they soon settled on a date. Kilimnik would fly to New York on August 2 and they would meet for dinner shortly after he landed. In a follow-up email, Kilimnik made sure Manafort cleared a good couple of hours for their meeting—because, as Kilimnik put it, "it is a long caviar story to tell." Other emails showed Kilimnik lying about the purpose of his trip to friends and colleagues he frequently communicated with, giving a fake excuse for traveling to the United States. We also painstakingly pieced together, from other emails and location data, that Gates had attended the dinner as well, arriving late. Kilimnik then returned to Russia.

Omer and I were excited—but in the dark as to what these messages meant. Why did Kilimnik insist on an in-person meeting? We knew he regularly communicated with Manafort by email, and they mentioned using encrypted apps as well. What were the "several important messages" that were so urgent and sensitive as to require Kilimnik's traveling from Moscow to New York, and then back again? And who was the mysterious giver of the large container of caviar?

We pulled together a quick one-page time line about the meeting and placed copies of all the key emails and other documents, including classified material, in a binder for Mueller and the other team leaders. Team R and Team 600 needed to know what we were seeing, so they could keep an eye out for additional evidence in their investigations. The emails we distributed were thrilling enough, all by themselves, to elicit another bout of Jeannie's trademark celebratory hollering: "Oh . . . My . . . God," she kept repeating. "Oh. My. God."

Even by that early stage of our investigation, in the summer of 2017, it had become clear to Jeannie and her investigators that the Trump team had had absolutely no compunctions about accepting aid from a foreign government during the campaign. Could that be what was happening here? Jeannie noted an unnerving coincidence: On August 2, Roger Stone, an adviser to the Trump campaign, was also cryptically emailing Manafort about a new strategy to engineer a Trump win, though Stone was smart enough not to transmit in writing the substance of the plan. Did this new approach have anything to do with whatever information Kilimnik brought to Manafort? In short, we were seeing the fact of these communications, and their suspicious circumstances, but we did not yet know their content.

We issued a slew of additional legal process for anything that might provide context around the Grand Havana Room meeting, requesting information from the club, Kilimnik's hotel, the airline he'd flown, the cellphones used. But unless someone had foolishly taken notes at the dinner—which was a fanciful prospect, given that Kilimnik insisted on an in-person meeting precisely to avoid any record of their communication—it was clear we'd ultimately need a witness: someone who'd been in the room, and could relay what the meeting was actually about. Gates was our best, and perhaps only, shot. It would be difficult to flip a Russian national like Kilimnik, who was now unlikely to set foot in the United States again, or even a country with an extradition treaty with the United States. But Gates was here; he was much younger than Manafort, with a wife and young children, and more of his life ahead of him.

Wrapping up Sherine's bank fraud investigation suddenly took on more importance: It was no longer strictly a tangent, as Mueller had feared, but central to advancing Team M's ultimate goals. Here we had a secretive meeting between a presumed Russian intelligence asset and Trump's campaign chairman. But to figure out what happened at it, we needed to flip Gates, which meant we needed a bigger hammer to hold over his head. And we soon got an unlikely lift in that regard.

My phone rang: It was Randy Toledo, a senior leader in the Office of International Affairs. She had been pushing through all of our MLATs assiduously. "Andrew, are you sitting down?" she said. "Cyprus has found responsive documents and they are sending them." I couldn't believe it; we had planned our strategy around this not happening, but this Cyprus evidence could be another blow to the defense.

Not long after this call, a couple of bankers boxes full of documents arrived in our office. They were gold: The names of Manafort, Gates, and Kilimnik were all over the foreign accounts in Cyprus. And there were other important documents: Mueller had been asking us if we'd found Manafort's instructions to the overseas account managers to pay bills from his U.S. vendors. We had not seen those in his U.S. emails, and suspected he had either deleted them or was using an account we just had not found yet. But the foreign account managers had kept a variety of Manafort's emails, showing that they had made these U.S. vendor payments at Manafort's direction. We turned all this new data over to Manafort's and Gates's counsel—more proof, more pressure.

The special counsel's investigation had started with the working hypothesis that, if there'd been a criminal conspiracy between the Trump campaign and Russia to alter the course of the 2016 election, Manafort would have likely known about it. If true, Team M's investigation of Manafort, and Team R's investigation of the Russian interference effort, would eventually meet like two parallel columns joined by a keystone in a gothic arch.

Jeannie and I had another way of imagining it—a sardonic inside joke between two art lovers. (The two of us had once played hooky during a lunch period to walk the marble halls of the National Gallery across the mall from our offices, remembering the beautiful world outside our hermetically sealed bubble.) We pictured the famous Michelangelo fresco of God giving life to Adam on the ceiling of the Sistine Chapel: Russia reaching its hand out toward the Trump campaign, which was reaching its own, smaller hand up to meet it.

With the Grand Havana Room meeting, we were potentially staring at a moment when those hands had eagerly stretched out toward each other. But a sliver of space between them was still occluded. We couldn't see if the two had touched.

■ CHAPTER 14

Flipping Gates

TEAM M SPENT THE final two months of 2017 pulling together the bank fraud case that Sherine had first sussed out and, by the time the new year started, we were preparing to indict Manafort and Gates a second time, on a slew of new bank fraud charges, in Virginia. Meanwhile, I had uncovered an important new line of evidence concerning the FARA charges, to augment our charges in Washington. All of this work would create another, more forceful opportunity for us to flip Gates and potentially learn from him the full story behind Manafort's meeting with Kilimnik at the Grand Havana Room in New York.

We were nearly ready to indict the two men when, one day in mid-January, Mueller stopped by my office with news. "I just got a call from Tom Green," he said. "He is representing Rick Gates now. You should give him a call."

This was unexpected. Gates had already switched attorneys once. His first defense counsel had surprised us on October 30, the day Gates was being arraigned on the Washington, D.C., charges, by announcing that he would no longer be representing Gates—not even during the proceeding that was about to start. (Gates was thus hastily represented that day by a federal defender, a lawyer who represents the indigent and is paid for from the public fisc.) We suspected that, as sometimes happens, the attorney was refraining from filing his formal appearance in the case until Gates paid him in advance; as a defense counsel I'd worked with early in my career used to put it, he was waiting for "Mr. Green to arrive."

Gates subsequently hired a new defense team: a trio of lawyers who, unconventionally, all worked at different firms. The lead attorney, Walter Mack, had been a federal prosecutor in New York a full generation before me—and I, at age fifty-nine, was already long in the tooth. Walter was shrewd and capable, though you had to put up with a lot of shtick before you got to the substance. He'd arrived to our last meeting, in early January 2018, wearing a wide necktie with a large yellow Pac-Man face printed at the bottom.

We'd called that particular meeting to conduct a reverse proffer—a "reverse," as we refer to it. Reverses are common, particularly in economic cases. They offer a look at the charges the government plans to bring: The prosecutor lays out the new proposed charges and the evidence supporting them, and the defense has an opportunity—either at the meeting, or after some limited time—to offer facts or arguments. We had done this precise thing in August 2017 before bringing the Washington charges against Manafort and Gates.

Some young prosecutors think these meetings are unwise, as a reverse essentially tips off the defense to the proof ahead of the formal discovery process. But in my mind, the potential benefits outweigh the costs. First and foremost, a reverse is a good opportunity to check our work. It's always possible that we shouldn't actually be bringing the new charges—that we've overlooked some legal precedent, pertinent fact, or discretionary argument that would change our decision. And even if the arguments the defense raises at the meeting aren't fatal to our case, hearing them at the outset gives us time to chart out how we'll overcome them at trial.

Most important, in a case like Gates's, cataloguing our evidence at a reverse proffer can convince the defense that fighting our charges will be hopeless—that their client's best option is to cut a deal and cooperate. And this is exactly what Team M did with Walter Mack at our reverse, inundating him and his colleagues with binders full of damning facts. Sherine and Morgan gave an especially masterful presentation, walking Walter and his team through the charges and responding swiftly and thoroughly to every question he asked. The overall evidence against

Gates was devastating, and I felt a surge of pride watching my team's command of the facts. "But there is more," Sherine kept saying, as she meticulously detailed the suite of new bank fraud charges. Morgan, meanwhile, dispensed facts and figures in support of our money-laundering charges with a kind of clinical precision—her dispassionate, objective recitation of the details making them feel all the more foreboding.

Walter had tried to keep a poker face, but the truth was apparent: Game over. On his way out that day, he confessed as much. "Thank you," he said. "That presentation was strong and helpful." This was a subtle concession, well understood by us as code for "You have the goods."

Now, shortly after the reverse, Mueller was informing me that a new defense attorney, Tom Green, had phoned, and that Gates had made another change and added Tom as counsel. We took this as a sign that the reverse proffer had had its intended effect and Gates was seriously considering flipping; there would be no reason for him to hire yet another lawyer otherwise, and especially a lawyer of this caliber.

Tom Green was an absolute lion of the criminal defense bar in Washington. I'd known him since my Enron Task Force days, when as prosecutors we routinely dealt with the cream of the white-collar bar. Everyone seemed to know Tom and respect him, and he was a good friend of Mueller's. (It was because of their friendship that Mueller had passed Tom's call directly to me, keen to avoid any appearance of impropriety in negotiating with him.) They were an amusing pair, Tom a chatty and rumpled counterpart to Mueller's starched solemnity.

Retaining Tom at this stage was an unusual move. Typically, the existing defense counsel would undertake plea negotiations. The only exceptions I'd seen were cases in which the defendant didn't completely trust his counsel—in organized crime cases, for example, when the would-be cooperating witness knew his attorney was beholden to the more powerful mobsters he'd be cooperating against. I'd watched it happen with Sammy the Bull Gravano in New York, when he'd decided to turn against his boss, John Gotti.

What made Tom Green's entrance into this case most unusual, however, was his stature and reputation. We had been seeing only a few defense counsel from top-tier law firms representing the main players, and we had a fairly good idea why. One prestigious defense attorney, a man who had represented leading Republicans and Democrats, CEOs and CFOs, as well as mobsters and fraudsters, explained to me: "My wife told me that if I wanted to take on as clients any of the people in your investigation, that's fine, but I should get a new wife." Similarly, we had watched as preeminent defense lawyers offered one excuse after another in declining to represent even the president himself—usually a plum gig to land.

I returned Tom's call promptly that day, and after some brief chitchat he asked to come in and speak with us. A few days later, Team M sat down with Tom and his two conscientious associates, for a redo of our reverse proffer. The meeting began with Tom fiddling with his two hearing aids—taking them out, fastidiously repositioning them, just so: "A casualty from shelling during Vietnam," he explained. (Military service was something else he and Mueller had in common.) We walked him through our case, just as we'd done with Walter Mack, and as soon as we'd finished, he told us, plainly: "I was hired to see what the best deal is that I could get for my client." That was Tom: forthright, efficient, a total straight shooter. He understood that his client faced a near certainty of conviction. It didn't take long for us to schedule our first meeting with Gates. Tom, it was clear, was prepared to work at Mueller's tempo.

The prospect of flipping Gates was a goal Team M had been driving toward since the earliest days of the investigation. It seemed the bank fraud charges had provided the necessary extra leverage. But there'd been another, new incentive as well—one for which Team M couldn't take full credit.

The new bank fraud charges legally could not be brought in Washington, D.C., as there was no venue. (The Constitution generally requires criminal charges to be brought only in places where the crime occurred, and none of the bank frauds had been perpetrated in Washington.) Similarly, we had charged only tax fraud conspiracy in Washington, and not substantive tax fraud charges, because although the conspiracy had in part occurred in Washington, none of the substantive tax filings had happened there.

But the bank fraud and the substantive tax charges could both be brought in Virginia. Recognizing this, as we readied our new charges, we had offered counsel for Manafort and Gates the option of "waiving venue," so that all of the charges could be brought together in the Washington. This was an unconventional tactic for us, as prosecutors, to take. It meant that everything would be folded into a single trial, instead of two separate ones—a matter of efficiency for us, but an arrangement that most defendants would consider greatly advantageous.

Gates had quickly taken us up on the offer to waive venue. But Manafort decided against it. It was—at the time, at least—a bewildering decision; he was essentially refusing our gift. As one news outlet put it, Manafort's choice to be charged in two different districts was like choosing to play Russian roulette with two bullets in the chamber instead of one. The sharp, no-nonsense Judge Amy Berman Jackson, who presided over the proceeding in Washington, even expressed surprise from the bench, telling Manafort: "I think the only thing I can imagine that's more unusual than the government offering you the choice is the choice you are making." And because Manafort had declined to waive venue, we would not grant that privilege to Gates alone. That would have meant preparing and presenting the bank fraud witnesses and documents twice—once in D.C. against Gates, and then in Virginia against Manafort—and giving the second defendant the advantage of seeing the case unveiled against the first. Manafort's decision meant Gates would be going to trial twice, too.

That is, Manafort's cryptic judgment was dragging down Gates as well. It was all abnormal: Defense teams usually present a unified front. But here, it seemed possible that the issue had driven a wedge between the two men—and that Manafort might have helped push Gates into our hands. In a way, it was luck. But I knew that, by working doggedly and methodically, we'd put ourselves in a position to leverage that luck.

The location of our office in Washington was well known by that point in the investigation, in large part because Manafort had made a point of slipping our address into his court filings—a spiteful little "fuck you" that ensured that, every day, junior CNN reporters would stake out our building at Patriots Plaza, watch the front door, and even stand by the entrance to our underground garage, recording the license plates of the cars that came and went. We were aware of this, of course, and even pitied these young men and women who'd been given an assignment one step up from tollbooth operator. Still, we worked hard to outfox them.

One of Tom Green's visits to our office had already been noted in the papers, however, and we knew publicity would not be our friend in convincing Gates—or anyone else—to cooperate with the investigation. And so, plotting our first meeting with Gates himself, we decided not to take any chances. We arranged to conduct it in a recently vacated FBI office downtown. The location was ideal: No one would be looking for us there, and there were few people, even at the FBI, who'd know we were in the building.

To reach the vacant office, you had to walk through a food court and movie theater on Seventh Street—familiar places that now took on a surreal and heightened feel for me as scenery in a clandestine mission. The FBI office itself was eerie, as though it had been abandoned. I made my way toward the conference room at the rear of the floor through a landscape of empty carrels, all devoid of computers, paper, and other signs of life.

Eventually, Gates and Tom arrived, escorted by a couple of our FBI agents. Gates was forty-five and relatively trim with a sturdy, leggy frame—still a youthful-looking man, in spite of his thinning hair. He looked like a Midwestern soccer dad, albeit the kind that might yell a little too loudly from the sidelines. He seemed uneasy—understandably so. I knew that Tom would have vouched for us, but also knew that Gates would inevitably approach us with suspicion, just as we were approaching him.

Cooperation is, fundamentally, an act of mutual faith. Each side must believe the other is being forthright and will stay true to its word. It's unrealistic to expect such trust to blossom in the room right away. Almost as a rule, defendants don't think highly of the people who are prosecuting them—and, in this case, we knew that Manafort had likely been priming Gates, playing on his natural antipathy toward us to dissuade him from flipping. Prosecutors, meanwhile, have spent weeks, months, or even years assembling a picture of the defendant as an untrustworthy criminal. As a result, it takes a certain psychological alchemy to transform that confrontational relationship into a cooperative one. Each side has to find its way into a kind of vulnerable working alignment. It happens haltingly and skeptically, if it happens at all.

The tone of the first meeting with a potential cooperator—the proffer session, we call it—is always, therefore, important to get right, on both sides. The defendant must decide right away whether he wants to cross the Rubicon. The first thing Gates would have to do is admit to his crimes, and both he and I would sign the standard proffer agreement at the start of the meeting that protected the defendant from our using these admissions at trial if the proffer sessions did not go well and no cooperation agreement was ultimately entered into.

That agreement had important limitations, however. The office would still be allowed to introduce his statements as evidence if, at trial, he later denied anything he'd admitted to us. In essence, the agreement meant that, from this moment forward, Gates would not be able to effectively deny his guilt. That is, he was required to take the first risk in our new relationship. We went into the meeting merely to evaluate whether he had credible evidence to offer us. He had to walk in already trusting us to evaluate that information fairly and cut him a square deal.

I was required to start the meeting by attending to some legal issues, such as spelling out the contours of our proffer agreement and asking Gates if he understood and agreed to each one. It had been adapted by the Special Counsel's Office from a standard agreement that I'd used in the Eastern District of New York many times. I'd advised so many witnesses of their rights and obligations under this agreement that the entire preamble I was now downloading to Gates was one I had committed to memory—even down to a hypothetical example I'd found helpful to use in illustrating one particular point.

Suppose, I would tell the defendant, he admitted during the proffer to stealing a library book. We normally could not use that admission directly against the defendant to prosecute him for stealing a library book. But, if the defendant said the book was in his house, we could use that information to get a search warrant and then look for the book in his house and use that book as evidence. And if, at the trial for the book theft, the defendant took the witness stand and denied stealing the book, he would "open the door" to our rebutting that false testimony with his direct admission to the theft at the proffer session, and everyone present today at the proffer session could potentially testify to that.

"As I said, Mr. Gates, that's a silly example," I explained, "but it serves to make concrete the important limits of the agreement. The worst thing to happen is for you later to be under some misimpression as to what protections you have and which you do not." I knew an experienced attorney like Tom Green would have gone over all of this with his client beforehand, but I liked having everything memorized; it meant that every witness I interviewed was given the same warnings, in exactly the same way, in case one later claimed he hadn't been properly informed.

Gates, for his part, consented to everything politely and succinctly, and asked no questions of his own. We each signed the proffer agreement; we gave one original back to Tom, and Omer kept the other. I took a moment to stress the importance of mutual trust in this process. We are trusting you to be candid, I told Gates, and I assured him that our office had every intention to act in good faith. I knew Tom had told him enough about Mueller and me that he understood that. "Even if we weren't honorable people and true to our word," I added, "this is a small town. If we went around mistreating or duping potential cooperating witnesses, it would be impossible to ever bring anyone in."

Gates said he understood and, from there, we began in earnest, alternating between Gates admitting his guilt for the crimes he and Manafort had committed and our teasing out information he had about others. This can be an awkward dance, but Gates seemed to be forthcoming. For example, after walking us through how, precisely, he'd helped Manafort launder money from his offshore accounts, Gates explained that he'd also personally stolen money from Ukraine by inflating the invoices he submitted for their political consulting work then pocketing that excess cash. Gates had never told Manafort about this skimming, he said, or reported that extra income on his taxes. We hadn't known about this—it was new information, and encouraging, since it signaled that Gates understood that he could not hide or minimize his own criminality anymore.

Omer and I had the same instincts when it came to interviewing potential cooperating witnesses, believing it was most productive to question them respectfully, even affably, rather than stand over them thundering questions and demands. Movies and TV shows tend to depict these meetings with an onslaught of raised voices, prosecutors and agents proceeding with hammer and tongs. Those who take such an approach justify it by saying they want to instill fear in a defendant, so he will cooperate and not lie. I am no social scientist, and perhaps that strategy works, but neither Omer nor I take that approach, or would be likely to pull off the role convincingly if we tried. To me, the most commanding presentations are the ones that let the facts, grueling homework, and candor do the work. Omer knew that type A side of me. "It's not fun working with you," he would tease me, "but you're worth it."

This approach to interviews was consistent with the way FBI agents are typically trained—building cases by building rapport—and it has served them well historically. It had been the FBI that had blown the whistle on waterboarding and other forms of harsh interrogation techniques being used by other agencies at Guantánamo Bay. Talking with Gates, Omer and I were an effective team, perfectly aligned in style and substance: good cop, good cop. It helped that the press had dubbed me "Mueller's pit bull," so witnesses and defendants assumed I was merely keeping a more ferocious side of myself at bay.

Having gathered some momentum with Gates, I switched gears, turning to the subject on which Omer and I had been fixated since the previous fall: "Rick, tell us about the Grand Havana Room meeting on August 2," Omer asked. We wanted to know what had compelled Konstantin Kilimnik to come all the way from Russia to meet Manafort in person, and what compelled Manafort to take the meeting at the height of the campaign.

We knew, from examining emails, that Gates had been at the dinner, though he'd arrived late. Gates didn't know we knew this, however, and we were careful not to reveal too much in our questions. We wanted to test whether his account would match up with the other evidence. It helps incentivize a witness to be completely candid if he believes you already know the answers to the questions you're asking.

"I learned of that meeting on the same day that it happened," Gates explained. "Paul asked if I could join him and 'KK,'" as Gates called Kilimnik. "The meeting was supposed to be over dinner, but I got there late."

I did not look over at Omer, but I knew he was thinking what I was, that it was good that Gates was being forthright so far and confirming what we knew.

"Do you know how long they had already been there?" I asked.

"I don't, but I think I was fairly late getting there. They were well into the meal."

"What do you recall being discussed?" Omer asked.

"A few things," Gates explained. One subject was money—certain oligarchs in Ukraine still owed Manafort a considerable amount. Another was a legal dispute between Manafort and the Russian oligarch Oleg Deripaska. We asked Gates if there was any new or unusual information raised about these issues, but he said no—those problems had been percolating for a while. This was not, it seemed, enough of a reason for Kilimnik to come to New York from Moscow.

"What else do you recall being discussed?" Omer asked.

"There was discussion about the campaign," Gates said. "Paul told KK about his strategy to go after white working-class Democrats in general, and he discussed four battleground states and polling."

"Did he name any states?" I asked.

"Michigan, Wisconsin, Pennsylvania, and Minnesota," Gates said.

"Did he specifically mention those states, and did he describe them as battleground states, or is that your description?" I asked.

"No," Gates said. "Paul described them that way. And, yes, I remember those four states coming up."

"And he described polling?" Omer asked.

"Yes, but I had been sending our internal polling data to KK all along," Gates explained. "So this was a follow-up on that, as opposed to something out of the blue."

"I'm sorry," I said, "but why were you sending polling data to Kilimnik?"

"Paul told me to send him the data, periodically. So I did. I'd send it using WhatsApp or some other encrypted platform. I assume it was to help Paul financially. I just did what Paul told me to do."

"KK didn't have any position on the campaign, right?" I asked.

"Right."

"And you sent the data repeatedly, not just once?"

"Right."

"Did you know in fact why Paul told you to send the data to Kilim-nik? You just told us you believed that it was to help Paul, but do you know that in fact?"

"No," Gates replied.

"Did Paul ever say anything to suggest that?" Omer followed up.

"No."

"What did you do after Paul left the campaign on August 19?"

"I continued to send the data out, but my access to it was diminished over time."

"Did you retain the communications to KK?" Omer wanted to know.

"No, I got rid of them as soon as I sent the data," Gates said. This explained why we could not see it.

"Do you know what KK did with the data?"

"No idea," Gates said, matter-of-factly.

I kept a poker face, but my mind was racing: *Jackpot,* I thought. We talked for a few more minutes before I suggested taking a break, then told my team to continue debriefing without me for a few minutes, so I could update Mueller right away.

It was breathtaking for a campaign manager to reveal internal poll-ing data to someone outside the campaign—much less to a Russian with apparent ties to the Kremlin. And Manafort had done it repeatedly.

There must have been some benefit to Manafort in doing this—he was the ultimate transactional player, just like his boss: the kind of per-son who did something only after determining what was in it for him-self. As this August meeting with Kilimnik was two months after the meeting that Don Jr. had organized with Manafort, Kushner, and the Russian attorney at Trump Tower, Manafort already understood that Russia was backing Trump over Clinton and trying to get him elected. And Manafort had been forwarded the email chain setting up the Trump Tower meeting, in which Russian operatives offered to provide dirt on Clinton as "part of Russia and its government's support for Mr. Trump."

It was possible that access to the campaign's polling data could help Russia refine and better target the online disinformation efforts that Jeannie was uncovering. Gates was claiming, after all, that Manafort also revealed specific tactical information to Kilimnik that was not oth-erwise available publicly: There was, for instance, no inkling in the

press, or obvious awareness in the political world, that Wisconsin and
Minnesota were battleground states. If Hillary Clinton had suspected
Trump had a path to victory in Wisconsin, she wouldn't have neglected
to campaign there.

Was it possible that Manafort was sharing that data solely for his
personal business interests, as a way to have Ukrainian oligarchs realize
they should pay their past debts to him and to have them and Deripaska
send him work, as he was now back in an influential position in the
United States? Manafort, after all, was not earning anything from the
Trump campaign and was going to need to monetize his experience.

But if Manafort were sharing the polling data solely as a way to generate money, why would he be sending the polling data so often, particularly since the data was not all positive or trending in a positive direction?
More to the point, it seemed unlikely that Manafort was so naïve that he
did not recognize how the data could be used. Omer and I theorized that
Manafort had been acting out of both motivations: to both benefit his
own pocketbook and aid the presidential campaign he was managing.
In the end, the two goals were symbiotic.

The question of whether Manafort was reporting to others on the
campaign about the August 2 meeting with Kilimnik was more complicated. If Manafort represented a Russian link into the campaign, the
clearest window of opportunity for him to discuss the August 2 meeting
with other campaign officials would have been narrow. His meeting
with Kilimnik was on August 2, but Manafort left the campaign on August 19, and had been publicly circling the drain for at least a week or so
prior to that. He could have shared his Kilimnik meeting with others on
the campaign after he resigned, of course, but his access was greatly diminished. It was also possible that Manafort had felt no need to inform
less sophisticated people on the campaign, particularly since they might
be skeptical of his intentions, understanding there was likely a personal
financial motive for his dealings with Kilimnik as well.

A similar conundrum applied to whether Manafort told anyone
about sharing polling data, except the time frame was longer—but if
Manafort were sending it solely for his own personal financial benefit,
there would be no reason to publicize his outlandish conduct of sending
internal campaign information to overseas actors.

In short, there were still a host of unanswered questions, but this insight into the Grand Havana Room meeting, and the sharing of polling data, was shocking, and a payoff we never would have reached without conscripting Gates as a cooperating witness. As Gates himself explained, aside from this in-person conversation, the polling data was routinely sent to Kilimnik via encrypted means we would not have been able to access. Gates's testimony wasn't enough to prove a criminal conspiracy beyond a reasonable doubt—not between Russia and Manafort, or anyone else on the campaign—but what he described was plainly outlandish and appeared to bring us closer to uncovering whether any such coordination had occurred.

As I stepped out of the proffer to relay this development to Mueller—"Interesting," was all he said—my mind was already jumping forward to the next unanswered questions. Could we corroborate what Gates was telling us? And would we ever be able to peer inside the Russians' active measures with enough clarity to see where they'd made use of that polling data Manafort was feeding them—if they'd leveraged it to reach voters in those four states with microtargeted Facebook ads, for example?

Still, even as Gates produced this enticing new piece of evidence, he seemed sincerely unable to answer the central question we had going into the proffer: Why had Kilimnik flown halfway around the globe to meet with Manafort? What message was he delivering—what "caviar story" did he have to tell—that was so sensitive and important?

But before we got to that, our proffer session with Gates was about to hit an unsettling bump.

Not long after I reentered the room, our interview with Gates turned to the FARA charges. Gates explained, in a convoluted fashion, that he and Manafort had believed there was no need to register under FARA since they were not personally doing any of the lobbying themselves. Manafort understood now that the law required him to file, Gates said, but he hadn't understood that at the time.

Nothing about this argument was credible. Manafort was not only a longtime lobbyist but an attorney himself; he had extensive experience navigating the FARA rules and had gotten entangled with the FARA Unit before. (In the eighties, Manafort had a presidential appointment in the Reagan administration, which normally would have prohibited him from also working as a lobbyist, but he'd requested a waiver from that facet of the FARA rules. Interestingly, when his request was denied by a responsible White House attorney, Manafort resigned from his public office in order to continue the more profitable private lobbying work.) We had even uncovered an email from Gates to Manafort that clearly set out the FARA regulations. It was inconceivable that they'd misunderstood the law. Even the factual premise of their purported misunderstanding was untrue: Manafort had personally acted as a lobbyist. We had emails showing that Gates had arranged a meeting for Manafort with the pro-Russia California congressman Dana Rohrabacher in March 2013, shortly after Rohrabacher became chair of the subcommittee that oversaw Ukraine issues.

It was clear that Gates was not being straight with us—not uncommon, initially, with people who try to cooperate; they tell the truth with various degrees of success at first. When we confronted Gates with the emails about the Rohrabacher meeting, Gates simply doubled down, floating an even more absurd claim. He acknowledged that, yes, Manafort and Rohrabacher had met in Washington in 2013, but Gates claimed that he remembered Manafort telling him at the time that the subject of Ukraine had never come up—and therefore, there'd been no reason for Manafort to register under FARA for this activity: It wasn't actually lobbying.

This wasn't true, either, and we had evidence to prove it. Gates and Manafort had prepared a memo after the Rohrabacher meeting for President Yanukovych of Ukraine, summarizing the discussion. That memo was one of the many damning documents we'd discovered from Manafort's condo search. We showed it to Gates: Was everything written here a lie? we asked. He had no response.

Gates's story was crumbling before our eyes. It was infuriating because it was so counterproductive for everyone, and, on a personal level, displayed a certain contempt for us, and a low opinion of our ability to discern the truth. The good faith we needed, on both sides, was evaporating.

I asked Tom Green, Gates's counsel, to speak in private, and then decided with him that we should break for the day. I asked Tom to get to the bottom of whatever was happening. All along, Gates had seemed to have trouble when it came to discussing Manafort and his crimes. He was clearly straining to shed his allegiance to his old boss. Still, Gates was discussing his own crimes, and it wasn't clear why he'd chosen to start lying, so stubbornly, now, about this particular point; the FARA charges weren't even among the most serious ones we brought.

If there was some explanation, Tom would need to figure it out quickly. The lies we'd just been told were deflating for us, given how hopeful we'd been about Gates's usefulness as a witness.

Right now, we told Tom, there was no way we could sign Gates up.

Tom came back to our office the next day. "Look," he said, "my client messed up."

Gates was scared, he explained. This entire process was wrenching for him. Gates felt pulled between his desire to cooperate and his allegiance to Manafort, and his client had just momentarily broken down. He'd fed us the various cover stories yesterday to avoid implicating Paul on the FARA charges.

I'd suspected as much. In fact, it hadn't taken me long after the meeting to come up with a theory about why the proffer had taken that particular turn on the FARA charges. Contrary to popular belief, the most common hazard I'd come across with cooperating witnesses is not that the witness will lie and falsely accuse someone of a crime (which is your worst nightmare as a prosecutor), but that the witness will lie to protect someone. And in this case, Gates was protecting Manafort from the FARA case because he knew that those charges would be uniquely destructive to Manafort financially. We'd frozen an estimated $30 to $40 million of Manafort's assets when he was arrested. But our ability to seize those assets hinged largely on a guilty verdict for the money-laundering charge, which was predicated on the FARA charges specifically. (It was Mueller who had figured out, based on his perusing the minutiae of the law, that a money-laundering charge could be based on an underlying FARA violation.) If the FARA charges didn't hold up, Manafort would keep his money. This was one way to explain Gates's behavior: He was still loyal to the man who had given him his start and he knew this charge was the one that would crush Manafort financially. As a defense lawyer, I'd once represented a phenomenally wealthy client who proposed, while I was negotiating a plea deal for him with the government, that he serve an extra year in prison in exchange for keeping more of his assets. It was an unimaginable trade-off to me: Give up your freedom to buy back some of your money? Since then, I've never been surprised by the moral and criminal contortions that people will put themselves through to satisfy their greed.

Tom assured us that Gates would explain all of this himself the following morning. "He's coming along," Tom said, "and he will get there—with your help." But Tom also wanted to know if his client had irrevocably spoiled whatever deal we'd been prepared to offer. I said I'd have to get back to him.

Mueller had previously signed off on a proposed deal for Gates, assuming he dealt with us with integrity. Rather than facing guidelines calling for more than ten years in prison, we would allow him to plead to a criminal charge that carried a maximum statutory sentence of only five. That may sound like a big break, but in reality, that statutory maximum was largely irrelevant. Here, the real benefit would be that the judge would be able to consider Gates's cooperation, not just his crimes, at sentencing. Defendants like Gates who successfully cooperate can be reasonably assured they are not going to serve anything close to a statutory maximum of five years. Under such circumstances, those maximums wind up merely capping a worst-case scenario for a good cooperator. The real advantage in the cooperation agreement was the prospect that the judge might give Gates a significant break on his sentence and would not simply follow the federal guidelines.

We still wanted Gates as a cooperator if he would stay on the straight and narrow, but we'd need to proceed cautiously now, demonstrating both to him and, eventually, to a jury that we took his lying seriously.

I consulted with Omer, then together we asked Mueller to sign off on a new approach. Assuming Gates did not mislead us again, we'd still allow him to cooperate, but require him to plead to an additional 1001 crime first. (This alludes to the section of the criminal code that covers lying to a federal officer like Omer.) And we'd make sure Gates understood that there wouldn't be a next time: Lie again, and we'd throw the book at him—no cooperation, no favorable sentencing recommendation. Mueller loved this arrangement, feeling it stuck the right balance.

Gates returned the following day with Tom and promptly confessed what he'd done. He wasn't happy to learn he'd have to plead to the 1001 charge, which would up his statutory maximum to ten years, but accepted it and appeared genuinely contrite—even a little frightened.

We decided to keep the meeting brief and told Tom we'd send him drafts of all the necessary agreements to proceed. It felt like a fresh start. Our investigation now had its first real cooperating witness.

Little did we know, however, that the Gates cooperation saga was not over. The next two weeks would be the most baffling and unusual of my career.

It took a few days to finalize Gates's paperwork, as we negotiated various details with Tom. He was a great defense lawyer: thorough, smart, and reasonable, and he made some excellent points as we sent the documents back and forth, ultimately achieving more for his client than attorneys who are more bombastic and confrontational.

But before we received the final versions back, with signatures, the process was disrupted yet again. Gates's second defense counsel, Walter Mack, called our office unexpectedly and asked what the heck was going on: Was it true that his client was cooperating with the special counsel's investigation?

It's hard to convey the strangeness of Walter's phone call: not only that he didn't seem to know that Gates was seeking to cooperate, but that he was calling us for answers, instead of asking his own client, or his co-counsel Tom Green. We told Walter that he should direct those questions to Gates or Tom. It was not our place to be an intermediary between defendants and their various attorneys, or to mediate whatever spat Walter had just brought to our doorstep.

I'm still not sure what was going on behind the scenes. Later, Walter would claim a lack of payment from Gates—maybe that had something to do with it. But it was also hard to ignore that Walter happened to be simultaneously representing a man named Steven Brown in a separate case in New York. Brown had enlisted Gates in a fraudulent scheme and therefore could be harmed by information Gates might share if he cooperated.

Regardless, whatever dispute was playing out might have remained irrelevant to our case—except that Walter's subsequent discussions with Tom apparently unraveled to the point that Walter filed a motion asking to be relieved as Gates's counsel; this required all of us to appear briefly in court. The short proceeding had very little to do with our office and was under seal at the time, but our mere appearance at the courthouse roused interest from the reporters staking out the building. At the proceeding, the court told Tom to brief Walter on the cooperation progress. Shortly thereafter, someone leaked a story about Gates and his intention to cooperate to the *Los Angeles Times*.

This media attention was unsettling for Gates—as whoever leaked the story presumably knew it would be. It is hard enough to betray your former mentor, and walk away from your former life, by talking to government investigators. It is more daunting once you've seen your decision to cooperate spelled out in a national headline and are forced to discuss it with every friend and family member who calls to ask you if it's true. Such press also sends out an alarm to those who'd seek to pull Gates back in line and away from the government.

As we feared, once the story ran, Gates got cold feet. Tom and I spoke nearly every day for the next two weeks. He explained that he was still working to convince his client to cooperate, and I expressed bafflement. I'd never seen anything like this before. Gates had passed the point of no return; because he'd already signed the proffer agreement and admitted his criminal liability to all of the charged crimes (and then some), he would be going to trial with effectively no defense if he backed out now. Tom assured me that Gates understood this—but he also said that Gates had lots of people loyal to the White House whispering in his ear.

Eventually, I set a deadline—then caved and extended the deadline a little, as more calls and entreaties from Tom ensued. For every call with Tom, there was also a call with Mueller, pressing me for an update.

On the last deadline date, Tom phoned one last time, defeated: Gates had decided not to cooperate. Tom knew his client was making the wrong decision, but he had run out of ways to convince him. At that point, we had no choice. I told Tom we would go ahead with our second indictment in Virginia and the superseding indictment in Washington, as planned. Gates would be saddled with all the new charges, alongside his old boss.

.   .   .

Less than a week later, in February 2018, two members of Team M were with the grand jury in Virginia, presenting the proof for our bank fraud and tax indictment of Gates as well as Manafort. I had stayed behind in Washington dealing with the new Washington charges and was sitting in my office when the phone rang. It was Tom Green, reporting that Gates had had another change of heart; he'd decided he wanted to cooperate after all.

This time it seemed real. "He's coming to my office to sign the papers right now," Tom said.

I was relieved, but still skeptical. I told Tom I'd need to see him and Gates in our office again, to hear Gates explain what the hell had just happened. I also alerted him that we were, at that moment, pushing forward with our indictment in Virginia and, because the courthouse there didn't allow phones or electronic devices, there was no way for me to call the prosecutors and stop it. Still, I assured Tom, this wouldn't affect our deal: If Gates proved trustworthy, we'd move to dismiss this second set of charges in Virginia without prejudice and proceed in Washington as planned.

Gates came back into our office the next day. I leveled with him: "I've never had this experience before, and I need to understand what happened," I said. "Why did you balk at the last minute? What's going on?"

He seemed more vulnerable this time. He explained the intense pressure that Manafort and others were putting on him not to cooperate, how Manafort had told him that money could be raised to defray their legal expenses, and that the White House had their backs—code, Gates knew, to keep quiet and hold out for a pardon.

But, Gates went on, he'd also spoken to Charlie Black. Black had been in business with Manafort years ago, at the firm Black, Manafort, Stone and Kelly, then gone on to become a dean of Republican Party strategists and enjoyed a sterling reputation. (In a masterstroke, it turned out, at a moment when Tom was almost out of ideas, he had recruited Black to reach out to Gates and offer advice.) Black told Gates that, were he in a similar predicament, he would cooperate. Gates wasn't an old man like Black and Manafort, Black explained; he needed to think about himself and his young family. And moreover, Black insisted, Gates would be foolish to count on a pardon. Trump was too self-absorbed to be dependable.

"I took this all in," Gates said, "and I decided to follow Black's advice." Black's encouragement seemed to have finally empowered Gates to turn on his old boss. "I know there's a possibility that Paul will get a pardon in the end, and I'll have to watch him walk free. But I decided I just have to deal with what I've done, and own what I have done." He'd broken the law, he said. He needed to deal with the consequences now and do right by his family.

Months earlier, I'd spent days reading Gates's emails, and found them to reveal a fair amount of macho bluster. But now, as he explained the doubts and tribulations he'd worked through in the preceding weeks, I saw none of that. It had all drained away, revealing a reflective capacity that had previously been nowhere in sight. He projected a kind of vulnerability that was heartrending. I've flipped dozens of witnesses in my career, many of them mobsters, murderers, and inveterate fraudsters who had shattered innumerable lives—that is, far less sympathetic figures than Rick Gates. At times, the process has what I can only describe as an almost spiritual dimension to it. The drama turns on moments of confession, forgiveness, and mercy, and involves a fair amount of shame.

All of us tell ourselves lies every day, as Eugene O'Neill famously observed. It's natural to compartmentalize our bad behavior, to look away from the worst parts of ourselves in order to get through the day. But a cooperating witness must give up that privilege. He must admit his wrongdoings, in full—first to his lawyer, then to a bunch of government prosecutors, then, finally, in open court. Along the way he has to reveal the full extent of what he has done to his friends and family, too. Worst of all, he must admit it to himself, which often means acknowledging the darker motivations that led him to such behavior in the first place. He must strip away whatever justifications he's lived with—whatever lies he tells himself—in order to confront a shameful truth: He's a criminal.

Gates was a political creature—a lobbyist who, like Manafort, made his living by spinning facts. He was good at it, too. But the job before him now was precisely the opposite: to face reality unvarnished and head-on. It was a painful shift to make, and in Gates's case, a lot of people in his prior orbit seemed to be conspiring to turn him away from that hard work and back toward perpetuating a lie. That same day, when

Gates came in and explained the forces that had been tearing him apart, someone in Manafort's camp leaked a fabricated story to the press claiming that Gates had fired Tom Green and was refusing to cooperate—presumably to give Gates permission, in public, to do just that.

I knew I'd just witnessed a modern-day medieval morality play unfold, with the devil and an angel vying for the soul of the protagonist. For the past two weeks, Tom and his allies had sat on one of Gates's shoulders, and Manafort and his camp sat on the other, flaunting money and the prospect of a presidential pardon. This isn't the way it should happen; a defendant facing a tough case who decides to do the right thing and cooperate with a government investigation shouldn't be dissuaded from doing so by the possibility that the target of that investigation might, instead, simply pardon him. None of us in the Special Counsel's Office had expected to encounter such interference when it came to the high-ranking staff of a sitting president's campaign.

This experience with Gates was the first time we encountered the effect of the president's power to brandish his power to pardon corruptly. His apparent willingness to do so had begun upsetting the normal machinery of the justice system, just as the president's power to fire the special counsel had started to seep into our office, influencing our own decisions and subverting our pursuit of the truth.

This time, we'd managed to fight that power off—but just barely. We arranged for Gates to plead guilty before Judge Jackson in Washington the following day. There'd be no going back.

It wasn't until a few months later that we got more insight into just how much we'd been up against while attempting to flip Gates.

At the same time the Manafort allies were working Gates over, dangling the prospect of money and a White House pardon, they were also fomenting a press strategy to undermine our office's work, and Team M's case against him in particular. In the spring of 2018, we discovered a new Manafort account he was using after his indictment in October 2017. As we had done countless times before, we obtained a court order from Chief Judge Howell, served it on the carrier, and soon unexpectedly had in our hands hundreds of texts between Manafort and the Fox News host Sean Hannity.

In one text exchange, during the weeks in which we were working to flip Gates, Manafort assured Hannity that Gates would stay strong and never cooperate. In others, he supplied Hannity with a cache of right-wing conspiracy-laden ammunition with which to attack Mueller, me, and the Special Counsel's Office as a whole—some of it, Manafort claimed, had been passed on from sources within the Justice Department. Manafort, who was under house arrest at the time, assured Hannity that Manafort's counsel would be in touch with him. Hannity worked this information into the tirades against us that he performed almost nightly on the air.

At the time, remember, Manafort was under indictment for the same charges as Gates; both were out on bail with strict pretrial conditions. Communicating with Hannity about the case was a violation of the gag order Judge Jackson had put in place on both sides so as not to taint the jury. But Manafort was undeterred by such legal niceties as a court order; he was doing what he did best: surreptitiously cooking up a smear campaign, then using Hannity to disseminate it, thereby contaminating the political discourse.

A Team M analyst correlated the texts to the Hannity Fox News programs that then aired in support of Manafort. The texts revealed a media plan that was just like the work he'd done in Ukraine, targeting President Yanukovych's enemies. Now, however, Manafort was working on his own behalf, launching an assault on a government investigation poised to undo him.

I had wanted to submit the Hannity texts to the court as they revealed a continued flagrant violation of the court's order, and it was something I believed the judge needed to know as it could well change her view on whether Manafort should remain on bail, or at least whether the conditions of his bail should be tightened up. When I told Aaron this, he had his usual reaction: No one could see these texts. "They are too explosive," he said. He did not want the inevitable shit storm that would result on Fox and other media outlets, but that was no excuse for not alerting the court to the violation of her order. (I made clear that the court would have to see them at least in connection with sentencing Manafort as it was our obligation not to hide this from the court, which is how these ended up seeing the light of day.) Soon this latest Grant-McClellan standoff would be largely moot when we discovered

Manafort's breach of his bail conditions in a manner that made the gag order violation pale in comparison.

One afternoon, in the midst of this back-and-forth with Aaron, Omer brought a huge sheaf of these texts into my office and flagged one particular exchange that had caught his keen investigative eye. Omer knew how hard it was to lie effectively—to place yourself in the position of what an innocent person would do and say, if you were not innocent.

In this conversation, Manafort was assuring Hannity that, even if Gates flipped, Manafort himself was not a threat to cooperate with our investigation. "They would want me to give up DT or family, esp JK," Manafort wrote, referring to Donald Trump and Jared Kushner. "I would never do that."

But Hannity, catching the same slipup that Omer did, felt obliged to correct Manafort: "There is nothing to give up on DT," he texted back.

Omer pointed to it on the printout. "Interesting wording," he said. "That's why Manafort is the next person we need to flip."

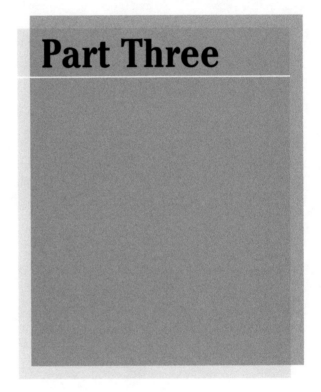

Part Three

CHAPTER 15

The Russian Hack and Dump

ONE NIGHT IN JUNE 1972, shortly after midnight, a young security guard who'd just started his shift at the Watergate office building in Washington noticed a piece of tape over the lock of a door in the basement. The guard ripped the tape off. When, a short while later, he discovered a new piece of tape over the same lock, he phoned the police.

As we all know, as a result of that one security guard, five intruders were caught in the act of burglarizing the offices of the Democratic National Committee at the Watergate, attempting to steal the Democrats' playbook for the upcoming presidential campaign. The break-in had been orchestrated by the Committee to Re-elect the President of the United States, Richard Nixon, an organization that went by an acronym Freud would have appreciated: CREEP.

In time, the scandal that sprung from that burglary would lead to the indictment of dozens of government officials and their conspirators, including Nixon's campaign manager, and expose Nixon's strong-arming maneuvers to obstruct the Justice Department and congressional investigations into the break-in and insulate himself from the rule of law. For this abuse of power as president, Nixon resigned rather than face sure impeachment and removal. On the day he resigned, the Watergate security guard who'd first noticed a sign of the intrusion, Frank Wills, told a reporter: "We treat the president like a king, when he should be a man for all the people."

Forty-four years later, at the height of the 2016 presidential campaign, our democratic process was undermined by another break-in and theft of Democratic National Committee plans. This was not a brick-and-mortar burglary, however. It was a crime possible only in the twenty-first century, in which such thefts—of political plans and even national security secrets—can happen in secret with a stroke of a computer key thousands of miles away, and gigabytes of that stolen material can then be tactically disseminated over the Internet with ease. Knowledge of this DNC hacking had become public during the 2016 campaign. The DNC first announced it in mid-June and reported that its cyber experts attributed the hack to Russian actors, working at the behest of their government. But the scope and specifics of those crimes had not been pinned down.

Jeannie and her cyber experts spent the first half of 2018 getting to the bottom of this attack, and their work would illuminate this second disruptive Russian assault on our 2016 election. Their investigation would show that it was far more pernicious than an isolated break-in to the DNC's server, and that it had been perpetrated from afar, by hackers outside the reach of the American criminal justice system.

Team R's investigation wasn't easy. The job of detecting and solving such virtual crimes is exponentially more complicated than noticing a piece of tape on a door; often, those who've had their documents stolen aren't even aware they've been the victims of a crime. The story of precisely how Team R mounted its investigation into the DNC hacking, therefore, hinges on a new kind of detective work: Rather than conducting physical searches of buildings, putting cuffs on people, and persuading them to cooperate, a team of cyber investigators appear to be largely sitting on their behinds at their desks, chasing down clues through dark, virtual alleyways—sweeping meticulously through the same netherworld in which the perpetrators operate.

It would undermine the integrity of our elections to publicly discuss the specifics of Team R's investigative methods; the more we let the bad guys know how, exactly, we track them down, the easier it will be for them to evade detection next time. But I can say that it was impressive to watch Team R—with the able assistance of attorneys from the Justice

Department's National Security Division—wield new technological tools with the same creativity and tenacity they brought to more traditional FBI detective work.

The fruits of their investigation were deeply alarming. Just as Team R was able to pierce the active measures operation of the IRA in St. Petersburg, they now revealed, with microscopic granularity, how a separate unit of the Russian government had pulled off a cyber break-in that made the Watergate burglary look like a child's game. This unit, a component of the Russian military, is known colloquially as the GRU (for the Russian Main Intelligence Directorate). In the run-up to the 2016 American election, the GRU had two Moscow-based units—more appropriately described as battalions—assigned to hacking into foreign computers and then publicly revealing the most damaging information they obtained. This style of two-phase attack—stealing documents, then strategically disseminating them—is known as a "hack and dump." The United States was not the only target of its operations. The GRU sought to destabilize other Western democracies, too; another of its projects supported the Brexit campaign.

The scheme began simply enough in 2015 and early 2016, with the Russian military identifying various Democratic websites to target and casting out hundreds of emails to known affiliated individuals. The emails were sent to scores of employees, advisers, and volunteers at the DNC, DCCC, and the Clinton campaign, purporting to be from a trusted source. (These emails might be disguised, for example, as a standard Google security alert.) But in fact, these emails were like hooks on a fishing line—a tactic known as "spear phishing" that is used by criminals around the world. The recipient of the email is enticed to click on a link, and that click is all the bad guy needs. That click is the digital equivalent of unlocking your front door.

Team R could use the end result to work backward, tracing the route the hack and dump had taken. By using the "dumped" documents as jumping-off points, they could figure out the identity of the computer servers from which these dumped documents had been taken. Then, looking at these servers, Team R was able to see that numerous DNC and Clinton campaign personnel, including Clinton's campaign manager, John Podesta, had clicked on disguised Russian links. This had enabled the GRU to plant malware—malicious software—on those recipients' computers. This, in turn, enabled the Russians to take a host of surreptitious actions.

The Russians could watch the activity on the computers, undetected. The GRU could see every keystroke that user made, take screenshots of what was on his or her screen, and, importantly, could hoover up vast quantities of emails and digital documents. The malware also allowed them to hop from one account on the network to others—and from one network to another. Because the DNC and DCCC computer networks were linked, once the GRU obtained the credentials for a DNC employee, it could use that ID and password to cross the electronic bridge into the DCCC network and penetrate the accounts of employees there, as well. Even after the DNC realized it had been hacked and swept its networks to rid itself of the malware, the Russians managed to keep one of their exfiltration tools on the DNC network undetected—they are simply that good.

The Russian military malware system connected the infected computers to its own GRU-controlled servers located in the United States. Through this electronic tunnel, the GRU could abscond with copies of anything it found on DNC and DCCC computers. The Russian military obtained internal emails between DNC workers, financial and fundraising records, strategy plans, opposition research, and more. All of this was done furtively, scarcely leaving any electronic trace; the GRU covered its tracks by setting up dummy accounts to make it look as though the original spear-phishing emails had come from actual American email addresses, and by creating other, fake intermediary accounts all over the world to mask the origin of the operation.

Team R was also able to piece together how that stolen material was weaponized—the equally well-coordinated "dumping" phase of the attack. The GRU had set up two fake online entities to publish the stolen documents, so that the material would appear to be coming from independent operators. The GRU called these fronts DCLeaks and Guccifer 2.0—though Jeannie, being the office's lone fashionista, would call the latter "Gucci" for short.

The first dump of stolen DNC materials had come in June 2016 when thousands of pages of personal and sensitive material was posted on DCLeaks.com. The GRU had anonymized the identity of the website's registrant, to mask its Russian roots, using a service that is currently still legal, and paid for the site's hosting with Bitcoin to make it difficult to trace the origin of the money. When the DNC's cyber experts managed to attribute the hack of those documents to the Russians, the GRU sprung into action, now using their second persona—Guccifer 2.0—to throw everyone off the trail.

The following day, Guccifer 2.0 publicly took credit for the hack, claiming it hadn't been perpetrated by the Russians, but by Guccifer 2.0, who claimed to be a Romanian hacker, acting alone. And the DCLeaks site—a separate-seeming outfit, though actually just another alias controlled by the same units of the GRU—began disseminating more stolen DNC and DCCC material. DCLeaks and Guccifer published some of it on their own blogs but also privately approached news outlets and passed the information to reporters for publication. This slow drip of damaging stolen material would continue until Election Day, five months later.

The Russians also worked with a true third party—one it hadn't invented—to coordinate its dumps. The founder of WikiLeaks, Julian Assange, had long been vehemently opposed to Clinton's candidacy and committed to derailing it; WikiLeaks was already in the process of amassing a database of Clinton emails via public records requests, as a resource for those looking to dig up dirt on the candidate. During the campaign, the GRU approached WikiLeaks, through its aliases, about a partnership, and soon began feeding the organization material it had extracted from the DNC computer networks through Guccifer 2.0.

On July 22, WikiLeaks released a cache of twenty thousand emails and other stolen documents. The documents exposed a bias among DNC officials in favor of Clinton and against her opponent in the primaries, Bernie Sanders. They also served to amplify the divide within the Democratic Party, with the aim of suppressing the Clinton vote. (As Mueller later warned in his congressional testimony, this interference has continued unabated, and is manifest in the 2020 election, given Trump's refusal to seek to prevent election interference). WikiLeaks released these documents three days before the Democratic convention, precisely when political parties try to unify in advance of the national election—a move clearly designed to diminish the kind of laudatory focus political parties are usually afforded by the media at that time.

One of the most explosive, and the most shrewdly timed, document dumps came on October 7. That was the day that the infamous *Access*

Hollywood tape hit the airwaves—the recording of Donald Trump bragging about committing sexual assault. Within an hour of the recording becoming public, WikiLeaks released thousands of pages of John Podesta's internal emails, which it had obtained from the Russians. Among the Podesta emails was correspondence about private speeches that Clinton had given but refused to discuss publicly; material on the Clinton Foundation; and material that painted an unflattering portrait of Hillary Clinton. Clearly, this dump was timed to draw the focus away from the *Access Hollywood* tape—and WikiLeaks kept doing it, thirty-three more times, providing a constant feed of unfavorable Clinton news throughout October in the run-up to the election.

The Russian attack did not stop here. Team R determined that Russian hackers had also targeted numerous federal and state election officials across the United States, including state boards of elections, secretaries of state, and county governments. The goal wasn't to manipulate the electorate, but to compromise the administration of the election itself. Specifically, among the GRU's targets were private firms that provide the software and hardware used by state and local governments to conduct voter registration, manage voter rolls, and run electronic polling stations.

These attacks were distressingly widespread. Often, they consisted of bombarding particular entities with spear-phishing emails or probing their computer networks for vulnerabilities. (A separate FBI investigation discovered that the Russians had sent spear-phishing emails to more than 120 email accounts used by county election officials in Florida. And in Illinois, the GRU successfully hacked into a State Board of Elections voter database and extracted information on thousands of voters before the break-in was detected.)

Whenever Jeannie and her investigators came across such evidence, they alerted our law enforcement counterparts, so they could follow up. For instance, at the time of our investigation it was plain that no one had actually examined the entirety of state election computer tabulation systems—the electronic systems used in various states for recording individual votes, and the computer systems that amass such data—which is necessary to determine if there was an attempted or successful hacking.

This would be described for the public in our report, when the scope of the Russian assault was laid bare. We make plain how much more there is to investigate by law enforcement, beyond what we were able to look at ourselves. We relayed this with an appropriately ominous note of alarm, given the stakes going forward. It was apparent to Jeannie, however, that there was simply not the will nor the leadership at the Department of Justice or elsewhere in our government to take this threat on. I agreed with her—and nothing we have seen since gives even the slightest hint that there is any interest from the White House in ferreting this out to prevent election interference again. The administration views the issue solely through a political lens: So long as the foreign interference will help the side in power, why on earth would one complain about it?

As with Team R's examination of the active measures campaign, the details unearthed by their investigation into this hacking offensive were downright shocking. They'd illuminated another wave of Russian attacks meant to destabilize our free and fair elections. Moreover, I took Team R's exemplary work as proof that our government is fully capable of detecting and catching such cybercriminals and thwarting such foreign interference. If we lack anything, it is the will to do so.

Repeatedly during the campaign, Trump simply swatted away the compelling evidence of Russian election interference, and would similarly dismiss, out of hand, indications that Russia had hacked his opponent. In July 2016, five days after the first WikiLeaks dump, he'd also taken the extraordinary step of explicitly courting such help from a foreign adversary on live television. "Russia, if you're listening," he said, "I hope you're able to find the thirty thousand emails that are missing."

This was illegal; candidates are prohibited from soliciting foreigners for anything of value, in order to keep our elections immune from outside influence. Not surprisingly, when called to task for this, Trump claimed that he was joking. It turns out Russia had been listening to Trump when he requested their help that day in July 2016—and they didn't seem to think he was joking, either. Until then, the GRU had attempted to hack only institutions, like the DNC, the DCCC, and the Clinton campaign. But Team R was able to determine that, later that very same day, the GRU began targeting Hillary Clinton's personal email accounts for the first time.

When Jeannie told me about this discovery—"You are not going to believe this," she said as she made her umpteenth excited foray to my office—I was once again awestruck by the high resolution of Team R's investigation. It was like going from seeing with the naked eye to using an electron microscope. So long as there was an electronic trail within legal grasp, her team was all over it.

Late in the spring of 2018, Jeannie wound down Team R's hacking investigation and started to focus on preparing a new indictment for the crimes it had uncovered. The Special Counsel's Office would charge twelve GRU operatives with various crimes, including conspiracies to commit computer fraud, identity theft, and money laundering. Jeannie wanted the indictment to lay out, in as much detail as possible, what the Russians had done—to make it undeniable, even if the chances of bringing those Russians to the United States for a trial were nil. There needed to be a clear public accounting of their attacks on our election.

Team R had filed its first indictment earlier that year, in February, charging thirteen Russian nationals and three Russian companies in connection with their active measures investigation. The Intelligence Community is quick to block such indictments if there's any risk that allowing the case to go forward could divulge sensitive information, but I'd been surprised to discover that my initial pessimism about the chances of them clearing Jeannie's active measures indictment had been unwarranted. In fact, Jeannie's indictment had sailed through the IC's approval process. I chalked that up in part to Jeannie's having used criminal process—and not national security tools—whenever possible. I believe the IC also realized that with a White House that was fact-resistant when it came to acknowledging the existential threat of the Russian election interference, a public indictment was now needed to undermine cynicism and conspiracy theorists. Now, for this second indictment—the hack and dump attack—the IC was on board again. In addition, once again, this indictment was fully approved by the Justice Department.

Bear in mind that the IC had already issued its own assessments (one public, one classified) of Russian interference in the election, in 2017, only to watch the president denigrate its reports as more fake news. The IC had gotten the Iraq War intelligence wrong, he insisted, so how could we trust its conclusion here? This dismissal was childish, seemingly rooted in Trump's conviction that to admit that Russia interfered in the 2016 election would undermine the legitimacy of his electoral victory.

Even after the IC report, Trump succeeded in muffling the impact of its findings—or at least sufficiently sowing doubts about the issue for a meaningful segment of the public. The fact that America had been attacked—and that Russia had attacked us—was not getting the attention it deserved.

So while it was unusual for the Intelligence Community to clear Jeannie's indictments, I believed they did so because Trump's denial had shifted the normal calculus in such a situation. The IC knew that Russian interference was a threat to our electoral process—the lifeblood of our democracy. Having our indictments lay out, in stark terms, what they had done would, we hoped, have the salutary effect of putting the fact of that attack beyond debate or conjecture, cementing that reality in the minds of all but the most hardened conspiracy theorists.

A problem arose, however, when it came to the timing of this indictment. Having secured the Intelligence Community's and Justice Department's go-ahead, Jeannie aimed to have the indictment completed by July 2018. However, Team M's first case against Manafort was scheduled to go to trial in Virginia in mid-July and, with Manafort showing little sign of wanting to plead, much less cooperate, with our office, we had few doubts that the trial would go forward. If we brought Team R's indictment just before the trial, the judge in the Manafort case would go bonkers, justifiably concerned that such an indictment from the Special Counsel's Office could generate adverse pretrial publicity, even if it didn't relate directly to the Manafort charges.

But we couldn't afford to wait to bring the hacking indictment until after both of Manafort's trials concluded—the trial in Virginia was slated to start in July and the trial in Washington in early September. By then, we would be running up on the midterms, and we would not announce any new charges that close to the election (consistent with Department policy). But waiting until mid-November would be intolerable to Mueller. I told Jeannie I thought we could safely defend ourselves from any objections from the Virginia judge if she brought her case at least two weeks before the start of our July trial—that, I hoped, would give us a reasonable buffer.

Jeannie said she could manage that, then quickly noted that the new timetable created yet another problem: Two weeks before our trial, the president was scheduled to be in Helsinki, where he would be meeting privately with Vladimir Putin. Our indictment would require alerting the State Department, given their diplomatic concerns in preparing for and running a summit, as the indictment would accuse the Russians explicitly of election interference. That was standard operating procedure, but there was also the real perception issue that the indictment could look like a commentary on Trump's decision to meet alone with Putin, which we did not intend.

We brought the dilemma to Mueller. He suggested we determine whether the White House would take issue with our proceeding just before the president's trip—would it pose any diplomatic issues? The answer we got back was no: The administration would not object to the timing. I suspect the White House Counsel's Office did not want to be perceived as dictating to us how or when to bring our indictment, or as hiding evidence of Russian election interference. In retrospect, a less generous interpretation of their blessing to move forward was that they knew dropping the indictment just before the trip would provide Trump and Putin an opportunity to jointly deny the attack on a global stage—that they were playing us, as Barr would later on.

Once we had the green light, Jeannie went ahead. The result was surreal—and, ultimately, soul crushing. On July 16, 2018, soon after the grand jury had brought an indictment that recounted detailed evidence of an attack on the United States by a furtive arm of the Russian military, the president of the United States was standing alongside the president of Russia at a joint press conference in Helsinki, following their closed-door meeting, with all the world watching.

When asked about the Russian disruption of our election, Trump openly sided with Putin over our own Intelligence Community, asserting that Putin had denied such interference and that he, President Trump, believed him. By this time, Trump not only had the conclusions of the original intelligence assessment, but the incontrovertible proof that Team R had worked up to expand on and corroborate it. Still, Trump said, Putin "was extremely strong and powerful in his denial," and that was apparently enough for him.

The scene in Helsinki should have been stunning to the average American viewer, but for those within our office who'd poured their energy into pinning down these facts, it was profoundly alarming. Here was our own president kowtowing to Putin, denying the election interference he had perpetrated on our nation and siding with a bloody dictator over a bipartisan consensus in the Senate and the nonpartisan conclusions of the IC that Putin had attacked our democracy. Our latest indictment, as had the active measures' indictment, laid out incontrovertible proof of Russian interference, much of which Trump himself had seen and benefited from. But now, with the lead perpetrator standing right next to him, Trump had not said a word against it. There was not a peep from our president about defending our electoral system.

The president said he saw no reason why Putin would have attacked our election and he believed him. Trump's body language and near shell-shocked countenance upon exiting his meeting with Putin sent alarm bells off for Jeannie and me. What was going on? Mueller looked exasperated at our daily five P.M. meeting in his office that day, and commented that, if the president was in the tank with Putin, "It would be about money"—that is, that Trump was motivated by money and his fawning behavior toward Putin could be explained by his seeking to make a buck in Russia. We all knew we had to dig deeper to get to the truth—but Mueller's comment did not result in our getting the green light to do a full-scale financial investigation of the president.

In our office, there was general amazement about the Helsinki meeting among the career FBI agents: It was like they'd built up a mountain of incriminating evidence only to watch the prosecutor suddenly decide to call off the case and go home, just because the defendant said he wasn't guilty. The initial reaction of the press and congressional leaders was heartening—how could the president be siding with Putin on this, in the face of so much evidence and just Putin's word on the other side? Had the president expected Putin to simply admit it? In the face of a bipartisan uproar at home, Trump tried to calm the waters by implausibly claiming he misspoke.

It was clear to Jeannie and me that the GRU had now gotten what it had worked so hard for: a servile, but popular, America leader. We believed the two indictments would make it plain to patriotic Americans that we are very much under assault. I did not think we should be encouraging our adversary by willfully ignoring that attack, making tongue-in-cheek admonitions to President Putin about not interfering anymore in our elections, or taking Putin's word that he was not trying to destabilize our democracy.

We had been attacked, repeatedly, and in a way that is as pernicious as anything we faced in World War II or on 9/11. We have a White House that is vehemently devoted to building a physical wall to keep illegal immigrants out, but unwilling to lift a finger to defend our country from actual destabilizing foreign intrusions—to safeguard the sovereignty of American elections. Even now, there are no new laws requiring paper ballots in all states, as a safety net in case of potential hacking or electronic voting manipulation; no substantial funding to upgrade our defenses; no dedicated group of agents, analysts, and prosecutors devoted solely to election interference, the way we have for other scourges, such as the opioid crisis. Nor has there been any bipartisan commission to examine securing our voting systems, in the same way a stellar bipartisan commission was convened following 9/11 to make insightful and long-lasting recommendations as to how we can better protect our nation from terrorist attacks.

Watching the president in Helsinki, I recognized that the post-fact world was swallowing the one I'd always inhabited—not only as a prosecutor but as a citizen. The emperor had no clothes, but no one in the Republican Senate or House who was running for reelection was willing to say it. The world I knew and understood was shaped by hard evidence and reason. It had given rise to the eighteenth-century French Encyclopedists, who attempted to chart all known human knowledge, and believed in reason over the irrational embodied by Mesmer. It had devised the machines of the nineteenth-century industrial revolution, altering our fundamental economic structures. It had enabled the twentieth-century advent of modern medicine, which charted our genome and cured tuberculosis and polio. And it had given rise to the very structure of our democracy embodied in the U.S. Constitution, with its belief in checks and balances and the rule of law, not men.

All that now seemed to be on unsure footing, with so much quicksand beneath it falling away.

CHAPTER 16

The Prospect of a "Mueller Massacre"

JIM QUARLES AND HIS Team 600 had been slowly plugging along on their investigation into whether the president's firing of Comey and request for him to go easy on Flynn constituted obstruction of justice, putting together a precise chronology of the events between December 2016 and May 2017. Anyone who stopped by Jim's office would be regaled with some new fact or suspicious contradiction that they had uncovered from their interviews and slotted into the time line on Jim's whiteboard. A junior person at the State Department or Department of Defense who had heard from their boss about Trump's desire to fire Comey, for instance—evidence that cut against the president's initial claim that he was simply following the advice of Sessions and Rosenstein—matched predictably with that boss claiming to not recollect that conversation.

But the narrow aperture that Team 600 was looking through widened dramatically as we learned that Trump was continuing to seek to fire his perceived enemies—and, this time, that enemy was Mueller himself. Team 600's investigation had begun as a straightforward examination regarding Comey and Flynn but expanded in scope as new evidence sprung up of his trying to thwart our own work. It would become increasingly clear that Trump was wielding the presidential power to pardon as an enticement to deter witnesses from cooperating with our office, while simultaneously wielding his power to fire Mueller as a threat to keep us reined in.

One thing that the whole office soon realized was that the third act in this play would be an inevitable investigation of us, by the Trump administration, when our investigation was complete: Trump would surely try to undermine every move we had made in order to burnish his standing and consolidate his power. This led to more gallows humor within the office. Whenever someone gave an opinion or spun out a possible theory to test out, someone would pipe up: "Write that down, that will be for the investigation of the investigators." That banter took on a darker hue in advance of the November 2018 congressional election. "If they retain the House, we all need to retain criminal lawyers," Jeannie said at one point. "That's how bat-shit crazy they are now. I am not joking." And I knew she wasn't. Jeannie was savvy about the ways of Washington, to a degree that I was not, and I took her seriously.

When the House flipped, it bought us more time, and we all collectively let out a deep breath. But Jeannie's concerns were prescient, given what we have all lived through. The leader of the free world has asked the Department of Justice to go after Democrats, has advocated the indictment of Comey, McCabe, Strzok, and others, and even accused Mueller of perjury. He and Barr have subverted the rule of law by providing unequal treatment to his cronies Stone, Flynn, and Manafort. They dismissed the Russian hack and dump case against a Russian company. And the U.S. attorney in Washington tried to indict McCabe, but the grand jury balked and found that the government had not even met the standard of probable cause—one of the lowest thresholds in the criminal law. The U.S. attorney then apparently refused to seek to indict McCabe before a different grand jury; Trump was furious and used the refusal as a reason to argue why his friend Roger Stone should be pardoned to even the playing field. The illogic of comparing the two is, of course, that Stone was found guilty by a jury beyond a reasonable doubt—the highest standard under the law—whereas McCabe was not found by even probable cause to have done anything wrong. The world has indeed gone topsy-turvy—"might makes right" overwhelming the rule of law.

Looking back now on the events in 2016, it is hard not to view the firing of Comey and Trump's request for leniency for Flynn through the lens of what we ourselves have since experienced—it was all of a piece. The proper way to understand Trump's firing of Comey—the incident that, in large part, gave rise to the creation of our office—was not as an isolated, impulsive act of personal score settling, but as an opening gambit in an ongoing, brazen effort by the president of the United States to undermine the rule of law and create a reality in which his personal views, whims, and resentments supersede objective truths. We were seeing Trump in real time turn against his choice for attorney general, Jeff Sessions, for not doing his bidding, just as he had freed himself of an independent FBI director who'd stood up to his request to let Flynn go and to publicly absolve the president of culpability. It was only logical that such a worldview might lead to dismissing Mueller as well. That is, the obstruction of justice portion of the special counsel's investigation had folded in on itself: The facts now required us to investigate the president's attempts to sabotage our own investigation.

The fears of imminent firing that dogged us through our first months of operation did not relent, even after we'd more than proven the legitimacy of our endeavor by indicting or convicting Paul Manafort, Michael Flynn, Rick Gates, George Papadopoulos, and numerous others, as well as detailing the orchestrated attack by Russia on the 2016 election. We had heard rumors—and were reading the press like everyone else—about pressure on Sessions to "un-recuse" himself in order to fire us or rein us in. But it was only in the spring of 2018 that Team 600 got its first substantial insight into the administration's behind-the-scenes attempts to fire Mueller and shut us down—which was around the time that Team M was seeing him wield his pardon power to thwart our investigation.

This information came principally when Team 600 interviewed White House counsel Don McGahn and his chief of staff, Annie Donaldson. Ordinarily, communications between a client and a lawyer would be privileged and out of bounds for an investigation, but this is not the case with White House counsel like McGahn and Donaldson. A White House counsel works for the public, and represents the White House as an institution, not the president personally—just as when I was the FBI's general counsel, I had represented the Bureau itself, and not Mueller, the Bureau's director.

Both McGahn and Donaldson were brought to our office quietly on the days of their interviews—the standard protocol we had in place so as not to subject them to media scrutiny. The FBI used "Bu cars" with tinted windows to take people into the underground parking garage of our offices at Patriots Plaza. That would prevent even the CNN reporter stationed at the entrance to the garage from monitoring in real time who we were speaking with. Our security staff then brought those witnesses up through the back elevator, to avoid the lobby. Even within our office, we would send out alerts that a certain area should be avoided, so that other witnesses we were interviewing would not see who else was arriving. In short, there was careful choreography to avoid leaks and to protect witnesses from the glare of the media.

As a result of what we would learn, Team 600 would morph into what we had lightheartedly dubbed Team 1600. McGahn is a traditional conservative Republican who clearly understood his obligation as a public servant to provide truthful information to our investigation. In retrospect, his conduct was in striking contrast to that of senior public administration officials in connection with the House and Senate impeachment proceedings—where officials such as Mike Pompeo and Mick Mulvaney refused to cooperate with a lawful inquiry. McGahn and Donaldson understood that as public servants they had an obligation to be truthful, and we would find them both to be forthright in their interviews.

McGahn sat down in our conference room with a rather large cast from our office, including a couple of lawyers from our legal team, FBI agents, and the core Team 600 members, Jim Quarles, Michael Dreeben, and Andrew Goldstein. As we are all trained to do when interviewing witnesses, they did not provide any information to McGahn and tried to not even show on their faces their internal thinking. We are trained to ask questions and more questions, to flesh out and probe the information we were receiving. Michelle Taylor, the lead FBI agent on Team 600, was particularly adept at questioning; personally disarming, she exuded integrity and thoroughness. Her quiet, earnest demeanor coaxed the best out of witnesses. McGahn was no exception.

McGahn calmly relayed to the team concrete efforts by the president to fire Mueller occurring as early as June 2017, a month after Mueller's appointment. And when that strategy failed, the president worked persistently to curtail our investigation, so that we'd be permitted to look only at future election interference, and not investigate Russia's role in Trump's ascent to power. McGahn explained in a specific, detailed account—backed up by contemporaneous notes—how Trump had initially sought to concoct an appropriate-seeming excuse for terminating Mueller, a strategy that was eerily reminiscent of how he'd used Rosenstein's well-argued memo on Comey's conduct before the election as public justification for firing Comey. The president seemed to have fixated on the idea of Mueller's having some kind of disqualifying conflict of interest, and cited a series of alleged conflicts to McGahn, as though testing them out.

I've mentioned these allegations previously, as most emerged as public lines of attack against Mueller and were easily and fulsomely debunked. (They included the supposed grudge Mueller held over an unreimbursed membership fee to one of Trump's golf clubs, and his reputed bitterness about not being hired as Comey's replacement to lead the FBI.) None of it was true. Still, Mueller, a stickler for propriety, had advised the Department of Justice and its ethics office of each allegation floated against him, so that the institution could investigate and rule on these issues. The head of the Department's ethics office rejected them all, determining that none posed a conflict. Its conclusion was publicly announced in late May 2017.

None of this prevented Trump from continuing to push for Mueller's termination on the basis of these claims. Nor did it give him pause that the defectiveness of his reasoning was plain to those around him. In his interview with Team 600, Steve Bannon, who was Trump's chief strategist at the time, described cautioning the president that his justifications for firing Mueller were "petty." Other advisers told us that Trump's concerns about Mueller were "silly" and "not real."

Nevertheless, McGahn told Team 600 that Trump had asked him to raise these issues with Rosenstein, Mueller's direct supervisor. McGahn refused to do so. In his notes from the time, he wrote that he explained to the president that these were matters to take up with his personal counsel, not the White House counsel—a responsible position that recognized that it would be inappropriate for the White House counsel, who represented the public, not the president, to participate in such a scheme.

Implicit in McGahn's drawing this distinction was that if Trump

tried to orchestrate a firing he would not be doing so in the public interest, but in his personal interest—an issue we would see play out again
and again in connection with the impeachment proceedings, where the
president saw no distinction between the personal and the political. I
was a French history major in college, and it was hard not to reflect on
the historical roots of this worldview: Louis XIV, the "Sun King," who
ruled France with an increasingly iron fist in the seventeenth and eighteenth centuries before the French Revolution. He famously said, "L'état,
c'est moi"—"I am the state." He was the embodiment of an absolute
monarch and was a prime illustration of why we have a Constitution in
America to prevent such autocratic rule. McGahn was lifting the veil on
the president's worldview, one that was antithetical to the ideals of our
founding fathers.

McGahn told Team 600 that his advice to Trump was to drop the
issue of firing Mueller. He even warned the president that resorting to
baseless allegations to rid himself of Mueller would look like obstruction
of the special counsel's investigation. Nevertheless, Trump persisted.
The timing of events laid out by McGahn—and confirmed by Donaldson in her interview—spoke volumes. It helped contextualize a call Jim
Quarles had received on June 13, 2017, from Trump's personal attorney
John Dowd. Dowd was essentially putting our office on notice, explaining to Jim that Trump was complaining about Mueller and the alleged
conflicts of interest. Coincidentally, this was the same day Rod Rosenstein testified before a Senate appropriations subcommittee; we all
watched on the flat-screens in our office as Rosenstein told the senators
that he saw no basis for removing Mueller—more evidence that the
president's opposition to Mueller was a purely self-interested tactic.

This squared with what we were now hearing from McGahn. It had
been the following evening, June 14, 2017, a day after Dowd's call to Jim
and Rosenstein's appearance in the Senate, that reports first emerged in
The Washington Post that the Special Counsel's Office was examining
whether the president had obstructed justice. This was the first public
indication that our office was investigating the president himself and not
merely Russian nationals and campaign staffers like Manafort or Gates.

Learning that you are the focus of an investigation would be of concern to anyone, but Trump had already demonstrated extreme sensitivity to being eyed by any criminal probe; notably, he'd made a point of

tortuously inserting into the memorandum justifying his firing of Comey that Comey had privately assured him—three times, no less—that he was not under investigation. Numerous witnesses had confirmed that the president had been fixated on getting this detail into the memo. In case there was any doubt as to the president's extreme wariness of our investigation in general, we'd also learned from Jody Hunt, the chief of staff to Attorney General Sessions, of Trump's reaction when he first got the news of Mueller's appointment. Backed up by his voluminous and verbatim handwritten notes, Hunt told us that he was with Sessions in the Oval Office when the attorney general broke the news to the president. Trump had crumpled into his chair and said, "Oh my God. This is terrible. This is the end of my presidency. I'm fucked."

The *Post* story exploded on cable news that June evening. It seems to have enraged the president. Using telephone records our office had obtained by subpoena to accurately create a time line of events, in conjunction with what McGahn was telling us, we saw that at 10:31 that night, Trump phoned McGahn on McGahn's personal cellphone. (McGahn's recollection of this call was hazy, but he believed they might have discussed the media reporting.) The following morning, Trump began griping about our office in a series of tweets, calling our investigation "the single greatest WITCH HUNT in American politics history—led by some very bad and conflicted people!" He suggested, not for the last time, that Hillary Clinton was the real criminal.

Three days later, on June 17, 2017, a Saturday, the president called McGahn again, at home, and told him to phone Rosenstein and explain that Mueller's purported conflicts of interest disqualified him from serving as special counsel. According to McGahn, the president said something like: "You gotta do this. You gotta call Rod." McGahn was unnerved. He sensed that he'd been forced into an untenable situation: If he conveyed the president's message, he explained to Team 600, he knew he'd be sparking another Saturday Night Massacre. And if he did not convey the president's message, he would be defying a direction from the leader of the free world. McGahn told us that he placated the president by assuring him he'd see what he could do, but—McGahn confessed to our team—he'd had no intention of carrying out the order.

Trump called McGahn again, to check if he'd spoken to Rosenstein. This time, McGahn recalled, the president explained more directly that he wanted Mueller fired: "Mueller has to go," Trump said. "Call me back when you do it." Again, McGahn left the president with the impression that he would take care of it, but actually remained committed to ignoring the president's order. As McGahn put it to us, "I just wanted to get off the phone."

He felt he had only one option, he said: When he got off the phone with the president, he decided to resign. There was no way he could comply with the order; he saw no basis for Mueller's removal. McGahn went to the White House, packed his office, and informed a handful of associates that he was resigning. Only after Steve Bannon and the president's then chief of staff, Reince Priebus, implored him to reconsider did McGahn agree to stay. He felt "trapped," he told our team. He recounted all this solemnly, as though still burdened by the weight of that dilemma.

When Jeannie told me about the substance of McGahn's interview, I was floored. It was only the integrity, backbone, and judgment of people like McGahn that had saved the president from himself and curtailed, or simply wore down, his destructive impulses. Time and again, Team 600 would uncover examples of people who'd simply refused to comply with directives from the president that they deemed improper or illegal. But in this particular case, the situation was particularly astonishing: The White House counsel was adamantly refusing to follow an order from the president. It signaled to me that, behind the scenes, the structures of our government had unraveled to a remarkable extent, leaving some people to operate, on an ad hoc basis, as a last check on the president's worst impulses.

I had been brought up in the U.S. attorney's offices under the ethos that you needed to be prepared to resign if you could not comply with a direction consistent with your personal morals. But to refuse an order from the president would require an extreme measure of fortitude that I was not sure I'd be capable of, until tested in the moment. I knew Mueller had such mettle. Once, by happenstance, I had come across a letter in my office safe while I was general counsel of the FBI. There, mixed in with papers about a then-secret surveillance program, was a handwritten letter of resignation Mueller had prepared, explaining that he could not implement the program because he believed it to be illegal. The dispute about the program's legality had precipitated the now well-known showdown between Vice President Dick Cheney and Comey (then the deputy attorney general) that culminated at the hospital bed of Attorney General John Ashcroft. The Office of Legal Counsel had analyzed the program and found it did not comport with the Constitution, but the vice president had disagreed. Mueller's letter eloquently explained it had been his privilege to have served the FBI and the president, but he was now required to resign since he could not carry out the administration's plans. It was only after Mueller had gone to speak privately with President Bush about the matter that the president, to his credit, relented and Mueller remained.

Now we had a White House counsel telling us that the president's orders were so wildly out of bounds that he, too, could not bring himself to follow them. It was highly unusual, to say the least. It seemed to me that if McGahn had been concerned solely with the optics and strategy of the president's desire to fire Mueller, he could have talked himself into complying with the president's instruction by acknowledging the measure of uncertainty involved: After all, McGahn could not say with complete certainty that the president's firing Mueller would have triggered another Saturday Night Massacre. Circumstances were different than they had been during Watergate: Nixon did not have Fox News at his disposal to spin his termination of the special prosecutor as righteous. The fact that McGahn did not resort to such rationalizations, however, and remained unwilling to play any role in Mueller's firing, underscored how seriously awry he felt the situation at the White House had become. In short, he was not going to be party to such abuse.

With McGahn's refusing to order Muller's firing, the president then turned to a series of alternate plans, each involving an escalating measure of bureaucratic brute force. This next phase was recounted to us in interviews with Rob Porter and Corey Lewandowski, as well as McGahn. And we had the benefit of contemporaneous notes: McGahn, Donaldson, and Jody Hunt were scrupulous note takers. Hunt's notes were more akin to a personal diary, recounting the day's pertinent events and his personal reactions to them. Donaldson's were similar: "Is this the beginning of the end?" she wondered at the time that Hunt was noting Trump's more profane reaction to our appointment.

We learned from McGahn, Lewandowski, and Porter that plan B was to tell Attorney General Sessions to "un-recuse" himself from the Russian investigation, snatch oversight of our office back from Rosenstein, and curtail the scope of our investigation so we could examine only foreign interference in future elections: Everything we'd ultimately discover about Russia's attack on our nation in 2016—and the role they'd played in Trump's attaining the presidency—would have been left untouched. Trump began expressing to reporters his desire for Sessions to un-recuse himself, then publicly lobbed a series of degrading insults at him. When it was clear Sessions was refusing to do as the president wished, a plan C emerged: fire Sessions himself.

We learned from Lewandowski that, at this point, Trump had turned to him, his first campaign manager, for help. Lewandowski was a curious accomplice; he was, by then, a private citizen. Trump had thrown him overboard in the middle of his campaign, in the spring of 2016, in favor of Paul Manafort, who Lewandowski still regarded with hostility. Lewandowski viewed Manafort as a backstabber who'd sought to take credit for Trump's victory after Lewandowski had done much of the hard work. Lewandowski arrived at our office to be interviewed in the spring of 2018, not long after Manafort had been indicted in Washington and Virginia. In addition to Team 600's questioning, Jeannie interviewed him about Russian influence during the campaign, and Lewandowski made a point of telling her that he was hoping to meet me, as well. He wanted to shake the hand of the guy who'd finally held "that piece of shit" to account, he said.

Lewandowski explained to Team 600 that the president had called him in the summer of 2017 and instructed him to tell Attorney General Sessions to un-recuse himself from the Russia investigation, then dramatically narrow its scope. It was an outlandish move: a president enlisting someone who did not work at the White House—who did not have a job in government at all—as his messenger. How could a civilian possibly order the attorney general of the United States to do anything? As it turns out, this struck Lewandowski as odd, as well; he viewed the directive as ill advised and never followed through on it. Here was one more subordinate refusing to carry out the president's orders and simply hoping—correctly, as it turned out—that he would move on, or forget about it. As with Trump's orders to McGahn—and, more recently, with his pressuring the Ukrainian president for an investigation into the Bidens—he was attempting to leverage his power as president for a "personal errand." There was no separation of the personal and political.

More important, Sessions had recused himself from the special counsel's investigation on the advice of the Department of Justice's ethics officers, since he had been an active and early member of the Trump campaign. Trump had no rationale for opposing this conclusion—he didn't even feign having a reason; he just wanted Sessions to un-recuse himself so that he could exert more control over our work.

The Sessions plan was a continuation of Trump's efforts to peel the world around him away from the rule of law—away from reason itself—and mold it to accommodate his desire for unchecked power. As my Freudian psychologist mother would put it: all id, no superego.

It is natural to wonder why people like McGahn and Donaldson were honest in their interviews with us, why they were willing to share unvarnished accounts—accounts that provided incriminating evidence against the president—when they could have simply lied as other witnesses, such as Papadopoulos, did. A culture of mendacity seemed to be infecting the highest reaches of our government, gradually normalizing such deceit.

We asked this same question ourselves.

It cannot be gainsaid that some people are inherently truth tellers, and in law enforcement we depend on such people to bring the guilty to justice and to assure that the innocent are not wrongly accused. Others, meanwhile—and I would put Manafort in this category—will lie whenever it serves their self-interest. Still others fall on a spectrum in between: They might be dishonest if they feel reasonably sure they can get away with it, but won't if the risks or repercussions appear to be too great.

As investigators, our job is to maximize the incentives for honesty and the deterrents for duplicity, to ensure that anyone making such a calculation will realize that his or her best option is to tell the truth. One fundamental way of doing so is to conduct as meticulous an investigation beforehand as possible—to demonstrate to the witness that you already know the answers to the questions you're asking and will be quick to catch on to any elisions or misrepresentations. But the only way to have witnesses truly believe that a lie will be discovered and have consequences is for us to take action when a witness lies.

By early 2018, it would have been apparent to everyone we were interviewing that we at the Special Counsel's Office took the crime of lying to us seriously, and that the warnings we issued at the beginning of every session about the possible consequences for lying were not empty admonitions. We had already charged George Papadopoulos, Michael Flynn, and Rick Gates with lying to the FBI; all three men had admitted this conduct and were awaiting sentencing in Washington. (Flynn would famously later claim he lied to the court when he admitted lying to the FBI.)

The president's personal attorneys denigrated these charges as "process crimes"—as almost frivolous technicalities—though, in reality, we knew this was merely a cynical attempt to further undermine our office by limiting our ability to use one of our most powerful tools to obtain truthful testimony to advance the investigation. The president's lawyers knew, as well as we did, that meting out penalties for lying serves as a strong deterrent, further incentivizing future witnesses to tell the truth. Mueller had made this point explicitly, both while deliberating whether to charge Gates and, again, shortly afterward, as we discussed the subsequent case of another witness, an attorney we'd interviewed from the powerhouse international firm Skadden Arps named Alex van der Zwaan.

Van der Zwaan was a senior associate in their London office and part of the team hired by Manafort to work on behalf of Yanukovych's Ukraine government in 2012. His firm was tasked with assembling a supposedly independent report that would assess the trial that had resulted in the imprisonment of President Yanukovych's political rival Yulia Tymoshenko. Van der Zwaan had developed a close relationship with Manafort and his two right-hand men, Gates and Konstantin Kilimnik.

After Team M requested an interview with van der Zwaan, he arrived at our office represented by four lawyers, fastidiously prepared and a bit too smartly dressed. Nevertheless, in spite of clear warnings about the consequence of lying, he chose to do so when asked about his last contacts with Gates and Kilimnik, issuing flat denials or attempting to put distance between them and himself in ways that clearly contradicted recent communications we'd obtained. (In an email between van der Zwaan and Kilimnik, for example, written in Russian, Kilimnik had asked van der Zwaan to call him urgently on an encrypted device.)

In addition, van der Zwaan had destroyed documents that he was supposed to turn over to us, and hidden others. When, later, we sought access to his mobile devices, he claimed one of his phones had been irreparably damaged when he accidentally dropped it into a London toilet. We never were able to fully recover the data on it.

We on Team M were all in favor of charging van der Zwaan with lying. Van der Zwaan's esteemed counsel issued an appeal to Mueller not to charge his client for these deceptions, presenting a hodgepodge of arguments, including the potential collateral consequences to him in England as a lawyer, his relative youth, and his willingness (albeit after he was caught) to admit to what he had done and turn over certain electronic devices. Mueller listened to it all and swiftly denied the appeal; holding van der Zwaan accountable was not just clearly the right thing to do, Mueller explained, but would continue to send a strong signal of deterrence to everyone else.

Van der Zwaan was charged and pleaded guilty on February 20, 2018. His plea agreement, in which we made a point of thoroughly detailing his lies and obstruction, received considerable press, even though it occurred in the shadows of Team R's active measures indictment. Whether there was a cause and effect I do not know, but not long after, Team 600 got a phone call from McGahn. He wanted to come in and speak with Jim and his investigators again, he said; there was some new information to share. McGahn had already been interviewed by our office twice at that point, providing his bone-rattling account of the president's efforts to dismiss or restrict the special counsel. But what he proceeded to tell us in this third interview still stands out in my mind as perhaps the most chilling revelation we'd hear during the twenty-two months of our investigation.

McGahn began by describing the fallout in the White House from a *New York Times* story in January 2018 that revealed the same information that he'd divulged to us in his previous interviews: that the president had ordered McGahn to fire Mueller in June 2017, but that McGahn had told Trump he would not and attempted to resign. Publicly, the president decried the article in his usual fashion. ("Fake news, folks," he told reporters. "Fake news.") We knew, of course, that the *Times* journalists had gotten the story almost entirely right. In fact, the lone inaccuracy in the story—an implication that McGahn had told the president he planned to resign, rather than privately determining he would resign, only to be talked out of it by others without Trump ever knowing—was quickly clarified by *The Washington Post,* which followed up with its own reporting the following day.

The president was apparently incensed by the story. McGahn recounted how Trump instructed him—first through his personal attorney, then through press secretary Sarah Huckabee Sanders—to issue a public denial. McGahn refused, pointing out that the story was, in fact, true. Trump then complained about the reporting to his aide Rob Porter, insisting that the *Times* story was "bullshit" and that McGahn—who Trump referred to as a "lying bastard"—must have leaked it to the media in order to burnish his own reputation.

Porter, in turn, approached McGahn to deliver the message from the president again: Issue a denial. When McGahn again shrugged the order off, Porter advised him that the president had suggested McGahn would be fired if he didn't write a memorandum for the White House files denying that Trump had ordered him to fire the special counsel. Still, McGahn refused, pointing out to Porter how untenable this threat was politically: Trump would be firing him for refusing to lie. McGahn still thought this was a guardrail that the president would not cross—at least at this point in the presidency.

The following day, February 6, 2018, McGahn was summoned to the Oval Office. There, Trump told him—for the first time, directly—that he needed to speak out and contradict the *Times* reporting. The president insisted the story was incorrect: "I never said to fire Mueller. I never said 'fire,'" he claimed. This was merely a hairsplitting attempt to deflect from his stratagem—a move that, in the eyes of any reputable prosecutor, would only serve to display the president's consciousness of guilt. It indicated that Trump understood that what he'd done was wrong, but was seeking to open some small semantic loophole through which he might wriggle free. In fact, it made no difference whether the president said the word "fire." McGahn understood this, of course; he even explained it to the president. What Trump had told him, McGahn said, was to tell Rosenstein that Mueller could no longer serve as special counsel and "had to go."

At that point, Trump's resentment of McGahn's disobedience—and resentment for the law and the strictures of legal process more broadly—

came into sharper relief. The president, McGahn recounted, wanted to know why he'd even told the Special Counsel's Office about his order to remove Mueller—why, that is, he'd been honest with us. It was so shocking as to be disorienting; reality appeared to have turned inside out: The president of the United States, who oversees the Justice Department and all its federal investigators, was angrily demanding to know why someone had told those investigators the truth. The reasons for McGahn's honesty should have been self-evident—for one thing, he would have been committing a felony if he'd lied to us. But they were not self-evident to Trump; in fact, it seemed as though McGahn's integrity struck him as a bewildering aberration.

This strange upbraiding continued. "What about these notes?" McGahn remembered the president asking him. "Why do you take notes? Lawyers don't take notes. I never had a lawyer who took notes." Clearly, the implication was that these notes of McGahn's were a grave inconvenience—it's far easier to get away with lying about what happened, and refuting the truth, if no one takes notes. McGahn explained to the president that he takes notes because he is a "real lawyer," and understands that creating a record of events is a good thing.

"I've had a lot of great lawyers," the president responded, "like Roy Cohn. He did not take notes." Trump was speaking to McGahn as though McGahn were his own personal criminal defense lawyer; he did not care that as White House counsel, McGahn worked for the public, not Trump.

The McGahn story—which was whispered about throughout the office, in spite of the effort to keep such gossip to a minimum—was stunning. There had been an enormous effort on Mueller's part not to have tunnel vision, where you start to believe only evidence favorable to your theory, and dismiss evidence that poses a challenge to it; Mueller was particularly on the lookout for this form of bias in our work, and remained open to changing his mind. But this latest McGahn interview made it impossible to see the president's conduct for anything other than what it was. Even Aaron, whose caution could be helpful in pushing and prodding to test our conclusions, was convinced—a useful sanity check, for all of us, that this evidence was in fact as powerful as it seemed. Months later, when Attorney General Barr would claim in his four-page letter—the one that purported to summarize our report—that there'd been full cooperation by the White House with the investigation and no effort to obstruct our office's investigation by the president, Jim Quarles would rightly point to McGahn's evidence as succinct and irrefutable proof that Barr's contention simply was not true.

For me, personally, McGahn's recitation was as upsetting as the tape recordings of Richard Nixon discussing how to cover up the break-in at the Watergate, or, in a certain way, the revelations that Bill Clinton had oral sex with an intern near the Oval Office, then coached his secretary on a cover story to conceal his sexual harassment. Each brought to light—in different ways and degrees—an extreme debasement of the Oval Office.

McGahn's evidence demonstrated that the kind of abusive behavior that I'd worried might be unfolding, but prayed was not, was in fact happening and even more acutely than I'd imagined. This all jibed with what we had heard from McGahn and Donaldson, that the lawyers in the White House Counsel's Office referred to the Oval Office as the "Magic Kingdom"—a reality-free zone, with just the ravings of our own Mad King George to deal with. Even their taking notes confirmed for me that they knew they had to do so. In truth, taking such detailed notes of the president's statements was not typical. But it would be necessary to protect the institution they represented as lawyers for the White House.

I had the same sinking feeling of a system gone horribly awry as I did when I worked on a police corruption case involving a young Haitian immigrant named Abner Louima in 1997, which had garnered widespread attention. While in New York Police Department custody for a minor offense, Louima was violently assaulted and sodomized with a broken wooden broom handle by an NYPD officer in the bathroom of a precinct. I was not so naïve as to be shocked that the police could engage in crime, but this was different: The violence and depravity of this crime was profoundly disturbing, as was the fact that the police had thought the safest place to pull off such a horrendous act without getting caught would be in a police precinct—a place that should be a haven from crime.

My reaction now was of similar disbelief and disillusionment: How were the president's actions possible in a country as great as ours, with a Constitution and judicial system that are—or at least were—a beacon for so many other countries around the world? The conduct that McGahn described—the efforts to fire the special counsel and then to get the White House counsel to lie for the president to cover it up—fundamentally assaulted our history and ideals; it left me sad to my core.

There are times in our lives when circumstances bring out the best in us, granting us a necessary measure of humility or lucidity to see ourselves as part of a more magnificent whole. On the morning of 9/11, for example, I had just dropped off my father for work at the NYU School of Medicine and was approaching the Brooklyn Bridge on the FDR Drive when I saw the second plane hit the south tower. I remember thanking God that I was a member of the Department of Justice at the time, grateful that I could play some role, however small, in helping our country restore its sense of justice and security after such a destabilizing attack. And for a time, the whole country seemed to be one: The tragedy had brought us together; we cherished our commonality over our differences.

Visits to the Oval Office have been similar occasions for me, moments inflected by a deep sense of awe—an awareness of the genuine grandeur of our country and its ideals. I first set foot in that room during the George W. Bush administration, and then again during the presidency of Barack Obama. But it made no difference who held the office; I felt the same flood of emotion both times. Consequently, it was soul crushing to digest McGahn's account—the latest and most searing evidence of how the office had been debased by a person sworn to uphold the law.

There was no looking away now; we all knew what we were dealing with. The president was abusing his power, obstructing our investigation, and corroding the rule of law. His thinly veiled excuses for getting rid of Comey; his outright lies and his fixation on frivolous conflicts to lay the groundwork for Mueller's termination; his entreaties to have Sessions take over our investigation and, when Sessions refused, his efforts to belittle and fire his own attorney general; the dangling of pardons to try to keep Flynn and Gates and Manafort and Cohen in line—all of it made perfect sense if the president's sole objective was his own self-preservation; if he were, in the end, like an animal, clawing at the world with no concept of right and wrong. Any damage done to the country, or the Constitution, would merely be collateral damage. He was not serving the people of this country. He was engaged in a brawl for his own power and survival.

The only question that remained to be settled was one of labeling that behavior: How would Mueller choose to characterize the president's actions in our report?

CHAPTER 17

The First Manafort Trial

ON JULY 31, 2018, two weeks after Jeannie brought her Russian hacking indictment, Team M began trying in federal court in Virginia the first of our two cases against Paul Manafort.

From the outset of our investigation, Team M's mission had been to work our way up the ladder of the Trump campaign along a succession of cooperating witnesses—moving, ideally, from Gates to Manafort, then from Manafort into the sprawling unknown. To be clear, we had no idea what information Manafort might provide us about coordination between Russia and the Trump campaign—because we had no idea if any criminal coordination had taken place. Our mission was to uncover the facts, wherever they led us, and to use every tool at our disposal to uncover the truth. We'd accept whatever those facts illuminated, but what the Special Counsel's Office owed the American people was a thorough and credible accounting of what, exactly, had happened. Our goal was clarity.

But now, a little more than a year into our investigation, Team M found itself stuck on a rung of the ladder we'd set out to climb. We'd managed to flip Gates that February, but Manafort had refused to cooperate or plead guilty. He had, in fact, pleaded not guilty to both sets of charges we'd brought against him and opted to defend himself at two separate trials—as was his constitutional right. This trial in Virginia, on the tax and bank fraud charges, would be followed closely by a second one, for FARA, money laundering, tax conspiracy, lying, and witness tampering violations, in Washington, D.C., in mid-September.

In the parlance of trial attorneys, certain cases are "triable" and others are not. A triable case is one that's potentially winnable for the defendant, with legitimate, open factual questions that can and should be argued out in court. Lawyers on both sides tend to be clear-eyed when making an assessment as to whether a given case is triable, just as doctors have a responsibility to realistically gauge the prognoses of their patients.

I knew that both of our cases against Manafort were not triable cases—not remotely. The evidence against him was stark and stitched together so tightly that there was simply no opportunity for Manafort's defense counsel to poke a hole in it. We had too many damning documents, from too many different sources, and too many witnesses implicating him from too many discrete facets of his life: tax accountants, bill payers, store owners, bank managers, and even his right-hand man, Gates. I'd love to report, in retrospect, that it was a difficult case to prove, and that only our masterful prosecutorial skills allowed us to prevail. But while our prosecution team would do a wonderful job, we all knew, going into the trial, that Team M's performance in the courtroom would not mean the difference between winning and losing. Our best work had been amassing the evidence we would use at trial.

I'd spent years, as a supervisor in the Justice Department, tamping down the tendency of young prosecutors to believe that every case they won was proof of their talent. It took a certain amount of experience to understand that, more often than not in federal court, the evidence in a given case was so forceful that the verdict had little to do with the brilliance of the lawyers on either side. In my youth, I, too, would often forget this; when we were working on the Enron investigation, which resulted in numerous convictions, a snarky but unfortunately perceptive defense counsel I was negotiating with correctly chided me: "I don't know what you are so impressed by; you have the facts and the law on your side."

With Manafort, we had the facts and law on our side, and yet, he'd chosen to go to trial, hoping that a Virginia jury would acquit him or at least he would persuade one juror not to convict. (Under the federal law, a jury must be unanimous to convict or to acquit.) It was always possible that Manafort would still choose to cooperate after this trial or the next, if convicted. I had a plan in place—which I had used during the Enron investigation—for how to find out what he knew regardless of his co-operation. If Manafort still did not cooperate after the trials, we would put him in front of the grand jury and ask him all the questions we had amassed during the investigation. The grand jury is entitled to every person's testimony, absent a privilege. The only privilege that could prevent Manafort from answering the questions would be the Fifth Amendment, but we could avoid that by granting him immunity—meaning we could not use anything he said in the grand jury against him (but we could use it against anyone else).

There would be little downside in granting immunity at that juncture, as we would have already tried Manafort twice for a host of crimes, and he would have been adjudged guilty or acquitted. Manafort would thus have to testify about what he knew—and if he refused, he would be summarily put in jail by the court for contempt. That strategy had worked in Enron, when Ben Glisan, the Enron treasurer, had pleaded guilty but not cooperated with us. Kathy Ruemmler and I then put him in front of the grand jury, and he decided, at that point, to come clean rather than commit perjury or refuse to testify and thereby commit contempt. To do this now with Manafort we needed to get through the trials.

The pressure on Manafort had recently increased, thanks to my mantra of putting ourselves in a position to get lucky. Manafort was now in jail for having tampered with two witnesses while he was out on bail. That Manafort had been so bold—in such a high-profile case—to have tried to coach two witnesses to lie still astounds me. We uncovered what he'd done in the course of investigating the "Hapsburg Group"—a nefarious part of Manafort's FARA violations. Manafort had arranged for Ukraine to secretly retain a series of former high-level senior European leaders to lobby for Ukraine. Those leaders would write op-eds and meet with American politicians—including President Obama—but were secretly paid by Ukraine to advance its agenda. None of that activity was disclosed to the Department of Justice at the time, as the law required.

We had sought to interview two people who'd served as intermediaries between the Hapsburg Group and Manafort, but both were overseas.

We had a border lookout in place should they come into the United States and, sure enough, in the spring of 2018 both did within weeks of each other, and both cooperated. Not only did they describe efforts by Manafort and Kilimnik to get them to deny that the Hapsburg Group lobbied in the United States (something that was demonstrably untrue, from the written records we had), but they also retained copies of messages Manafort and Kilimnik had written on encrypted devices seeking to have them keep to the scripted story. Our two new witnesses had been so concerned by the Manafort and Kilimnik outreach that they'd taken and kept screenshots of the messages, and when they came to the United States, they turned them over to us.

That led to the mother of all Grant-McClellan disputes: Aaron was adamant that we do nothing with this evidence at all. But Omer and I wanted to charge Manafort and Kilimnik with witness tampering and obstruction—we had such devastating proof that it would make the Washington trial what's known in the business as a "rock crusher." And I once again let Aaron know we simply could not keep such a clear bail violation from Judge Jackson: "She would rightly have our heads if we did not alert her to this, and Manafort skipped town." I told Mueller, "In Brooklyn, we would need to bring our toothbrush to the next court appearance," meaning the judge would haul us off to jail for such conduct.

That moved Mueller and he agreed we could add the new charges to the Washington case, but then Aaron got him to agree that although we would alert the judge to the new evidence of Manafort's bail violation, we would not move to remand Manafort—that is, ask for him to be put in jail. I could see where this was going to end up, once the court saw this evidence, and I did as I was told.

When our filing was made public, it had an enormous impact: Not even Fox News could continue to say the Manafort case was weak or political; the proof of his crimes while out on bail was there for all to see. I still remember watching Jeffrey Toobin, a former EDNY prosecutor, commenting on CNN that he could not understand why we were so lily-livered in the Special Counsel's Office that we had not asked the court to remand Manafort to jail. But once the court saw the evidence and heard from the defense (which offered no innocent explanation), Manafort's fate was sealed.

On Friday, June 15, 2018, the court found that Manafort had violated his bail by committing the new federal crimes, and he was remanded. Manafort then claimed that he was locked up in solitary by the judge, but in truth the Bureau of Prisons had housed Manafort in a suite previously inhabited by Michael Vick, in which he had a private library, a bathroom, and a laptop, and did not have to wear prison garb. As we noted in our papers responding to Manafort's complaint about his housing conditions, Manafort was overheard saying on a prison phone that the jail was treating him "like a VIP."

Everything was going according to plan in the lead-up to the trials. But there was one curveball thrown at us during the trial in Virginia that made our job far more difficult than we'd anticipated: the conduct of the presiding judge, Judge T. S. Ellis III. Before the trial, we'd done due diligence on Judge Ellis and had every expectation that he'd oversee our proceeding with professionalism, intelligence, and impartiality. If anything, we learned that he could display a pro-government bent, meting out tough sentences and having little sympathy for defense pleas for leniency. In our second court appearance, however, Judge Ellis's antipathy was revealed.

Michael Dreeben, our legal mastermind, was going to address the court on the defense motion challenging the special counsel regulations. It was a rarity for Michael to appear in district court, though he had argued more than a hundred cases before the Supreme Court as a senior member of the Solicitor General's Office. Michael and I were sitting side by side at the government's table when Judge Ellis made what can only be described as a startling and antagonistic comment, telling us, out of the blue, that the Special Counsel's Office did not actually care about prosecuting Manafort for his crimes. We merely wanted to flip him, Judge Ellis insisted, in order to gather information "against" President Trump that could be used to indict or impeach him. He criticized this tactic, from the bench that day, as "distasteful."

This condemnation of our tactics was hard to make sense of—it was one thing to hear this nonsense on Fox News, but quite another to hear it from a federal judge. As Michael said, once we were safely back in his office, wanting to flip a defendant is unremarkable—as the judge knew—so it was hard to square his implication that our intention to do so was somehow improper; making such a claim cut against the notion of judicial impartiality. Moreover, the Special Counsel's Office had no interest in impeaching Trump, or even the ability to do so, and there was no evidence anywhere—no statements we'd made or conduct we'd undertaken in our investigation of Manafort—to indicate that this was our ulterior motive. Only Congress could determine whether the facts we uncovered warranted impeachment proceedings; our office simply had our collective heads down, digging out facts as doggedly as we could.

As Michael and I talked, I told him that perhaps the judge's most disheartening comment was the idea that we only sought evidence "against" Trump. There was simply no basis to find that we were not following the facts where they led. Flipping Manafort and others might provide us with information that incriminated or exonerated the president, but it was imperative that we learn what the facts were, one way or the other. Judge Ellis was therefore making a claim about our intent that was unsupported by the factual record. Perhaps he'd reached that opinion by reading the news or listening to the many pundits attempting to undermine our work. But it was just that: an opinion. Voicing such an opinion from the bench was truly unwarranted and it served to inflame a segment of the public against us.

Moreover, Judge Ellis's belittling the use of cooperating witnesses was unusual—and oddly aligned with a comment the president had made, seeking to thwart such cooperation, saying publicly that the practice of flipping witnesses "almost ought to be illegal." But unlike the president, Judge Ellis knew from years on the bench, the government regularly brings lower-level criminal cases, as we were doing with Manafort, in order to see if it can advance a larger investigation. Good prosecutors flip subordinate after subordinate, as far as the evidence leads, as a way of uncovering the full breadth of a criminal conspiracy and climbing toward whoever sits at its top. This does not make those cases along the way bogus—the crimes committed by those subordinates are no less criminal or deserving of prosecution—nor is there anything improper about conducting an investigation this way. In fact, it's standard operating procedure. Without such cooperators, mob cases would not have a chance of succeeding.

After that second appearance, Judge Ellis's treatment toward us only got worse. I frown upon disparaging judges, as it can undermine the institution of the court. I will, however, point to the media coverage of Manafort's trial in Virginia, much of which rested on a pattern of inappropriate behavior. As a retired U.S. District Court judge and Harvard Law School lecturer put it in one *Washington Post* op-ed, Judge Ellis's behavior was "decidedly unusual" and exhibited "extraordinary bias" against the Special Counsel's Office. The writer, Nancy Gertner, went on:

> During the trial, Ellis intervened regularly, and mainly against one side: the prosecution. The judge's interruptions occurred in the presence of the jury and on matters of substance, not courtroom conduct. He disparaged the prosecution's evidence, misstated its legal theories, even implied that prosecutors had disobeyed his orders when they had not. . . .
>
> The judge continually interrupted the prosecution's questioning of witnesses. . . . Ellis pressed the prosecution to rush through testimony about important financial documents. He made critical comments about prosecution evidence and strategy—all in front of the jury.
>
> Ellis also questioned the relevance of Manafort's work as a political consultant for Russian-backed politicians in Ukraine, for which he was paid tens of millions of dollars from 2010 to 2014. But if Manafort didn't disclose some payments because he was not registered in the United States as a foreign agent, it would provide a motive to hide the amounts from the U.S. government—just what the trial was about.

I had planned on trying the Virginia case myself, along with Greg Andres, one of my other Team M prosecutors. But with Manafort's second trial slated for early September, and with the Virginia trial date slipping on Judge Ellis's calendar so it would begin only at the end of July, I found it necessary to split Team M in two, so that I could oversee preparations for the D.C. trial. I did not want the date of the second trial delayed. In order to keep the maximum pressure on Manafort, we needed to be able to roll off the first trial onto the second.

We expanded the first trial team with Brandon Van Grack, who had led the Flynn investigation, and Uzo Asonye, who joined us from the Virginia U.S. attorney's office (Judge Ellis had insisted we have a member of that local office join our team). One clear sign of how sensitive we had become to the White House's perception of our work was that Aaron did not allow Uzo to be identified as a member of the Special Counsel's Office; he did not want any stories in the press suggesting our team was expanding. Better for them to understand that we were winding down, not ramping up, particularly as we were now starting year two of the investigation.

The practical consequences of Aaron's hypersensitivity, however, were that Uzo could not even get access to our computer system at first, or have an office email or phone number. This made it impossible for him to do his work—preparing documents, communicating with witnesses' counsel, working with agents—all merely to avoid a story that, in fact, would be accurate and understandable: Our team had expanded out of the necessity of handling two back-to-back trials. "Perception should not be trumping substance," I groused to Jeannie, who was ever sympathetic to me. Eventually, Aaron reconsidered, and Uzo got what he needed. Even so, we were not permitted to identify him as a member of our office.

All three of our trial attorneys are exceptionally capable lawyers and performed superbly, under hostile and dispiriting circumstances. But even with this stalwart team in place, the situation with Judge Ellis became so contentious that I took to attending the Virginia trial more often than I had anticipated. My days and nights quickly filled up with attending the trial, preparing for the imminent next trial, and helping put out brush fires that kept igniting in court.

Late one afternoon, for example, Uzo advised the court that the following day we would be calling an IRS audit agent as an expert witness, which is a standard practice in a tax case. Judge Ellis exploded—in front of the jury—insisting that the agent would not be allowed to testify because he'd been in the courtroom previously while other witnesses were on the stand (also standard practice when calling an expert). This, Judge Ellis scolded the prosecution, violated the rules for the trial that had previously been established. Uzo explained to Judge Ellis that we had, in fact, asked the court for permission at the outset of the trial for the agent to be present for those other witnesses' testimony and that the judge had granted it. Uzo added that he would double-check the transcript, to be absolutely sure.

"Let me be clear," Judge Ellis shot back. "I don't care what the transcript says."

I knew Uzo had it right, as I had been in the courtroom when we had sought and been granted that permission. I stayed up that night with our legal team drafting a motion to have Judge Ellis give a corrective instruction to the jury, explaining his error in reprimanding Uzo. We attached the transcript page that demonstrated that the judge had been in error and I signed the motion myself, so that any blowback would be on me as the team leader, and not my prosecutors in court. And yet, even after Judge Ellis granted this motion for a corrective instruction the next morning, he offered only a grudging clarification to the jury. "I was probably wrong in that," he told them. "I may have made a mistake there and any criticism to counsel should be disregarded."

This proved a tipping point; the press coverage of the trial, which had initially brushed off Judge Ellis's previous comments as the colorful idiosyncrasies of an irascible, no-nonsense judge, quickly morphed into criticism of his conduct. We knew things had truly gone off the rails when one pundit in particular accused Judge Ellis of "showing an extraordinary bias against the government. If you feel that negatively about the government," the commentator said of the judge, "you shouldn't be on the case." This pundit was Judge Andrew Napolitano, a regular commentator on Fox News.

As the trial wore on, and Judge Ellis's conduct toward us became more problematic, it became hard not to step back and marvel at Manafort's decision to elect to have two trials in the first place, which would compel us to do this all over again in Washington in just over a month. For anyone with experience as a prosecutor or a defense lawyer, it seemed similarly counterintuitive and unwise that Manafort had chosen to go forward with a trial at all, rather than plead, given the strength of the case we'd built against him. It was like Manafort had pulled us all through a looking glass, where little of what was happening added up according to any conventional understanding of the law.

Manafort was not following a normal criminal defense strategy, based on a sober assessment of the cases against him. Remember, to be acquitted or convicted, a jury has to be unanimous. Having opted for two separate trials, Manafort now had to convince twenty-four jurors that he was not guilty in order to walk free, instead of just twelve. Even if Manafort did not want to cooperate with our investigation, why not have one trial, or plead guilty and avoid all the work, expense, anxiety, and public humiliation of enduring two trials? That's what a defendant would ordinarily do, and they'd likely be rewarded for their decision at sentencing, too; the judge would give such a defendant credit for accepting criminal responsibility, and would furthermore not have had his or her opinion of the defendant shaped by all the damaging evidence a trial produces.

As odd as Manafort's decision-making seemed, there was one way to make sense of it: He was throwing a Hail Mary pass, adopting the only strategy he saw that might ultimately keep him out of prison. In short, he had his eyes on a presidential pardon. I made sense of his gambit as follows: Yes, Manafort knew it was unlikely he could obtain an acquittal in both the first and second trials. But if he were able to eke out a hung jury in the first trial, he could spin that result as a vindication—indeed, it would widely be viewed as a defeat for our office. Manafort and his allies at Fox News could hold that up as proof that a partisan Special Counsel's Office had gone after an innocent man. And that, of course, would also conform perfectly to the larger "witch hunt" story that the president and his mouthpieces were promulgating daily.

All of a sudden, in this twisted universe, the president wouldn't just have the political cover necessary to pardon Manafort; pardoning Manafort would, perversely, play to his advantage. A pardon would galvanize Trump's base: The president would be seen as taking a stand for justice and upbraiding a Special Counsel's Office that had gone rogue. This was why Manafort wouldn't now plead guilty: If he admitted his guilt, he'd be giving credence to our work and undoing the entire foundation on which this narrative might be built. And the president liked people who hung tough, repeatedly praising Manafort for not caving in to pressure to cooperate. This, too, played into his calculus.

Meanwhile, as Manafort maneuvered for a pardon, President Trump was laying the groundwork to provide him one. He'd begun manipulating public opinion to make such a move appear more reasonable, continually reminding his base how outrageous our prosecution was, while also signaling his continued support for Manafort to discourage him from flipping. As the Virginia trial got under way, we watched the dance between Trump and his former campaign chairman unfold publicly, in the media and on Twitter—an analogue to the private tug-of-war we'd experienced while persuading Rick Gates to cooperate. Trump was making veiled assurances to Manafort that he'd be rewarded if he continued to keep quiet, and Manafort was praising the president for his support.

It's important to understand that the president didn't particularly like Manafort. Their relationship was prickly; the two, we'd learned, had never clicked. Trump didn't care for Manafort's overdone clothes, dyed hair, whitened teeth—a head-spinning irony that I chalked up to Trump's own vanity, and his desire to be the only peacock in the room. Manafort was also different from much of Trump's inner circle on the campaign. Many of the others were family members; Manafort was a hired gun. His loyalty was an open question.

This explained why Trump had now taken to publicly saying how much he admired Manafort. On the second day of trial, for example, the president tweeted: "Looking back on history, who was treated worse, Alfonse Capone, legendary mob boss, killer and 'Public Enemy Number One,' or Paul Manafort, political operative & Reagan/Dole darling, now serving solitary confinement—although convicted of nothing? Where is the Russian Collusion?" And then: "I feel very badly for Paul Manafort and his wonderful family. Such respect for a brave man." He publicly implored Attorney General Sessions to "stop this Rigged Witch Hunt right now, before it continues to stain our country any further." Putting aside how strange it was to compare Manafort to Al Capone, or that Manafort was not in solitary confinement, it was clear to me what was happening: Trump was whispering to Manafort that he had his back, that he'd look out for him.

We'd already seen him make similar overtures that spring to his longtime attorney and fixer, Michael Cohen. By then, the case against Cohen that we'd referred out to the Southern District of New York had progressed significantly, and a *New York Times* story reported that, as a result, Cohen might be considering cooperating with the Special Counsel's Office. In a series of tweets, the president insulted the *Times* reporter, and accused her and the newspaper of "going out of their way to destroy Michael Cohen . . . in the hope that he will 'flip.'"

Trump called Cohen a "fine person with a wonderful family. . . . Most people will flip," the president opined, "if the Government lets them out of trouble, even if . . . it means lying or making up stories. Sorry I don't see Michael doing that despite the horrible Witch Hunt and the dishonest media."

But later, when it became clear that Cohen had decided to cooperate in our investigation, Trump did a one-eighty, lambasting him in another series of tweets, labeling him a "rat"—all the while continuing to praise Paul Manafort, who, unlike Cohen, had "refused to 'break' [and] make up stories in order to get a 'deal.'" One thing about this behavior: It was not subtle. There was no subtext, only text. The president was flaunting his power to pardon, advising Manafort—and, by extension, anyone else—to think twice before cooperating with Mueller. The language the president was using was reminiscent of that of the many mobsters I'd dealt with as an assistant U.S. attorney in Brooklyn. This was exactly how Sammy the Bull Gravano talked. It was alarming to hear such words from the leader of the free world.

I had read Jim Comey's book several months earlier and chalked up as pure hyperbole his comparison of the president to a mob boss, when describing Trump's fixation on pledges of personal loyalty. But now, tracking Trump's tweets during the Manafort trial, I knew I was wrong: We were watching the president mirror the behavior of criminals—not just by prioritizing loyalty to him personally over loyalty to the law, but by dangling certain rewards and punishments to back up such demands. Mobsters used the threat of "whacking" potential cooperators to keep everyone in line; the president had the power to pardon to reward those who stayed loyal.

The president possessed a singular power that could thwart the fundamental precepts of a criminal investigation by inducing people not to cooperate with law enforcement, no matter how guilty or how strong a case we amassed. It was a neutralizing force that we would find difficult to counter, and would only meet with exasperation, dark humor, or despair. (Eventually, contending with the specter of a pardon became such a familiar and vexing element of our work that Jim Quarles, Team 600's leader, took to sardonically exclaiming "Pardon me! Pardon me!" as he trotted past clusters of our staff through the hallways of the office—a running joke that, even after many months, Jim endearingly never tired of.) The power to pardon functioned as a kind of alternate gravity, pulling everything and everyone around it off their more predictable paths. Gradually, this weapon, deployed bluntly and boldly, in private and in public, was creeping into the work of our entire office, undermining the rule of law that Mueller was appointed to uphold.

Perhaps the pinnacle of this disruptiveness came after we finished presenting our case against Manafort in the Virginia trial and the jury was in the midst of its deliberations. Talking to reporters on the White House lawn on August 18, 2018, the president described Manafort's trial as "a very sad day for our country." Manafort, he insisted, "happens to be a very good person. And I think it's very sad what they've done to Paul Manafort."

Bear in mind that Paul Manafort had been charged with numerous federal crimes, including millions of dollars in tax and bank fraud, lying to the government, and even tampering with witnesses while he was out on bail. A judge had already found the last crimes as warranting putting Manafort in jail pending trial. What sort of person is in favor of such crimes, and seeks to defend that behavior—particularly if you are in the government that Manafort defrauded and lied to? Particularly if you are the chief executive of that government? And yet, here was the president of the United States lamenting what "they" were doing to Paul Manafort. "They" was the government of the United States. "They" was the rule of law. In retrospect, this was another watershed moment in the escalation of the president's prioritizing his own personal power over the laws of our nation and the norms and integrity of the institutions that uphold them.

The timing of this particular statement, at such a sensitive moment in Manafort's trial, left little to the imagination: It was plain that Trump was attempting to influence the jury's decision. The court in Washington had issued a standing gag order, restricting public statements that might affect the jury—meaning that, if I or anyone else in the prosecution had issued a response to the president, underscoring the sweeping evidence of Manafort's guilt, we would have landed in front of a judge for contempt of court. The president, however, felt no such compunction. He eventually defended his statements, arguing that he has a First Amendment right to say what he likes. But this is wrong: None of us is entitled to say something that constitutes a crime or contempt of court. You cannot use words to obstruct justice or to order a murder in the mob—neither is protected by the First Amendment.

Our recourse was to add Trump's statement to a growing list of evidence that could support the crime of obstruction of justice—Team M's work, in other words, was now spilling over into Team 600 territory. I dropped by Jim's office to let him know, teasingly, that Team M had come to his team's rescue: Our trial apparently pushed the president into a position where he felt it wise to try to obstruct the jury in full public view.

"You think?" Jim retorted, knowing I had just stated the obvious.

It all raised the question of why the president's personal interests, and the interests of the government he led, were so misaligned. And more immediately, why did the president fear the prospect of Manafort's cooperating with the Special Counsel so acutely? What was he worried Manafort might say?

CHAPTER 18

Our High Point

ON THE MORNING OF August 21, 2018—four days after Trump's tweet expressing sympathy for Manafort and comparing him to Al Capone— the jury in the Manafort case in Virginia was still out, deliberating, and I was back at our offices in Washington cramming to prepare for the second trial, which was just three weeks away. One phone call, however, would bring that work to an abrupt halt.

The call was to alert me that the jury in Virginia had reached a verdict. As there were no phones allowed in the Virginia courthouse, one of the Team M agents on site had to scurry back to our temporary office space in Virginia to give me a quick call and then run back to court. After I put down the phone, I actually ran down the long hallway between my office and Mueller's, poked my head in, and gave him the news. He looked up and nodded, and I could see in his eyes a look of eager anticipation, ever the trial lawyer. From there, I relayed the information to Aaron, Jim, Jeannie, and others on Team M, and news spread in minutes across our floor until my tiny, windowless office became crammed with so many attorneys that it resembled a clown car.

I rarely turned on the TV in my office, but now had it tuned to CNN. The chyron was reporting that a verdict had been reached, but no one yet knew what it was—including us. Nor did we know that this day would mark the high point in the special counsel's investigation.

Mueller and Jim Quarles were hovering near my desk when one of our FBI agents phoned from Virginia with an update: The jury had reached only a partial verdict; the jury informed the court that it had decided unanimously on only eight of the twenty-two counts. With respect to the other fourteen, the jury was hung. The court can take a partial verdict—that is, allow the jury to announce its verdict on the eight counts—and the government can then choose to retry the hung counts if necessary. Here, both sides agreed that the court should take the partial verdict. The defense must have been betting the jury had acquitted Manafort on the eight counts and was hung on the rest.

After I hung up, I gave Mueller and Jim the news. I couldn't make sense of it; a unanimous verdict on only eight counts didn't add up. Knowing the evidence in the case backward and forward, in the moment I found it difficult to imagine how a jury could have unknotted all the proof and come to an agreement on eight of the counts, but not more or less. I was still confident we would have guilty verdicts: Our case against Manafort seemed unassailable and part of a cohesive whole. But with juries, particularly in high-profile cases, you never know. Eight acquittals and hung on the rest, without a single guilty finding for any of the twenty-two counts, would be a devastating outcome for us.

Upon hearing my update, Jim rolled his eyes with stoic exasperation—but also a clear hint of worry; he was an experienced trial lawyer, too, and had great instincts on this stuff. Mueller just stared at me—jaw clenched more than usual, silent, and listening to my babbling attempts to come to a theory about the counts; he was as tense as I can ever recall seeing him.

This was a must-win case. We all knew how a partial acquittal would be spun by Manafort, the right-wing media, and the White House. It would be twisted into a referendum on our entire investigation, proof that our work was a sham. This would not be a fair or even rational contention, but we could not afford any doubts to be sown on our thoroughness, expertise, or impartiality.

A partial acquittal would therefore be a nightmare, and I knew Mueller and Jim were thinking the same thing, though none of us said it aloud. In fact, we found ourselves saying nothing at all—just waiting, nervous and grim-faced. CNN would be the fastest way for us to learn the verdict; the network's reporters would be able to bolt out of the courthouse to the waiting news cameras with the news much faster than any member of our trial team could get back to our office to call us. The network appeared to have a full production team in place in Virginia, and now, in an exact reversal of the dynamic of the previous fifteen months, the leadership of the Special Counsel's Office was staring at cable news in ignorance and torturous anticipation.

Suddenly, CNN went to split screen. Alongside the shot of the front door of the courthouse in Virginia, another materialized of the federal courthouse in Manhattan. In an almost implausible twist, news had just broken that our colleagues in the U.S. attorney's office were about to make an announcement about their criminal case against Michael Cohen, which we had referred to them months earlier. The precise timing was a surprise, leaving even us dumbstruck, though we knew what was coming: Cohen, it would soon be revealed, had pleaded guilty to a number of felonies.

In my mind, our strategy of splitting off the Cohen investigation to the U.S. attorneys, instead of pursuing it ourselves, had been far from ideal—a tactic, in fact, that risked undoing the very purpose of appointing a special counsel in the first place. The point of standing up our office was to ensure that an independent, objective investigation could be conducted, cordoned off from political interference—or at least as much as possible, given that the special counsel was still within the Department of Justice. Now we were removing a piece of the investigation from the protections of the special counsel regulations, entrusting it to other prosecutors who did not have these same protections.

In the end, however, this concern proved to be merely theoretical. We were fortunate to have colleagues in New York who acted aggressively, thoroughly, and, most important, independent of political pressure. They had amassed strong proof of the hush payment Cohen made to Stephanie Clifford, to keep her from going public before the election with her claim that she'd had an affair with Trump, and of a similar catch-and-kill scheme with a second woman, Karen McDougal. Beyond that, Cohen was also charged with a constellation of other fraud and tax evasion crimes.

Meanwhile, Cohen had come up again in our own investigation when Team R interviewed the real estate businessman Felix Sater. Sater had been a cooperating witness during the time when I was a prosecutor in the EDNY and, after pleading to securities fraud and cooperating with the government, had gone to work, of all places, with the Trump Organization, even though he was a convicted felon. When I interviewed for the job with Mueller in May 2017, I'd noted Sater as someone who would be worth reaching out to for an interview, to learn more about Trump and his organization, and Mueller had agreed. As this was more in Team R's bucket, I made the introductions and passed the lead to Jeannie. Sater proceeded to offer up proof indicating that Cohen had lied to Congress about one of the president's real estate endeavors in Russia, plans for a luxury high-rise that would be known as Trump Tower Moscow.

The press had started asking questions about the Trump Tower Moscow project in early 2017, prior to Trump's inauguration. In response, Cohen and Trump claimed that the project had died on the vine a full year earlier—long before Trump had become the presumptive Republican nominee. Later, Cohen would testify before Congress that the deal was over by the beginning of 2016—which conformed to what Trump had said publicly. But Sater told Team R that the negotiations over the Moscow deal had stretched into the first half of 2016, and he provided our office with emails to support that assertion.

Jeannie was thrilled and expressed it with her usual enthusiasms, regaling me chapter and verse with what Sater had recounted. She then orchestrated a plan to get Aaron and Jim to agree that it was necessary to subpoena the Trump Organization emails and not just rely on the paperwork that Team R had obtained from Sater. But they had cold feet. They knew that making a move like this would get back to the White House and there could be consequences. And, sure enough, Aaron eventually told Jeannie to stand down in her pursuit of Trump Tower Moscow emails. He said that Mueller agreed with him, that this was not worth the potential blowback; we were still negotiating with the White House to get an interview and, once again, Aaron claimed this would hurt that negotiation.

For Jeannie, this directive was the last straw. We shut the door to her office and had the mother of all bitch sessions. "So what?" she railed.

"Better to get fired, than to voluntarily pull our punches." All I could do was reiterate her point, in various different ways, and with rising amounts of ire and profanity. From then on, "Better to get fired" was the refrain we tossed back and forth every time we sensed our office pulling back from our mission.

"And Aaron's idea of negotiating with the White House is absurd," I vented. "Unless you pull the trigger and say you'll issue a subpoena, the White House knows you are bluffing."

"And we all know that's not going to happen," Jeannie added. "Aaron is just using it as an excuse to keep us doing as little as possible."

On and on it went. We both knew that the lack of follow-up here meant that any chance we had of ever performing a classic financial investigation to assess Trump's ties to Russia and motive evidence was dead. We also knew that this was the kind of insider nuance that a considerable part of the public wouldn't understand. Needless to say, this meant that Trump's tax returns were out of bounds. It was agonizing to be told, again and again by Aaron, not to follow any of these leads, and always according to the same defective rationale: that we couldn't afford to be fired over it, that we didn't want to rock the boat while negotiating for an interview. "How did that turn out, Aaron?" Jeannie and I would eventually say to each other when it was all over. In the end, we would fail to conduct a full investigation, and we never got an interview with the president.

I told Jeannie she should just talk to Mueller and make her case, but she explained that she'd previously gotten into a heap of trouble with Aaron when, after being unable to reach Aaron quickly with a separate, time-sensitive issue, she had gone to discuss it directly with Mueller.

"He told me I am forbidden to raise anything directly with Mueller," she said. I told her that was bullshit, and she should raise that issue with Mueller as well. "You have a different relationship with Mueller," she said. "You worked with him for years. I don't have that relationship so I can't do that." I was seething. Our work centered on crucial matters that struck at the core of American democracy. It was too important to be mucked up by Aaron's need for control.

In the end, Jeannie did not go to Mueller. And as much as I thought Aaron was dead wrong, I still strove to be a good soldier and did not go behind his back to raise these issues with Mueller myself, either. In retrospect I should have—and I can't find a totally compelling or credible reason for my reticence; though I don't think it would have changed anything, it was incumbent on me to try. Aaron had never attempted to quash my line of communication—sensing, I think, that Mueller would not approve, as Omer and I had a long-standing relationship with him. But Jeannie had not been granted that same privilege.

As time went on, Jeannie and I became concerned about how information was getting filtered by Aaron to Mueller, or not reaching him at all. While Aaron was afraid of charging people like Sam Patten and Alex van der Zwaan, for fear of upsetting the White House negotiations, Mueller would praise the charges as augmenting his position in the negotiations for an interview with the president. Later I would experience an even more jarring and important disconnect between the two in a matter that went to the heart of our effectiveness.

After our investigation was over, it was with bitter satisfaction that I read a lengthy ruling from Chief Judge Howell on a House request for special counsel documents in which she pointedly set out a series of gaps in our investigation. It was simultaneously embarrassing that we had not done more, but also a relief to know that Jeannie and I had not been crazy to be as exasperated as we were. Aaron had a way of gaslighting you, of making you question your own reality, that you were being too aggressive in your drive to pursue leads and push harder—like you were not enough of an adult. The small consolation of reading Chief Judge Howell's opinion was little comfort in terms of feeling like we had let people down.

An investigation into Trump's finances could have produced important evidence perhaps better delineating a motive for the president to curry favor with Russia, or for Russia to assist Trump in the election. Criminal investigations routinely examine motive. At a trial, for instance, a jury is much more likely to acquit a defendant if you cannot establish why the defendant committed the crime. Similarly, a motive can make a crime more likely, and if a criminal conspiracy to interfere with the election existed between the Trump campaign and any Russians, the public would want to understand the motive of each party. A motive can make otherwise disparate-seeming facts cohere, demonstrating that there was, in fact, a secret logic dictating the conduct in question.

As discussed, Trump's pro-Russia behavior during the campaign had been baffling: the sympathetic foreign policy positions he took; his over-the-top professions of admiration for Putin personally; his calling on Russia to find Hillary Clinton's missing emails. Was there a relationship that could explain why he was seeking Russian assistance to his campaign? Or was he attempting to enhance his business interests in the event that he was not elected?

To answer these questions, we would need to understand his financial ties with Russians. And this was not a speculative fishing expedition: Although Trump claimed to have no ties to the country, Donald Trump, Jr., had publicly said, prior to the campaign, that the Trump Organization had Russian financial support. Eric Trump, too, had explained to a reporter that the Trump Organization did not have to worry about support from U.S. banks during the financial crisis of 2007 because they had all the backing they needed from Russia.

To be clear, I am not claiming that the president was compromised by Russia. I am pointing out that we never took the opportunity to search fully for evidence that might answer the question. The Supreme Court had said that a grand jury investigation "is not fully carried out until every available clue has been run down and all witnesses examined in every proper way to find if a crime has been committed." We were not meeting that standard.

We still do not know if there are other financial ties between the president and either the Russian government or Russian oligarchs. We do not know whether he paid bribes to foreign officials to secure favorable treatment for his business interests, a potential violation of the Foreign Corrupt Practices Act, which would provide leverage against the president. We do not know if he had other Russian business deals in the works at the time he was running for president, how they might have aided or constrained his campaign, or even if they are continuing to influence his presidency.

That gap in the investigation highlights another flaw in the presentation of our work. The special counsel's report can be rightly criticized for not clearly specifying what we looked at in our investigation and what we did not look at. Even if you believe that Mueller was right not to explore this area fully, there is no acceptable reason not to make that decision unambiguously clear in our report. The report is even unintentionally misleading in this regard; it may suggest to some readers that we did more than we actually did. Reading the evidence we set out about Trump Tower Moscow, one may surmise that those findings were the product of a complete investigation into Trump's finances and business dealings in Russia—that we'd scrubbed his sprawling portfolio for questionable or criminal undertakings, or troubling Russian entanglements, and that this, in the end, was all that we found. But that is not the case.

Teams M and R had many back-and-forths with Aaron with respect to this problem while drafting the report. Aaron was adamant that our report be conclusive, making only definitive conclusions, while the teams on the ground pushed back, noting the many gray areas and gaps in our evidence and the realms we decided not to examine, including the president's financial ties to Russia; our failure to obtain the truthful cooperation of witnesses who'd been influenced by the president's conduct in dangling the prospect of a pardon; what questions remained outstanding; what evidence we could not obtain; and our inability to interview certain other witnesses at all, up to and including the president. Only some of these limitations made it into the final report, as Team M and Team R did not have the pen—that is, the final say. To remedy this, at least for posterity, I had all the members of Team M write up an internal report memorializing everything we found, our conclusions, and the limitations on the investigation, and provided it to the other team leaders as well as had it maintained in our files.

We should have been more transparent. We knew our report would be made public and, while our superiors at the Justice Department understood the ultimate parameters of our investigation, the American people did not and cannot be expected to glean them all from our report.

In the end, the wrongdoing we found in the areas in which we chose to look, particularly in the one Russian financial deal we examined as a result of Cohen's cooperation, left me with a deeply unsatisfying feeling about what else was out there that we did not examine. One of my strengths—and simultaneously one of my flaws—as an investigator is the desire to turn over every rock, go down every rabbit hole, try to master every detail. In this investigation, that tenacity was as much an asset as a curse: The inability to chase down all financial leads, or to examine all crimes, gnawed at me, and still does.

. . .

Ever resourceful, Jeannie and her team made do with what they had. Armed with the information from Sater and the documents from him on Trump Tower Moscow, as well as the evidence amassed by the New York prosecutors on illegal campaign finance payments and other Cohen wrongdoing, the two offices jointly approached Cohen and his counsel: This was his window of opportunity to come in and cooperate.

And it largely worked. Cohen was unwilling to cooperate completely—he seemed concerned about having to give up information about his family—but he met with us repeatedly and was more than willing to share everything he knew about Trump, the campaign, and the Trump Tower Moscow deal. And he would agree to plead guilty in two cases: one brought by our office involving his lying to Congress about the Moscow project, and another to the array of charges our colleagues in New York were bringing. Normally, a witness who wants to cooperate needs to be completely truthful and cannot pick and choose whom he's willing to give information about. Here, we agreed to alert the court at his sentencing that he provided useful information that the court could consider in sentencing, but we would note that he had not fully cooperated.

Cohen's information would cement a new pathway for our investigation. He provided a clear insider's account of the major Moscow real estate deal that Trump was negotiating with Russian officials while he was running for president. As Cohen revealed, in October 2015, three months after launching his campaign, Trump signed a letter of intent to partner on the project with a Russian development firm, I.C. Expert Investment Company. Trump had long sought to open such a complex in Russia and had worked with various people over the years to get it off the ground, including, at one point, the Agalarovs—the same Russian developers who'd initiated the June 2016 meeting at Trump Tower in New York to offer the campaign dirt on Hillary Clinton. In this most recent iteration of the project, a Russian firm would handle construction, while Trump's company would manage the building and grant license for its name, a deal that would potentially net hundreds of millions of dollars in revenue for the Trump Organization. As with any major financial undertaking in Putin's Russia, brokering the deal had involved contact between the Trump Organization and high-level government officials.

Cohen was the Trump Organization's point person on the project and told us, during a series of proffers, that he had been working to nail down the deal until at least June 2016, when the campaign was in full swing. Cohen explained that the false cover story was a recitation of a "script" that he and the president had worked on—an obfuscation— meant to put more distance between Trump and Russia. Cohen pushed this same fabrication on Congress, while testifying under oath.

As Jim Quarles noted, Cohen may have lied to Congress and thus been a perjurer, but he had only one reason to have lied: to protect the president. He had nothing to gain personally from such a deception—in the end, it only opened him up to a prosecution for perjury. What was self-evident to Jim was confirmed by Jeannie. She had pulled Cohen's telephone records and saw that he had repeated calls with the president's personal counsel—signaling that this was a matter involving Trump personally. And the calls were in the days leading up to the submission of Cohen's deceptive written statement to Congress in which he adhered to the false story about the Trump Tower Moscow project. And Cohen told us that Trump's personal counsel had carefully massaged that written statement to keep it on script and as anodyne as possible, while assuring Cohen that the president appreciated Cohen's loyalty. I had seen this all before, but not for decades. It was precisely how "house counsel" for a mob family would ensure a witness didn't turn state's evidence and was kept in line.

In short, this was another instance of the president and his men undermining our system of checks and balances. In this case, they were sabotaging the oversight power of Congress by inducing Cohen to lie.

Back in my office that morning in August 2018, watching tensely as CNN went to split screen to cover the Manafort verdict and the announcement of Cohen's guilty plea, I turned to Mueller and noted how surreal all of this felt. No one would believe it was a coincidence, I said— which, of course, it was. While New York had kept us abreast of the details in the Cohen case, we'd had no heads-up about, or influence over, the timing of this announcement; the NY prosecutors, of course, had no idea when our jury would come back with a verdict. We waited for the Cohen announcement to begin on the left side of the screen. What would happen on the right side, in the Manafort case, remained a mystery. Only the jury knew.

The crowd that was wedged into my office was mostly silent, watching and waiting. Finally, we saw the courthouse doors in Virginia open on the right side of the television and a pack of young reporters run toward their respective cameras. We held our breath. CNN made a preliminary announcement: So far, they reported, the jury had rendered at least one guilty verdict in the trial of Paul Manafort.

A loud cheer went up outside my office; this meant my imagined worst-case scenario would not happen. Mueller smiled broadly and shook my hand. "Good work," he said.

I thanked him, equally tersely, and told him we'd had the best team of lawyers and agents imaginable investigating and prosecuting the case. Before I could leave my office to hug the rest of my colleagues outside in the hall, CNN announced that Manafort had been found guilty on all eight counts on which they'd reached a verdict. Guilty on eight counts, without being acquitted on a single one of the remaining charges, was a resounding defeat for the defense. Such a loss couldn't be spun. Moreover, we'd soon learn that the jury had written on its verdict sheet that it had voted eleven to one in favor of conviction on each of the remaining fourteen counts. It was unusual for a jury to go out of its way to indicate how it had split. Clearly, it was sending a message, communicating its damning view on the entire case.

The jury's failure to vote unanimously on fourteen charges had been due to the qualms of a single juror—and the same juror on each count. There was no evident rhyme or reason to the charges on which this juror had chosen to vote in opposition to the rest of the jury, suggesting that she just as easily could have held out on the other eight charges, too, producing a hung jury on every single one of our charges.

When a jury hangs, the government often retries the case, but both the prosecution and defense consider a hung jury a bad development for the government. The defense has the advantage of having seen all of the evidence the government will present. And retrying a case is a real chore: It is like putting on a wet bathing suit. In other words, the history books would have read very differently had there been a slight change in the view of a single juror. If it had gone the other way—even hung on all counts—what was quickly heralded as a big win for the Special Counsel's Office, having overcome the challenges posed by a difficult judge, would have been trumpeted by the president, Manafort, Hannity, and their minions as Mueller spectacularly failing the first true test of the Special Counsel's Office's worth. The assessment of victory and defeat can be tissue thin.

The only juror to speak publicly identified herself as a Trump supporter, but announced that she had put her personal views aside and voted to convict on each charge, based solely on the facts and law as she was instructed to do by the court. That is, she had acted with impartiality—precisely what the president, in his attacks on our office and others, always presumed people did not have the capacity to do. The juror added some advice: She felt it would be a mistake for the president to pardon Manafort.

Soon the trial team in Virginia called my office and recounted the blow-by-blow of how the verdict had been delivered. I put them on speakerphone, with Mueller and everyone else listening. We tried to take their story in and let the enormity of the day fasten itself in our minds. But even before it could sink in, the still image on the left side of the television screen finally sprung to life and the Cohen news broke.

Cohen had implicated another person while pleading to the campaign violation charge—the individual who'd authorized his payments to Stormy Daniels, referred to in the indictment as "Individual 1." The press would quickly identify Individual 1 as President Trump. That is, not long after the president's campaign chairman was convicted of multiple felonies, word came that his personal attorney had pleaded to a variety of felonies as well—one of which involved the president himself, according to Cohen. It was a remarkable moment: The president's campaign chairman and personal lawyer were guilty of serious felonies. It was a high point for our office, and a low one for our country.

But the feelings of relief erupting in the office were palpable—as was a sense of fierce and unshakable momentum. It took a while for it to peter out that afternoon; the outpouring of bonhomie faded slowly, with celebratory chitchat still lingering in the hall. Eventually, Omer, Jeannie, and I slipped away from it all, into Omer's office, still in a state of elation and excitement. Then, Jeannie said, very seriously: "Tomorrow, Team 600 has to pull the trigger. It's now or never. There never will be a better time."

Omer and I nodded. We knew exactly what she meant.

■ **CHAPTER 19**

Subpoenaing the President

THE OUTCOMES OF THE Manafort and Cohen cases underscored the peril of continuing to deal with the president meekly. The truth is, by the time Jeannie, Omer, and I were discussing pulling the trigger on subpoenaing the president in Omer's office that afternoon in August 2018, we'd grown pessimistic that it would ever happen; Mueller did not seem likely to engage with the White House with sufficient assertiveness to either secure an interview with the president or compel him to appear before the grand jury. For too many months, we'd watched Team 600's negotiations with the president's attorneys sputter along with no signs of a shift in momentum.

Now we were seizing upon the possibility that these two blockbuster developments—Manafort's guilty verdict and Cohen's plea, which implicated the president—might upend Mueller's uncharacteristic indecision and offer new hope. We all felt a forceful wind at our backs and knew it was now or never. If our office continued to be reticent about pressing the president for his cooperation, it would be obvious that we had no intent of ever issuing a subpoena and that the president could simply call our bluff.

For months, Team 600 and Aaron had been going back and forth with the president's personal lawyers, as well as with the deputy attorney general and his staff, in a protracted, excruciating negotiation to convince the president to sit for an interview with our office. We all knew that the endless exchange of letter writing was not how you were going to get an interview with Trump, and that he was too recalcitrant, and too slippery, to coax into any purely voluntarily agreement. And yet, we kept bending over backward, offering all kinds of accommodations and limitations. Indeed, even offering an interview was an accommodation; in theory, we might have started by simply insisting on his appearance before a grand jury, under oath—a proceeding that a witness must go through alone, without the benefit and comfort of his attorneys' presence. (The attorney can be outside the grand jury room, and the witness can leave the room to consult on legal issues that arise, but legally the attorney cannot be in the grand jury.)

The back-and-forth was maddening. The president kept publicly stating how much he wanted to give the special counsel his side of the story, and how comfortable he'd be with such a conversation. But his counsel—from John Dowd to Rudy Giuliani to the lesser known but highly astute Jane and Martin Raskin—wisely kept putting the kibosh on any such plan. Lying to us in an interview would be a crime, and the president obviously had a tenuous relationship with the truth. It was unsurprising that his counsel did not want him to speak to experienced prosecutors who had done their homework and knew how to ask questions, with follow-ups; there was a grave risk that our investigation had turned up facts that could blindside the counsel, if their client was not telling them the truth. In other words, it made sense that the president would not voluntarily sit for an interview.

We believed we had two points of leverage to work in our favor, however. One was the potential political fallout of the president not sitting for an interview; though Trump's base would hardly care about his reticence to participate in our supposed witch hunt, a flat-out refusal to cooperate could have an effect on so-called swing voters, leaving them to wonder what he had to hide. The other was our power to issue a grand jury subpoena, if our negotiations broke down. The president might very well challenge a subpoena, but that would simply underscore his stubborn refusal to speak to us. And there was a distinct possibility that the courts would uphold our subpoena and force Trump to choose between testifying or asserting the Fifth Amendment—something no president has ever done. That said, we had to deploy this weapon prudently. We could not threaten to issue a subpoena as a negotiating tactic unless we were prepared to carry through on it. It was Prosecution 101: backing down after issuing a threat drains you of any credibility going forward.

The brokering dragged on, for months and months, and we always stopped short of giving such an ultimatum or deadline. That itself was a tell—a sign of our weakness: the president's counsel knew, so long as we weren't raising the threat of a subpoena, that they still had wiggle room. Issuing a subpoena was, simply put, a power Mueller and Aaron had so far been reluctant to deploy, though none of the rest of us—not Jeannie, Jim, Michael Dreeben, or I—could seem to get our minds around why. Dreeben and his team had researched every single circumstance going back to the eighteenth century when a president had ever given testimony or an interview, up through the Clinton testimony to the grand jury. Nothing in that history suggested that a grand jury subpoena would be inappropriate, particularly since we had first tried to accommodate the president by offering an interview and had even provided the topics we would ask about (which we suspect the White House then promptly leaked to the press).

A grand jury subpoena was the trigger that Jeannie was now saying we had to pull. And Omer and I both agreed. "We have the most leverage now," Omer added as we huddled in his office after the Manafort and Cohen announcements, "and we'll never have more public support for subpoenaing him."

The way I saw it, our office had a mandate to conduct a thorough investigation, and we needed to be appropriately aggressive in order to fulfill it. Our job was to determine whether Trump or any other American had conspired with Russia to interfere with the election—or sought to obstruct our or Congress's efforts to answer that question. Hearing from the president himself would be critical on both of those issues, particularly as his intent was a central issue. Why had he wanted Comey to go easy on Flynn? Why had he fired Comey? Why had he doctored the press statement issued by Donald Trump, Jr., on the Trump Tower meeting, or tweeted praise about those who did not cooperate with us while denigrating those who did? Did he dangle a pardon to thwart cooperation by Gates, Manafort, and others? Why was he supportive of

Russia's takeover of Crimea? Why was he not taking Russian election interference seriously—and even actively denying it?

The questions went on and on—and we knew, even if it was unlikely he'd answer them all forthrightly, it was crucial for us to at least assess his honesty or evasiveness for ourselves. If we provided him with a list of those questions in advance, no even mediocre defense lawyer would bring a client like Trump in to answer them and risk getting caught lying, which would constitute the crime of making a false statement.

A subpoena was needed.

The Department was not making it easy for Mueller, however, to pull that trigger. Rosenstein was refusing to say whether he would support it. We did not need Rosenstein's sign-off, but under the special counsel regulations, the deputy attorney general could overrule our decision if he concluded that issuing the subpoena was either illegal or did not comport with established Department policy. There was a high bar for him to override such a decision, let alone one made by Mueller and Dreeben, who had vastly greater legal reputations than Rosenstein. If Rosenstein did overrule us, the regulations required that Congress be notified at the conclusion of our investigation that he had done so. That provision was included so that the Department of Justice could not quietly dictate the investigation's course while keeping up the appearance that it had been independently conducted by the special counsel. Ironically, this requirement would work counter to its intent; Mueller and Aaron did not want any public disagreements now or ever.

Mueller and Aaron, reluctant to trigger such a scenario, had taken a preliminary step of asking Rosenstein's office what its position would be if we decided to subpoena the president—to, in effect, provide its judgment in advance. But Rosenstein and his principal deputy, Ed O'Callaghan—"Eddie O" to his friends—would reply only that they did not know yet. They felt there was a lot of merit to the view of the president's counsel that we did not need the president's testimony and had not established enough evidence to warrant it; it would depend on what other interim measures we proposed, what counterarguments the president made, and so forth. Until those next steps played out, Rosenstein and O'Callaghan would not commit to supporting or undercutting a subpoena from our office. They had thrust the ball squarely back in our court. We'd simply have to take our shot, or not.

As a result, in yet another attempt to accommodate the Department of Justice and the White House, we agreed to the proposal from the president's battery of lawyers that he answer written questions from our office, but only ones about the Russian links to the campaign and not about anything having to do with obstruction of justice. This exercise was futile from the start: The answers that came back were useless, as they equivocated on anything material. They in fact raised more questions than they answered, as the president claimed not to recall or remember facts that surely would have stuck out, such as conversations he'd had about WikiLeaks' possession of Clinton campaign emails. And with written answers there was no opportunity for follow-up or to assess credibility—which is precisely why the White House agreed to them. It also made it easier for the president to claim later that he had cooperated with us, when he hadn't.

Dreeben had his team dig deeply into the legal issues and teed up our arguments for defending a subpoena; he believed we were on solid ground, particularly given the daunting standard in the special counsel regulations that Rosenstein would have to meet to overrule us. Jim supported that approach and was clearly at his wit's end. One day after a meeting with Rosenstein and O'Callaghan, Jim came into my office, shut the door, and said, as angry as I had ever seen him: "I did not come here to take orders from Ed O'Callaghan."

I knew this wasn't Jim just letting off steam; it was also his way to get support, to see if I'd be willing to broach the subject with Mueller. I told Jim I would make my arguments to Mueller, but I had a sinking feeling that it was a lost cause. If Mueller had not taken that step by now, I took it as a sign that he simply wasn't willing to risk putting us on a collision course with the deputy attorney general, inciting the prospect of a public disagreement with the Department, and litigation with the White House all the way to the Supreme Court—all that, assuming we were not simply fired along the way.

At our next supervisors' meeting, in the fall of 2018, Jim and Aaron gave a short recap of their meeting with Rosenstein and O'Callaghan, and a summary of where our office stood in the tedious dance they were engaged in with the president's counsel. Much of it boiled down to more letter writing—tepid and largely ineffectual busywork that I was amazed to see Mueller not just tolerating, but condoning. Mueller's diffidence was perfect for running the FBI—it steered that agency away from political controversies—but it was not ideal in this setting.

There was one other factor at play: The proof of obstruction was so clear that all the downsides of proceeding with a subpoena would be unnecessary if grown-ups would simply look at the evidence dispassionately. That might have happened in another time and place, but that world had come and gone. The world of gentleman and -women, governed by reason and logic, was no longer something we could count on, to the country's eternal discredit.

When the summary from Jim and Aaron was over, I spoke up, drawing on the many conversations I'd been having with colleagues—the agonizing, informal strategy and venting sessions that had been happening in our offices as cabin fever set in. I knew this was my last opportunity to make my case—but also my first opportunity to do so full-throatedly. Like many important decisions Mueller faced in our office, this wasn't something he'd continually called us in to discuss at length or shout about. The discussion had unfolded, in spurts, over time. And for weeks after the Manafort and Cohen announcements, we'd known the likelihood of our issuing a subpoena, and his appetite for doing so, was diminishing. We had registered it draining away, the way a tide goes out.

"I am concerned about the precedent we are setting," I began. "What are we saying to future presidents, and to future investigators, who will have our decision thrown in their face? If we do not subpoena the president in this investigation, how can others justify the need to do so? The facts warrant it. The president, and his intent, are at the very center of so many questions in this investigation. Without his testimony, our report is like *Hamlet* without Hamlet. The character at the very center of the drama would never come onstage. If we don't pull the trigger, it will be on us, not the DAG [deputy attorney general]," I said calmly. If we wrapped our investigation without ever interviewing the president, we'd look back and have only ourselves to blame. "If taking our shot with a subpoena leads to our getting fired, so be it," I concluded. It would be better than standing down from our responsibility, I thought.

Mueller sat patiently through all of this, nodding but offering no reaction, no indication of whether it was affecting his thinking. This, I knew, was not a good sign. He said nothing in response. But out of respect, he'd let me finish—which I appreciated. I knew that I would be burdened with regret if I had not expressed my views in full, no matter how unlikely I knew I was to change his mind.

The meeting ended unceremoniously, shortly after I'd concluded my soliloquy. It was clear a decision had been made, and that the rest of us were simply late in recognizing that and accepting it. A short while later, the tenacious lead FBI agent on Team 600, Michelle Taylor, poked her head into my office. "Nice try," she told me.

"Thanks." I felt for her; she had worked so hard on Team 600. She, too, wanted to issue a subpoena, but it was now clear that would not happen.

It had been difficult for Jeannie, Omer, and me to watch Mueller vacillate on this question—to see him suspended in a kind of endless negotiation with respect to issuing the subpoena. With each letter back from the president's counsel giving reasons why he would not sit down voluntarily, Mueller had made yet another offer—given him a list of topics, a list of questions, a time limit, the ability to provide written answers first, to only answer questions about the Russian side of the investigation and not the obstruction side. All of that was tried, but no interview was forthcoming. The president would never agree, and Mueller was not going to press the issue.

Over time, this decision has come to feel even more momentous: My concern about setting a destructive precedent was realized much faster than I'd imagined. After successfully avoiding giving testimony to us, the president sidestepped giving testimony or even a written denial to Congress in connection with his impeachment. He makes elaborate statements to the press and at his rallies, but cagily never submitted an accounting in the forum where his misdirections and lies would subject him to legal consequences. The president knew it was a crime to lie to Congress, and so—tellingly—he never gave any statement there.

I will later discuss how Mueller justified his decision not to subpoena the president in our report; his rationale was difficult to agree with then, and even more so now, looking back. Pressing for the subpoena might not have changed things—we could have been fired or lost the litigation over the subpoena. Still, it was the proper route to take. The tactics of Grant, not McClellan, were needed.

By the end of the summer of 2018, events had started to feel unsettled and in turmoil, inside and outside our office. One morning, CNN and Fox News were blaring on the televisions throughout our office with reports that Rod Rosenstein had been summoned to the White House where, it was widely expected, he would be dismissed by the president, clearing the way for a less scrupulous appointee at the Justice Department to finally fire Mueller. Whatever forbearance Trump had mustered for our work—and for the checks and balances of American government more broadly—had apparently worn thin.

We had internally sussed out how easy it would be for Trump to appoint a more personally loyal operative as acting attorney general. Dreeben told us that the president did not need to await the confirmation of a new AG; he could appoint on an acting basis anyone who'd already been confirmed by the Senate to immediately take over (a tactic the president has since used with abandon to sidestep any congressional approval process). As the news of the Rosenstein–White House meeting flooded our office, BAM came around alerting us that Mueller wanted to talk to everyone in fifteen minutes. We all gathered, with a sense of foreboding. This was it, after so many months of anticipation of being fired. And by this point, we knew we could not expect Congress to deploy its powers of oversight and rush to our defense—its early days of courageously supporting Sessions, to protect us, were long gone. We crowded somberly into the hallways leading to Mueller's office.

He appeared, in his white button-down shirt and dark suit pants, closely shaved, with perfectly coifed hair, though it was hard not to see the twelve years of grueling pressure running the FBI, and the year and a half running our investigation, in the drained look on his face—he bore the physical toll of his public service. He began to address us with an air of finality. He told us, in a halting and clipped voice, that he appreciated all our hard work and the exemplary way in which we'd handled ourselves during the investigation. We should all be proud of how we conducted ourselves—we had his respect for that. Aaron, Jeannie, and I exchanged sidelong glances; I felt oddly resigned to the whole thing. I had expected it for so long, and now that it was here, I accepted it. When the meeting broke up, everyone wandered back to their offices.

All our work on the investigation had been securely recorded and backed up every day, ensuring it would survive when this disaster inevitably came to pass. Consequently, Mueller's remarks incited no pandemonium, or even visible agitation, in the office; there was nothing to scramble around attending to, or saving. I had a tightness in the pit of my stomach, of course, about the uncertainty of who, if anyone, would ever pick up the many leads we still had to chase down. Would they just wither away with our demise?

I had been Mueller's general counsel at the FBI when his twelve-year tenure as director came to end—a term that had been extended two extra years, singularly for Mueller, by a special act of Congress. (The act passed 100 to 0, which now seems like a throwback to a distant time in America). As his term wound down, Mueller wanted to understand the details of that idiosyncratic exception meticulously, and asked me to research and summarize in a memo when, precisely, his tenure was supposed to end—not just the precise date, but the time of day, down to the minute. He intended to be at his desk working the whole time till that moment.

Now, as we awaited an announcement of Rosenstein's firing, we did what Mueller taught us to do: We put our heads down and went back to our desks and continued our work.

Eventually—and miraculously, it seemed—we learned that Rosenstein had returned from the White House to the Justice Department, still the deputy attorney general—and our ultimate boss. What, if anything, he may have told the president about our investigation in their meeting to extract more patience from Trump, or talk him down, I don't know. But something had clearly caused the president to back off. Jeannie and I strongly suspected that Rosenstein must have told the president that our report would somehow exonerate him or find there'd been "no collusion"—that, in short, Trump could be confident he'd survive our conclusions.

We came to this theory soon after this White House meeting, as we noticed the president dramatically shifting his public posture toward our investigation, making a show of saying, oddly, that he anticipated being treated fairly by Mueller—even as he continued to decry our entire operation as a witch hunt. He continues to cling to a form of this paradoxical view of our investigation, and our report, to this day: Any bad fact we discovered was merely a product of a gravely conflicted and vengeful inquisition; the more favorable facts, however, were unassailable truths.

In the end, I still don't know what motivated Mueller's decision not to issue a subpoena to Trump. It was left to Michael Dreeben to articulate that reasoning in our report. Even now, the language he arrived at, and which Mueller ultimately signed off on, strikes me as problematic.

Our report noted that Mueller had concluded that a subpoena was unwarranted since taking the president's testimony was not essential: "We determined that the substantial quantity of information we had obtained from other sources allowed us to draw relevant factual conclusions on intent and credibility." This statement makes sense, though, only if we had concluded in the report that the proof we'd amassed was sufficient or insufficient to charge the president with a crime, and, in addition, if we had made the presumptuous conclusion that his testimony would be unlikely to change our calculus. This was not the case.

In volume one, which dealt with Russian election interference and the possibility of coordination with the campaign, we concluded that the evidence was insufficient to bring a charge. But nowhere do we indicate that gleaning more knowledge from Trump directly could have changed that judgment; in fact, there were many issues in volume one that Trump would have been able to further elucidate: What did he know about the Trump Tower meeting in June 2016? What did he discuss with Stone and Manafort about Russia and WikiLeaks? Why did he support, rather than condemn, Russia's invasion of Crimea, a region of Ukraine? What financial ties did he have with Russian oligarchs and why did he prevaricate about the Trump Tower Moscow project?

These are just some of the more obvious questions Trump has never answered under oath, and without those answers it is impossible to conclude that nothing untoward went on. After all, Roger Stone has not cooperated and, as I will discuss, neither did Manafort; so the president was an important untapped source of information on these topics.

In volume two, meanwhile, our report drew no conclusion as to whether the president's actions constituted obstruction of justice, noting that it was for others to make that formal, legal assessment. But the record for those others to assess could have been made clearer—one way or the other—if Trump had answered under oath in an interview a similarly lengthy list of questions on this issue: Why had he fired Comey? What did he say to Comey about the Flynn investigation? What was his role in crafting the misleading Trump Tower message to the press? Why did he dangle the prospect of a pardon and tweet about Manafort even during jury deliberations? And what steps did he take to remove Mueller, and why did he tell McGahn to lie about it?

Our report claimed these answers were unnecessary, given the record we had already amassed. But the problem with that reasoning is threefold. First, our report never actually came out and said Trump obstructed justice. Second, why should we assume he would not provide useful testimony to consider—not even a few critical new facts? And, finally, the report noted that, although the Department of Justice kept us from indicting a sitting president, we were supposed to investigate and preserve evidence for future decision-making on that indictment. Wouldn't a future prosecutor—or Congress in an impeachment proceeding—want us to have done everything we could to nail down all the evidence, particularly since our investigation was uniquely empowered to try to get Trump's testimony? And there was an important legal advantage we had: Unlike a congressional subpoena, a grand jury subpoena had been found to be enforceable against the president in the Supreme Court Watergate decision forcing Nixon to turn over the White House tapes to the prosecution. Bill Clinton, while he was president, even had to give a deposition in a civil suit.

The report gave another justification for not subpoenaing the president that I find less than transparent: that the inevitable constitutional litigation over our power to subpoena the president would have led to a significant delay in our completing the investigation. There is little question that the president would have fought a subpoena in court, up to and including the Supreme Court, and that this litigation would have indeed taken significant time—months if not a year or more if it went to the Supreme Court. But the report implies that this clock would have started ticking in mid-December 2018, once the president provided his paltry and inadequate written answers and still refused to sit for an interview. This does not answer why we'd allowed the process to drag along for so long up to that point. We had been given clear signs of the White House's reticence much earlier, and we could have taken greater control over the time line if we hadn't been slow to accept that a subpoena would be necessary. We could have started such litigation even as early as the beginning of 2018.

All of this left Jeannie and me dispirited. We knew that we and our colleagues had done great work and would buck each other up by noting the other team's respective accomplishments in record time. But we were both too type A to take solace in these bromides. As much as we respected Mueller and understood that his decisions were governed by his sense of duty and right and wrong, we also knew how each of us would have proceeded if we'd been in charge. We would have subpoenaed the president after he refused our accommodations, even if that risked us being fired.

It just didn't sit right. We were left feeling like we had let down the American public, who were counting on us to give it our all. We as a group had done amazing work, indicting dozens of people and companies in a short amount of time, but we had left important work undone.

CHAPTER 20

Throwing in the Towel

PAUL MANAFORT FOUND HIMSELF in a daunting predicament as his second trial approached in September 2018, and our last-gasp effort, within our office, to get Mueller to subpoena the president was foundering. Manafort gambled in choosing to have two trials, and had already lost the first in Virginia. Now he faced a second trial on multiple serious felonies—including witness tampering while on bail—and in the Washington jurisdiction he had desperately wanted to escape.

Manafort had made a motion to the Washington judge to have this second trial moved to Virginia, where—notwithstanding his recent defeat—there were more Trump voters and he believed he might stand a better chance of acquittal. (This, it's worth noting, betrayed the familiar, cynical belief that jurors are incapable of setting aside their personal opinions and deciding a case on the facts—the same mistaken assumption behind the president's attacks on Mueller and the rest of us.) I had learned in several of the Watergate memoirs I'd been reading that another presidential campaign manager, John Mitchell, had made an identical motion after the Watergate investigation led to a case against him. The judge in that case, Chief Judge Sirica, a sturdy Republican Nixon supporter, later wrote that he found Mitchell's motion offensive and rejected it. Manafort's motion was rebuffed as well.

There were other pressures bearing down on Manafort, too—time pressure prime among them. The second trial was scheduled to start in mid-September, just a few weeks after the guilty verdicts had been delivered in Virginia. It was unlikely that Manafort's defense team had time to get fully ready; Team M had coped with the harrowing schedule by splitting our legal team in two, preparing for the Washington trial while we tried the one in Virginia. Our strategy was to do everything we could to keep the September trial date from being pushed back, to increase the pressure on Manafort. When the junior lawyer working on the second trial with me left our office in July to return home to New York, I convinced Jeannie to take his place and—with Mueller's blessing—try the second case with me.

By mid-August—in the midst of the first Manafort trial—Jeannie and I had filed a prodigious cache of exhibits with the Washington court, signaling that we were ready to go. We had spent the previous two months working seven days a week, pulling double duty: preparing for the Washington trial while continuing to supervise our respective teams. Along with two FBI agents, we had catalogued four thousand pieces of evidence into charts for the jury, much of it focusing on Manafort's surreptitious lobbying on behalf of Ukraine. There were charts that documented Manafort's illegal lobbying of U.S. senators, congressmen, and other political leaders; charts showing op-eds and blogs he'd published, disguising the fact that they'd been paid for by Ukraine; charts that showed the millions of dollars he had funneled from Ukraine to other illegal lobbyists like the Hapsburg Group.

For every possible defense we anticipated Manafort would raise, we built a chart to knock it down. As stressful and exhausting as it was, Jeannie and I and two FBI agents on our team—Brock Domin and Omer—were having more fun than four people should; you can get a little giddy when you have so much evidence on your side. The challenge was how to synthesize all the proof for the jury—a good problem for a prosecutor to have. We decided that Jeannie would give the opening statement; in the run-up to the trial, she meticulously sharpened every word of it like the teeth of a blade.

In August, with the trial only a few weeks away, Manafort's defense team requested an extension of the court deadlines for filing various submissions—which, we warned the court, was clearly a harbinger of an inevitable motion to delay the trial itself. And in early September,

Manafort read through the questionnaires the hundreds of prospective jurors were required to fill out and—digesting the information as he would one of his opinion polls—got spooked and felt he was done for. He made the inevitable motion to put the trial off.

It didn't take a genius to figure out why Manafort really wanted to delay the start of the trial. It wasn't simply a matter of needing more time to prepare; he didn't want to hurt his chances of wringing a pardon out of Trump. The second trial would take place just before the November midterms, and Manafort understood that having his lengthy trial unfold in Washington in the run-up to those elections would not be good for the president and his fellow Republicans. So much of the evidence against Manafort that would surface in the trial was repellent stuff.

During the 2012 U.S. presidential election, for example, Manafort had concocted a story about Hillary Clinton's supposed anti-Semitism, arranged for the story to be disseminated through an Israeli government official, then planted it in a New York newspaper. Then Manafort instructed a colleague to tell the Obama campaign that the story had been planted by the Romney campaign, and that Ukrainian president Yanukovych had sought to prevent it from getting out. According to Manafort, the ultimate goal of this chicanery was twofold: The Obama administration would both feel indebted to Yanukovych and distance itself from Clinton to appease the "Obama Jews." Manafort was proud of the scheme he'd orchestrated: "Bada bing, bada boom," he'd crowed in an email to a conspirator. There was a load of evidence like this—and, once the trial started, there'd be a slow drip of it appearing in the media, day after day, for weeks, dominating the headlines.

Judge Amy Berman Jackson denied Manafort's motion for a months-long extension. So that was it; he was hurtling toward the trial now, with no more procedural moves with which to break free of its pull. I knew in my bones that Manafort understood he would throw out his chances for a pardon if he put the president through the political debacle of his trial now, just before the midterms. Thus, when I got a call from Manafort's counsel during jury selection, asking if we'd still be open to him cooperating, I wasn't totally surprised. But I wasn't totally credulous, either.

It is unusual, but not unheard-of, to allow a defendant to cooperate after he has already lost once—or "blown trial," as we say. Permitting a defendant to first take his chances in court, and then cooperate, sets a precedent that discourages defendants from cooperating earlier and does not suggest true acceptance of responsibility for one's crimes. But the government will set aside that concern in cases where the witness has significant intelligence. I had authorized such cooperation in rare circumstances when I was chief of the Criminal Division in the EDNY. I used to call it the T exception, the "T" being short for terrorism: We are all willing to break convention if a cooperating witness might give us information that could prevent death. Clearly, Manafort might be worth an exception, too—and he and his counsel knew it. But as with Gates, we would need to hear from him first before we'd sign him up as a cooperating witness. We had to determine how committed he was to being truthful, and if the evidence he could provide merited such a deal.

Jeannie and I took the offer to Mueller, and a meeting was quickly convened in his office with Omer, Aaron, Jim, and Greg. Jeannie and I began by laying out the proposed deal. Manafort's counsel had explained that the key issue for Manafort was locking in a maximum statutory sentence of ten years in the Washington case, while understanding that if Manafort breached his plea agreement with us—lied or double-crossed us, or otherwise violated our deal—that guarantee would fall away. We saw little downside to accepting the ten-year cap—Manafort was unlikely to get more than ten years anyway in Washington—and he still faced his sentencing in Virginia, which could lead to substantially more time. If Manafort was truly going to cooperate truthfully, then he would get a whole lot less time than ten years.

I confess that, personally, Jeannie and I were disappointed. Like all trial lawyers, we knew we had done the hard part—the tough slog of preparing the witnesses and documents—and now we had finally arrived at the rewarding piece from all that preparatory work. But we, like everyone else in the room, also understood how valuable Manafort might be to the special counsel's investigation—that flipping him had been an objective from the beginning. For well over a year, Team M had been battling to find out what was in his head. It was likely our last, best shot to hear from an insider in the campaign, as the president clearly was not coming in voluntarily, and Mueller was not forcing the issue with a subpoena.

There would be ancillary benefits, too. "Taking the deal will free Jeannie and Andrew to write their sections of the report," Aaron noted. Mueller and Aaron had been pressing us on this for months, recognizing the workload ahead of us—indeed, the legal team, which was coordinating the report writing, was now almost unavailable to do anything else for us, given that assignment.

"There's another nice factor, too," I began. Jeannie and I had told Manafort's attorney that any deal would require Manafort to agree to the forfeiture we'd sought in our indictment. That is, he'd be stripped of his ill-gotten gains: the houses and condos—everything Manafort had been able to buy, over the course of the past decade, as a result of his criminal activity.

"The forfeiture is considerable," I went on. "We won't know the precise value for sure until the real estate can be sold, but we're talking about thirty or forty million." We were all aware of the feigned right-wing outrage over how much the government was spending to keep the Special Counsel's Office up and running. That line of attack was misleading; most of us were federal employees already and were paid our same salaries no matter where in the government we were assigned. Still, stripping Manafort of those assets might result in the government taking in more money than our office had spent to date. And it would result in just punishment for his criminal acts over decades.

"And we will provide in the plea agreement that he would be agreeing that it was all forfeitable, criminally and civilly," I added. The significance here was technical, but important: even winning at trial in Washington would not result in such a civil concession, only a criminal judgment. And if Manafort were later pardoned, that criminal forfeiture might be undone. But the civil forfeiture would almost certainly still stick—though, I was careful to stipulate, the issue had not been decided by the Supreme Court. So cutting this particular deal with Manafort meant that he was likely going to lose it all. Mueller asked me to send some legal material on this issue, so he could read up on it, but he understood the point that this was just one more reason to go forward with the deal.

"But," I told him, "there are also downsides here." The truth was, we would be foolish to take Manafort's change of heart at face value. Jeannie, Omer, and I had talked through potential scenarios earlier, and we were concerned that Manafort was working an angle. I believed there was a real risk that he would feed us a lot of false, exculpatory information. "Then, when we call him out on those lies, he'll claim to the press, 'This is just a witch hunt. I told the special counsel what I knew, and it proved their case was bogus, but they're not interested in the truth.'"

"And that ups his odds for a presidential pardon," Omer added.

"We need to be on our guard," I said. "It could be a setup. He knows there's no way he can get a pardon if he drags everyone through a three-week trial just before the midterms. I can imagine Trump's personal counsel shouting at him: 'If you ever want to be considered for a pardon, you need to get rid of this trial.' So, as risky and dangerous as pretending to cooperate with us would be, he might be making the calculation that it's actually his best shot."

"Any other factors I should consider?" Mueller asked. He looked around the office and we all indicated no. He asked if anyone was against the deal. No one was.

Mueller wanted to know how we planned to protect ourselves from getting taken in by Manafort, if he were to lay the trap I'd just described. Omer and I had discussed this as well and now conceded that, while this is a potential danger with any cooperator, the deck was stacked against us more than normal here. Manafort had already seen so much of our evidence in discovery for the two trials that, if he intended to lie, he could puddle jump, spinning those lies with an awareness of what we'd be able to prove or disprove.

"But even then," I told Mueller, "it would be hard for anyone to keep all that evidence straight and lie consistently. He may be an inveterate liar, but that would be hard to pull off." We knew that Mueller, as an experienced prosecutor, would understand the nuances innately and trust we could manage the risks.

Many months later, much would be said about Mueller's unsteady testimony before Congress about our report. Was he the same man who'd led the FBI for twelve years? Did he understand what was in the report? Was he compromised by a medical issue or by aging? But none of those speculative concerns affected his ability to make the tough, day-to-day decisions he was called on to make while leading our office.

"Go forth," he now said, tersely approving our plan for handling Manafort. He'd judged that the potential risks of beginning the cooperation process weren't catastrophic enough to trade away the possibility that Manafort would actually be truthful and bring more light to our investigation.

"Congratulations," Mueller said to Omer, Jeannie, and me. "Keep me posted."

There is something surreal about finally meeting someone you have been investigating for a long time. You begin an investigation as strangers. But through the course of your digging into the evidence, you develop a strong sense of the person secondhand: closely reading thousands of emails written by or to him; interviewing his associates, and, if you are lucky, hearing him speak candidly to colleagues on tape. It's extraordinary, really: Through court process, you are permitted access to deeply personal information about a person—granted entry into so many different chambers of their lives. Even after all my years as a prosecutor, I find something unsettling and prurient about the undertaking. And having absorbed all that information, it is a curious sensation to have the person you've known only secondhand suddenly appear in the flesh. That extraordinary process was never truer than when Paul Manafort materialized in the Elm conference room that September.

I'd first seen Manafort at his first court appearance on our initial indictment almost a year ago, in the fall of 2017. His hair had been dyed brown and carefully coiffed; his skin, plump, tan, and largely unlined; his suit, worth more than a month of my salary. Back then, his counsel had thanked me for all the extraordinary hoops I'd insisted our office jump through to orchestrate his self surrender after the hand-up of our indictment, ensuring he be taken in respectfully and held for no longer than necessary.

But in September 2018, Manafort had been sitting in federal prison for three months, after being remanded for witness tampering. Getting him to our offices for this meeting necessitated a so-called take-out order from the court, which stipulated that the FBI could retrieve Manafort from the jail, but had to keep him shackled and in close custody at all times and return him to his jail cell at the end of the day.

Manafort shuffled into the room wearing a dark green cotton jumpsuit and leg irons around his ankles. His hair was disheveled and gray, which matched his complexion. He'd lost considerable weight. It was impossible not to feel some pity for him, even if his suffering was a consequence of his own choices. I told him I was sorry he hadn't been allowed to change his clothes. (His attorneys had asked if Manafort could put on civilian clothes for our meeting, but the prison wouldn't allow it.) He was a human being. I didn't see any reason to humiliate him.

Manafort and his team sat down on one side of our conference table. He was flanked by all three of his Washington attorneys and a young intern, taking notes. I sat on the opposite side, directly across from him, surrounded by Jeannie, Greg, Omer, and a few other Team M FBI agents. Omer began by reading Manafort his Miranda rights—a requirement before any questioning, since he was in custody—and then I ran through all the same rights and obligations I had recited by heart at the Gates proffer. Here, we added one more admonition: What happened in this room needed to stay here, I said. Manafort and his counsel agreed. We nonetheless were under few illusions that if Manafort did not intend to truly cooperate, everything we did and said would be reported back to the president and Sean Hannity, among others. Events proved us right to harbor such cynicism.

We'd explained in advance to Manafort's counsel that we would need him to address the charges against him in Washington and, to streamline the process, we agreed with his counsels' suggestion to begin the proffer with a prepared statement from Manafort. He read it aloud. Although I'd heard Manafort's voice many times, both on tape recordings and on television during the campaign, this was the first time I'd heard him speak in person other than to say he was not guilty, a year before. His voice had a slightly coarse twang; he read his statement in a tone that was even-tempered and self-possessed. His equipoise was in striking contrast to the reality of his situation, dressed in prison garb and in cuffs.

His statement amounted to a sweeping admission. Manafort explained that he'd intentionally conspired to fail to pay taxes on millions of dollars of income and to hide his foreign bank accounts; that he'd intentionally failed to register his lobbying work for Ukraine under FARA; that he'd knowingly lied to the Department of Justice to cover these activities up; and that he'd purposefully conspired to obstruct justice by tampering with the two potential witnesses while he was out on bail. As incontrovertible as the proof we'd gathered against Manafort was—and as certain as I was, intellectually, that he had done what we'd charged him with—there was something deeply satisfying about hearing him admit it in person. Omer, who'd been taking notes the whole time, astutely asked for a copy of Manafort's statement for accuracy—and so there could be no dispute later as to what he had just admitted.

As Manafort finished reading, it became clear: He would not be going to trial in Washington. Whether he would cooperate with us truthfully or not was still an open question, but by admitting his guilt in such a comprehensive and straightforward way he appeared to have given up. This was a good start.

We would question Manafort for three days that week, returning him to the prison each time by late afternoon. We asked him up front about his sharing of internal polling data with Kilimnik; he claimed that he told Gates only to keep Kilimnik up to date and Gates took it upon himself to provide polling data repeatedly—a claim he backed off later. Given the upcoming trial and our limited time to debrief Manafort, we were able to touch on this and other topics only somewhat superficially, testing the waters to see how candid he was prepared to be. Manafort spoke carefully and provided only a few pieces of truly revelatory information.

Most notably, at one point we asked him about an email he'd received in August 2016 from Roger Stone. Manafort gave a long explanation, the gist of which was to implicate two senior Trump campaign officials; it was related to an investigation in New York. (As the precise material is still under seal I cannot discuss the details, although it is unclear to me what the continued basis is for keeping all this material under seal.) We were trying to assess his credibility, fixating on signs of dishonesty—any indication that Manafort was still angling for a pardon, or attempting to play us. Volunteering this information, which implicated senior officials, suggested he may have written that possibility off, even though we all had continuing doubts.

There was one issue on which Manafort turned palpably evasive. While tracing Manafort's assets, Renee Michael, one of Team M's superstar financial analysts, had gotten curious about a $125,000 payment by a campaign pollster in June 2017 to the law firm representing Manafort in his criminal matter. The press has since reported the identity of the pollster as Tony Fabrizio, who'd worked for years with Manafort on polling in Ukraine. (I am using herein the names and details the press has divined from our filings, without confirming that they are accurate, as none of these people have been charged with a crime.)

Renee couldn't make sense of it: Was this payment to settle a debt owed to Manafort? And why had it been sent directly to the law firm, and not to Manafort? We did not know, but in tracing Manafort's assets it was an open question that Renee wanted to explore.

When Renee asked Manafort about it during one of our first proffer sessions, he became visibly flustered. He claimed it was money he was owed by a friend, Laurence Gay, who had run a political action committee during the campaign—though he stammered through his explanation. I glanced at Omer, who was already looking at me; our antennae were up—though frankly, in this case, you didn't need a lot of training to notice that something was off.

Afterward, we discussed the situation with Renee. She had double-checked her records, and Manafort's story didn't add up. For one thing, Manafort had recorded a loan to Gay in his books, but the amount was only $20,000, not $125,000. More important, we knew the payment to the law firm hadn't been made by Gay, but by the pollster publicly identified as Fabrizio.

After we ended the proffer session that day, we explained these inconsistencies to Manafort's counsel, citing the documents we had and alerting the defense team that Manafort appeared to be saying something demonstrably untrue. What was going on? we asked. They should figure this out with their client, we said—still open to the possibility that he had made an honest mistake. That said, we knew we had no hope of getting to the bottom of this question quickly; it was Thursday, September 13, 2018; his trial was scheduled to begin the following Monday. We'd made a judgment to forge ahead with a plea, but we wanted to set down with the defense a clear marker as to our thinking.

We asked to speak to Manafort's counsel in the "pizza slice," a narrow triangular room adjacent to the large conference room, and explained our position. We still didn't trust Manafort and had more work to do to determine his credibility, but given the time constraints we'd allow him to plead pursuant to the cooperation agreement. We'd arrange for him to enter his plea in court the next day.

Soon, after the attorneys had discussed the matter with Manafort, we were all back in the conference room, shaking hands. I turned to Manafort and said, "I know tomorrow is going to be difficult, and I wish you the best."

"Thank you for your sensitivity," he said, revealing a softer side at odds with his gruff political operative persona. "I appreciate it."

When I saw him next, in Judge Jackson's courtroom the following morning, Manafort was dressed in a blue suit and tie (the court, appropriately, had granted his request to appear in a suit). Typically, when taking a guilty plea, Judge Jackson will ask the government to recite the facts of the case, indicating what the defendant had done to make him guilty of the crimes he'd been charged with. Here, our statement of the facts stretched to twenty-four pages—with Manafort, there was a lot of criminality to cover—and, mercifully, one of the judge's deputies had pulled me aside beforehand and suggested I merely summarize it. Even then, it took me a while—and this was deliberate. I was conscious of the conspiracy theorists out there, including the president himself, who questioned our motives and denigrated our office for what we were "doing" to Manafort with these charges. I felt it was necessary to document, in meticulous detail, the incontrovertible and damning facts that established what Manafort had himself chosen to do.

Importantly, the statement included an admission by Manafort that he was in fact guilty of the ten tax and bank fraud charges on which the jury in Virginia had hung. That was not an unusual thing to require in a plea deal in and of itself; it was standard practice for our office to compel a cooperator to admit to every crime he'd committed, beyond the specific criminal charges to which he was pleading guilty. (When Flynn, for example, pleaded guilty to lying to the government, he also admitted that he'd failed to register under FARA for his own lobbying work but was not required to plead to that crime as well, so long as he acknowledged his guilt—which he did, until he claimed to be lying when he told the court he was guilty of lying!)

In Manafort's case, however, we knew this admission could wind up having useful repercussions. It would likely make his criminal conduct effectively pardon proof. Even if the president pardoned him down the road, a state like New York might still be able to prosecute him for state crimes arising from those same bank frauds that the jury had hung on in the Virginia trial and, armed with the admission of guilt he'd just made, be assured of getting a conviction. In retrospect, therefore, the partial conviction and hung jury in Virginia had been the worst possible outcome for Manafort. Better he receive a flat-out acquittal or flat-out conviction—now he could face state prosecution on the hung charges (as generally double jeopardy does not apply to hung counts, only to counts on which the jury reached a verdict one way or the other). It left him exposed—and in a way the president does not have the power to fix for him.

I had examined the law on this and drafted the plea agreement with it all in mind. Mueller had asked me about the matter, and read closely the legal analysis I provided him as to how this federal plea could ultimately affect a state prosecution. He was on top of every subtlety of our agreement. It was the Manhattan district attorney who'd have jurisdiction to bring a state case against Manafort, and Mueller had authorized me to place a call and inform them of the plea and Manafort's admissions—though we would not make any recommendation as to whether the DA should bring any charges. That wasn't our place, and to avoid any claim that we had done so, I was sure to have an FBI agent on the call with the DA's office as well.

When Aaron stopped by, I told him about the discussions with the Manhattan DA, and he freaked out. He said he had been asked by the deputy attorney general's office not to coordinate with any state as it would undermine the president's pardon power, and he had agreed. I told him Mueller had approved it, which made it clear to me that Aaron had not told Mueller about this commitment; I certainly didn't know about it. It also seemed like poor judgment for him to make this commitment: Having Manafort admit these facts and alerting the DA served our interests as it gave Manafort more incentive to cooperate. And if it might also serve to defeat a pardon that would be used improperly to obstruct our investigation, that was a positive, not a negative.

In any event, we would not be making the decision as to what any state prosecutor might decide to do; a separate sovereign state had the absolute right to make that determination. It struck me as ironic that a Republican administration wanted to undermine states' rights—usually a core part of its value system. Aaron looked sheepish, and after consulting with Mueller, reported back that it was okay to give the DA information, but only what was publicly available, such as exhibits that were publicly filed and the like.

The whole incident left me profoundly troubled; the dangling of potential pardons was a unique weapon to obstruct our investigation that we had spent months trying to overcome. It was unfathomable that we would not do our all to counter it by the perfectly appropriate means Mueller had approved. In the end, we were able to get the state of New York much of the evidence they needed, but in spite of the DAG and Aaron, not because of them.

The prosecutors in New York State ultimately decided on their own initiative to push ahead, unsealing a new set of charges against Manafort in March 2019 and informing the judge that they would rely on Manafort's written statement from his Washington plea agreement as confirmation that he'd committed the crimes on which they were indicting. That case is currently mired in litigation over the New York double-jeopardy rules: A trial court ruled it was barred, but that decision is now on appeal.

We don't yet know if Trump will pardon Manafort, of course, so it's unclear whether this New York case will be superfluous or take on real significance. A pardon, if one is handed down, would presumably happen, at the latest, right after the 2020 election, regardless of whether Trump wins or loses. To any rational observer, absolving Manafort would look extraordinarily crooked—and, given all the evidence of Trump's having wielded his pardon power expressly to undermine our investigation, would be further evidence to establish obstruction of justice. It would show that Trump did not just dangle a pardon, he delivered it. (The pressure to issue a pardon is far less now that Manafort was released from prison in May 2020, ostensibly based on COVID-19, although he did not meet the reported criteria for release and there were no virus cases in his prison—yet another instance of disproportionate treatment for Trump loyalists meted out by corrupt Justice Department leadership.)

This is not to say that Trump will therefore be deterred. By failing to restrain him for so long, the institutions surrounding the president have given him permission to do whatever he wishes, particularly if he does so boldly and publicly—if he tramples the rule of law as yet another act of droit du seigneur.

CHAPTER 21

A Wink from Trump

THE PUBLIC REACTION TO Manafort's guilty plea was explosive and feverish. By flipping, he'd done precisely what the president had publicly praised him for resisting doing, and leaned on him not to—he'd become, in the La Cosa Nostra verbiage Trump had already used describing Cohen, a "rat."

Suspense built up in the media as to everything Manafort must now be revealing to our office about the president, the Russians, the August 2 meeting with Kilimnik. But all that bullish anticipation would prove to be at odds with the reality.

After the guilty plea, one of our first orders of business was to solve the mystery of the $125,000 payment to Manafort's attorneys. But the varying new explanations Manafort offered in our subsequent meetings only confused the matter further. Manafort—who now knew that we knew that the pollster, Fabrizio, had made the payment—started by admitting that the money had not, in fact, come from Laurence Gay. But when Renee pressed him on how he'd treated Fabrizio's payment for tax purposes, Manafort was flummoxed, first describing it as a loan, only to contradict himself shortly thereafter, referring to it as income that he'd told his tax preparer to include in his returns.

The money was income. But it was also a loan. It came from Gay. Then it came from Fabrizio. By now we were thoroughly confused, convinced that Manafort's changing stories could only mean he was hiding something, though we had no idea what it was. We were going to have to keep pulling this thread. Renee reached out to Fabrizio and Manafort's tax preparer for their documents and arranged for us to interview them as well.

That did the trick. We learned that Gay ran a PAC that supported the Trump candidacy and that Manafort had installed him in that position. Gay had hired Fabrizio on a $19 million contract to perform polling work for the PAC with a secret condition that Fabrizio kick back 3 percent of that payment to Gay—an amount that totaled $570,000. To hide the kickback, Fabrizio agreed to hold the money for Gay, then send portions of it periodically to wherever Gay instructed. The $125,000 was one such payment, paid by Fabrizio to Manafort's counsel at Gay's direction. So why would Gay make such a payment to Manafort's counsel? Either out of gratitude for Manafort's having installed him as the head of the PAC or, more likely, to pass along a cut of the kickback money.

Omer noted that this scheme fit with what we'd learned about Manafort's tenure as Trump's campaign manager. We knew that although he was hard up for cash and increasingly awash in debt, he'd agreed to work for Trump for free in order to get the job. The kickback scheme would allow him to take in money behind Trump's back; he could simply siphon it out of Gay's PAC, instead of drawing a salary from the campaign. And it would explain why Manafort had been so insistent that the campaign form PACs, in spite of candidate Trump's resistance to them.

We'd uncovered yet another financial crime. Manafort had committed so many of them, big and small, and yet he felt compelled to hide this one from us. Why? Confessing to the scheme wouldn't materially alter our opinion of him or cause us to undo our cooperation agreement. Renee had the answer. "Here's what I think," she said. "Admitting this means admitting that he was stealing money from a PAC that was supposed to be working to get Trump elected. That's not going to help his chances for a pardon."

Renee nailed it—we knew right away. Manafort's fear wasn't that confessing to this new crime would change our view of him in the Special Counsel's Office—we already knew he was a fraudster and a crook.

It was that it would change Trump's view of him, revealing that Manafort had made the president a mark in one of his scams.

"That weasel," Omer muttered, nodding his head. Manafort was still playing for a pardon.

Shortly after that, we encountered another, clear indication that Manafort was lying to us. We brought in prosecutors from New York, along with their partners in the FBI's New York office, to join our next session with Manafort, so they could hear Manafort's story about an email Roger Stone had sent in early August 2016, a story that implicated two senior Trump campaign officials. But when the New York investigators arrived in our offices and asked Manafort to walk them through his account again, he gave a whitewashed version of events.

The story was so at odds with what Manafort had said previously—his testimony was derailing to such an extent—that his own counsel interrupted the interview and tried to pull his client back on track. "Paul," he said, "that is simply not what you said before. These folks need to know the truth." That is what good defense counsel does—sometimes a client needs help to keep from hurting himself.

Initially, when he'd shared these revelations at our proffer the previous week, it had given me hope that he might actually be sincere about cooperation and abandoning his hope for a pardon. Now, it was a paradigmatic illustration of his duplicity. He'd realized that his prior version would reinforce Cohen's allegations, further implicating the president and damaging his chances of a pardon. Team M had spent more than a year ferreting out Manafort's lies to his tax preparers, his bankers, the Department of Justice FARA lawyers, and even his own defense counsel—documenting those lies so meticulously, in fact, that it had ultimately compelled him to admit them all in court. Now, perhaps inevitably, he simply continued to lie, but this time to us.

Usually, a cooperation agreement leverages a defendant's self-interest and instinct for self-preservation, placing him in a position in which it's riskier to lie and far safer to tell the truth. If he's truthful, he'll obtain a favorable sentencing letter from the prosecution, all but guaranteeing a lower jail term from the court. But if he goes on lying, the whole agreement will be thrown out—the defendant has still admitted his guilt but trashed any prospect of leniency. In my career, I'd watched everyone from the acting boss of the Lucchese crime family to the chief financial officer of Enron assess this predicament and make the same decision: Plead guilty and tell the truth under a cooperation agreement. Snaring a defendant in that system of incentives usually works out well. And it should have worked with Manafort, too, but for a form of interference we could not fully counteract: the president's flaunting of his power to pardon.

The president's power to pardon had distorted the circumstances in which Manafort found himself, just as his power to fire Mueller had subtly distorted our own decision-making at various points in the preceding fifteen months. Manafort had entered our proffers having made a calculation about what lines, vis-à-vis the president, would be too dangerous for him to cross. We made the same calculations all the time for ourselves.

The lies continued. Manafort was accomplished and well-practiced at dishonesty; even his chosen profession of lobbying and consulting was, at least in the way he practiced it, a form of deception. Still, as Omer observed, he had typical "tells" when he lied: stammering, averting his eyes, or staring a bit too defiantly at the person who'd asked the question, with his jaw firmly set. I recalled the advice the mobster Sammy the Bull Gravano had given a junior member of the Gambino crime family as the man prepared to meet with government prosecutors and agents: 60 or 70 percent of the time, Gravano had explained, you can tell the truth; 25 percent of the time, you have to bob and weave—ask them to be more specific, dodge the question, say you don't recall. In the slim remainder of cases, you have to look them in the eye and lie outright.

The only upside was that Manafort's lies were so blatant that he wouldn't be able to play the trick we'd worried he might: claiming that we'd rejected the exculpatory information he'd provided us simply because we wanted him to adhere to a set script—that we weren't actually concerned about the truth. The lies he fed us could be easily disproven in court; it wouldn't be just his word against ours. We could report to Mueller that we'd protected the reputation of the office, at least.

It was also true that the matters about which Manafort was lying, so far, were not core to the special counsel's mission; they did not concern Russian interference in the election or cooperation with the campaign. I was therefore eager to ask Manafort about his August 2 meeting with

Kilimnik. It would be a difficult thing to lie about convincingly, particularly since we had a new, weighty piece of evidence, which we'd discovered since his trial in Virginia, and which Manafort would not know about in advance or have figured out how to dance around. This evidence was a batch of emails that clearly indicated what Russia sought to obtain from an eventual Trump presidency, presumably in return for its election interference, information warfare, and other support the country was mounting on behalf of Trump during the campaign—a "quo" for all the elaborate "quid" that Team R had shown Russia engaged in.

During the course of interviewing the pollster, we had broadened our request to him for documents, asking him to double-check for any additional communications with Manafort he might have. He provided us with a series of emails from the winter of 2018, after Manafort had been indicted by our office. The documents showed that Manafort had reached out to ask if he would help conduct a new poll on Ukraine presidential politics.

The pollster told us he'd been surprised that Manafort was reaching out to him. He hadn't been in touch with Manafort for some time and hadn't done any substantive Ukraine polling with him in years, not since Yanukovych had fled the country for Russia in 2014. And, of course, it struck the pollster as odd that Manafort was doing Ukraine polling while under criminal indictment in Washington.

The poll focused on a future presidential election in Ukraine and asked a series of questions about various issues and a host of potential candidates. Manafort would not tell the pollster who his client was— who was commissioning this poll; he made a point of keeping that secret. The pollster said that Manafort was already working with Kilimnik on the poll, and the two had prepared a draft. Included in the draft was a question that outlined a plan for Russia to take control of the eastern portion of Ukraine—roughly half the country—along with questions about former president Yanukovych returning from Russia to be the head of that region. When the pollster turned them over to us, he noted that he now could see why they would be of interest. An understatement if there ever was one.

Their content was startling to me. I had learned a lot about Ukraine since I joined the Special Counsel's Office. The eastern part of Ukraine is the main economic driver of the country, akin to northern Italy or northern France or, closer to home, Wall Street and Silicon Valley combined. It is a region that is close to Russia, not just geographically but politically, too. Russia had sought for years to control Ukraine, as Putin needed that territory to transmit oil and gas to Europe. But Ukraine needed Russia even more, as it obtained basically all of its energy from that nation. Russia had enjoyed de facto control of Ukraine when Yanukovych was president, funneling him millions of dollars in bribes to curry his favor. But after Yanukovych's overthrow, Russia no longer had such a willing puppet under its control. Thus, Russia had turned to brute force: its infamous invasion of Crimea, a region of eastern Ukraine, in 2014—the one that had outraged most Western democracies, but which candidate Trump oddly had regarded as no big deal.

The proposal for Russia to take over the eastern half of Ukraine was the Crimea invasion on steroids. Russia would annex half the country, reinstall its favorite figurehead, and thus control the economic heart of the country. Notably, Manafort and Kilimnik's proposal explained that, for such a move to succeed, it would need the consent of the United States. It called on Trump to give Russia an approving "wink"—the word the proposal used—and, furthermore, to appoint Manafort to negotiate the logistics with Russia on America's behalf. In a separate email, Kilimnik endorsed Manafort for this role; Manafort would be able to deal with Russia at the "very top level," Kilimnik explained.

Manafort wasn't aware we'd discovered these emails or the proposal. After the election, when news broke about one Trump adviser after another having hidden ties to Russia, Manafort of course had not volunteered any of these communications. We were eager to see whether he would raise with us this outlandish Russian proposal on his own and, if not, what lies he might invent to attempt to sanitize it.

Omer dug in first. "What did you and Kilimnik discuss at your August 2 meeting?" he asked.

"We discussed money I was owed by Ukraine oligarchs," Manafort replied.

"Really? Kilimnik flew all the way from Russia to discuss that?"

"Well, he was concerned about hacking of emails and phones."

"But you had emailed with each other about that topic already," I said, leaping in. "When you were hired by candidate Trump in March 2016, you and Kilimnik and Gates had a series of emails about letting

Deripaska and several Ukraine oligarchs know about your new job, and about how you could use that position to be 'made whole.'"

"That's true," Manafort said, then pivoted: "We also talked about an idea Yanukovych had. KK [Konstantin Kilimnik] told me Yanukovych wanted to know if I would run an election campaign for him in Ukraine. He would return to Ukraine to run for the presidency again."

"How did you respond?" Omer asked.

"I was actually offended," Manafort said. "He hadn't reached out to me since 2014—and he fled the country without giving me so much as a heads-up. I didn't think he'd even needed to flee. I couldn't believe that he wanted something from me—now that I was in a position to help him and he, out of the blue, was seeking my help, with no apology first. There was no way I was going to do it. That's what I told KK."

What an ego, I thought. How dare the president of Ukraine flee without telling Manafort and getting his advice.

"So as far as you were concerned, this was a nonstarter?" I said.

"Absolutely."

"Was anything else discussed?" Omer asked. "Anything about the U.S. election?"

"Just chitchat. Nothing that was not public, all stuff that I would have said on the Sunday talk shows. My strategy to go after blue-collar Democrats, and the like."

"Anything about battleground states, or polling?" Omer asked.

"Not that I can recall."

"Well, did you tell Gates to share polling data with him?" I asked. I knew that Manafort would know Gates had told us this, because in discovery we'd provided Manafort with all the 302s from Gates's interviews.

"I had told Gates to keep KK up to speed generally about the campaign, but I didn't tell him to share polling."

"So he just decided to do that on his own, without checking with you?" I asked.

"I did not specifically tell him to share it."

We didn't believe him. It was not just that Gates had told us the opposite about the polling data and the discussion of private campaign information; there was no way that Gates would have risked sending Kilimnik such sensitive polling material without approval from his boss.

Gates had absolutely no motive to do this on his own and, because Manafort had his own relationship with KK, Manafort would have easily found Gates out, if he had.

It was time to confront Manafort with documents and see what he said.

"Mr. Manafort," I told him, "I would like to show you an email that Kilimnik wrote in December 2016, so after the August 2 meeting, after the election is over. Trump, at this point, is now the president-elect."

I slid a copy across the table to Manafort and his counsel to let them read it themselves. The email was written by Kilimnik, but also addressed to Kilimnik. We had learned from our review of hundreds of thousands of documents—and confirmed the conclusion with Gates—that Manafort, Kilimnik, and Gates often communicated the same way many ISIS members and General David Petraeus did; the news had apparently never reached them that draft foldering, as a privacy tactic, didn't actually work. They all shared access to one another's email accounts and wrote emails to each other without ever hitting send.

"You saw this in December 2016, right?" I asked.

"Yes," Manafort said. He read the document carefully. In the email, Kilimnik laid out explicitly Russia's plan for Yanukovych to lead a new eastern region of Ukraine and the necessity of getting Trump to approve it.

"So," I went on, "Mr. Manafort, I don't understand. When I read this, I don't see Kilimnik anywhere acknowledging that you'd already definitely shut down the idea of working with Yanukovych. He's talking to you as if you had never rejected that idea, right? And the plan is quite a bit different than what you said: It's not to have Yanukovych run for president of all of Ukraine; it's to create a new eastern region of Ukraine that he would head up."

"Well, that is true," Manafort said. "This plan . . . this plan was basically the same plan that he told me about in August. I'd told him that it wasn't the right time, and I wasn't sure Yanukovych was the right person, either."

"So this plan was a topic at the August 2 meeting?" Omer asked.

"Yes," Manafort said.

"This is basically a backdoor way for Russia to take over half of Ukraine," I said.

"Yes," Manafort said again. "Which is what I told Kilimnik, and why I was so against it when he raised it at the dinner in August. I did not want to do anything that would help Russia."

"But you did not say that just now; you said you were not sure Yanukovych would be the right person to lead that region."

"Right."

"So your issue was who would lead the region, not the plan itself."

"Right, and I wasn't sure the time was right."

"But you just insisted to us that you were against Russia," I went on, "and had previously said you had only been trying to make Ukraine more Western, and less beholden to Russia. So why wouldn't you be against this plan?"

"I was against this plan," Manafort said.

"But if you were so against it—if you didn't like it because it was pro-Russia—why is Kilimnik still writing to you as if you're for it?"

We kept going back and forth, but Manafort's story got no more consistent. He had no explanation for why Kilimnik was addressing him as an active partner on a project that Manafort was insisting to us—at least at the times he was not claiming to be against only the timing or leadership of the plan—that he'd never wanted any part of. And there was no document—nothing we had that Manafort had written, or which he could now produce—to indicate he'd been anti-Russia and back up his new story.

The facts we'd established, even amid Manafort's attempts to muddy them, were staggering. On August 2, if not earlier, Russia had clearly revealed to Manafort—and, by extension, to the Trump campaign— what it wanted out of the United States: "a wink," a nod of approval from a President Donald Trump, as it took over Ukraine's richest region.

It was a tremendous thing for Russia to ask for. It would seem to require significant audacity—or else, leverage—for another nation to even put such a request to a presidential candidate. This made what we didn't know, and still don't know to this day, feel monumentally disconcerting: namely, why would Trump ever agree to this? Why would Trump ever agree to this Russian proposal if the candidate were not getting something from Russia in return? Both Manafort and Trump were too transactional to give away something for nothing.

. . .

Manafort had clearly trampled on our cooperation agreement. Omer and I ended the session after that hodgepodge of lies. There was no point in continuing such a fencing match; that was not what cooperation is supposed to be. We struggled to figure out if we had any other way to persuade him to come clean, and if that did not work, how we were going to proceed. Then we reported our whole exchange with Manafort about the Russian plan, and the implosion of our proffer, to Mueller and Aaron.

I proposed to Mueller that, as a last attempt to get the truth out of Manafort, we put him in front of the grand jury, hoping that, facing down twenty-three jurors, under oath, with a court reporter transcribing his testimony word for word, Manafort might feel compelled to be more honest than he'd been with us. If it did not work, the proceeding would at least produce an independent transcript of his lies—an indelible, neutral record of what Manafort had said—beyond the notes already in our 302s. Manafort would not be able to say the FBI 302 was incorrect and that the FBI was corrupt, borrowing the playbook of his last employer, the president of the United States. Aaron was okay with the plan and Mueller signed off on it, understanding full well it was a long shot, but also recognizing that there was no real downside.

This was in the beginning of November 2018. On November 10, Mueller held his last U.S. Marine Corps Birthday celebration—an annual event he had commemorated at the Bureau and now in the Special Counsel's Office. The whole office attended, cake was served, and—as tradition would have it—the first piece was handed from Mueller to Ben Cohen (our security officer), symbolizing the passing of the torch from the oldest to the youngest marine. The tradition was lovely, and we all knew it would be our last with the office and Mueller.

In the meantime, we arranged for Manafort to be brought to the grand jury in Washington on two consecutive Fridays. But neither the formality of the proceeding, nor the oath Manafort took at the outset, had any salutary effect. He continued to lie—and not very elegantly, either, progressively digging himself deeper into an expanding warren of disordered and ridiculous holes. (Though grand jury proceedings are confidential, the transcript from his first day of testimony was eventually made public, in response to a court order we obtained to use in connection with his sentencing. It was easy to obtain such an order from the chief judge, which made it all the stranger when, after our report was issued, Attorney General Barr said he would not request any grand jury transcripts to be made available to Congress or the public. After all, we had already done that when it was in our interest.)

The U.S. Marshals had to escort Manafort as he was in custody, but as they were not allowed by law in the grand jury, they waited outside the room while the grand jury was in session. I had done something similar years before with Ben Glisan in Enron and even with a mobster in the Eastern District of New York, with the marshals on that occasion insisting on handcuffing the witness to his fixed chair in the grand jury room for safety. Manafort sat in a chair in the front of the room behind a long table, with the Special Counsel's Office prosecutors to one side of him, and the court stenographer next to us, at the end of the table. We all faced the grand jurors, who were in rows of tiered seats, like a small law school classroom.

Manafort was sworn in by the grand jury foreperson, as is standard. He then proceeded to repeat either the same false stories he'd told us previously or to embroider those stories in ways that were just as implausible and inconsistent with what he had already told us. We had not shared with him a piece of evidence that we had obtained since his first trial—the draft polling questions he had worked on with Kilimnik and the pollster. So when Manafort told the grand jurors that he was against the plan to split Ukraine in two and would not be a part of such a plan, as it would be a "backdoor" way for Russia to take over a swath of Ukraine, we showed him the pollster's documents. Those documents made clear Manafort was working on the plan even as late as 2018.

Manafort's attempts to get out of that were a classic example of someone who, when he is in trouble, keeps doubling down instead of coming clean. We all had seen that numerous times as investigators. Confronted with the draft polling questions he had worked on with Kilimnik and the pollster, Manafort would claim he was only performing a poll for a particular candidate and it had nothing to do with a plan by Russia to take over part of Ukraine. He claimed the questions about Yanukovych were not because of anything Kilimnik had said to him, but just general testing of ideas. He claimed Kilimnik did not even know the identity of the person he was doing the testing for, even though we then showed Manafort communications with Kilimnik that belied that claim. On and on it went.

At the end of the second day of Manafort's testimony, we all met in Mueller's office to go over our options. "We have two choices," I began. "We can breach Manafort"—terminate our cooperation agreement with him—"and prosecute him for the additional crimes to which he hasn't pleaded guilty yet. That would be easy, as in addition to all our other evidence, we now could use all of Manafort's admissions to us." The sole substantive reason to choose this option is that it would raise the statutory maximum Manafort faced in Washington far beyond the ten years, but the guidelines governing his sentencing would not change.

"The second option is to breach Manafort and not charge him with anything else. The ten year maximum he's facing in Washington could wind up running consecutive to the Virginia sentence, if the Washington judge decides it should. So that is a lot of time already. That's our unanimous recommendation." We didn't think piling on at this point made sense, given the time he already faced, or honestly would even make a difference in terms of the sentence Manafort would receive. Manafort had now lied to us and under oath to the grand jury, I said. "The courts can consider that in sentencing him."

Recommending this second option was frankly a no-brainer—charging Manafort with the crimes we had agreed to forgo under the cooperation agreement would have no effect on his sentence. He would still face the same stiff sentencing guidelines, and the court could consider the lies he had told us in sentencing him, as well as the uncharged crimes, which he had admitted to. (The sentences imposed on Manafort would bear this out.)

At that point, Aaron interrupted: "There is a third option," he said. "We could also do nothing. Just let the agreement stand."

I looked over at Omer, who was staring at me already, and found I had to quickly avert my eyes again, to keep from rolling them. This was classic Aaron: clambering for the path of least resistance. But in this case, what Aaron was proposing was not tenable. We'd known what we were getting ourselves into when we entered into the agreement with Manafort and, while no one wanted him to lie and breach his agreement, he had. We now had to deal with the situation responsibly and confront that disheartening reality head-on. This was the umpteenth time Jeannie and I had said to Aaron that we had to just deal with the facts, and then figure out the next steps; we could not let difficult decisions cloud our assessments.

"Aaron," I began, "if we don't breach him, we'd be required to submit a 5K letter to the court at sentencing, explaining the nature of his cooperation." (A 5K letter refers to the section of the federal sentencing guidelines that permits the government to move for a lower sentence for a defendant based on his truthful cooperation.) "We can't say he was truthful and seek to obtain a lower sentence for him based on his cooperation." Manafort's lies were pertinent to his sentencing, and we have a duty of candor to the court. Aaron had already forbidden me from alerting Judge Jackson about Manafort's breach of her pretrial gag order, which I justified at the time as a harmless error, so long as we disclosed it to her in advance of sentencing. But this latest proposal was simply a step too far and went against my training in the EDNY of complete candor with the court. And I knew Mueller well enough to know that that issue would trump all others, as it should.

"I'm not saying we should do nothing," Aaron said. "I just wanted to set it out as another option." I let the comment go. My point, after all, was that it wasn't actually an option.

Mueller cut to the heart of the matter: "We tried to get his truthful cooperation, and we didn't," he said. "We didn't get the truth." He agreed with the team: There was no reason to expend more resources and drown Manafort in new charges. "Let's get him sentenced and focus on the report. What's the process for getting him sentenced?" Mueller was, characteristically, keeping his eye on the ball: finishing up our report, and expending little energy on Manafort. We had played this out as far as it would go.

"We'll give defense counsel an opportunity to be heard on the question of whether he's actually breached," I replied. The agreement required that we make that decision in good faith, and we could bring any new defense evidence or argument on this issue to Mueller for consideration, but with the strong evidence that Manafort lied, this never became an issue. "Then we'll alert the court he's in breach and that we're ready to move ahead with sentencing. Manafort will have the opportunity to challenge us on it."

But there was more; I had played the scenario forward in my head and gleaned another potential benefit. "We could well end up with a court decision that Manafort lied—it would not be coming just from us, but the court." Moreover, his lies about the August 2 meeting and the Ukraine plan went to a central issue of our investigation, potentially covering up proof of coordination between Russia and the campaign. "It would be helpful to have the court determine that we had proved he had lied to us about that in particular," I explained. Again, it wouldn't be just our office claiming it.

Mueller looked at me, and said dryly, "I don't want to play poker with you."

We began the process at the end of November 2018, informing the court and filing, at Judge Jackson's request, an affidavit setting out the basis for the breach so that the defense could decide if it wanted a hearing to challenge it.

Omer, Jeannie, and I had discussed the various scenarios in advance and realized another beneficial by-product to our filing: We were putting yet more evidence gathered by the Special Counsel's Office into the hands of the judiciary, including key evidence of connectivity between the Trump campaign and foreign intelligence: the communications and face-to-face meetings of Manafort and Kilimnik.

We prepared a lengthy affidavit from an FBI agent who'd been involved in our proffers, recounting a tangle of Manafort's lies. Aaron looked it over and sent a version back, having cut down the number of lies it recorded and scaled back dramatically the proof of those that remained.

Omer, Jeannie, and I were stupefied. Why wouldn't we want to spoon-feed the judge as much proof as possible? The stronger our submission, the less likely Manafort would challenge the breach and the more likely we'd be to prevail if he did. Moreover, we saw no risk to overloading the document with evidence; the affidavit would be filed under seal, since it pertained to our ongoing investigation, so all we were doing by filing a watered-down version was keeping facts from the court.

When we asked Aaron about his edits, his answer was startling. "I don't want it to be too strong," he said. "That would put more pressure on the conclusions we want to set out in our final report." We were all taken aback. The facts were the facts, and the idea of sugarcoating Manafort's breach—or anything else we found—was unacceptable. Did Aaron really want to eliminate evidence from the record and soften our report?

Jeannie and I swallowed hard and filed the truncated submission, as Aaron instructed. We figured we would just need to supplement it later if we wound up having a hearing about the breach—which, ironically, was now more likely given that our submission was weaker. In fact, when we went to court, in January, the judge very politely told us that she'd found the affidavit lacking; she probably hadn't been clear, she said, but she wanted all of the evidence of Manafort's deceptions, even if it meant including interview reports or other documents. I apologized and said we'd file another version as speedily as possible. Jeannie, Omer, and I then proceeded, after alerting Aaron to the court's reaction to his crabbed submission, to resurrect our initial draft, brush it up a bit, and resubmit it right away.

Manafort's defense team took the high road. Once they'd examined our filing, they chose not to challenge our good faith determination of the breach. There was no argument: We had reached the conclusion that Manafort had lied in good faith. They had admirably resigned themselves to this unfavorable fact—an increasingly rare phenomenon in Washington—and Judge Jackson rightly praised them for taking this tack. In addition, the defense wisely decided not to ask for a hearing, as we had predicted to Mueller. The defense opted to have the court rule on the defendant's conduct based on the fulsome record we'd just submitted. They had determined that a hearing would only hurt them with the court and in the media.

Judge Jackson decided the matter swiftly: We were justified in breaching Manafort. He would receive no credit for cooperation at sentencing. Moreover, the court went on to find that three of our five grounds for concluding that Manafort had lied to us—and numerous lies that made up those three grounds—were established not merely in good faith, but by a preponderance of the evidence—the standard that was needed for the court to consider those lies at sentencing.

With only the Washington and Virginia sentencing proceedings left,

Team M's investigative job was essentially finished. We felt like we had both succeeded and failed. Paul Manafort would now surely be sentenced for some chastening number of years for crimes that a jury had found him guilty of, and to which he admitted he was guilty. And even if he was eventually pardoned, he would have been in jail since June 15, 2018. And yet, having essentially taken the political equivalent of a vow of omertà, he would sit in that prison with the answers to so many of our questions—and America's questions—still sealed in his head.

CHAPTER 22

The Report

IN THE BEGINNING OF March 2019, Michael Dreeben stopped by my office, shut the door, and with an exasperated sigh, said: "I need your help."

Michael and his team had taken the lead in writing up all the legal aspects of the report, articulating the law on each potential crime we examined, the scope of our jurisdiction, and other such questions. His team had done exhaustive research into the circumstances under which the president could be permitted to obstruct justice and so forth, cogently synthesizing and drawing solid conclusions about what, precisely, the law allowed.

It also fell to Michael's team to stitch together, into one coherent report, the various drafts of pieces that Team R, Team M, and Team 600 were finishing and sending off to both Michael and Mueller. That work was unfolding with enormous secrecy; even within the office, we each had little knowledge about the other sections of the report. This felt of a piece with my experience working for Mueller at the Bureau, which, under his direction, had been a strictly "need to know" place as well.

Team R was basically taking its internal prosecution memoranda for its two Russian indictments—the active measures indictment and the hack and dump indictment—and turning it into more descriptive and better contextualized prose. And Team 600 was writing up each of the episodes that could constitute obstruction of justice, some of which would be revelatory, based on the team's interviews and the handwritten contemporaneous notes it had gathered from witnesses, and some of which would be based on the president's public pronouncements.

Now, however, Michael was turning to me for a reality check because he was stumped on one particular point. "Do you have time to read this and give me your thoughts?" he asked.

"Sure," I told him.

"You never saw this," he said, as he put a few pages on my desk. "I want to know what you think. Does it work?"

The text was too long and dense to read and respond to right there, so I told Michael I would get back to him later that day.

"Great," he said, and left.

When I finished what I was working on, I turned to Michael's pages. He'd been drafting the section of the report explaining why the special counsel was not making a finding on obstruction—not saying, explicitly, whether certain actions of the president should be deemed obstructions of justice or not.

This was the first I had heard that Mueller was declining to make such a decision. That approach confounded me. In the second volume of the report, we would be providing a laborious and thorough accounting of the evidence we'd collected, strongly indicating as a whole that the president had obstructed justice in many different instances. The most glaring was Trump's directing his White House counsel, Don McGahn, to write up a document for the White House files falsely claiming that the president had never sought to have Mueller fired. And yet, after reciting all of this evidence, our report would stop short of saying outright that Trump had obstructed justice. Instead, the section that Michael was now writing would explain that our office was not offering any judgment as to whether the president's conduct constituted obstruction of justice or not.

Mueller's position was, in short, that we shouldn't exercise our discretion to make such a finding—it was not the proper function of a special counsel's office to do so. This idiosyncratic conclusion reflected an attempt to balance a complex set of circumstances, and Michael had the unenviable responsibility of articulating and justifying that decision in writing.

I could see Michael's draft proceeding in various logical steps, explicating Mueller's thinking. First: The Special Counsel's Office was part of the Department of Justice. Second: Being part of the Department of Justice, the office was required to follow decisions by the Office of Legal Counsel (OLC). And these decisions included two formal opinions, written years ago, stating that sitting presidents cannot be indicted for a crime. (Not surprisingly, one of those opinions had been issued during the Nixon administration and the other under Clinton.)

Michael and I had previously discussed those opinions. Their arguments did not strike me as terribly persuasive, and neither opinion had ever been tested in court—meaning, there was no legal precedent on this precise issue. But none of that mattered, since we were bound by the OLC decisions. Mueller was not an independent counsel, like Ken Starr, operating outside of Justice Department rules and free to chart his own course; he did not have the option of making his own assessment of the OLC opinion and arriving at some other, well-reasoned interpretation. The regulations setting up the Special Counsel's Office made clear that we simply had to follow all such Department rules and OLC opinions. We could be fired if we did not.

The question of whether a sitting president can be indicted is a complicated legal issue, however, and worth discussing here, at a thirty-thousand-foot level. Although it's been debated at length, the Supreme Court has never decided on it—meaning no one can say for sure, one way or the other, what the definitive answer is. The OLC opinions contend that, while a president can be held accountable if he appears to commit a crime, he cannot be charged with that crime until he is no longer in office. The opinions point out that the American system already has a means to remove a sitting president who commits a "high crime or misdemeanor": The president can be impeached by the House of Representatives, convicted by the Senate, and removed from office. He then can be charged in court with the crime, like any other private citizen.

In this view, the Constitution provides a kind of temporary immunity—and for good reason: Otherwise, any federal or state prosecutor could effectively defeat the will of the electorate by bringing a bogus criminal case against the president at any time, enormously distracting our chief executive from his responsibilities and causing him serious public vilification for however long it takes for him to be vindicated at trial. And what if the criminal case against the president is not bogus—what if it is meritorious and clear? The OLC view holds there is still no need to charge the president while he's in office because, under such circumstances, even the most popular president could be impeached, removed from office, and face criminal prosecution soon enough anyway.

The counterargument is, in a way, far simpler: No one is above the law. This is a core presumption of our democracy. We do not have kings and queens in this country, and if the president committed a crime, he should be charged with it. It is useful to think of the worst-case scenario: What if the president committed a murder—either while in office or just prior, during the campaign? Why should he be immune from prosecution until out of office, forcing the victims to wait years before seeing justice done? And criminal cases usually get weaker over time.

Prohibiting an indictment while the president is in office undermines the presumption that no American is above the law. Given this consequence, one should be able to point to a clear provision in the Constitution specifically prohibiting the indictment of a sitting president. But there simply isn't one. If one looks at the meager legal precedent we do have, it undermines such a prohibition. The Supreme Court has already determined that a sitting president can be required to be deposed in a civil case—a decision made in connection with President Clinton's having to give testimony in a civil suit alleging sexual harassment. If a civil suit can proceed, this argument goes, a criminal one—in which society has a far greater interest—should be able to go forward. (Those on the other side, it should be noted, address this final point by arguing that a criminal case is far more distracting and serious than the latter, and thus could serve to undermine the effectiveness of the president in a way that a mere civil suit seeking money does not.)

Legal scholars debate both sides endlessly. It is another issue that, thankfully, had previously seemed largely academic—until Trump's behavior forced it upon the real world. Given its importance, it is remarkable that the question has not received more attention in the popular press. This issue is not strictly one for lawyers or academics, but for all of us: We must arrive at an answer that aptly expresses our values. The Constitution, after all, is merely a document that derives its force from the will of the people, and can be molded through a formal process to conform to our beliefs about how society should be structured.

I would choose a system that allows for a sitting president to be indicted. That is, I disagree with the OLC opinions. And I would leave it to the courts handling the criminal case to decide whether that particular case should be tried before or after the term expired, after weighing various factors, such as the seriousness of the offense, how soon the president's term will expire, and the specific risk of loss of evidence before then. But, as I said, it did not matter how I, or anyone else in our office, personally would resolve this question. As a special counsel, Mueller had to follow the Justice Department's rules—including the OLC opinions.

Still, we did not test the issue. In fact, there was a path by which we could have sought to force the question of presidential indictment before a court, seeking to compel it to adjudicate and settle the matter. The thought process here is slightly complicated, so bear with me.

The courts in the United States do not resolve abstract legal questions; they wait until there is a real "case or controversy." They wait for a real dispute to be brought before them that hinges on such an unanswered question, then set forth an interpretation of the law in order to rule on the actual dispute.

There was a possible way to present an actual dispute that would raise the issue of whether a sitting president could be indicted. Federal statutes hold that every crime must be brought within a certain amount of time after it's been committed, or else it becomes barred from prosecution forever. The typical statute of limitations is five years, and that is the statute of limitations on the crimes of obstruction of justice and campaign finance violations—two of the more salient issues in our report regarding the president. So if the OLC opinions are wrong, and a sitting president should be able to be indicted, the statute of limitations would continue to run on any crimes that president had committed. The federal government would typically have five years from his last criminal act to bring an indictment.

In the particular case of President Trump, that timing could become problematic. If Trump is reelected, and serves a second term, the statute of limitations on any crimes could run out while he was still a sitting president; if the Department of Justice sought to indict him after he left office, a court could dismiss the charges for being brought too late. There were two ways for our office to address this problem. One would have been to ask the president to agree now to extend the statute of limitations for such crimes. (Parties can extend the statute of limitations by agreement, and defendants often choose to do so for various reasons.) Or we could have sought an indictment of the president under seal—that is, out of public view—and litigated under seal the question of its lawfulness. The president would have moved to dismiss our charges, claiming he was temporarily immune from indictment until he was out of office, and we could have disagreed and asked the court to settle the question. It wouldn't be an abstract matter anymore; two parties would be engaged in a real-world dispute with that uncertainty at its center.

But I knew this path would not be taken: to force the issue in a court proceeding seemed far too aggressive a tack for Mueller to take. It darted too close to the line of violating the OLC opinions and could have constituted crossing it. Theoretically, the path I've laid out was an option— and would have the benefit of allowing the courts to weigh in on the issue, not just the Department of Justice. But that was not how Mueller saw his remit; the Department could do that if it chose, but he was tasked under the rules with conducting an investigation and reporting on it, not testing and clarifying the law. But even that narrow view of our remit would pose significant problems in drafting the report.

Our report had to explain our lack of discretion to decide whether we could charge a sitting president and, as I read the pages Michael had given me, I could see he'd done so lucidly. But that only brought us to another, equally bewildering question, and one on which there was no Justice Department rule or OLC opinion to guide us: Even if the president could not be criminally indicted now, should we state whether the facts supported an indictment? Should we say that the president committed obstruction of justice?

We had already largely finished drafting volume one of the report, covering Russian interference in the election and our examination of whether there had been cooperation between Russia and the Trump campaign. We set out much of the proof that supported our two Russian indictments, and also stated clearly that our evidence did not yield proof beyond a reasonable doubt of a criminal conspiracy with any Trump campaign officials. But as to the obstruction evidence which was the subject of volume two, Michael was grappling with the flip side of the dilemma posed by what we said in volume one: If there was sufficient evidence that the president had committed obstruction, but we did not have the option to charge him, was it appropriate to say so? Or was it better to withhold a legal determination as to whether this constituted obstruction and abstain from saying the president had broken the law?

Mueller had made a nuanced decision. Where the facts did not support a criminal charge beyond a reasonable doubt, he would say so in the report, effectively exonerating the president of those specific charges, as he did in volume one. But where the proof did support such a charge, as with obstruction of justice in volume two, Mueller determined that the report would not say so. It fell to Michael to give voice to Mueller's reasoning in the report. He is brilliant and practical and steeped in the law, so he was ideally suited to the task. Even so, it was proving to be difficult for Michael to pull off.

After I'd finished reading, I carried the pages back to Michael's office, a cramped space decorated with a feeble-looking miniature ponytail palm in a tiny pot on the front edge of his desk, and a large handmade chart, replete with photos of the key subjects of our investigation, which he had ginned up in his spare time. Michael was at his standing desk and motioned me in. I shut the door and took a seat, eye level with the palm. The plant looked sad; Michael's office was windowless, with no natural light, and the palm had been there for as long as I could remember— perhaps all twenty-two months of our investigation.

"I thought it was a really good draft," I began.

But before I could continue, Michael interjected. "Thanks," he said. "I know it's not what you or I would write, but it had to be faithful to what the boss wants. Does it hang together and make sense?"

Michael's draft stated that because the Department's policy did not permit us to charge a sitting president, it would be unfair for us to say that the proof supported one. That isolated statement may seem shocking to some, but it was not to Dreeben or me. It flowed from standard Department policy, imbued in all good prosecutors and agents, that you do not have the prerogative of accusing someone of a crime publicly; that is the job of a grand jury. A person is either charged criminally or not. It is fundamentally a derogation of power to start maligning people who have not been charged. For those who disagree, it is worth recalling that that was the sin at the root of all our legitimate criticism of Comey's actions before the election: announcing publicly that the FBI would not recommend charging Hillary Clinton, but then going on to denigrate her actions in the strongest terms.

But that simple principle did not get Dreeben all the way to where he needed to be to articulate Mueller's decision. It did not completely justify Mueller's decision. Michael's draft explained that it would be unjust to report that the president had committed obstruction; unlike any other defendant, the president would not have his day in court until he was no longer in office—which could be years. The determination to accuse him of a crime would have to be made in the future by people other than us. Left unsaid in Michael's draft, but clearly implied, was that those other people would be either Congress—which could impeach the president if it believed the facts rose to that level—or a future prosecutor, who could indict the president once he left office. It was left unsaid, because Mueller did not think it was within his mandate under the special counsel rules to make such a referral—he was a subordinate within the Department of Justice under these rules. That decision would have to be made by the Department leadership. Or, it was Congress's job to weigh all options for itself after assessing the facts the Department provided it.

"I think there is one main problem," I told Michael, "and some other smaller ones." The main one was that his argument completely disregarded the fact that the special counsel regulations called for us to make a recommendation one way or the other regarding potential charges. "It's in the regulations," I said. "The text specifies that the special counsel 'shall' give a recommendation, so I don't see how Bob can ignore that." Moreover, I told Michael, "the special counsel regulations say that we are to submit our report to the attorney general privately—not release it publicly."

The report would become public only if the attorney general decided it should. "So the downsides that Mueller is worried about—this concept that the president would be maligned by our making an adverse recommendation on the facts, but not be able to clear his name in court right away—do not exist so long as the report is private. The reasons you lay out, in terms of unfairness to the president, center on a decision that is not actually Mueller's to make. It's an issue that the attorney general should be thinking about when deciding whether to make the report public."

I reminded Michael that the boss was usually so careful to stay in his lane. But here, he seemed to be doing the opposite, by making his own, freelance judgments about what was appropriate and not delivering on what he was tasked with doing by the acting attorney general. What happened after Mueller made a recommendation, or as a consequence of his giving one, was not Mueller's responsibility, or his call. In the back of my mind, I was thinking of the difference between Mueller and Comey in this regard. Comey's press conference before the 2016 election was a product of his improper regard for his role in our system—of, ultimately, his distrust for our system to handle difficult conundrums and his decision to attempt to solve them himself. It was inconceivable that Mueller would have taken that same course.

But here, Mueller was not staying within his lane either, and this, too, could destabilize the function and effectiveness of the larger institution in which he was working. He wasn't overstepping his role, but understepping it: failing to fulfill his explicit mandate to offer a recommendation on obstruction in what was technically an internal DOJ document under the special counsel regulations, for fear of what might happen if it became public.

Michael sat there listening, intently. He was processing what I was saying. I doubted I was telling him something he had not thought through already. The truth is, I was flummoxed by Mueller's thinking. It was clearly well intentioned, and certainly came from a place of true respect for a defendant's rights, which is admirable, and respect for Congress in performing its duty to decide whether the facts warranted impeachment. But I saw the issue differently.

I also didn't buy Mueller's more fundamental conclusion that it would be unfair to make a finding about the president's having committed a crime in the first place, although this was a closer call. Simply put, it would be treating the president differently than every other person in the United States. But if there is anyone in the country who has sufficient ability to defend himself, at least in the court of public opinion, it is the president, who speaks from the world's largest bully pulpit—and this was particularly true with this president, given his Twitter following and influence on the media in general.

Moreover, there is clear precedent for publicly indicting people who would not be tried in court for years—or ever. We ourselves had done it twice, when Team R publicly indicted the Russian operatives and hackers who were unlikely to ever appear in an American court. We never debated whether this was unfair, as we understood that if those Russians wanted their day in court they could come here and subject themselves to our jurisdiction. The president has this option, too; if he truly wanted his day in court quickly, and if it was not enough to defend himself in the court of public opinion, he could agree to have his case proceed. In short, the possibility that the president could opt not to face a trial until out of office was insufficient reason to not say he'd committed a crime.

Still, discussing all this with Michael, I went back to my narrower legal argument that upended his reasoning. "The point is," I said, "these fairness issues don't even arise unless the attorney general decides to make our assessment public. And that is his call, not ours. Here, Mueller is declining to make a determination in order to preempt those potential problems on his behalf. He's placing himself in leadership's shoes. He's not staying in his lane and his stated mandate to give a recommendation."

Michael thought some more. It was silent. I looked again at the plant.

"Anything else?" he asked me. I did not hold back. He had asked for my views and he was entitled to them—and I knew Michael welcomed them whether he agreed with them or not. "Yes, actually. I also think it seems like a transparent shell game," I said. "When there is insufficient proof of a crime, in volume one, we say it. But when there is sufficient proof, with obstruction, we don't say it. Who is going to be fooled by that? It's so obvious."

All one had to do was look at the proof we'd amassed in our report to know that it supported charging President Trump for criminally obstructing justice—that the case against him was more than strong enough to be brought. How, for example, was telling McGahn to lie, and then memorializing that lie in a false document, not obstruction? I had seen mobsters do the same thing: lean on witnesses to give false statements to absolve them under oath so that they could never credibly recant their story afterward. Even McGahn, as White House counsel, appeared to recognize it was criminal. That's why he took the extraordinary step of refusing a direct order from the president of the United States—not just once, but repeatedly.

Michael chimed in. "I agree with the latter logic point," he said, "but there is not much we can do about that. We have to follow the boss's decision on this. That's the way he wants it written." But Michael agreed that my first objection seemed like a real problem, and said he would look for some law or Department policy that might address the issue, in order to shore up Mueller's position that we not make a recommendation.

"Andrew," Michael finally told me, "if you and I were in charge, this is not how it would read." I said I knew that. And he knew I did.

Michael revised the draft. He ran it by me again; it was the language that now appears in the final report. Michael revised the draft to note that the OLC assessments that a sitting president cannot be indicted applied even to a sealed indictment, as the OLC opinions noted there would be reasonable concern that such a sealed indictment would leak. And Michael had seized on that articulated risk of leaks to get around the issue I had raised—my argument that, because we were tasked only with making an internal recommendation to the attorney general, it was up to the attorney general to decide whether to release it publicly: We could not feel confident that such an internal recommendation would not become public, either. This was the best Michael could do.

With that settled, Michael had to find a way to resolve the contradiction I'd raised, and explain why we were not saying anything about our assessment of the facts on obstruction, in volume two, given that we had made a conclusion about coordination with Russia, in volume one. I didn't envy him. Michael's explanation, as revised by Aaron and Mueller, was a carefully contorted mess that would be widely denigrated by people on both sides of the aisle:

> Because we determined not to make a traditional prosecutorial judgment, we did not draw ultimate conclusions about the President's conduct. The evidence we obtained about the President's actions and intent presents difficult issues that would need to be resolved if we were making a traditional prosecutorial judgment. At the same time, if we had confidence after a thorough investiga-

tion of the facts that the President clearly did not commit obstruction of justice, we would so state. Based on the facts and the
applicable legal standards, we are unable to reach that judgment.
Accordingly, while this report does not conclude that the President
committed a crime, it also does not exonerate him.

It is hard to read this now, knowing how Barr eventually used the
mealymouthed language of that passage to misrepresent our report's
conclusions, prior to its being made public. Far better to have just made
the difficult factual and legal calls we were supposed to make and let the
attorney general deal with their inconvenient consequences from there
on. If Barr wanted to then claim he disagreed with our conclusions, so be
it, that was his right—but we would have done our job and provided a
conclusion, derived objectively from the facts, to stand up to his spin.
That, after all, is what we had signed up for in May 2017.

In retrospect, there was an even more troubling behind-the-scenes wrinkle to Mueller's decision not to say clearly that the president had obstructed justice.

To fulfill his responsibility as laid out in our appointment order,
Mueller had taken the step of running this entire, tortured approach to
resolving this issue by Attorney General Barr, Deputy Attorney General
Rosenstein, and their staffs in advance. Mueller set out what he was proposing to do in the report, and how these issues would be handled, and
asked if those parties had any objections. If Barr or Rosenstein had concerns, or actually wanted our assessment of the facts—if they wanted us
to draw an explicit conclusion about whether the president had obstructed justice—all they had to do was tell us. After all, they were
Mueller's bosses.

But that did not happen. None of them told Mueller to do anything
differently. And so, by early March, as we readied to deliver our report,
we believed that our superiors at the Department understood and approved of the tack we'd taken.

That is, Mueller trusted them—naïvely, in retrospect. We never
imagined that the attorney general would slide in to make the factual
determination himself, conveniently announcing, in the infamous letter

I'd soon learn about on the radio in my car on March 24, 2019, that the president's conduct did not constitute criminal obstruction of justice. Mueller had no reason to foresee such a betrayal by Barr, who was also a personal friend. Clearly Barr had raised no objections to Mueller's approach to handling the obstruction quandary because he was planning to overstep his own role—because he understood that our leaving that question purposefully unanswered would allow him to answer that question himself. Moreover, he did so weeks before releasing our report publicly, warping the American people's understanding of the facts and helping to establish the terms of any subsequent political debate.

Whether you agree with Mueller's reasoning here, whether you wish he'd taken a stronger stand, his motivation and intent were pure. In the end, he may have pulled his punches, but wholly because he did not feel the alternative was appropriate or productive, and out of deference to the ideal of fairness and our democratic institutions—including the office of the presidency, regardless of who occupies it, and regardless of how recklessly that occupant may be debasing it.

Arguably, it is when our institutions are being corroded that we are most required to honor them. Clearly, part of me wishes that Mueller had acted differently. But I recognize that his restraint, and such faith in the larger systems in which we participate, requires an admirable measure of courage, too.

CHAPTER 23

"The Number of Lies"

IT WAS NOW EARLY March 2019. Our report was all but finished. Before long, we would all be packing up our offices and returning to our lives, outside of the pressure cooker in which we'd been confined for almost two years. One of our stalwart staff collected all our private contact information so we could stay in touch. Gradually, everyone who'd been toiling away together for the previous twenty-two months was finishing off their last outstanding tasks, and each posing for a goodbye photo with Mueller before departing on their last day. These exits became ceremonial, with Mueller and the relevant team leader saying a few words, expressing gratitude and pride. Every day, it seemed, someone else was leaving—some days, two or three people at a time. Every day, we ate another farewell cake.

Aside from Michael's legal team, which would be polishing every word of the report until the very end, Team M remained intact the longest, as we still had Manafort's two sentencing proceedings to attend to. I watched the office be depleted of its energy and life little by little until, although the physical space was the same as it always had been, it began to feel foreign and forlorn.

As a result of his conviction in Virginia, Manafort was facing a statutory maximum of eighty-five years in prison, and he faced another ten years from his plea in Washington. That said, there was not a defense lawyer, prosecutor, or judge in America who expected that Manafort, or any other defendant in his situation, would be sentenced so harshly. More important than these statutory maximums are the federal sentencing guidelines, standardized recommendations issued by the government to ensure that no two comparable defendants receive wildly disparate punishments, and to curtail the variability between various judges' approaches. And yet, for Manafort, these sentencing guidelines, too, were unrealistically stiff—notoriously high in financial cases and often all but disregarded. Judge Ellis in Virginia and Judge Jackson in Washington would both have a tremendous amount of discretion in deciding his fate.

In the end, the two sentences they imposed were basically the same. Judge Ellis imposed a term of incarceration of four years, and Judge Jackson added three and a half years after that, running the D.C. sentence consecutively to the Virginia term. And yet, the differences in what each judge said at sentencing, and the tone of their remarks, were staggering and illuminative.

In Virginia, Judge Ellis was almost apologetic toward Manafort, explaining that one factor he'd considered in determining his sentence was that, but for the crimes before the court, Manafort had "lived an otherwise blameless life." Until that point, I'd sat impassively at the government's table, trying to maintain a neutral mask and show no emotion. But now, I looked up reflexively. One of Judge Ellis's young law clerks, apparently startled by his ill-chosen comment as well, had looked up, too, and our eyes locked. The comment was incomprehensible, as the court well knew that Manafort had committed crimes for decades and was, at that time, awaiting sentence for an entirely separate batch of crimes in Washington as well.

The press shared my reaction and voiced suspicion that race and class had played a significant role. They asked if a black man would have received the same consideration, or someone less politically connected. No one can say for sure. However, our team had seen Judge Ellis sentence numerous other people in Virginia; his sentencing always included a severe reprimand from the court, and strong moral admonitions to the defendants about their behavior. And the press noted that when Judge Ellis had sentenced William J. Jefferson, a black congressman convicted of corruption charges in 2009, in a case centering on Jefferson's acceptance of roughly $400,000 in bribes, he had imposed a thirteen-year term of imprisonment, the highest sentence ever for a sitting congressman.

Just one week later, we were in Washington for Manafort's second sentencing, Judge Jackson avoided the Sturm und Drang that had been kicked up in Virginia by clearly and pointedly expressing her disapproval of Manafort's crimes. In the moment, I was impressed and grateful to her; I knew her comments would serve to educate the public. But only in retrospect do I also appreciate how incisively she managed to articulate a central and dismaying truth about our entire experience at the Special Counsel's Office.

She spoke of Manafort's numerous lies, and his multiple obstructions of our investigation—both through his own willful deceit and by coaching witnesses to lie for his protection. He'd done the latter, Judge Jackson noted, while he was under indictment and out on bail. Finally, she explained that Manafort had even lied to the government about telling the truth: claiming that he would finally cooperate with our investigation only to obfuscate and impede it further. "It is hard to overstate the number of lies and the amount of fraud and the extraordinary amount of money involved," she said. Manafort had not lived an exemplary life. Here was a chastening recognition that his conduct was serious and flagrant, and repeated over years.

Earlier, when the news had first broken that Manafort had breached his cooperation agreement, the press focused on the most immediate consequence: Manafort appeared to have lied his way into more prison time. But I worried the larger ramifications of his obdurate dishonesty had gone unnoticed, consequences that went to the core of the special counsel's mission. To me, it was ultimately less important that Manafort lied than what he was lying about and why—and the many facts that, even now, his lies have prevented us from knowing.

We learned that Russia worked, laboriously, to interfere in our election for the purpose of electing Trump. And we learned that on August 2, at the height of the presidential campaign, Manafort—Trump's campaign manager—met with Konstantin Kilimnik, a man known to be affiliated with Russian intelligence. We learned that the two of them discussed a Russian proposal to take over half of Ukraine, and Russia's need for Trump's support for the plan to go forward. But we did not learn why Russia had felt emboldened to ask for such a concession, why that support would be given—whether, if at all, those two hands we saw reaching out to aid each other ever touched.

At sentencing, Manafort's defense team made plain its strategy for a pardon, claiming in its sentencing memorandum to the court that because the Special Counsel's Office had failed to find enough evidence to charge Manafort, or anyone else on the Trump campaign, with criminally conspiring with Russia to influence the election, we had brought these other charges against him instead. No fool, Judge Jackson noted that this argument was irrelevant, noting that "the no collusion mantra is a non-sequitur. Collusion with Russia was not the charge that Manafort was facing, and not what he had pleaded guilty to." She went on. "It's also not particularly persuasive to argue that an investigation hasn't found anything when you lied to the investigators."

This applies, too, to the president and our report as a whole: It is meaningless for the president to claim that our report is a total exoneration, and that we found no "collusion," when he refused to be interviewed and dangled pardons to discourage key witnesses from cooperating with our probe—when, time and again, he kept us from finding all the facts. This obvious point was driven home during the impeachment proceeding in the Senate: If you keep witnesses from testifying, if you block access to all documents in the hands of the executive branch, you cannot credibly claim you were vindicated. You've simply succeeded in sabotaging the possibility of a conviction. But like Congress, we were guilty of not pressing as hard as we could for that evidence when we had the chance.

Would it have made any difference? Unlikely. But that is not the point, any more than asking whether it would have made a difference had the Senate voted to hear from witnesses like John Bolton, or to press for documents. The facts should still matter.

Since leaving the Special Counsel's Office, I have thought back many times to Comey's October 2016 announcement reopening the Clinton email investigation on the eve of the election. Many have argued that his decision to hold that press conference was clearly wrong, but that it did not change the election outcome. I am not sure if it did or didn't. My take has always been that I and every other voter are entitled not to have to ask that question.

There are, similarly, open questions at the heart of the special counsel's investigation, as a result of Trump's actions as well as our own, and we don't know whether the answers would be incriminating or exculpatory. Did Trump obstruct justice by firing Comey or by interfering in the Flynn investigation? Did he obstruct by seeking to fire Mueller and attempting to thwart the very investigation into Russian interference and his obstruction? What are the reasons he sought to prevent the cooperation of Manafort, Gates, Stone, Cohen, and others, if there is no there there with respect to Russian interference, obstruction, or other possible crimes? Our investigation and report do not resolve those issues once and for all. But we, as a country, are entitled not to have to wonder what the facts would have revealed.

This was the point of the special counsel all along.

■ EPILOGUE

Looking Forward

ON SATURDAY, JANUARY 21, 2017, the day after the inauguration of Donald J. Trump as the forty-fifth president of the United States, the streets in downtown Washington, D.C., were deluged with women (and a few good men) wearing pink "pussy" hats. I was working at the Department of Justice at the time and decided I should not publicly protest my new boss; instead, I walked over to the recently opened National Museum of African American History and Culture on the Washington Mall, a spectacular set of inverted pyramids wrapped in brown metal filigree. The bottom floors chronologically recount the scar of slavery on this country, while the top floors celebrate contributions of individual African Americans to the world.

The museum is an overwhelming, gut-wrenching experience meticulously documenting the inhumanity that we are capable of as a people. The history of buying and selling human beings, of whippings and murderous lynchings, is almost too much to bear. I'd had a similar experience when first visiting the Holocaust Memorial Museum, which is just a few hundred yards away. Decades ago, FBI director Louis Freeh had wisely made a visit to the Holocaust museum a mandatory part of the training of every new FBI agent. Freeh felt it would be crucial for them to bear witness to the atrocities that an autocratic state can produce, the horror that ensues when the rule of law is twisted beyond recognition. A similar, cautionary instinct had compelled the Department of Justice to inscribe in the limestone walls of its headquarters: "Where law ends, tyranny begins," paraphrasing the famous John Locke quote.

That afternoon, as I ascended floor after floor of the African American history museum, taking in the chronicle of the subjugation of one race by another, as well as the struggle to overcome it, I could hear the chanting of millions of marchers outside. Looking out through the museum's transparent walls, I saw a city overrun by a sea of pink hats and protest signs. The parade route had long been abandoned, as the crowd had swelled far beyond its anticipated size. The juxtaposition of what our country had been through and was now confronting was palpable. Many have observed that we, for generations, have continued to refight the Civil War, and that this particular rift in our society has still yet to heal. And in truth, our nation is riven with a multitude of divisions. Some are shamefully wide; others, networks of insidious fissures. It was clear, that day in Washington, that a fault line was cleaving wide open, between law and lawlessness, fact and fiction.

Two years later, I had no illusions that our special counsel's report would bridge that widening chasm, but I hoped that for most citizens, facts and law would still matter. The same should be said for this book, which can hardly overcome the machinery of misinformation that separates fact from fiction, and science and law from populist tyranny.

The limitations of our report were underscored for me almost immediately, on the night of March 24, 2019, in Washington, as I stood in the doorway of my condo, reading Attorney General Barr's letter on my iPad. Just two days after Mueller had handed in our final report—the product of twenty-two months of intensive work by a total of fifty-nine prosecutors, agents, and analysts—Barr issued his four-page letter purporting to summarize it. That letter was a shot across the bow, signaling that the short interregnum of the rule of law represented by Mueller was over. The checking function Mueller provided on the actions of the president had come to an abrupt end at the Department of Justice and the White House.

As a private citizen, Barr had written a memo that indicated to the president that he'd seen no need for a special counsel. And now, he had delivered on that pronouncement: The report would be ignored, even its most serious and ostensibly nonpartisan findings that we had been attacked by Russia—and would be again in upcoming elections. Barr's gambit—enabled by Rosenstein and his staff—gave the president a green light to resume conducting himself beyond legal confines. His actions would not be constrained or held to account by Mueller or any other law enforcement officer.

And it worked. Three months later, on the day after Mueller testified about our report in Congress, the president held up hundreds of millions of dollars in funding to aid Ukraine in its war against Russia—funding that had been authorized by Congress and previously signed off on by the president himself. Why? Because he wanted the Ukrainian government to open an investigation into his political opponent Joe Biden and his son—even though he could not meet the low threshold of getting his Justice Department to open an investigation into either of them.

The military aid for Ukraine constituted public funds that could not properly be withheld for personal political reasons. But the fact that the president primarily wanted a public statement by Ukraine—a televised announcement that an investigation was being opened, more than any actual investigation itself—revealed his true purpose. Indeed, seeking a public statement was directly contrary to the reasons the president gave for firing Comey—that is, the Rosenstein memo criticizing Comey for violating Justice Department norms by publicly disparaging Clinton although she had not been charged with a crime.

Moreover, and most important, the president was asking for foreign assistance in the upcoming election, the same illegal act at the very heart of our investigation. It is breathtaking that the president still had no reservations about doing so. Indeed, even shortly after we issued our report, the president told George Stephanopoulos that he would consider asking for foreign assistance in the future; now, he had.

Still, it is a different investigation that Trump sought from Ukraine that I find even more disturbing. The president leaned on the Ukrainian government to investigate Ukraine's purported interference in the 2016 U.S. presidential election. These allegations are rooted in Russian disinformation. The unanimous conclusion of our Intelligence Community and Trump's own experts, like Dr. Fiona Hill, is that Russia interfered with the election; our indictments laid out clear and extensive proof, replete with Russian emails detailing the efforts. We had the facts. Why would Trump raise the boogeyman of Ukraine election interference other than to distract from what Russia had done (and would continue to do)?

Did Ukraine help Trump in the 2016 election? Of course not. And nothing about Trump's Ukraine allegations diminished the proof against Russia. Conveniently, Barr moved to dismiss our indictment against the Russian company involved in the hacking so that the proof would not be laid out for all to see in a federal court, in advance of the upcoming 2020 election. And the president's other actions since our report did not dispel the concern about Russian election interference: For instance, his sudden withdrawal of assistance for the Kurds in northern Syria allowed Russian dominance in that region, against clear U.S. policy and only serving Putin's interests. In short, no checks were left to limit Trump and his attack on reason and reality—the wheels had come off the wagon.

Barr's four-page letter was the first clear signal that the rule of law was no longer inviolate. The letter was a gut punch. Its many omissions and misleading statements make it paradigmatic of the brazen misconduct of a gaggle of presidential defenders and conspirators—not just Barr, but Trump's attorney/fixer Rudy Giuliani, and politicians like Devin Nunes: the entire group of old white men who've participated in, or condoned, improper or illegal conduct by the White House. It is worth recalling this first sign of the end of the rule of law at the Justice Department, even though it may seem quaint in light of Barr's actions bastardizing the government's sentencing submission in the Roger Stone case and dismissing the Michael Flynn case for reasons that can be understood only as political.

Barr explicitly stated in his letter that he was writing it to "summarize the principal conclusions" of the report. But after our report was finally made public, he was confronted with the striking discrepancy between his misrepresentations and the actual document. At that point, his defense was to claim that he'd never meant his letter to be a summary of the report, though he never specified what he did intend it to be. He couldn't, because the answer is simple: a whitewash.

It is useful to offer a close reading of Attorney General Barr's many misleading claims about our report and to dissect his strategy of confusing or obscuring our findings in order to protect the president:

- In his letter, Barr leads the reader to believe that given the thoroughness of our investigation, surely we had managed to learn whatever facts are out there. Then, on April 17, 2019—one day before the report would become public—he took to the airwaves to again masterfully reinforce and elaborate on the idea that our investigation was comprehensive. He even added the false nugget that the White House had "fully cooperated" with our investigation: "The President took no act that in fact deprived the Special Counsel of the documents and witnesses necessary to complete his investigation," he claimed. This is not just untrue, it's astonishingly far from the truth. Even if one leaves aside all the dangling of pardons and attempts to fire us, the president persistently did not cooperate with our requests for an interview with him—he downright refused—and fought being subpoenaed, in spite of repeated appeals and accommodations offered by our office. His son Don Jr. similarly refused to be interviewed. And Trump engaged in a persistent campaign to deter others from cooperating with our investigation. Barr's statement, in short, was simply false.

- Barr claimed that the president never asserted any presidential privilege to withhold information from the special counsel. This is also not true: Numerous claims of privilege were raised to challenge our ability to interview or subpoena the president. Nor is it even especially believable, given the confrontational posture of the president in general and his increasingly audacious belief in his own immunity while in office. Since our investigation wrapped, the world has watched this White House make outlandish claims of privilege claiming in court that the president (and his family and companies) cannot be either investigated or prosecuted for any crime while he is in office; that, in one example recently argued in court, if Trump were to shoot someone while in office—literally shoot someone in the middle of Fifth Avenue—the police could not lawfully examine the crime scene, interview witnesses, or even pick up one of the bullets as evidence.

- Barr claimed the president did not intend to obstruct our investigation, but he utterly failed to deal with the obstructionist conduct by the president clearly chronicled in the report. Trump, Barr insisted, simply felt wrongly accused; the president was frustrated and angered by what Barr terms a "sincere belief" that the investigation was undermining his presidency. There are two problems here. First, Barr is claiming to have somehow divined the president's emotions and intent, even though the president did not provide any testimony that explained them—neither under oath nor even in an interview with our office. Barr did not explain how he knew the president did not intend to obstruct our investigation. Second, even if the president did feel wrongly accused, that fact is completely disconnected from the question of whether his actions constitute obstruction of justice. One isn't allowed to interfere with a law enforcement investigation simply because one feels he is innocent. If anything, the mindset Barr articulated supports the opposite conclusion, further implicating the president rather than exonerating him. Feeling wrongly accused—and believing that those investigating you are biased or corrupt—could provide a motive for the president to commit obstruction of justice: He would not trust the investigation to take its course, confident in the outcome.

- Describing our examination of Russian interference in the 2016 presidential election, Barr affirmatively misled the public about Russia's active measures campaign, noting wrongly that it was "designed to sow social discord, eventually with the aim of interfering with the election." Barr again repeated that line—the Russians wanted to "sow social discord"—in his April press conference. This mischaracterizes what the Russians did and obscures their real objective. Our report makes clear that the active measures scheme was designed to, and in fact served to, support candidate Trump and undermine his Republican rivals during the primary, and then to support Trump and undermine Clinton during the general election. The election interference was not a random or evenhanded effort to simply sow discord, as Barr claimed. It had a specific goal and, with Trump's victory, achieved it. Our documentary evidence showed this beyond any doubt. What other than political bias can justify that omission in Barr's public statements? But Barr went further: When Congress sought to obtain our fully unredacted report, and access to the evidence to support the report, he balked and opposed providing it. What was he afraid of in not providing this to a co-equal branch of government?

- Barr described the Russian hack and dump operation and noted our indictment of Russian military officers for illegally hacking into computers in the United States to influence the election. But nowhere did he reveal that Trump campaign personnel—from the candidate on down—were seeking such assistance and were entirely willing to condone the crime and be the beneficiaries of the damaging Clinton material the Russians had stolen from those computers. That omission is all the more significant given that Barr repeatedly stated that the special counsel "did not find" that the Trump campaign conspired with the Russian actors. What actually happened is that we did not find sufficient evidence of a conspiracy to bring a criminal case—which requires proof beyond a reasonable doubt. It is not true that we did not find any evidence—which was what the Barr letter was widely interpreted to claim. And in his April 17, 2019, press conference, Barr went even further, stating that the public now knows from the Mueller investigation that the Russians did not have "the cooperation of President Trump or the Trump campaign." This statement flies in the face of the truth—ignoring the campaign's willful and enthusiastic pursuit of Clinton dirt at the Trump Tower meeting, its pursuit of emails from WikiLeaks, and Manafort's dissemination of internal campaign polling data to the Russian operative Kilimnik.

- Barr slyly stated in his letter that we did not find that the Trump campaign or anyone associated with it had conspired or coordinated "with the Russian government" in its illegal hacking or "with the IRA" in its disinformation campaign. Such narrow wording was intentional; it leaves out coordination with Russians more generally. And Barr carefully repeated that claim in his press conference. Again, nowhere did Barr explain that, in fact, we es-

tablished that the president's son, son-in-law, and campaign chairman had all welcomed illegal foreign campaign assistance from an
oligarch tied to the Russian government at the Trump Tower
meeting, or that the president's campaign chairman and deputy
campaign chairman had routinely passed internal polling data to
a Russian linked to Russian intelligence—and also met with that
same man, Kilimnik, during the campaign to discuss both internal Trump campaign information and to plot a backdoor means
for Russia to seize half of Ukraine.

- Barr made deceptive statements at his press conference while describing the Trump campaign's efforts to coordinate the dissemination of the hacked Clinton campaign emails. Knowing that the
  report was replete with evidence of the Trump campaign's complicity in these efforts, Barr chose to narrowly focus on whether
  the Trump campaign had participated in the underlying illegal
  hacking itself. Engaging with the question on these disingenuous
  terms allowed Barr to conflate the two phases of the hack and
  dump attack. Barr's conclusion was that, because the special counsel "did not find" that the president participated in the hacking
  itself, there was no evidence that the Trump campaign "illegally"
  participated in the dissemination of the materials. But this ignores
  all the evidence of the campaign's efforts to encourage, obtain, and
  disseminate the illegally hacked emails and the reality that such
  efforts could constitute a campaign finance violation, which prohibit soliciting or accepting any foreign aid of value. Barr's play
  here was a shameless sleight of hand, a kind of rhetorical misdirection that focused the public on one crime the campaign hadn't
  clearly committed—the hacking—in order to distract from another crime—the violation of campaign finance laws—which
  it had.

- Barr was even more misleading with respect to the evidence of
  obstruction of justice. He noted that we did not reach a conclusion
  on the issue of obstruction and claims that our report lays out facts
  "on both sides of the question." He thus made it sound as though
  bringing an obstruction charge was a toss-up—and concludes it

was thus up to him and Rosenstein to make a final determination, as if breaking a tie. Their conclusion, of course, was that the president was innocent.

Nowhere in his letter did Barr say what the facts actually were—and for good reason, as the evidence we gathered was so overwhelmingly damaging to the president: his dangling pardons to deter witnesses from cooperation, his efforts to fire those investigating the facts, and his demanding his White House counsel create a fake memorandum to cover up the president's attempts to fire Mueller. Eventually, when our report finally came out, Barr defended his judgment on obstruction, claiming implausibly that even if the president had wanted to fire Mueller, Trump was not seeking to end the special counsel's investigation, merely to replace the special counsel who was leading it with a different person. That is a whopper: There is literally no credible evidence to support this theory—and, again, how Barr managed to definitively understand the president's intentions, without any testimony from the president himself, is never explained. Nor does Barr provide any analysis that he and Rosenstein applied to reach their conclusion and exonerate the president. Doing so would have required discussing the actual facts. And when the facts are so inconvenient—and these were downright damning—it is apparently best not to sully oneself dealing with those facts at all.

The attorney general is not supposed to be an enabler or a fixer. He is a public servant, paid for by taxpayer dollars, accountable to the public, and tasked with upholding the rule of law. For us in the Special Counsel's Office, watching the sudden demise of those principles, within just days of our concluding our mission, was soul crushing.

Barr's conduct after we submitted our report proves why a special counsel was necessary in the first place—how crucial it is for our government to have a mechanism for independently investigating allegations of criminality by the president. But it also exposes why that mechanism is not nearly strong enough.

Barr's disregard for the facts and attempted erasure of our findings makes plain the need for stronger special counsel rules, better safeguards to keep a special counsel's work—and the knowledge it produces—from being inappropriately undermined by those in power. The Trump presidency has uncovered numerous ways in which our system of checks and balances is flawed; how it is norms, and not necessarily laws, that stand between democracy and autocracy. A time will come when our institutions will revisit what we need to do as a country to stiffen such norms into binding, legal rules. There must be impregnable guardrails to keep executive branch conduct within the rule of law.

The question of who should investigate criminality in the White House is a thorny one; no traditional institution of the government seems guaranteed to have sufficient independence and power to conduct that work effectively. The Department of Justice, which is overseen by the president, has an inherent conflict. Its leader, the attorney general, as well as many of its officials, are all appointed by the president, and thus the public could not be confident that an investigation by the Department would not be tainted, consciously or unconsciously, by bias.

At the time of Watergate, we relied on the special prosecutor system. However, it proved to be too vulnerable to the abuse of presidential power when, during the Saturday Night Massacre, President Nixon directed the firing of the special prosecutor, and the leaders of the Department of Justice nobly resigned rather than carry out the order. Subsequently, Congress established the independent counsel system, which granted an investigation true independence by placing it outside of the Department of Justice. But this solution had its own imperfections, as the Ken Starr investigation of President Clinton proved. The independent counsel law proved to be a kind of overcorrection: The instinct to keep an investigation unfettered by executive branch oversight left insufficient checks on an independent counsel who ran amok, investigating for years and straying far beyond his initial mandate.

The creation of the special counsel rules, in turn, was a reaction to this deficiency—a further refinement of the system. But clearly those new limitations have left the institution fallible, once again. As our experience shows, the special counsel's work can be overpowered by the same unethical actors it is designed to hold to account.

There is no other way to put it: Our country is now faced with the problem of a lawless White House, which addresses itself to every new dilemma or check on its power with a belief that following the rules is optional and that breaking them comes at minimal, if not zero, cost. Sadly, though wrongheaded, this belief has been continually reinforced by the many institutions that have opted not to prove to the president, through their legitimate powers of oversight, that he is, in fact, not above the law, and specifically by an attorney general and White House counsel who think of themselves as defense attorneys, representing the personal interests of the president, rather than as public officials who represent the interest of the presidency and serve the public.

This is not a normal situation in America; it's unlike anything we've faced before. It is debatable whether a stronger set of special counsel rules would be sufficient to deal with such a president. Still, better rules can only help. If another special counsel were appointed tomorrow, he or she would be subject to the same difficulties and vulnerabilities—and likely be challenged far more aggressively, now that Trump's playbook has been shown to work. I understand that individual special counsels can overcome such structural challenges while others may succumb to them, but there is no reason future generations should be forced to overcome imperfect rules. The lessons from the special counsel's investigation behoove us to adopt rules and structures that increase the odds for an independent investigation and successful fact finding.

It is fair to expect, in response to the many lies by Barr, that the special counsel should have hewed to the course set by Archibald Cox and taken to the press to articulate a response—and not left it to the public to sift through more than four hundred pages of turgid legalese. In other words, part of the reason the president and his enablers were able to spin the report was that we had left the playing field open for them to do so, and they took advantage of it.

But the reasons that criticism is not entirely correct is that our investigation arose under special counsel rules that were put in place to thwart the excesses of the independent counsel law—a Ken Starr investigation that resulted in a four-year investigation that began as a political corruption investigation (as to which it concluded there was no evidence) and ended in a salacious public report and testimony by the independent counsel about perjury concerning an extramarital liaison. The special counsel rules were intended to prevent that public airing of investigative findings. As an internal Justice Department employee, Mueller could not take readily to the airwaves or even release the report of his findings—that could only be done by the attorney general. Nor could the special counsel violate internal Department policies by indicting a sitting president.

To be fair, revising the special counsel rules is not an entire answer to what went wrong. Although there may have been consequences to his decision to do so, Mueller was in fact free to conduct a financial investigation of the president; free to make a finding on obstruction; and free to subpoena the president. And when Mueller was authorized to testify before Congress, he was free to provide a critique of the Barr "summary" and to use that opportunity to educate the public as to his findings regarding the conduct of the president—as he chose to do with respect to Russian interference.

But while that is all true, the special counsel rules did not help with the goal of transparency to the public or with the independence of the investigation. My proposals for reform are an effort to start the conversation about these lessons learned, just as the current special counsel rules improved upon those of the independent counsel. The key problem with the system now in place centers on a disconnect between the mission described and authorized by the special counsel rules and the public's understanding of that mandate.

The rules imagine that a criminal investigation would be done in secret and result only in an internal Justice Department report in which the special counsel would make private recommendations to the attorney general about its charging determinations: who to charge with a crime, who not to, and why. These regulations do not contemplate a public report assessing the facts the special counsel has gathered and making proscriptions for the future. However, it was always clear to us, given intense public interest in the questions we set out to answer, that the attorney general would need to make our report public (except for minor redactions for privilege issues). So the role of the special counsel immediately diverged from what was contemplated by the rules.

The public understandably believed that we would operate as an independent fact-finding commission, akin to the bipartisan 9/11 Commission, which issued a superb, thoughtful, detailed, and well-written report explaining how the 9/11 terrorist attacks had been allowed to happen and drawing specific recommendations to prevent future attacks.

When I read our report now, I see a document caught in the tension between our stated and de facto missions. In part, the report reads as a highly legalistic internal Justice Department document, akin to the scrupulously detailed prosecution memoranda prepared by prosecutors before bringing an indictment. At the same time, it is addressed to the American people—a public accounting of the facts we uncovered. Ultimately, the report does not serve either purpose adequately.

First, a report that was truly addressed to the public would have been structured and written in a more straightforward manner, without the legal nomenclature of an internal prosecution memo. It would have drawn conclusions more clearly and explicitly, rather than risk overwhelming those conclusions with long, narrow disquisitions about the interpretation and application of the law. Such a report would have been more transparent about what we did not investigate, such as the president's finances, and why, and would better emphasize which questions we were not able, or permitted, to sufficiently answer, such as the Department's obstacles in seeking to interview and subpoena the president. And it would have proposed remedial steps to deal with problems like Russian interference, just as the 9/11 Commission Report addressed the threat of future terrorist attacks.

A Mueller report that was exclusively an internal document, meanwhile, would have summed up the facts and included our internal assessment of those facts, including a definitive assertion that the proof established that the president had, in fact, obstructed justice—just as any other internal prosecution memoranda would do. But it was the expectation that our report would become public that weighed on Mueller, and kept him from allowing the report to voice such a conclusion explicitly, since he determined that it would be unfair to level such an accusation publicly if the president would not have the opportunity to promptly defend himself in court. That is, ironically, knowing that the American people would be reading our report weighed against our answering one of their most pressing questions as clearly as they deserved.

This flaw must be corrected. The regulations should state clearly what is expected from a special counsel's report, and who its actual audi-

ence is, so as not to confront another special counsel with such a dilemma. The current rules provide solely for a private report to the
attorney general, but I would revise them to make clear that the report
will be made public, and that it therefore must include an assessment
of the facts and propose remedial measures. New regulations should
resolve the tension that Mueller confronted by requiring the special
counsel to make a public finding—to say whether the president has
committed a crime even if he may not be able to be indicted until he is
out of office. That temporary immunity may not even exist under the
law, after all, and the very purpose of appointing a special counsel, independent of the Department of Justice, is to provide the public with an
objective assessment of the facts.

Moreover, the Department's general policy of not publicly accusing
someone of wrongdoing unless they have been formally charged is not
entirely fully applicable to wrongdoing by the president. If a court eventually considers the question and finds that a president in fact can be
indicted while in office, the concern evaporates; that is, a report can conclude that the president committed a crime and can charge the president. Conversely, if the court finds that he does have temporary
immunity, his day in court will simply be delayed until he is out of office.
(And, of course, if a president feels strongly about clearing his name in
court, he could waive such immunity and proceed to trial while in office.) During that temporary immunity, the president could use his
unique bully pulpit to defend himself—a privilege that a normal defendant does not enjoy.

Beyond that, there are other reforms that should be made in light of
our experience. Currently, only the attorney general or acting attorney
general can appoint the special counsel. This is an insufficient trigger.
The attorney general is a presidential appointee. Imagine you have a
lawbreaking president who has appointed an attorney general who,
rather than honor his role as a defender of justice for all the people,
views himself as the president's personal defender—in other words, the
situation we are in with Trump and Barr. Had Barr already been serving
as attorney general when James Comey was fired, it is impossible to
imagine that he would have appointed a special counsel in the first place.
Surely, he would have waved away the strong appearance of wrongdo-

ing at the outset, just as, in his four-page letter, he waved away all the evidence of that wrongdoing we'd collected over twenty-two months.

I propose that two other institutions be granted the power to appoint a special counsel, provided that the same thresholds to warrant such an appointment are met. First, if the matter to be investigated deals with national security, the director of national intelligence—the head of the Intelligence Community—should be able to appoint a special counsel.

The current special counsel rules were established prior to 9/11; they contemplated only a criminal investigation. But that is not the world we inhabit now. America may face other issues of national security that bring investigators into conflict with the executive branch, just as the question of Russian interference in the 2016 election did. Permitting the director of national intelligence to appoint a special counsel would provide another chance to obtain an independent investigation into such a matter. And dispersing that appointment power beyond the attorney general would reduce the risk of political interference keeping a special counsel from being appointed at all.

Institutionally, the Intelligence Community is typically filled, more so than the Department of Justice, with longtime career employees dedicated to keeping the country safe; compared to Main Justice, its operation is less buffeted by political winds. And even if my assessment of its integrity is suspect, simply giving the appointment power to more than one person makes it harder for those with conflicts of interest to circle the wagons and prevent the appointment of a special counsel when an investigation is merited.

Congress should also be able to appoint a special counsel—with limitations. Congress can already hold hearings and conduct investigations (although with fewer tools than the Justice Department). The appointment of a special counsel should not measurably increase the power it currently has. Therefore, a congressionally appointed special counsel should not have the power to bring indictments. That is an executive branch function, and I do not think the courts would permit Congress to have such power, in any event. But a congressionally appointed special counsel would be able to refer matters to federal or state law enforcement or civil authorities. Having this congressional safety valve would strengthen our checks and balances, in instances when the executive branch is unwilling to take action. And by specifically granting the ability to refer matters to state authorities, the rules would shelter the indictment process from executive power—or abuse of power, including the president's ability to pardon his way out of trouble.

Fully safeguarding a special counsel's investigation from the abuses of that pardon power is difficult, however, since the president is granted that power by the Constitution and, absent a constitutional amendment, will continue to be able to exercise it. But there are potential ways to curtail how that power is used.

We must first recognize that the power to pardon is conferred on the presidency—it is not a personal power of the man or woman who inhabits the office. As president, that person has a sworn duty to uphold the law fully and faithfully, not to undermine or invalidate it. And so, where a pardon is being used to protect the president personally, or to protect the president's family, friends, or conspirators, it should not be seen as a valid exercise of that constitutional power.

Being able to tell one scenario from the other may not be difficult; until Trump's presidency, all recent presidents used a formal process for evaluating and granting pardons. Where pardons are awarded to conspirators of the president and without any consistent rationale to support them, a court could find the pardon to be an invalid exercise of the power of the presidency, which can overcome a strong presumption in favor of regularity. And, in any event, even if the pardon is legal, a prosecutor could consider the granting of such a pardon as a part of an effort to obstruct illegally an investigation. Dangling a pardon should be recognized as an even more egregious abuse of that power, since there is no reason to signal the possibility of a pardon in advance, except to deter a witness from cooperating and obstruct an investigation.

Among many other more minor reforms, the special counsel regulations should also make clear that the full, unredacted report should be provided simultaneously to the attorney general and to the oversight committees in Congress—and, if assessing a national security matter, to the director of national intelligence, as well. We cannot afford another Barr letter—or any other future attempts to pervert the findings of such a report before it reaches other hands. The underlying evidence obtained in a special counsel's investigation should also be made available to each body, so that another Barr cannot stonewall to keep it from Congress. A salutary effect of such disclosure is that each body would have the ability to assess the work and judgments of the special counsel for itself, thus holding the special counsel's investigation to greater, aggregate account-ability.

These reforms, however, will do little to protect our democracy from the now endemic problem of foreign governments interfering in our elections. To do this, we need to create a group of investigators within the Department of Justice, composed of representatives of the Intelligence Community—the NSA and the CIA, among others—whose sole mission would be investigating and preventing attacks on our elections.

The work of the Special Counsel's Office in uncovering and documenting Russia's election interference in the 2016 election was remarkable—but it was possible only because of Mueller's leadership and drive, matched by the expertise and elbow grease of a dedicated group of career agents, analysts, and prosecutors. America deserves an equally exemplary group of intelligence professionals working on this problem on a permanent basis. The threat is not going away. In fact, our government experts know that the meddling we faced in 2016 is child's play compared to the kinds of disruptions and attacks we will face in the future.

Such a group of election interference specialists could be required, for instance, to issue yearly reports about the activity it has detected, and recommendations to the executive branch and Congress about what measures are needed to thwart such attacks (in sealed and unsealed versions to protect important countermeasures). Having a dedicated team will deter foreign actors, as well as any politicians here in America who find it expedient to ignore, minimize, or even accept such illegal assistance. And establishing the group on a permanent basis would make it that much harder for a sitting president who has benefited from such foreign interference, as Trump indisputably did, to welcome future interference, or demand it as a favor, as Trump has also done.

I have watched our report, since its completion, be manipulated and disregarded by a brazen, imperial presidency, a presidency that uses the powers of the office, and the force of the American government more broadly, to reshape reality for the president's own personal benefit. The reforms I've proposed here seek to keep a future special counsel's work from being manipulated—which is to say, to defend the truth from being similarly undercut, overwhelmed, and ignored.

How we uphold the rule of law amid such a ferocious storm of wrongdoing is a question that, if not taken seriously, will undermine our democracy from outside and from within. Already we have signaled our permission to foreign nations to influence our elections without fear of consequence, so long as they assist the administration in power. Already we have negated what generations of Americans have fought for, beginning with the American Revolution, when we slipped the yoke of tyranny under a British monarch. What we do next, or choose not to do, will either repair that damage or tacitly allow the corrosion of our ideals to keep advancing.

As one small witness to history, I now know that the death of our democracy is possible.

Fixing it is possible, too.

■ ACKNOWLEDGMENTS

NO BOOK IS AN ISLAND; it is the product of influences throughout the life of the author and, more immediately, the skill and craft of numerous editors and readers. This effort is no different.

Given the limits placed on my ability to show the manuscript to people prior to the Department of Justice conducting its prepublication review, I am particularly indebted to those who were able to provide me guidance within those parameters. My agents at ICM, Esther Newberg and Zoe Sandler, were fiercely devoted to the project and committed to providing their no-nonsense, clear-eyed assessment. The team put together by Random House, particularly Andy Ward and Jon Mooallem, was invaluable in helping me to gain distance from the maelstrom that enveloped me for twenty-two months. They pushed and pulled with generosity and insight, and shook me loose from decades of writing dry legal prose in order to evoke the look and feel of the historic events I lived through.

I thank the legal team at the Knight Center—Alex Abdo, Ramya Krishnan, Meenu Krishnan, and Katie Fallow—for their skill and fortitude in navigating the book successfully through the prepublication review process.

I am most indebted to the many mentors and colleagues with whom I have worked in my life. As I am long in the tooth, there are too many to name here. But they extend far and wide: Professors Natalie Davis and Carl Schorske at Princeton; Andrea Bonime-Blanc, Stephanie Breslow, Anne Chwat, Ed Newman, Kelly Williams, Phillipp Windemuth, and Richard Ziegler at Cleary Gottlieb; Valerie Caproni, Mark Feldman, John Gleeson, Katya Jestin, Leo Laufer, Kelly Moore, Peter Norling, Lauren Resnick, Bridget Rohde, George Stamboulidis, and Sung-hee Suh, in the U.S. attorney's office for the Eastern District of New York; Sam Buell, Leslie Caldwell, Matt Friedrich, Lisa Monaco, and Kathy Ruemmler on the Enron Task Force; Ray Andjich, Tom Bondy, Catherine Chen, Paula Schanzle Ebersole, Chris Favo, Joe Ford, Jason Herring, Paul Holdeman, Janet Kamerman, Julie Katzman, Patrick Kelley, Elaine Lammert, Howard Leadbetter, Omer Meisel, Anthony Montero, Tim Murphy, Lisa Page, John Pistole, Greg Ruppert, Monica Ryan, Elisabeth Theodore, and Jeff Tomlinson at the Federal Bureau of Investigation; Matt Alsdorf, Christina Andolino, Josh Block, Michael DeSanctis, Elizabeth Edmondson, Lisa Genn, Mark Lightner, Joe McFadden, David Newman, Peter Pope, Alix Smith, Paul Smith, and Danielle Tarantolo at Jenner and Block; Rachel Barkow, Ryan Goodman, Jim Jacobs, Anne Milgram, and Erin Murphy at NYU School of Law; Joe Beemsterboer, Dan Kahn, Kathleen McGovern, Sandra Moser, Ben Singer, and Rob Zink at the Department of Justice Fraud Section—to name just a few members of the very large village that helped form who I am.

This book, which records for posterity the work of the Special Counsel's Office, would not have been possible without the dedication and skill of the lawyers, agents, analysts, and staff who worked at or with the Special Counsel's Office. The office was embodied in the inimitable Robert S. Mueller III, who had the foolhardiness to hire me three times, to my unending gratitude. Those who had the honor of a lifetime in working for Mueller in this endeavor and who worked to meet the challenge include: team leaders Michael Dreeben, Omer Meisel, Jill Murphy, Jim Quarles, Jeannie Rhee, Michelle Taylor, and Brandon Van Grack; our legal team Adam Jed, Scott Meisler, and Elisabeth Prelogar; our FBI supervisors Dave Archey, Brian Auten, and Bill McCausland; our administrative leaders Connie Kozlusky, Beth McGarry, and Linda Williams; our attorneys Rush Atkinson, Andrew Goldstein, Aaron Zebley, and Aaron Zelinsky; our meticulous and worked-to-the-bone paralegals—and now budding law students—Lorna Mosher, Emma Shreve, and Evan Binder; and my dedicated and fearless Team M colleagues Greg Andres, Uzo Asonye, Kevin Constantine, Brock Domin, Sherine Ebadi, Mike Ficht, Kyle Freeny, Morgan Magionos, Renee Michael, Brian Richardson, Rob Valdini, and Jeff Weiland, as well as the intrepid prosecutors in the U.S. attorney's office for the District of Columbia, Fernando Campoamor-Sanchez, Michael DiLorenzo, Molly Gaston, Jonathan Kravis, Jessie Liu, and Michael Marando. I am most indebted to Jeannie Rhee and Omer Meisel for their unwavering support and dedication to justice. They are models of all that public service should be.

And finally I thank my friend Sharon Weinberg for her endless erudite title suggestions; Jerry March for guiding me to my home at ICM; my best friend and soul mate, Susan Amron; and my sister and sister-in-law, Lisa and Deb, for their example of lives well lived.

■ NOTES

INTRODUCTION

xi   **Two days before:** Eric Tucker, Michael Balsamo, and Chad Day, "Mueller Concludes Russia-Trump Probe with No New Indictments," Associated Press, Mar. 22, 2019.

xii   **After months of speculation:** William Barr to U.S. Congress, Mar. 22, 2019.

xii   **The special counsel's report:** U.S. Department of Justice, *Report on the Investigation into Russian Interference in the 2016 Presidential Election* (2019), 1:14–51.

xii   **We had found insufficient evidence:** Ibid., 4–10.

xii   **Instead, our report:** Ibid., 2:1–8.

xiv   **The voices on the radio:** William Barr to U.S. Congress, Mar. 24, 2019.

xv   **Which is not to say:** William Barr to Rod Rosenstein and Steve Engel, "Mueller's 'Obstruction' Theory," June 8, 2018.

xvi   **But I also knew:** Darren Samuelsohn, "New Trump-Russia Subplot: Mueller and Barr Are 'Good Friends,'" *Politico,* Jan. 15, 2019.

xvi   **The letter indeed:** William Barr to U.S. Senate Committee on the Judiciary and U.S. House of Representatives Committee on the Judiciary, Mar. 24, 2019.

xvi   **Barr's letter claimed:** William Barr to U.S. Congress, Mar. 24, 2019.

xvi   **On the issue of obstruction:** Ibid.

xvii   **Moreover, Barr took it upon:** Ibid.

xxiii   **The president's dangling:** U.S. Department of Justice, *Report on the Investigation into Russian Interference in the 2016 Presidential Election* (2019), 2:6.

xxiii   **Thus, when within days:** "Transcript: Attorney General William Barr's

Press Conference Remarks Ahead of Mueller Report Release," *Politico,* Apr. 18, 2019, https://www.politico.com/story/2019/04/18/transcript-barr -press-conference-1280949.

xxiii   **The president, encouraged by a team:** Peter Baker, "Trump Proceeds with Post-Impeachment Purge Amid Pandemic," *The New York Times,* Apr. 4, 2020.

CHAPTER 1. THE BEGINNING: SPRING 2017

3   **Robert Mueller had been appointed:** U.S. Department of Justice, Office of the Deputy Attorney General, Order No. 3915-2017, *Appointment of Special Counsel to Investigate Russian Interference with the 2016 Presidential Election and Related Matters,* May 17, 2017.

7   **As I dug in:** Franklin Foer, "Paul Manafort, American Hustler," *The Atlantic,* Mar. 2018.

7   **I learned from:** Ibid.

7   **One of the firm's:** Kate Zernike, "'Steady Hand' for the G.O.P. Guides McCain on a New Path," *The New York Times,* Apr. 13, 2008.

7   **He would work for:** Ibid.

7   **He was drawn:** Jeffrey Toobin, "The Dirty Trickster," *The New Yorker,* May 23, 2008.

8   **Manafort also acquired:** Foer, "Paul Manafort, American Hustler."

8   **By the end of the nineties:** Ibid.

8   **And along the way:** Shelby Holliday, "Roger Stone Was Longtime Associate of Donald Trump," *The Wall Street Journal,* Jan. 25, 2019.

8   **He used his ballooning wealth:** Sarah N. Lynch, "Manafort Spent Millions on Homes, Rugs, Clothes: Court Filing," Reuters, Oct. 30, 2017.

8   **The annual gardening:** Katelyn Polantz and Liz Stark, "Landscaper Describes Manafort's Impressive Pond and Flower Bed in the Shape of an 'M,'" CNN, Aug. 2, 2018.

9   **The first was Oleg Deripaska:** U.S. Department of Justice, *Report on the Investigation into Russian Interference in the 2016 Presidential Election* (2019), 1:131–32.

9   **Manafort's other main source:** Superseding Indictment, *United States v. Manafort,* No. 1:18-cr-83 (E.D. Va. Feb. 23, 2018), ECF No. 14, ¶ 1.

9   **Yanukovych was a pro-Russian thug:** Foer, "Paul Manafort, American Hustler."

9   **Here, in the United States:** U.S. Department of State, Press Statement, *Treatment of Former Prime Minister Yulia Tymoshenko,* May 1, 2012, https://2009 -2017.state.gov/secretary/20092013clinton/rm/2012/05/188998.htm.

10   **After Yanukovych's election:** Foer, "Paul Manafort, American Hustler."

10   **His right-hand man there:** Superseding Indictment, *United States v. Manafort,* No. 1:17-cr-201 (D.D.C. June 8, 2018), ECF No. 318, ¶ 8.

10   **Manafort's position of privilege:** Ibid., ¶ 9.

10   **The FBI dossier noted:** Natasha Bertrand, "Hacked Text Messages Allegedly Sent by Paul Manafort's Daughter Discuss 'Blood Money' and Killings, and a Ukrainian Lawyer Wants Him to Explain," *Business Insider,* Mar. 21, 2017.

12   **Work in the past few months:** Superseding Indictment, *United States v. Manafort,* No. 1:18-cr-83 (E.D. Va. Feb. 23, 2018), ECF No. 14, ¶ 4.

12   **The investigation uncovered:** Ibid., ¶¶ 7–14.

14   **They were the largest:** Indictment, *United States v. Calk,* No. 1-19-cr-366 (S.D.N.Y. May 21, 2019), ECF No. 2, ¶ 8.

14   **After obtaining the loans:** Indictment, *United States v. Calk,* No. 1-19-cr-366 (S.D.N.Y. May 21, 2019), ECF No. 2, ¶ 9.

15   **It's worth noting that:** Julia Ainsley, Andrew Lehren, and Anna Schecter, "The Mueller Effect: FARA Filings Soar in Shadow of Manafort, Flynn Probes," NBC News, Jan. 18, 2018.

15   **Part of Manafort's assignment:** Superseding Indictment, *United States v. Manafort,* No. 1:17-cr-201 (D.D.C. June 8, 2018), ECF No. 318, ¶ 9.

16   **To accomplish this:** Ibid., ¶¶ 14, 28.

16   **It was one of the reasons:** U.S. Department of Justice, *Report on the Investigation into Russian Interference in the 2016 Presidential Election* (2019), 1:141.

16   **After Manafort's resignation:** Superseding Indictment, *United States v. Manafort,* No. 1:17-cr-201 (D.D.C. June 8, 2018), ECF No. 318, ¶ 27.

16   **Consequently, by the spring:** Isaac Arnsdorf, "Podesta Group Files New Disclosures in Manafort-Linked Ukraine Lobbying," *Politico,* Apr. 12, 2017.

CHAPTER 2. LIVING AN IDEA

24   **He regularly hit the town:** Selwyn Raab, "John Gotti Dies in Prison at 61; Mafia Boss Relished the Spotlight," *The New York Times,* June 11, 2002.

24   **I FORGOTTI:** Andy Geller, "Rise & Fall of the Godfather," *New York Post,* June 11, 2002.

24   **The indictment our office:** Arnold H. Lubasch, "Gotti Sentenced to Life in Prison Without the Possibility of Parole," *The New York Times,* June 24, 1992.

24   **Gravano, who faced the same charges:** Emily Saul, " 'Sammy the Bull' Reveals He Plotted Ultimate Mob Hit on Boss John Gotti," *New York Post,* Oct. 21, 2019.

25   **The jury did:** Arnold H. Lubasch, "Gotti Sentenced to Life in Prison Without the Possibility of Parole," *The New York Times,* June 24, 1992.

25   **At the time, the Colombo family:** Robert McFadden, "Brooklyn's Mob War Interrupted with a Quiet Day in Court," *The New York Times,* Dec. 17, 1991.

27   **Over the next two years:** Selwyn Raab, "Carmine Persico, Colombo Crime Boss, Is Dead at 85," *The New York Times,* Mar. 8, 2019.

30   **And Enron was a whale:** Reed Abelson and Jonathan D. Glater, "Enron's Collapse: The Auditors: Who's Keeping the Accountants Accountable?," *The New York Times,* Jan. 15, 2002.

30   **Suspicions about the inner workings:** John R. Emshwiller, Gary McWilliams, and Ann Davis, "Symbol of an Era: Lay, Skilling Are Convicted of Fraud; Jurors Reject Defense Claim That Enron Was Clean; Question of Credibility; Two 'Very Controlling People,'" *The Wall Street Journal,* May 26, 2006.

30   **A few days later:** "Timeline: A Chronology of Enron Corp.," *The New York Times,* Jan. 18, 2006.

30   **But its internal documents:** Jeff Leeds, "Andersen Auditor Details Shredding of Enron Papers," *Los Angeles Times,* May 14, 2002.

31   **Andersen appealed:** Linda Greenhouse, "Justices Unanimously Overturn Conviction of Arthur Andersen," *The New York Times,* May 31, 2005.

31   **The *Houston Chronicle*:** Mary Flood, "June 9, 2002: Alternate Juror Would Have Acquitted Andersen," *Houston Chronicle,* June 9, 2002.

32   **We were ultimately able:** Emshwiller, McWilliams, and Davis, "Symbol of an Era."

32   **It wasn't until very shortly before:** Lesley Curwen, "The Corporate Conscience: Sherron Watkins, Enron Whistleblower," *The Guardian,* June 21, 2003.

37   **Within one year:** Nathan Bomey, "VW Pleads Guilty to Conspiracy, Obstruction of Justice; 6 Execs Charged," *USA Today,* Jan. 11, 2017.

37   **Mueller had followed:** Jack Ewing and Hiroko Tabuchi, "Behind Volkswagen Settlement, Speed and Compromise," *The New York Times,* July 15, 2016.

39   **As one example:** Indictment, *United States v. Firtash,* No. 1:13-cr-515 (N.D. Ill. June 20, 2013), ECF No. 2, ¶ 7.

39   **What none of us knew:** Renae Merle, "Trump Called Global Anti-Bribery Law 'Horrible.' His Administration Is Pursuing Fewer New Investigations," *The Washington Post,* Jan. 31, 2020.

42   **Trump, for example, had denigrated:** Nina Totenberg, "Who Is Judge Gonzalo Curiel, The Man Trump Attacked for His Mexican Ancestry?," NPR, June 7, 2016.

43   **In January 2017:** Michael D. Shear and Helene Cooper, "Trump Bars Refugees and Citizens of 7 Muslim Countries," *The New York Times,* Jan. 27, 2017.

CHAPTER 4. THE START OF THE OBSTRUCTION INVESTIGATION

50   **As part of Team 600's:** Michael S. Schmidt and Maggie Haberman, "Mueller Has Early Draft of Trump Letter Giving Reasons for Firing Comey," *The New York Times,* Sept. 1, 2017.

50   **Comey was fired:** U.S. Department of Justice, *Report on the Investigation into Russian Interference in the 2016 Presidential Election* (2019), 2:62.

51   **The memo's subject line:** "Trump's Letter Firing FBI Director James Comey," CNN, May 10, 2017, https://www.cnn.com/2017/05/09/politics/fbi -james-comey-fired-letter/index.html.

52   **The FBI was recommending:** Mark Landler and Eric Lichtblau, "F.B.I. Director James Comey Recommends No Charges for Hillary Clinton on Email," *The New York Times,* July 5, 2016.

53   **When asked much later:** Interview with Loretta Lynch, Attorney General, *Nightly News with Lester Holt,* NBC News, Apr. 9, 2018, https://www.nbc news.com/nightly-news/video/former-attorney-general-loretta-lynch -speaks-out-1206752323896.

53   **As we all know:** James Comey to U.S. Congress, Oct. 28, 2016.

54   **Comey would defend his actions:** Josh Gerstein and Austin Wright, "Comey Forcefully Defends 'Painful' Decision on Clinton Probe," *Politico,* May 3, 2017.

54   **According to the inspector general's report:** U.S. Department of Justice, Office of the Inspector General, *A Review of Various Actions by the Federal Bureau of Investigation and Department of Justice in Advance of the 2016 Election* (2018), 94–95.

54   **This, in fact, was the option:** Ibid., 384, 389.

55   **It seemed distinctly possible that Trump:** U.S. Department of Justice, *Report on the Investigation into Russian Interference in the 2016 Presidential Election* (2019), 2:23, 62.

55   **Trump had written this draft:** Ibid., 64–65.

56   **This preceded the Rosenstein memo:** Ibid., 66.

56   **In the memo, Trump:** Ibid., 65.

56   **It's a big deal to fire:** Michael Isikoff and Ruth Marcus, "Clinton Fires Sessions as FBI Director," *The Washington Post,* July 20, 1993.

56   **These were the personal memos:** Nicholas Fandos, "Comey Memos Provide Intimate Look into Trump Presidency," *The New York Times,* Apr. 19, 2018.

57   **In fact, Comey's memoranda:** U.S. Department of Justice, *Report on the Investigation into Russian Interference in the 2016 Presidential Election* (2019), 2:40.

57   **Flynn had got caught up:** Ibid., 24.

57   **The first phone call:** Ibid., 24–25.

58   **In January 2017, when the call:** Ibid., 29.

58   **As a result, the vice president:** Interview with Mike Pence, Vice President Elect, *Face the Nation,* CBS News, Jan. 15, 2017, https://www.cbsnews.com /news/face-the-nation-transcript-january-15-2017-pence-manchin -gingrich/.

58   **Ultimately, our office brought:** Plea Agreement, *United States v. Flynn,* No. 1:17-cr-232 (D.D.C. Dec. 1, 2017), ECF No. 3.

58   **According to the memo Comey:** Memorandum from James Comey, Director, Federal Bureau of Investigation, Feb. 14, 2017.

59 **There was also substantial evidence:** U.S. Department of Justice, *Report on the Investigation into Russian Interference in the 2016 Presidential Election* (2019), 2:24–26.

59 **In fact, the next day:** Corky Siemaszko, "Trump Says Putin 'Smart' for Not Retaliating Against U.S. Sanctions," NBC News, Dec. 30, 2016.

59 **The statute, however, had never resulted:** Jeremy Duda, "Michael Flynn Has Absolutely Nothing to Fear from the Logan Act," *The Washington Post,* Feb. 16, 2017.

60 **The president claimed in the press:** Ashley Parker and David Nakamura, "Trump Denies Telling Comey to Back Off Flynn Investigation," *The Washington Post,* May 18, 2017.

59 **But the president was never willing:** U.S. Department of Justice, *Report on the Investigation into Russian Interference in the 2016 Presidential Election* (2019), appendix C:1–2.

60 **Over the next six months:** Ibid., 2:64–69.

60 **Indeed, one senior national security staffer:** Ibid., 68, n.439.

60 **The Office of White House Counsel:** Ibid., 68.

60 **They advised that the Trump draft:** Ibid., 68, n.442.

60 **And, as detailed in our report:** Ibid., 70.

61 **The president then had to admit:** Ibid., 71.

61 **The media later reported:** Matt Apuzzo, Maggie Haberman, and Matthew Rosenberg, "Trump Told Russians That Firing 'Nut Job' Comey Eased Pressure from Investigation," *The New York Times,* May 19, 2017.

61 **McGahn told our office:** U.S. Department of Justice, *Report on the Investigation into Russian Interference in the 2016 Presidential Election* (2019), 2:71.

61 **Eventually, in 2019, the press:** Shane Harris, Josh Dawsey, and Ellen Nakashima, "Trump Told Russian Officials in 2017 He Wasn't Concerned About Moscow's Interference in U.S. Election," *The Washington Post,* Sept. 27, 2019.

61 **The evening after the Lavrov-Kislyak:** Interview with Donald J. Trump, President, *Nightly News with Lester Holt,* NBC News, May 11, 2017, https://www.nbcnews.com/nightly-news/video/pres-trump-s-extended-exclusive-interview-with-lester-holt-at-the-white-house-941854787582.

63 **When pressed during his confirmation hearing:** Isaac Stanley-Becker, "Trump Reportedly Told Michael Cohen to Lie. His Own Attorney General Pick Testified That's a Crime," *The Washington Post,* Jan. 18, 2019.

63 **During a proceeding:** Oral Argument at 47:24, *Trump v. Vance,* 941 F.3d 631 (2d Cir. 2019) (No. 19-3204), https://www.c-span.org/video/?465172-1/circuit-hears-oral-argument-president-trumps-tax-returns-audio-only&live&start=2833.

63 **Acting attorney general Rod Rosenstein:** U.S. Department of Justice, Office of the Deputy Attorney General, Order No. 3915-2017, *Appointment of Spe-*

cial Counsel to Investigate Russian Interference with the 2016 Presidential Election and Related Matters, May 17, 2017.

64   **At no point did he tell us:** Testimony of Rod Rosenstein, Deputy Attorney General, *Hearing on Fiscal 2018 Justice Department Budget Before the Senate Appropriations Committee,* June 13, 2017.

CHAPTER 5. TEAM M RAMPS UP

66   **What Jim was referring to:** Sidney Powell, "In Andrew Weissmann, the DOJ Makes a Stunningly Bad Choice for Crucial Role," *The New York Observer,* Jan. 12, 2015.

66   **Bannon referred to me:** Michael Wolff, *Fire and Fury: Inside the Trump White House* (New York: Henry Holt, 2018).

70   **The email included a series:** Superseding Indictment, *United States v. Manafort,* No. 1:18-cr-83 (E.D. Va. Feb. 23, 2018), ECF No. 14, ¶ 21.

71   **In the end, we would find:** Ibid.

73   **These files appeared to include:** Superseding Indictment, *United States v. Manafort,* No. 1:17-cr-201 (D.D.C. June 8, 2018), ECF No. 318, ¶ 27.

74   **"He lied to the government already":** Ibid.

76   **Manafort's $15,000:** Samantha Schmidt, "Paul Manafort's $15,000 Ostrich Jacket Raises Tantalizing Questions," *The Washington Post,* Aug. 1, 2018.

77   **Deripaska, who had paid him millions:** U.S. Department of Justice, *Report on the Investigation into Russian Interference in the 2016 Presidential Election* (2019), 1:131.

77   **Ukraine was one of their targets:** Foer, "Paul Manafort, American Hustler."

77   **One 2005 memorandum:** U.S. Department of Justice, *Report on the Investigation into Russian Interference in the 2016 Presidential Election* (2019), 1:131.

CHAPTER 6. THE TRUMP TOWER MEETING

79   **In early July:** Jo Becker, Matt Apuzzo, and Adam Goldman, "Trump Team Met with Lawyer Linked to Kremlin During Campaign," *The New York Times,* July 8, 2017.

80   **These numerous leads:** Brett Samuels, "Jailed Belarusian Escort Says She Has Tapes That Prove Russian Meddling," *The Hill,* Mar. 5, 2018.

80   **And Don Jr. had previously:** Becker, Apuzzo, and Goldman, "Trump Team Met with Lawyer Linked to Kremlin."

80   **His statement described:** Ibid.

81   **The principal Russian operative:** U.S. Department of Justice, *Report on the Investigation into Russian Interference in the 2016 Presidential Election* (2019), 1:110, 112.

81   **She had employed legal:** Ibid., 112.

82   **No doubt understanding:** Jeremy Diamond, "Donald Trump Jr. Releases Email Chain on His Russian Meeting," CNN, July 11, 2017.

82   **The email to arrange the meeting:** U.S. Department of Justice, *Report on the Investigation into Russian Interference in the 2016 Presidential Election* (2019), 1:110, 111.

82   **His initial approach to Don Jr.:** Ibid., 113.

83   **Don Jr.'s reply to Goldstone:** Ibid.

84   **Beginning in March 2016:** Ibid., 83, 89.

84   **Papadopoulos was brand-new:** Ibid., 81.

84   **He was only twenty-eight years old:** Sharon LaFraniere, Mark Mazzetti, and Matt Apuzzo, "How the Russia Inquiry Began: A Campaign Aide, Drinks and Talk of Political Dirt," *The New York Times,* Dec. 30, 2017.

84   **Papadopoulos, for example:** Ibid.

84   **That this supposed council:** U.S. Department of Justice, *Report on the Investigation into Russian Interference in the 2016 Presidential Election* (2019), 1:84.

84   **The FBI had first interviewed:** LaFraniere, Mazzetti, and Apuzzo, "How the Russia Inquiry Began."

85   **About three weeks after:** Ibid.

85   **The story that Papadopoulos:** Statement of the Offense, *United States v. Papadopoulos,* No. 1:17-cr-182 (D.D.C. Oct. 5, 2017), ECF No. 19, ¶ 2.

86   **Records of their communications:** Ibid., ¶ 2a.

86   **More important, Papadopoulos:** U.S. Department of Justice, *Report on the Investigation into Russian Interference in the 2016 Presidential Election* (2019), 1:87.

86   **Jeannie obtained emails:** Ibid., 89–90.

86   **In fact, Papadopoulos appeared:** Ibid., 89.

86   **But Papadopoulos had deactivated:** Statement of the Offense, *United States v. Papadopoulos,* No. 1:17-cr-182 (D.D.C. Oct. 5, 2017), ECF No. 19, ¶ 33.

87   **He told Jeannie he didn't:** U.S. Department of Justice, *Report on the Investigation into Russian Interference in the 2016 Presidential Election* (2019), 1:93.

87   **In one instance, for example:** Ibid., 92.

88   **But Papadopoulos claimed:** Ibid., 92, n.489.

88   **In the end, given that:** Plea Agreement, *United States v. Papadopoulos,* No. 1:17-cr-182 (D.D.C. Oct. 5, 2017), ECF No. 18.

88   **First, it was clear:** U.S. Department of Justice, *Report on the Investigation into Russian Interference in the 2016 Presidential Election* (2019), 1:113.

88   **And yet, Manafort, too:** Becker, Apuzzo, and Goldman, "Trump Team Met with Lawyer Linked to Kremlin."

89   **Indeed, as Goldstone explicitly:** U.S. Department of Justice, *Report on the Investigation into Russian Interference in the 2016 Presidential Election* (2019), 1:113.

89   **The *Times* story mentioned:** Becker, Apuzzo, and Goldman, "Trump Team Met with Lawyer Linked to Kremlin."

89   **Some fast work by Omer:** U.S. Department of Justice, *Report on the Investigation into Russian Interference in the 2016 Presidential Election* (2019), 1:117.

92   **Most notably, in the course:** Ibid., 122.

94   **We knew that Don Jr.:** Ibid., 117.

94   **We'd also zeroed in:** Ibid., 116, 120.

94   **Indeed, we learned that Aras:** Kara Scannell, "Emin Agalarov Cancels U.S. Concert Tour After Not Reaching Testimony Deal with Mueller and Congress," CNN, Jan. 21, 2019.

94   **But shortly thereafter, he went:** Interview with Donald Trump, Jr., *Hannity,* Fox News, July 11, 2017, https://www.youtube.com/watch?v=ExcDi9a9His.

95   **Even Steve Bannon:** Wolff, *Fire and Fury.*

95   **All of these witnesses:** U.S. Department of Justice, *Report on the Investigation into Russian Interference in the 2016 Presidential Election* (2019), 1:118–20.

95   **Kushner claimed he'd known:** Ibid., 114–15.

96   **This was corroborated by:** Ibid., 118.

96   **But our interviewees agreed:** Ibid., 117.

96   **The much-anticipated dirt:** Ibid.

96   **Various participants said that:** Ibid., 118.

96   **All Don Jr. would tell:** Ibid.

97   **What this whole episode established:** Ibid., 180.

CHAPTER 7. THE TRUMP TOWER COVER-UP

100   **Don Jr.'s written statement:** U.S. Department of Justice, *Report on the Investigation into Russian Interference in the 2016 Presidential Election* (2019), 2:102–3.

100   **Corey Lewandowski would later:** Nicholas Fandos and Maggie Haberman, "Key Moments from Corey Lewandowski's Testimony Before Congress," *The New York Times,* Sept. 17, 2019.

100   **And Deputy Attorney General:** Carrie Johnson and Philip Ewing, "Rosenstein Denies That He Discussed Recording Trump, Invoking 25th Amendment," NPR, Sept. 21, 2018.

101   **Another suspicious dimension:** U.S. Department of Justice, *Report on the Investigation into Russian Interference in the 2016 Presidential Election* (2019), 2:99.

101   **And it is now a matter:** Josh Gerstein and Darren Samuelsohn, "Justice Dept. Confirms Trump Jr. and McGahn Did Not Testify to Mueller Grand Jury," *Politico,* Oct. 20, 2019.

102   **As to the president:** U.S. Department of Justice, *Report on the Investigation into Russian Interference in the 2016 Presidential Election* (2019), appendix C:2.

102   **The president did provide:** Ibid., appendix C:1.

103   **The emails revealed:** Ibid., 1:121.

103   **Later in June, Goldstone emailed:** Ibid.

103   **This conspiratorial scheming:** Ibid., 122.

104   **In July 2017, Trump announced:** Interview with Jay Sekulow, *New Day,* CNN, July 12, 2017, https://www.cnn.com/videos/politics/2017/07/12/jay -sekulow-trump-attorney-full-interview-newday.cnn.

104   **Later, he admitted to our office:** U.S. Department of Justice, *Report on the Investigation into Russian Interference in the 2016 Presidential Election* (2019), 2:105.

105   **Hicks explained that:** Ibid.

105   **The first statement Hicks:** Ibid., 102.

105   **According to her, the first:** Ibid., 100.

105   **The second time, however:** Ibid., 101.

106   **But Hicks also admitted:** Ibid., 100.

106   **She recalled being shocked:** Ibid., 100–101.

106   **Hicks knew the Trump Tower story:** Ibid., 101.

106   **The president's personal press agent:** Ibid., 104.

106   **Hicks described repeatedly urging:** Ibid., 100–102.

107   **Hicks tried to avoid:** Ibid., 100.

108   **Team 600 determined:** Ibid., 106–7.

111   **Meanwhile, Team R:** Ibid., 1:113.

CHAPTER 8. FIRING MUELLER

112   **Our discomfort was bolstered:** Carroll Kilpatrick, "Nixon Forces Firing of Cox; Richardson, Ruckelshaus Quit," *The Washington Post,* Oct. 21, 1973.

112   **But there was another precedent:** U.S. Department of Justice, *Report on the Investigation into Russian Interference in the 2016 Presidential Election* (2019), 2:62.

112   **In fact, though we did not know:** Ibid., 85.

113   **But McGahn had refused:** Ibid., 86.

114   **We kept reading in the press:** Karen Freifeld, "White House Lawyer Cobb Predicts Quick End to Mueller Probe," Reuters, Aug. 18, 2017.

114   **It was not surprising when:** Matt Apuzzo and Michael S. Schmidt, "Trump Adds Clinton Impeachment Lawyer, Bracing for a Fight on Multiple Fronts," *The New York Times,* May 2, 2018.

114   **I was taken by Judge Sirica's:** John Sirica, *To Set the Record Straight: The Break-in, the Tapes, the Conspirators, the Pardon* (New York: W. W. Norton, 1979), 239.

116   **We filed more than five hundred:** U.S. Department of Justice, *Report on the Investigation into Russian Interference in the 2016 Presidential Election* (2019), 1:13.

116   **And often we would refer:** Ibid., appendix D:1.

116   **And of course, after:** Ashraf Khalil and Michael Balsamo, "Roger Stone Guilty of Witness Tampering, Lying to Congress," Associated Press, Nov. 15, 2019.

117   **The president's daughter:** David S. Cloud, "Mueller Calls Back at Least One

Participant in Key Meeting with Russians at Trump Tower," *Los Angeles Times,* Jan. 6, 2018; U.S. Department of Justice, *Report on the Investigation into Russian Interference in the 2016 Presidential Election* (2019), 2:100.

CHAPTER 9. RUSSIA'S ACTIVE MEASURES

124   **Trump ran a campaign:** David E. Sanger and Maggie Haberman, "Donald Trump Gives Questionable Explanation of Events in Ukraine," *The New York Times,* July 31, 2016.

125   **This prompted the FBI:** LaFraniere, Mazzetti, and Apuzzo, "How the Russia Inquiry Began."

125   **At around that same time, emails stolen:** U.S. Department of Justice, *Report on the Investigation into Russian Interference in the 2016 Presidential Election* (2019), 1:176.

125   **The Intelligence Community:** Office of the Director of National Intelligence, Intelligence Community Assessment, *Assessing Russian Activities and Intentions in Recent U.S. Elections,* Jan. 6, 2017.

125   **And the Russian hacking was known:** Ellen Nakashima, "Russian Government Hackers Penetrated DNC, Stole Opposition Research on Trump," *The Washington Post,* June 14, 2016.

125   **But instead of accepting:** Sarah Wheaton, "Trump Not Convinced of Russian Hacking," *Politico,* Sept. 26, 2016.

126   **He famously ventured on national TV:** Ibid.

135   **We had a slight crisis:** Indictment, *United States v. Internet Research Agency LLC,* No. 1:18-cr-32 (D.D.C. Feb. 16, 2018), ECF No. 1, ¶ 58d.

135   **The Internet Research Agency:** U.S. Department of Justice, *Report on the Investigation into Russian Interference in the 2016 Presidential Election* (2019), 1:14.

135   **The agency itself aptly:** Indictment, *United States v. Internet Research Agency LLC,* No. 1:18-cr-32 (D.D.C. Feb. 16, 2018), ECF No. 1, ¶ 10c.

136   **The IRA had its main hub:** Ibid.

136   **It employed hundreds:** Ibid., ¶¶ 10a, 11b.

136   **The IRA was much like:** Ibid., ¶ 10b.

136   **It masked the Russian origins:** Ibid., ¶ 39.

136   **Its finances were similarly cloaked:** Ibid., ¶¶ 10, 11c.

136   **With the help of our:** Ibid., ¶ 12.

136   **The core work of the IRA:** U.S. Department of Justice, *Report on the Investigation into Russian Interference in the 2016 Presidential Election* (2019), 1:14.

136   **In 2014, a two-woman team:** Indictment, *United States v. Internet Research Agency LLC,* No. 1:18-cr-32 (D.D.C. Feb. 16, 2018), ECF No. 1, ¶ 30c.

137   **These specialists were divided:** Ibid., ¶ 33.

137   **Each specialist would create:** Ibid., ¶¶ 10, 11c.

137   **These personas—"Alex Anderson":** U.S. Department of Justice, *Report on the Investigation into Russian Interference in the 2016 Presidential Election*

(2019), 1:22, n.45; Indictment, *United States v. Internet Research Agency LLC,* No. 1:18-cr-32 (D.D.C. Feb. 16, 2018), ECF No. 1, ¶ 14.

137 **Other online accounts were:** U.S. Department of Justice, *Report on the Investigation into Russian Interference in the 2016 Presidential Election* (2019), 1:22, 24–25.

137 **One social media post:** Indictment, *United States v. Internet Research Agency LLC,* No. 1:18-cr-32 (D.D.C. Feb. 16, 2018), ECF No. 1, ¶ 46a.

137 **One phony offshoot:** U.S. Department of Justice, *Report on the Investigation into Russian Interference in the 2016 Presidential Election* (2019), 1:25.

137 **Others aimed to split:** Indictment, *United States v. Internet Research Agency LLC,* No. 1:18-cr-32 (D.D.C. Feb. 16, 2018), ECF No. 1, ¶ 46b.

137 **One February 10, 2016, email:** Ibid., ¶ 43a.

137 **A September 14, 2016, email:** Ibid., ¶ 43b.

137 **The IRA, meanwhile, amplified:** U.S. Department of Justice, *Report on the Investigation into Russian Interference in the 2016 Presidential Election* (2019), 1:25.

137 **These ads ran throughout the spring:** Indictment, *United States v. Internet Research Agency LLC,* No. 1:18-cr-32 (D.D.C. Feb. 16, 2018), ECF No. 1, ¶ 50.

137 **So successful was the fake media:** U.S. Department of Justice, *Report on the Investigation into Russian Interference in the 2016 Presidential Election* (2019), 1:28, 33–34.

138 **Team R discovered that Russians:** Ibid., 29.

138 **The Russians would alert both:** Ibid., 29, 35.

138 **After the Russian-staged rallies:** Ibid., 29.

138 **Three such pro-Trump rallies:** Indictment, *United States v. Internet Research Agency LLC,* No. 1:18-cr-32 (D.D.C. Feb. 16, 2018), ECF No. 1, ¶ 56.

138 **At two of these events:** Ibid., ¶ 55d.

138 **When Team R's FBI agents:** Ibid.

138 **An IRA operative, posing online:** Indictment, *United States v. Internet Research Agency LLC,* No. 1:18-cr-32 (D.D.C. Feb. 16, 2018), ECF No. 1, ¶ 12b.

139 **Interestingly, during the Republican primaries:** Ibid., ¶ 43.

139 **That fact-resistant conspiracy:** U.S. Senate, Select Committee on Intelligence, *Report on Russian Active Measures Campaigns and Interference in the 2016 U.S. Election,* vol. 2, *Russia's Use of Social Media,* Oct. 8, 2019, https://www.intelligence.senate.gov/sites/default/files/documents/Report_Volume2.pdf.

139 **"The Committee found that the IRA":** Ibid., 4.

139 **When it was clear Trump:** Ibid., 34.

140 **After Russia's annexation of Crimea:** Philip Rucker, "Hillary Clinton's Putin-Hitler Comments Draw Rebukes as She Wades into Ukraine Conflict," *The Washington Post,* Mar. 5, 2014.

140　**But Trump was a bonus:** David E. Sanger and Maggie Haberman, "Donald Trump Gives Questionable Explanation of Events in Ukraine," *The New York Times,* July 31, 2016.

141　**But even that check:** Richard Cowan, "Breaking with Republicans, Romney Votes 'Guilty' in Impeachment Trial," Reuters, Feb. 5, 2020.

CHAPTER 10. TRUMP'S FIXER

143　**The same account made a transfer:** Michael Rothfeld and Joe Palazzolo, "Trump Lawyer Arranged $130,000 Payment for Adult-Film Star's Silence," *The Wall Street Journal,* Jan. 12, 2018.

144　**While prosecutors in a U.S.:** U.S. Department of Justice, Office of the Deputy Attorney General, Order No. 3915-2017, *Appointment of Special Counsel to Investigate Russian Interference with the 2016 Presidential Election and Related Matters,* May 17, 2017.

147　**In fact, I came across:** Statement of the Offense, *United States v. Patten,* No. 1:18-cr-260 (D.D.C. Aug. 31, 2018), ECF No. 7, ¶ 7.

147　**Asked by a reporter:** Peter Baker, Michael S. Schmidt, and Maggie Haberman, "Citing Recusal, Trump Says He Wouldn't Have Hired Sessions," *The New York Times,* July 19, 2017.

148　**In fact, when the press:** Greg Farrell and Christian Berthelsen, "Mueller Expands Probe to Trump Business Transactions," Bloomberg, July 20, 2017.

CHAPTER 11. INDICTING MANAFORT AND GATES

149　**We indicted Paul Manafort:** Indictment, *United States v. Manafort,* No. 1:17-cr-201 (D.D.C. Oct. 27, 2017), ECF No. 13.

149　**Along with Manafort:** Ibid.

149　**When Manafort joined:** U.S. Department of Justice, *Report on the Investigation into Russian Interference in the 2016 Presidential Election* (2019), 1:134.

150　**Gates was managing that effort:** Indictment, *United States v. Manafort,* No. 1:17-cr-201 (D.D.C. Oct. 27, 2017), ECF No. 13, ¶ 21.

151　**With respect to the tax charges:** Ibid., ¶ 6.

151　**Thirty-two different LLCs:** Ibid., ¶ 12.

151　**For example, Team M:** Ibid., ¶¶ 11, 20.

151　**Smart people at the lobbying firms:** Statement of the Offense, *United States v. Manafort,* No. 1:17-cr-201 (D.D.C. Sept. 14, 2018), ECF No. 423, ¶ 32.

151　**Another email from the head:** Ibid., ¶ 32.

151　**It also permitted Manafort:** Ibid., ¶ 11.

158　**Only hours later:** Pamela Brown, Evan Perez, and Shimon Prokupecz, "First on CNN: First Charges Filed in Mueller Investigation," CNN, Oct. 27, 2017.

159　**Later that morning:** Matt Apuzzo, Adam Goldman, Michael S. Schmidt, and Matthew Rosenberg, "Former Trump Aides Charged as Prosecutors Reveal New Campaign Ties with Russia," *The New York Times,* Oct. 30, 3017.

160 **Right away, President Trump:** Amber Phillips, "With Money Laundering Charges Against Paul Manafort, Trump's 'Fake News' Claim Is Harder to Defend," *The Washington Post,* Oct. 30, 2017.

CHAPTER 12. VILIFICATION

164 **Our work had initially:** Paul Singer, Eliza Collins, and Erin Kelly, "Rare Bipartisan Moment: Both Sides Embrace Robert Mueller as Special Counsel," *USA Today,* May 17, 2017; ACLU, Press Release, *ACLU Comment on Appointment of Special Counsel on Russia Investigation,* May 17, 2017, https:// www.aclu.org/press-releases/aclu-comment-appointment-special-counsel -russia-investigation; Senator Chuck Grassley, Press Release, *Grassley Statement on the Appointment of Special Counsel in Russian Interference Probe,* May 17, 2017, https://www.judiciary.senate.gov/press/rep/releases/grassley -statement-on-the-appointment-of-special-counsel-in-russian-interference -probe.

164 **To be fair, this was:** John F. Harris and Bill Miller, "In a Deal, Clinton Avoids Indictment," *The Washington Post,* Jan. 20, 2001.

164 **He undermined journalistic outlets:** Michael M. Grynbaum, "Crowds, Stoked by Trump's Rhetoric, Increase Their Ire Toward the Press," *The New York Times,* Aug. 1, 2018.

164 **Trump decried the press:** Andrew Higgins, "Trump Embraces 'Enemy of the People,' a Phrase with a Fraught History," *The New York Times,* Feb. 26, 2017.

165 **And so, a different tack:** U.S. Department of Justice, *Report on the Investigation into Russian Interference in the 2016 Presidential Election* (2019), 2:80–81.

165 **There were similar whispers:** Michael D. Shear and Maggie Haberman, "Friend Says Trump Is Considering Firing Mueller as Special Counsel," *The New York Times,* June 12, 2017.

165 **A bogus claim was concocted:** Ibid.

165 **Finally, an outlandish allegation:** Philip Ewing, "An Apparent Scheme to Discredit Mueller May Have Backfired. He Referred It to the FBI," NPR, Oct. 30, 2018.

166 **Moreover, a check of FBI records:** "Hey, Isn't That . . . ?: Robert Mueller Summoned to Jury Duty; Rose McGowan Visits the W," *The Washington Post,* Aug. 3, 2010.

166 **who'd held a legendary press conference:** "Excerpts from Transcript of Cox's News Conference on Nixon's Decision on Tapes," *The New York Times,* Oct. 21, 1973, https://www.nytimes.com/1973/10/21/archives/excerpts-from -transcript-of-coxs-news-conference-on-nixons-decision.html.

167   **Even Mueller seemed to have:** U.S. Department of Justice, Statement, *Special Counsel Robert Mueller Statement on Russia Investigation,* May 29, 2019, https://www.c-span.org/video/?461196-1/special-counsel-robert-mueller -doj-policy-prohibited-indictment-president.

167   **Within weeks of Mueller's appointment:** Megan Keller, "Trump Revisits Charge That 'Mueller Witch Hunt' Is 'Illegal,'" *The Hill,* Sept. 16, 2018.

167   **Department regulations precluded:** Nicholas Fandos and Charlie Savage, "Justice Dept. Official Defends Mueller as Republicans Try to Discredit Him," *The New York Times,* Dec. 13, 2017; U.S. Department of Justice, *Equal Employment Opportunity Policy* (2019), https://www.justice.gov/jmd/file /790081/download.

169   **Hundreds of texts:** Attachment to Sentencing Memorandum, *United States v. Manafort,* No. 1:17-cr-201 (D.D.C. June 21, 2019), ECF No. 606.

169   **In short order, I was being:** Catherine Herridge, "Mueller Deputy Praised DOJ Official After She Defied Trump Travel Order: 'I Am So Proud,'" Fox News, Dec. 5, 2017.

169   **I was attacked for giving:** Brooke Singman, "More Clinton Ties on Mueller Team: One Deputy Attended Clinton Party, Another Rep'd Top Aide," Fox News, Dec. 14, 2017.

171   **I offered Mueller my resignation:** Michael S. Schmidt, Matt Apuzzo, and Adam Goldman, "In Texts, F.B.I. Officials in Russia Inquiry Said Clinton 'Just Has to Win,'" *The New York Times,* Dec. 12, 2017.

171   **Strzok, for example, called Trump:** Lucien Bruggeman, Benjamin Siegel, and Mike Levine, "FBI Agent Who Sent Anti-Trump Texts Defiantly Fends Off GOP Attacks," ABC News, July 12, 2018.

172   **But Pete, who was still:** Michael S. Schmidt, Matt Apuzzo, and Adam Goldman, "Mueller Removed Top Agent in Russia Inquiry Over Possible Anti-Trump Texts," *The New York Times,* December 2, 2017.

172   **I watched Rod Rosenstein:** Josh Gerstein, "Rod Rosenstein Says He Made Call to Release Strzok-Page Texts," *Politico,* Jan. 18, 2020.

172   **They of course showed poor judgment:** U.S. Department of Justice, Office of the Inspector General, *A Review of Various Actions by the Federal Bureau of Investigation and Department of Justice in Advance of the 2016 Election* (2018), 149.

172   **Later, the inspector general:** Ibid., 497.

172   **For what it's worth:** U.S. Department of Justice, Office of the Inspector General, *Review of Four FISA Applications and Other Aspects of the FBI's Crossfire Hurricane Investigation* (2019), 339, n.477.

172   **Soon after, a right-wing:** Andrew C. McCarthy, "Mueller Needs to Make a Change," *The Washington Post,* Dec. 13, 2017.

172   **This was especially true:** Matt Flegenheimer, "Andrew Weissmann, Mueller's Legal Pit Bull," *The New York Times,* Oct. 31, 2017.

CHAPTER 13. RATCHETING UP THE PRESSURE

178   **Among the many victims:** Daniel Miller, "Dustin Hoffman Scores Win in Legal Fight Over $3 Million Deal with Paul Manafort's Son-in-Law," *Los Angeles Times,* July 27, 2017.

178   **Sherine had kept pulling:** Superseding Indictment, *United States v. Manafort,* No. 1:18-cr-83 (E.D. Va. Feb. 23, 2018), ECF No. 14, ¶ 27.

179   **One part of his stratagem:** Ibid., ¶ 16.

179   **Another part of the scheme:** Ibid., ¶¶ 13–14.

179   **But after Yanukovych fled:** Ibid., ¶ 3.

179   **To obtain the cash flow:** Ibid., ¶ 3.

179   **In order to qualify:** Ibid., ¶ 23.

179   **On one application:** Ibid., ¶ 28.

179   **In another instance:** Ibid., ¶ 34.

179   **Later, Manafort and Gates:** Ibid., ¶¶ 38–39.

183   **It was a series of messages:** U.S. Department of Justice, *Report on the Investigation into Russian Interference in the 2016 Presidential Election* (2019), 1:138–41.

183   **The two men had met:** Ibid., 138.

183   **By odd coincidence:** Caleb Melby and David Kocieniewski, "Kushners' Troubled Tower: Debt, Empty Offices and Rising Fees," Bloomberg, Mar. 22, 2017.

183   **The colleague Manafort met:** U.S. Department of Justice, *Report on the Investigation into Russian Interference in the 2016 Presidential Election* (2019), at 1:132.

183   **The FBI had advised us:** Ibid., 133–34.

184   **Aspects of the Manafort-Kilimnik:** Rosalind Helderman, Tom Hamburger, and Rachel Weiner, "At Height of Russia Tensions, Trump Campaign Chairman Manafort Met with Business Associate from Ukraine," *The Washington Post,* June 19, 2017.

184   **In the resulting trove of documents:** Statement of the Offense, *United States v. Patten,* No. 1:18-cr-260 (D.D.C. Aug. 31, 2018), ECF No. 7, ¶¶ 7, 9.

184   **Emails revealed that the August:** U.S. Department of Justice, *Report on the Investigation into Russian Interference in the 2016 Presidential Election* (2019), 1:138.

184   **Kilimnik was writing from Moscow:** Ibid.

184   **Kilimnik insisted that he:** Ibid., 138–39.

184   **In a follow-up email:** Ibid., 139.

185   **We also painstakingly pieced:** Ibid., 139.

CHAPTER 14. FLIPPING GATES

188   **His first defense counsel:** Darren Samuelsohn, "Lawyers for Rick Gates Withdraw from Russia Case," *Politico,* Feb. 1, 2018.

188   **Gates was thus hastily:** Matthew Nussbaum, Darren Samuelsohn, and Josh

Gerstein, "Trump Campaign Aides Charged in Mueller's Russia Probe," *Politico,* Oct. 30, 2017.

189 **Gates subsequently hired:** Karen Freifeld and David Alexander, "Manafort Associate Gates Hires New Defense Team in Russia Probe Case," Reuters, Nov. 2, 2017.

190 **Now, shortly after the reverse:** Sarah N. Lynch, "Manafort Co-Defendant Gates Shows Up in Court with New Lawyer," Reuters, Feb. 14, 2018.

191 **Similarly, we had charged:** Kevin Breuninger, "Here Are the Lawyers Who Quit or Declined to Represent Trump in the Mueller Probe," CNBC, Mar. 27, 2018.

191 **Recognizing this, as we readied:** Status Report, *United States v. Manafort,* No. 1:17-cr-201 (D.D.C. Feb. 22, 2018), ECF No. 190, ¶ 3.

192 **But Manafort decided:** Government's Response to Manafort's Second Supplemental Memorandum to His Motion for Reconsideration of Conditions of Release, *United States v. Manafort,* No. 1:17-cr-201 (D.D.C. Feb. 22, 2018), ECF No. 191-1, at 3 n.2.

192 **As one news outlet put it:** Josh Gerstein, "Mulling Manafort's Unusual Two-Trial Strategy," *Politico,* Mar. 1, 2018.

192 **The sharp, no-nonsense:** Transcript of Status Conference, *United States v. Manafort,* No. 1:17-cr-201 (D.D.C. Feb. 14, 2018), ECF No. 294, at 16:21–23.

193 **One of Tom Green's visits:** Katelyn Polantz, "Exclusive: New Signs Gates May Be Negotiating with Mueller's Team," CNN, Jan. 23, 2018.

195 **Gates explained that:** Chad Day and Matthew Barakat, "Gates Admits Crimes with, and Embezzlement from, Manafort," Associated Press, Aug. 6, 2018.

196 **It helped that the press:** Flegenheimer, "Andrew Weissmann, Mueller's Legal Pit Bull."

196 **We knew, from examining:** U.S. Department of Justice, *Report on the Investigation into Russian Interference in the 2016 Presidential Election* (2019), 1:139.

197 **One subject was money:** Ibid., 141.

197 **"Paul told KK":** Ibid., 140.

197 **"Yes, but I had been":** Ibid., 136.

197 **"Paul told me":** Ibid.

198 **"Did you know":** Ibid.

198 **"I continued to send":** Ibid.

198 **"No, I got rid of them":** Ibid.

198 **And Manafort had done:** Ibid., 113, 115.

199 **Manafort, after all:** Ibid., 135.

199 **His meeting with Kilimnik:** Maggie Haberman and Jonathan Martin, "Paul Manafort Quits Donald Trump's Campaign After a Tumultuous Run," *The New York Times,* Aug. 19, 2019.

200 **As Gates himself:** U.S. Department of Justice, *Report on the Investigation into Russian Interference in the 2016 Presidential Election* (2019), 1:136.

200 **Manafort was not only:** Government's Motion for Leave to Supplement Its Notice of Proposed Prior-Act Evidence, *United States v. Manafort,* No. 1:17-cr-201 (D.D.C. July 11, 2018), ECF No. 350, at 2.

200 **In the eighties:** Ibid., 3.

201 **Interestingly, when his request:** Ibid., 4.

201 **It was clear:** Statement of the Offense, *United States v. Gates,* No. 1:17-cr-201-2 (D.D.C. Feb. 23, 2018), ECF No. 206, ¶ 16.

201 **He acknowledged that:** Ibid.

201 **Gates and Manafort had:** Ibid.

202 **He'd fed us:** Ibid.

202 **We'd frozen:** Indictment, *United States v. Manafort,* No. 1:17-cr-201 (D.D.C. Oct. 27, 2017), ECF No. 13, ¶¶ 52–53.

204 **It's hard to convey:** Katelyn Polantz, "Rick Gates Sued by His Former Attorney for Almost $370,000," CNN, Oct. 11, 2018.

204 **Later, Walter would:** Ibid.

204 **But it was also hard:** Josh Gerstein, "Manafort and Gates Are Sprung for Holiday as Bail Talks Drag On," *Politico,* Nov. 11, 2017.

204 **Regardless, whatever dispute:** Samuelsohn, "Lawyers for Rick Gates Withdraw from Russia Case."

205 **At the proceeding:** Transcript of Motions Hearing, *United States v. Manafort,* No. 1:17-cr-201 (D.D.C. Feb. 7, 2018), ECF No. 375, at 29:16–25.

205 **Shortly thereafter:** David Willman, "Former Trump Aide Richard Gates to Plead Guilty; Agrees to Testify," *Los Angeles Times,* Feb. 18, 2019.

205 **Tom assured me:** U.S. Department of Justice, *Report on the Investigation into Russian Interference in the 2016 Presidential Election* (2019), 2:123.

206 **It was Tom:** David Willman, "Former Trump Aide Richard Gates to Plead Guilty; Agrees to Testify," *Los Angeles Times,* Feb. 18, 2019.

206 **He explained the intense:** U.S. Department of Justice, *Report on the Investigation into Russian Interference in the 2016 Presidential Election* (2019), 2:123.

207 **That same day:** Albert Luperon, "Richard Gates' Attorney Says *Daily Beast* Story Is False, Client HASN'T Fired Him," *Law&Crime,* Feb. 22, 2019, https://lawandcrime.com/high-profile/richard-gates-attorney-says-daily-beast-story-is-false-client-hasnt-fired-him/.

208 **As we had done:** Attachment to Sentencing Memorandum, *United States v. Manafort,* No. 1:17-cr-201 (D.D.C. June 21, 2019), ECF No. 606, at 34.

209 **In others, he supplied:** Attachment to Sentencing Memorandum, *United States v. Manafort,* No. 1:17-cr-201 (D.D.C. June 21, 2019), ECF No. 606.

209 **At the time, remember:** Order Setting Conditions for High Intensity Supervision Program, *United States v. Manafort,* No. 1:17-cr-201 (D.D.C. Oct. 30, 2017), ECF No. 9.

209 **Communicating with Hannity:** Order, *United States v. Manafort,* No. 1:17-cr-201 (D.D.C. Nov. 8, 2017), ECF No. 38.

210 **In this conversation:** Attachment to Sentencing Memorandum, *United States v. Manafort,* No. 1:17-cr-201 (D.D.C. June 21, 2019), ECF No. 606, at 37.

CHAPTER 15. THE RUSSIAN HACK AND DUMP

213 **One night in June 1972:** Adam Clymer, "Frank Wills, 52; Watchman Foiled Watergate Break-In," *The New York Times,* Sept. 29, 2000.

213 **On the day he resigned:** Ibid.

214 **Knowledge of this DNC:** Ellen Nakashima, "Russian Government Hackers Penetrated DNC, Stole Opposition Research on Trump," *The Washington Post,* June 14, 2016.

214 **The DNC first announced:** Dmitri Alperovitch, "Bears in the Midst: Intrusion into the Democratic National Committee," *CrowdStrike Blog,* June 14, 2016, https://www.crowdstrike.com/blog/bears-midst-intrusion-democratic-national-committee/.

215 **This unit, a component:** Indictment, *United States v. Netyksho,* No. 1:18-cr-215 (D.D.C. July 13, 2018), ECF No. 1, ¶ 1.

215 **In the run-up:** Ibid.

215 **The United States was not:** Rick Noack, "Everything We Know So Far About Russian Election Meddling in Europe," *The Washington Post,* Jan. 10, 2018.

215 **The GRU sought:** Michael Schwirtz, "Top Secret Russian Unit Seeks to Destabilize Europe, Security Officials Say," *The New York Times,* Oct. 8, 2019.

215 **The scheme began:** U.S. Department of Justice, *Report on the Investigation into Russian Interference in the 2016 Presidential Election* (2019), 1:37.

215 **These emails might:** Indictment, *United States v. Netyksho,* No. 1:18-cr-215 (D.D.C. July 13, 2018), ECF No. 1, ¶ 21a.

215 **But in fact, these emails:** U.S. Department of Justice, *Report on the Investigation into Russian Interference in the 2016 Presidential Election* (2019), 1:36, n.112.

215 **Then, looking at these:** Ibid., 37.

215 **This had enabled:** Ibid., 38.

216 **This, in turn, enabled:** Ibid.

216 **The GRU could see:** Indictment, *United States v. Netyksho,* No. 1:18-cr-215 (D.D.C. July 13, 2018), ECF No. 1, ¶¶ 24c, 26b.

216 **The malware also allowed:** U.S. Department of Justice, *Report on the Investigation into Russian Interference in the 2016 Presidential Election* (2019), 1:38.

216 **Even after the DNC:** Indictment, *United States v. Netyksho,* No. 1:18-cr-215 (D.D.C. July 13, 2018), ECF No. 1, ¶ 32.

216 **The Russian military malware:** Ibid., ¶¶ 8, 28a.

216 **Through this electronic:** U.S. Department of Justice, *Report on the Investigation into Russian Interference in the 2016 Presidential Election* (2019), 1:38–40.

216 **The Russian military obtained:** Ibid., 40.

216 **All of this was done:** Indictment, *United States v. Netyksho,* No. 1:18-cr-215 (D.D.C. July 13, 2018), ECF No. 1, ¶¶ 21, 76.

216 **The GRU had set up:** U.S. Department of Justice, *Report on the Investigation into Russian Interference in the 2016 Presidential Election* (2019), 1:41.

216 **The first dump:** Ibid.

216 **The GRU had anonymized:** Ibid.

217 **When the DNC's cyber:** Ibid., 42.

217 **The following day:** Ibid.

217 **DC Leaks and Guccifer:** Ibid., 41–44.

217 **The Russians also worked:** Ibid., 44.

217 **The founder of WikiLeaks:** Ibid., 44–45.

217 **During the campaign:** Ibid., 45–48.

217 **On July 22:** Indictment, *United States v. Netyksho,* No. 1:18-cr-215 (D.D.C. July 13, 2018), ECF No. 1, ¶ 48.

217 **The documents exposed:** Tom Hamburger and Karen Tumulty, "WikiLeaks Releases Thousands of Documents About Clinton and Internal Deliberations," *The Washington Post,* July 22, 2016.

217 **As Mueller later:** Lee Ferran and Trish Turner, "Mueller Sounds Alarm for 2020 Election Threats from Russia, Others," ABC News, July 24, 2019.

217 **One of the most explosive:** U.S. Department of Justice, *Report on the Investigation into Russian Interference in the 2016 Presidential Election* (2019), 1:58.

218 **Within an hour:** Ibid.

217 **Among the Podesta:** Kyle Cheney and Sarah Wheaton, "The Most Revealing Clinton Campaign Emails in WikiLeaks Release," *Politico,* Oct. 7, 2016.

218 **Clearly, this dump:** U.S. Department of Justice, *Report on the Investigation into Russian Interference in the 2016 Presidential Election* (2019), 1:48.

218 **Team R determined:** Ibid., 37.

218 **Specifically, among:** Ibid., 37, 50, 51.

218 **Often, they consisted:** Indictment, *United States v. Netyksho,* No. 1:18-cr-215 (D.D.C. July 13, 2018), ECF No. 1, ¶ 76.

218 **A separate FBI investigation:** U.S. Department of Justice, *Report on the Investigation into Russian Interference in the 2016 Presidential Election* (2019), 1:51.

218 **And in Illinois:** Ibid., 50.

218 **For instance, at the time:** Ibid., 50–51.

219 **In July 2016, five days:** Michael Crowley and Tyler Pager, "Trump Urges Russia to Hack Clinton's Email," *Politico,* July 27, 2016.

219 **Not surprisingly:** Donald J. Trump, President, *Remarks by President Trump at the 2020 Conservative Political Action Conference,* Feb. 29, 2020, https://www.whitehouse.gov/briefings-statements/remarks-president-trump-2020-conservative-political-action-conference-national-harbor-md/.

219 **But Team R was able:** U.S. Department of Justice, *Report on the Investigation into Russian Interference in the 2016 Presidential Election* (2019), 1:49.

220 **The Special Counsel's Office would:** Indictment, *United States v. Netyksho,* No. 1:18-cr-215 (D.D.C. July 13, 2018), ECF No. 1.

220 **Team R had filed:** Indictment, *United States v. Internet Research Agency LLC,* No. 1:18-cr-32 (D.D.C. Feb. 16, 2018), ECF No. 1.

220 **Bear in mind:** Office of the Director of National Intelligence, Intelligence Community Assessment, *Assessing Russian Activities and Intentions in Recent U.S. Elections,* Jan. 6, 2017.

220 **The IC had gotten:** David E. Sanger, "Trump, Mocking Claim That Russia Hacked Election, at Odds with G.O.P.," *The New York Times,* Dec. 10, 2016.

221 **Even after the IC:** Aaron Blake, "Trump's Bogus Claim That Intelligence Report Says Russia Didn't Affect the 2016 Election Outcome," *The Washington Post,* Jan. 7, 2017.

222 **On July 16:** Jeff Mason and Denis Pinchuk, "Trump Backs Putin on Election Meddling at Summit, Stirs Fierce Criticism," Reuters, July 16, 2018.

222 **When asked about:** Ibid.

222 **Still, Trump said:** Ibid.

CHAPTER 16. THE PROSPECT OF A "MUELLER MASSACRE"

225 **It would become:** U.S. Department of Justice, *Report on the Investigation into Russian Interference in the 2016 Presidential Election* (2019), 2:131.

226 **When the House flipped:** Jonathan Martin and Alexander Burns, "Democrats Capture Control of House; G.O.P. Holds Senate," *The New York Times,* Nov. 6, 2018.

226 **The leader of the free:** Josh Gerstein, "DOJ Drops Probe into Former FBI Deputy Director Andrew McCabe," *Politico,* Feb. 14, 2020.

226 **The U.S. attorney:** Ibid.

226 **Trump was furious:** Peter Baker, "Trump Renews Attack on Justice System, Again Disregarding Barr's Pleas," *The New York Times,* Feb. 20, 2020.

227 **We were seeing Trump:** Devlin Barrett, Matt Zapotosky, and Josh Dawsey, "Jeff Sessions Forced Out as Attorney General," *The Washington Post,* Nov. 7, 2018; Memorandum from James Comey, Director, Federal Bureau of Investigation, Feb. 14, 2017.

227 **We had heard rumors:** Michael D. Schmidt and Julie Hirschfeld Davis, "Trump Asked Sessions to Retain Control of Russia Inquiry After His Recusal," *The New York Times,* May 29, 2018.

228 **In retrospect, his conduct:** Peter Baker, "The Impeachment Witnesses Not Heard," *The New York Times,* Nov. 21, 2019.

228 **McGahn calmly relayed:** U.S. Department of Justice, *Report on the Investigation into Russian Interference in the 2016 Presidential Election* (2019), 2:85.

228 **And when that strategy:** Ibid., 91–92.

229 **McGahn explained:** Ibid., 90.

229 **They included the supposed grudge:** Ibid., 80–81.

229 **Its conclusion was publicly:** Matt Zapotosky and Matea Gold, "Justice De-

partment Ethics Experts Clear Mueller to Lead Russia Probe," *The Washington Post,* May 23, 2017.

229   **In his interview** 302, Stephen Bannon, Former Chief Strategist for Trump Campaign, Oct. 26, 2018, at 13.

229   **Other advisers told:** U.S. Department of Justice, *Report on the Investigation into Russian Interference in the 2016 Presidential Election* (2019), 2:85.

229   **Nevertheless, McGahn told:** Ibid., 85–86.

229   **In his notes:** Ibid., 85.

230   **McGahn told Team 600:** Michael S. Schmidt and Maggie Haberman, "Trump Ordered Mueller Fired, but Backed Off When White House Counsel Threatened to Quit," *The New York Times,* Jan. 25, 2018.

230   **The timing of events:** U.S. Department of Justice, *Report on the Investigation into Russian Interference in the 2016 Presidential Election* (2019), 2:86.

230   **It helped contextualize:** Ibid., 83.

230   **Coincidentally, this was:** Testimony of Rod Rosenstein, Deputy Attorney General, *Hearing on Fiscal 2018 Justice Department Budget Before the Senate Appropriations Committee,* June 13, 2017.

230   **This squared with what:** Devlin Barrett, Adam Entous, Ellen Nakashima, and Sari Horwitz, "Special Counsel Is Investigating Trump for Possible Obstruction of Justice, Officials Say," *The Washington Post,* June 14, 2017.

230   **Learning that you:** U.S. Department of Justice, *Report on the Investigation into Russian Interference in the 2016 Presidential Election* (2019), 2:65.

231   **Backed up by his:** Ibid., 78.

231   **Using telephone records:** Ibid., 84.

231   **The following morning:** Ibid.

231   **Three days later:** Ibid., 85.

231   **He sensed that he'd:** Ibid., 85–86.

231   **McGahn told us:** Ibid.

232   **He felt he had:** Ibid., 86.

232   **McGahn went to the White House:** Ibid.

232   **Only after Steve:** Ibid., 87.

232   **He felt "trapped":** Ibid., 86.

232   **Trump eventually called:** Ibid., 86.

232   **The dispute about:** James Risen and Michael S. Schmidt, "2004 Showdown Shaped Reputation of Pick for F.B.I.," *The New York Times,* June 22, 2013.

233   **Donaldson's were similar:** U.S. Department of Justice, *Report on the Investigation into Russian Interference in the 2016 Presidential Election* (2019), 2:68, n.442.

233   **We learned from:** Ibid., 91–92.

234   **Trump began expressing:** Peter Baker, Michael S. Schmidt, and Maggie Haberman, "Excerpts from the *Times*'s Interview with Trump," *The New York Times,* July 19, 2017.

234 **When it was clear Sessions:** U.S. Department of Justice, *Report on the Investigation into Russian Interference in the 2016 Presidential Election* (2019), 2:95.

234 **We learned from Lewandowski:** Ibid., 90.

234 **Lewandowski was a curious accomplice:** M. J. Lee, Dana Bash, and Gloria Borger, "Corey Lewandowski Out as Trump Campaign Manager," CNN, June 20, 2016.

234 **Lewandowski explained:** U.S. Department of Justice, *Report on the Investigation into Russian Interference in the 2016 Presidential Election* (2019), 2:91–92.

234 **As it turns out, this struck:** Ibid., 92.

234 **As with Trump's orders:** Peter Baker, "Trump Acknowledges Discussing Biden in Call with Ukrainian Leader," *The New York Times,* Sept. 22, 2019.

235 **More important, Sessions:** Karoun Demirjian, Ed O'Keefe, Sari Horwitz, and Matt Zapotosky, "Attorney General Jeff Sessions Will Recuse Himself from Any Probe Related to 2016 Presidential Campaign," *The Washington Post,* Mar. 2, 2017.

236 **The president's personal:** David A. Graham, "Process Crimes and Misdemeanors," *The Atlantic,* Dec. 14, 2018.

236 **Van der Zwaan was a senior:** Sharon LaFraniere and Kenneth P. Vogel, "Former Skadden Lawyer Pleads Guilty to Lying in Russia Investigation," *The New York Times,* Feb. 20, 2018.

236 **His firm was tasked:** Ibid.

236 **Nevertheless, in spite of:** Statement of the Offense, *United States v. van der Zwaan,* No. 1:18-cr-31 (D.D.C. Feb. 20, 2018), ECF No. 9, ¶ 5.

236 **In an email between:** Ibid., ¶ 6b.

237 **In addition, van der Zwaan:** Criminal Information, *United States v. van der Zwaan,* No. 1:18-cr-31 (D.D.C. Feb. 16, 2018), ECF No. 1, at 2.

237 **Van der Zwaan was charged:** Plea Agreement, *United States v. van der Zwaan,* No. 1:18-cr-31 (D.D.C. Feb. 20, 2018), ECF No. 8.

237 **Publicly, the president decried:** Rosalind S. Helderman and Josh Dawsey, "Trump Moved to Fire Mueller in June, Bringing White House Counsel to the Brink of Leaving," *The Washington Post,* Jan. 26, 2019.

237 **We knew, of course:** Schmidt and Haberman, "Trump Ordered Mueller Fired, but Backed Off."

237 **In fact, the lone:** Helderman and Dawsey, "Trump Moved to Fire Mueller in June."

238 **The president was apparently:** U.S. Department of Justice, *Report on the Investigation into Russian Interference in the 2016 Presidential Election* (2019), 2:114–15.

238 **McGahn refused:** Ibid., 114.

238 **Trump then complained:** Ibid., 115.

238 **Porter, in turn, approached:** Ibid., 116.

238 **When McGahn again shrugged:** Ibid.

238 **Still, McGahn refused:** Ibid.

238 **The following day:** Ibid.

238 **There, Trump told him:** Ibid.

238 **The president insisted the story:** Ibid.

238 **McGahn understood this:** Ibid., 117.

239 **The president, McGahn recounted:** Ibid.

239 **This strange upbraiding:** Ibid.

239 **McGahn explained to the president:** Ibid.

239 **"I've had a lot":** Ibid.

239 **Months later, when Attorney General:** William Barr to U.S. Congress, Mar. 24, 2019.

240 **I had the same sinking feeling:** Marie Brenner, "Incident in the 70th Precinct," *Vanity Fair,* Dec. 1997.

CHAPTER 17. THE FIRST MANAFORT TRIAL

243 **He had, in fact:** Josh Gerstein, "Mulling Manafort's Unusual Two-Trial Strategy," *Politico,* Mar. 1, 2018.

245 **That strategy had worked:** John R. Emshwiller, "'Benron' Behind Bars," *The Wall Street Journal,* Apr. 21, 2007.

245 **We uncovered what:** Statement of the Offense, *United States v. Manafort,* No. 1:17-cr-201 (D.D.C. Sept. 14, 2018), ECF No. 423, ¶ 9.

245 **Those leaders would:** Ibid., ¶¶ 11, 13.

246 **Not only did they:** Government's Motion to Revoke or Revise Defendant Paul J. Manafort Jr.'s Current Order of Pretrial Release, *United States v. Manafort,* No. 1:17-cr-201 (D.D.C. June 4, 2018), ECF No. 315, at 5, n.3.

246 **I could see where:** Government's Motion to Revoke or Revise Defendant Paul J. Manafort Jr.'s Current Order of Pretrial Release, *United States v. Manafort,* No. 1:17-cr-201 (D.D.C. June 4, 2018), ECF No. 315.

246 **On Friday, June 15:** Order of Detention, *United States v. Manafort,* No. 1:17-cr-201 (D.D.C. June 15, 2018), ECF No. 328.

247 **Manafort then claimed:** Tom Jackman, "Manafort Checks into VIP Section at Virginia Jail Where Chris Brown, Michael Vick Also Did Time," *The Washington Post,* June 16, 2018.

247 **As we noted:** Government's Opposition to Motion to Continue Trial, *United States v. Manafort,* No. 1:18-cr-83 (E.D. Va. July 11, 2018), ECF No. 117, at 3, n.3.

247 **Michael and I were sitting:** Josh Gerstein, "Judge Challenges Mueller's Actions in Manafort Case," *Politico,* May 4, 2018.

247 **We merely wanted to flip:** Ibid.

247 **He criticized this tactic:** Josh Gerstein, "Judge Rejects Manafort's Challenge to Mueller's Legitimacy," *Politico,* June 26, 2018.

248 **Moreover, Judge Ellis's:** Brooke Singman, "Trump Rips Cohen for 'Flip-

ping,' Praises Manafort in Exclusive FNC Interview," Fox News, Aug. 23, 2018.

249 **As a retired:** Nancy Gertner, "The Extraordinary Bias of the Judge in the Manafort Trial," *The Washington Post,* Aug. 16, 2018.

250 **Late one afternoon:** Sarah N. Lynch and Warren Strobel, "Judge Backs Off Comments to Prosecutors in Ex-Trump Aide Manafort's Trial," Reuters, Aug. 9, 2018.

251 **We knew things had:** Michael Burke, "Fox News Analyst: Judge in Manafort Trial Showing 'Extraordinary Bias' Against Prosecutors," *The Hill,* Aug. 8, 2018.

252 **He'd begun manipulating:** Singman, "Trump Rips Cohen for 'Flipping.'"

253 **On the second day:** Veronica Stracqualursi, "Trump Asks Who Had It Worse: Capone or Manafort," CNN, Aug. 1, 2018.

253 **"I feel very badly":** Julie Hirschfeld Davis and Eileen Sullivan, "Trump Praises Manafort, Saying 'Unlike Michael Cohen' He 'Refused to Break,'" *The New York Times,* Aug. 22, 2018.

253 **He publicly implored:** Julie Hirschfeld Davis, Eileen Sullivan, and Katie Benner, "Trump Tells Sessions to 'Stop This Rigged Witch Hunt Right Now,'" *The New York Times,* Aug. 1, 2018.

253 **By then, the case:** Maggie Haberman, Sharon LaFraniere, and Danny Hakim, "Michael Cohen Has Said He Would Take a Bullet for Trump. Maybe Not Anymore," *The New York Times,* Apr. 20, 2018.

254 **In a series of tweets:** Lauren Gambino, "Trump Attacks *New York Times* Journalist Over Michael Cohen Article," *The Guardian,* Apr. 21, 2018.

254 **But later, when it:** Jeffrey Toobin, "Michael Cohen's Last Days of Freedom," *The New Yorker,* May 6, 2019.

254 **I had read Jim Comey's:** Rick Klein, "Comey Book Claims President Trump Sought Loyalty Like Mafia Boss 'Sammy the Bull's' Induction Ceremony," ABC News, Apr. 12, 2018.

255 **Talking to reporters:** Caitlin Oprysko, "Trump" Manafort Trial Is a 'Very Sad Day for Our Country,'" *Politico,* Aug. 17, 2018.

255 **The court in Washington:** Order, *United States v. Manafort,* No. 1:17-cr-201 (D.D.C. Nov. 8, 2017), ECF No. 38.

CHAPTER 18. OUR HIGH POINT

258 **Mueller and Jim:** Matt Zapotosky, Lynh Bui, Tom Jackman, and Devlin Barrett, "Manafort Convicted on 8 Counts; Mistrial Declared on 10 Others," *The Washington Post,* Aug. 21, 2018.

259 **The precise timing:** Nicole Hong, Rebecca Ballhaus, Rebecca Davis O'Brien, and Joe Palazzolo, "Michael Cohen Pleads Guilty, Says Trump Told Him to Pay Off Women," *The Wall Street Journal,* Aug. 21, 2018.

259 **They had amassed:** Criminal Information, *United States v. Cohen,* No. 1:18-cr-602 (S.D.N.Y. Aug. 21, 2018), ECF No. 2.

260　**Sater proceeded to offer up:** U.S. Department of Justice, *Report on the Investigation into Russian Interference in the 2016 Presidential Election* (2019), 1:76–78.

260　**The press had started:** Megan Twohey and Steve Eder, "For Trump, Three Decades of Chasing Deals in Russia," *The New York Times,* Jan. 16, 2017.

260　**In response, Cohen and Trump:** Carol D. Leonnig, Tom Hamburger, and Rosalind S. Helderman, "Trump's Business Sought Deal on a Trump Tower in Moscow While He Ran for President," *The Washington Post,* Aug. 27, 2017.

260　**Later, Cohen would testify:** Criminal Information, *United States v. Cohen,* No. 1:18-cr-850 (S.D.N.Y. Nov. 29, 2018), ECF No. 2, ¶ 4.

260　**But Sater told Team R:** U.S. Department of Justice, *Report on the Investigation into Russian Interference in the 2016 Presidential Election* (2019), 1:69–78.

262　**It was with bitter:** Memorandum Opinion, *In re Application of the Committee on the Judiciary, U.S. House of Representatives, for an Order Authorizing the Release of Certain Grand Jury Materials,* No. 1-19-gj-48 (D.D.C. Oct. 25, 2019), ECF No. 46.

263　**And this was not:** David Ignatius, "A History of Donald Trump's Business Dealings in Russia," *The Washington Post,* Nov. 2, 2017.

263　**Eric Trump, too:** Bill Littlefield, "A Day (and a Cheeseburger) with President Trump," WBUR, May 5, 2017.

263　**The Supreme Court had:** *United States v. R. Enterprises, Inc.,* 498 U.S. 292 (1991).

265　**And he would agree:** *United States v. Cohen,* No. 1:18-cr-850 (S.D.N.Y. Nov. 29, 2018), ECF No. 2; *United States v. Cohen,* No. 1:18-cr-602 (S.D.N.Y. Aug. 21, 2018).

265　**As Cohen revealed:** U.S. Department of Justice, *Report on the Investigation into Russian Interference in the 2016 Presidential Election* (2019), 2:135.

265　**Trump had long sought:** Ibid., 1:67–68.

265　**In this most recent:** Ibid., 69, 71.

265　**As with any major:** Ibid., 72.

266　**Cohen was the Trump:** Ibid., 2:76–77.

266　**Cohen explained that the false:** Ibid., 138–39.

266　**Cohen pushed this same:** Criminal Information, *United States v. Cohen,* No. 1:18-cr-850 (S.D.N.Y. Nov. 29, 2018), ECF No. 2, ¶ 7.

266　**She had pulled:** U.S. Department of Justice, *Report on the Investigation into Russian Interference in the 2016 Presidential Election* (2019), 2:142, n.988.

266　**And Cohen told us:** Ibid., 143.

267　**Before I could leave:** Matt Zapotosky, Lynh Bui, Tom Jackman, and Devlin Barrett, "Manafort Convicted on 8 Counts; Mistrial Declared on 10 Others," *The Washington Post,* Aug. 21, 2018.

267　**Moreover, we'd soon:** Aruna Viswanatha, "Juror in Manafort Trial Says There Was One Holdout," *The Wall Street Journal,* Aug. 23, 2018.

267   **The jury's failure:** Ibid.

268   **The only juror to speak:** Peter Doocy, Jake Gibson, and Lucas Tomlinson, "Manafort Juror Reveals Lone Holdout Prevented Mueller Team from Winning Conviction on All Counts," Fox News, Aug. 23, 2018.

268   **The juror added some:** Sophie Tatum, "Manafort Juror on a Potential Pardon: 'It Would Be Grave Mistake,'" CNN, Aug. 24, 2018.

268   **Cohen had implicated:** Eric Tucker, "Inside Catch and Kill: Cohen, a Porn Star and 'Individual 1,'" Associated Press, Aug. 22, 2018.

CHAPTER 19. SUBPOENAING THE PRESIDENT

270   **For months, Team 600:** U.S. Department of Justice, *Report on the Investigation into Russian Interference in the 2016 Presidential Election* (2019), appendix C:1.

271   **The president kept publicly:** Maggie Haberman and Julie Hirschfeld Davis, "Trump Says He Is Willing to Speak Under Oath to Mueller," *The New York Times,* Jan. 24, 2018; Eric Tucker, Chad Day, and Jonathan Lemire, "Inside Trump's Refusal to Testify in the Mueller Probe," Associated Press, Nov. 21, 2018.

272   **The brokering dragged:** Carol D. Leonnig and Robert Costa, "Mueller Raised Possibility of Presidential Subpoena in Meeting with Trump's Legal Team," *The Washington Post,* May 1, 2018.

272   **Nothing in that history:** Michael S. Schmidt, "Mueller Has Dozens of Inquiries for Trump in Broad Quest on Russia Ties and Obstruction," *The New York Times,* April 30, 2018.

273   **We did not need:** 28 C.F.R. § 600.7(b).

273   **If Rosenstein did:** 28 C.F.R. § 600.9(a)(3).

274   **As a result, in yet:** U.S. Department of Justice, *Report on the Investigation into Russian Interference in the 2016 Presidential Election* (2019), appendix C.

276   **After successfully avoiding:** Andrew Desiderio and Kyle Cheney, "White House Won't Take Part in First House Judiciary Impeachment Hearing," *Politico,* Dec. 1, 2019.

277   **One morning, CNN and Fox:** Sadie Gurman, Michael C. Bender, and Aruna Viswanatha, "Deputy Attorney General Rod Rosenstein to Meet Donald Trump to Consider His Future at DOJ," *The Wall Street Journal,* Sept. 24, 2018.

278   **I had been Mueller's:** Terry Frieden, "Senate Gives Mueller 2 More Years at FBI," CNN, July 27, 2011.

278   **Eventually—and miraculously:** Michael D. Shear, Katie Benner, Maggie Haberman, and Michael D. Schmidt, "Rod Rosenstein's Job Is Safe, for Now: Inside His Dramatic Day," *The New York Times,* Sept. 24, 2018.

278   **We came to this theory:** Devlin Barrett and John Wagner, "Trump Says He Expects to Be 'Treated Very Fairly' in Russia Probe, Has No Plans to Fire Rosenstein," *The Washington Post,* Oct. 8, 2018.

279 **Our report noted that Mueller:** U.S. Department of Justice, *Report on the Investigation into Russian Interference in the 2016 Presidential Election* (2019), appendix C:2.

279 **In volume one, which dealt:** Ibid., 1:180.

280 **In volume two, meanwhile:** Ibid., 2:182.

280 **Our report claimed:** Ibid., appendix C:2.

280 **And finally, the report:** Ibid., 2:1–2.

280 **The report gave another:** Ibid., appendix C:2.

CHAPTER 20. THROWING IN THE TOWEL

282 **Manafort had made:** Motion for Change of Venue, *United States v. Manafort,* No. 1:17-cr-201 (D.D.C. Aug. 29, 2018), ECF No. 393.

282 **The judge in that case:** Sirica, *To Set the Record Straight,* 225.

282 **Manafort's motion was rebuffed:** Kevin Breuninger, "Judge Denies Trump Ex-Campaign Boss Paul Manafort's Request to Move Second Criminal Trial Out of D.C.," CNBC, Sept. 5, 2018.

283 **By mid-August:** Spencer S. Hsu, "Paul Manafort's Trial in D.C. to Take 3 Weeks, Probe Ukraine Lobbying World," *The Washington Post,* Aug. 24, 2018.

283 **In August, with the trial:** Ibid.

284 **During the 2012:** Superseding Criminal Information, *United States v. Manafort,* No. 1:17-cr-201 (D.D.C. Sept. 14, 2018), ECF No. 419, ¶ 37.

288 **But in September 2018:** Order of Detention, *United States v. Manafort,* No. 1:17-cr-201 (D.D.C. June 15, 2018), ECF No. 328.

290 **We asked him up front:** U.S. Department of Justice, *Report on the Investigation into Russian Interference in the 2016 Presidential Election* (2019), 1:129, 131.

290 **While tracing Manafort's assets:** Government's Submission in Support of Its Breach Determination, *United States v. Manafort,* No. 1:17-cr-201 (D.D.C. Dec. 7, 2018), ECF No. 460, at 7.

290 **The press has since:** Christina Wilkie, "A Mysterious Payment to Paul Manafort's Lawyer Reveals a Hidden Chapter of Trump's 2016 Presidential Campaign," CNBC, Mar. 10, 2019.

291 **He claimed it was money:** Government's Submission in Support of Its Breach Determination, *United States v. Manafort,* No. 1:17-cr-201 (D.D.C. Dec. 7, 2018), ECF No. 460, at 7.

292 **Here, our statement:** Statement of the Offense, *United States v. Manafort,* No. 1:17-cr-201 (D.D.C. Sept. 14, 2018), ECF No. 423.

292 **Importantly, the statement:** Ibid., 20–23.

292 **When Flynn:** Statement of the Offense, *United States v. Flynn,* No. 1:17-cr-232 (D.D.C. Dec. 1, 2017), at 5.

294 **In the end:** Tom Winter and Rich Schapiro, "Paul Manafort Indicted on Fraud Charges by Manhattan Prosecutors," NBC News, Mar. 13, 2019.

294   **That case is currently:** Shayna Jacobs, "Paul Manafort's Fraud Case in New York Was Dismissed, Blocking Local Prosecutors' Efforts to Undercut a Potential Trump Pardon," *The Washington Post,* Dec. 18, 2019.

CHAPTER 21. A WINK FROM TRUMP

295   **But the varying:** Government's Submission in Support of Its Breach Determination, *United States v. Manafort,* No. 1:17-cr-201 (D.D.C. Dec. 7, 2018), ECF No. 460, at 7.

295   **The money was:** Ibid.

296   **We learned that Gay:** Christina Wilkie, "A Mysterious Payment to Paul Manafort's Lawyer Reveals a Hidden Chapter of Trump's 2016 Presidential Campaign," CNBC, Mar. 10, 2019.

297   **Shortly after that:** Government's Submission in Support of Its Breach Determination, *United States v. Manafort,* No. 1:17-cr-201 (D.D.C. Dec. 7, 2018), ECF No. 460, at 8.

297   **The story was so at odds:** Declaration in Support of the Government's Breach Determination and Sentencing, *United States v. Manafort,* No. 1:17-cr-201 (D.D.C. Jan. 15, 2019), ECF No. 476, ¶ 62.

299   **This evidence was a batch:** U.S. Department of Justice, *Report on the Investigation into Russian Interference in the 2016 Presidential Election* (2019), 1:130.

299   **The documents showed:** Ibid., 140, 144.

299   **The poll focused:** Ibid., 144.

299   **The pollster said that Manafort:** Ibid.

299   **Included in the draft:** Ibid., 139.

300   **Thus, Russia had turned:** David E. Sanger and Maggie Haberman, "Donald Trump Gives Questionable Explanation of Events in Ukraine," *The New York Times,* July 31, 2016.

300   **Notably, Manafort:** U.S. Department of Justice, *Report on the Investigation into Russian Interference in the 2016 Presidential Election* (2019), 1:130.

300   **It called on Trump:** Ibid.

300   **In a separate email:** Ibid., 143.

300   **"We discussed money":** Ibid., 141.

301   **"That's true":** Ibid., 140.

301   **"Just chitchat":** Ibid.

301   **"I had told Gates":** Ibid., 129.

301   **It was not just that Gates:** Ibid., 136.

302   **"You saw this in December":** Ibid., 142–43.

302   **"Well, that is true":** Ibid., 130, 140.

302   **"Which is what I told":** Ibid., 140.

303   **We kept going:** Ibid., 130.

303   **On August 2, if not earlier:** Ibid.

304   **Manafort had clearly trampled:** Ibid., 130, n.842.

304   **In the meantime:** Government's Submission in Support of Its Breach Deter-

mination, *United States v. Manafort,* No. 1:17-cr-201 (D.D.C. Dec. 7, 2018), ECF No. 460, at 2.

304   **He continued to lie:** Government's Sentencing Memorandum, *United States v. Manafort,* No. 1:17-cr-201 (D.D.C. Feb. 23, 2019), ECF No. 525, at 2.

305   **It was easy to obtain:** Morgan Chalfant and Olivia Beavers, "Grand Jury Material Becomes Key Battle-Line in Mueller Report Fight," *The Hill,* Apr. 9, 2018.

305   **We had not shared:** U.S. Department of Justice, *Report on the Investigation into Russian Interference in the 2016 Presidential Election* (2019), 1:144.

306   **The sentences imposed:** Sharon LaFraniere, "Paul Manafort's Prison Sentence Is Nearly Doubled to 7½ Years," *The New York Times,* Mar. 13, 2019.

308   **We began the process:** Joint Status Report, *United States v. Manafort,* No. 1:17-cr-201 (D.D.C. Nov. 26, 2018), ECF No. 455; Government's Submission in Support of Its Breach Determination, *United States v. Manafort,* No. 1:17-cr-201 (D.D.C. Dec. 7, 2018), ECF No. 460.

309   **In fact, when we went:** Darren Samuelsohn, "Manafort Shared Trump Polling Data with Ukrainian Associate During 2016 Campaign," *Politico,* Jan. 8, 2019.

309   **Jeannie, Omer, and I:** Declaration in Support of the Government's Breach Determination and Sentencing, *United States v. Manafort,* No. 1:17-cr-201 (D.D.C. Jan. 15, 2019), ECF No. 476.

309   **Once they'd examined:** Response to Government Submission in Support of Its Breach Determination, *United States v. Manafort,* No. 1:17-cr-201 (D.D.C. Jan. 8, 2019), ECF No. 472, at 2.

309   **Judge Jackson decided:** Sharon LaFraniere, "Manafort Lied After Plea Deal, Judge Says," *The New York Times,* Feb. 13, 2019.

309   **Moreover, the court:** Order, *United States v. Manafort,* No. 1:17-cr-201 (D.D.C. Feb. 13, 2019), ECF No. 509, at 3–4.

310   **And even if he was:** Order of Detention, *United States v. Manafort,* No. 1:17-cr-201 (D.D.C. June 15, 2018), ECF No. 328.

CHAPTER 22. THE REPORT

312   **In the second volume:** U.S. Department of Justice, *Report on the Investigation into Russian Interference in the 2016 Presidential Election* (2019), 2:3–6.

312   **The most glaring:** Ibid., 113.

312   **And yet, after reciting:** Ibid., 8.

312   **Mueller's position was:** Ibid., 1.

313   **The regulations setting:** 28 C.F.R. § 600.7(a).

313   **We could be fired:** 28 C.F.R. § 600.7(d).

313   **The OLC opinions contend:** U.S. Department of Justice, *Report on the Investigation into Russian Interference in the 2016 Presidential Election* (2019), 2:1.

313   **The opinions point out:** U.S. Department of Justice, Office of Legal Counsel, *A Sitting President's Amenability to Indictment and Criminal Prosecution* (2000), 24 Op. O.L.C. 222, 257.

314 **The OLC view holds:** Ibid., 255.

314 **If one looks:** *Clinton v. Jones,* 520 U.S. 681, 707 (1997).

314 **Those on the other side:** U.S. Department of Justice, Office of Legal Counsel, *A Sitting President's Amenability to Indictment and Criminal Prosecution* (2000), 24 Op. O.L.C. 222, 249.

316 **We set out much:** Indictment, *United States v. Internet Research Agency LLC,* No. 1:18-cr-32 (D.D.C. Feb. 16, 2018), ECF No. 1; Indictment, *United States v. Netyksho,* No. 1:18-cr-215 (D.D.C. July 13, 2018), ECF No. 1; U.S. Department of Justice, *Report on the Investigation into Russian Interference in the 2016 Presidential Election* (2019), 1:9.

317 **Where the facts:** U.S. Department of Justice, *Report on the Investigation into Russian Interference in the 2016 Presidential Election* (2019), 2:182.

317 **Michael's draft stated:** Ibid., 2.

318 **For those who disagree:** U.S. Department of Justice, Office of the Inspector General, *A Review of Various Actions by the Federal Bureau of Investigation and Department of Justice in Advance of the 2016 Election* (2018), 246–49.

318 **Michael's draft explained:** U.S. Department of Justice, *Report on the Investigation into Russian Interference in the 2016 Presidential Election* (2019), 2:2.

318 **The main one:** 28 C.F.R. § 600.8(c).

318 **Moreover, I told Michael:** 28 C.F.R. § 600.9(c).

320 **Even McGahn:** U.S. Department of Justice, *Report on the Investigation into Russian Interference in the 2016 Presidential Election* (2019), at 2:117.

320 **That's why he:** Ibid., 86, 117, 158.

321 **Michael revised the draft to note:** U.S. Department of Justice, Office of Legal Counsel, *A Sitting President's Amenability to Indictment and Criminal Prosecution* (2000), 24 Op. O.L.C. 222, 259 n.38.

321 **And Michael had seized:** U.S. Department of Justice, *Report on the Investigation into Russian Interference in the 2016 Presidential Election* (2019), 2:2.

321 **Michael's explanation:** Ibid., 182.

322 **It is hard to read:** William Barr to U.S. Congress, Mar. 24, 2019.

322 **To fulfill his responsibility:** Julia Ainsley, "Mueller Told Barr, Rosenstein 3 Weeks Ago He Would Not Make Decision on Obstruction," NBC News, Mar. 25, 2019.

322 **We never imagined:** William Barr to U.S. Congress, Mar. 24, 2019; Mark Mazzetti and Michael S. Schmidt, "Mueller Objected to Barr's Description of Russia Investigation's Findings on Trump," *The New York Times,* Apr. 30, 2019.

323 **Moreover, he did so weeks:** Kyle Cheney, "AG: Mueller Report to Be Released 'By Mid-April, If Not Sooner,'" *Politico,* Mar. 29, 2019.

CHAPTER 23. "THE NUMBER OF LIES"

325 **In the end, the two:** LaFraniere, "Paul Manafort's Prison Sentence Is Nearly Doubled."

325   **In Virginia, Judge Ellis:** Sharon LaFraniere and Alan Blinder, "Manafort's 47 Months: A Sentence That Drew Gasps from Around the Country," *The New York Times,* Mar. 8, 2019.

325   **And the press noted:** Michelle R. Smith, "Manafort Case Sparks Conversation About Sentence Disparities," Associated Press, Mar. 8, 2019.

326   **Just one week later:** LaFraniere, "Paul Manafort's Prison Sentence Is Nearly Doubled."

326   **"It is hard to overstate":** Transcript of Sentencing Hearing, *United States v. Manafort,* No. 1:17-cr-201 (D.D.C. Mar. 13, 2019), ECF No. 554, at 61:6–7.

326   **We learned that Russia:** U.S. Department of Justice, *Report on the Investigation into Russian Interference in the 2016 Presidential Election* (2019), 1:1.

326   **And we learned:** Ibid., 6.

326   **We learned that the two:** Ibid., 6.

327   **At sentencing, Manafort's defense:** Defendant's Sentencing Memorandum, *United States v. Manafort,* No. 1:17-cr-201 (D.D.C. Feb. 25, 2019), ECF No. 527, at 5.

327   **No fool, Judge Jackson:** Transcript of Sentencing Hearing, *United States v. Manafort,* No. 1:17-cr-201 (D.D.C. Mar. 13, 2019), ECF No. 554, at 77:11–17.

327   **But that is not:** Nicholas Fandos and Michael S. Schmidt, "Bolton Is Willing to Testify in Trump Impeachment Trial, Raising Pressure for Witnesses," *The New York Times,* Jan. 6, 2020.

EPILOGUE. LOOKING FORWARD

330   **Just two days after:** William Barr to U.S. Congress, Mar. 24, 2019.

330   **As a private citizen:** William Barr to Rod Rosenstein and Steve Engel, "Mueller's 'Obstruction' Theory," June 8, 2018.

331   **Three months later:** Lisa Mascaro, Mary Clare Jalonick, and Eric Tucker, "Trump Directed Ukraine Quid Pro Quo, Key Witness Says," Associated Press, Nov. 20, 2019.

331   **Because he wanted:** Matt Zapotosky and Devlin Barrett, "Barr Acknowledges Justice Dept. Has Created 'Intake Process' to Vet Giuliani's Information on Bidens," *The Washington Post,* Feb. 10, 2020.

331   **The military aid for Ukraine:** U.S. Governmentt Accountability Office, *Office of Management and Budget—Withholding of Ukraine Security Assistance* (2020), B-331564, at 1.

331   **But the fact that the president:** Brett Samuels, "Sondland Says He Believed Ukraine Did Not Actually Have to Conduct Investigations," *The Hill,* Nov. 20, 2019.

331   **Indeed, seeking a public statement:** "Trump's Letter Firing FBI Director James Comey," CNN, May 10, 2017.

331   **Indeed, even shortly after:** Lucien Bruggeman, " 'I Think I'd Take It': In Exclusive Interview, Trump Says He Would Listen if Foreigners Offered Dirt on Opponents," ABC News, June 13, 2019.

331 **The unanimous conclusion:** Office of the Director of National Intelligence, Intelligence Community Assessment, *Assessing Russian Activities and Intentions in Recent U.S. Elections,* Jan. 6, 2017; Nicholas Fandos and Michael D. Shear, "Fiona Hill Testifies 'Fictions' on Ukraine Pushed by Trump Help Russia," *The New York Times,* Nov. 21, 2019.

331 **The president leaned on the Ukrainian:** "Official Readout: President Trump's July 25 Phone Call with Ukraine's Volodymyr Zelensky," *The Washington Post,* Sept. 25, 2019.

332 **Conveniently, Barr moved to dismiss:** Spencer S. Hsu, "Justice Dept. Abandons Prosecution of Russian Firm Indicted in Mueller Election Interference Probe," *The Washington Post,* Mar. 16, 2020.

332 **And the president's other actions:** Alex Leary and Gordon Lubold, "American Troops to Withdraw From Northern Syria Ahead of Turkish Incursion," *The Wall Street Journal,* Oct. 7, 2019.

332 **At that point, his defense:** Devlin Barrett and Matt Zapotosky, "Mueller Complained That Barr's Letter Did Not Capture 'Context' of Trump Probe," *The Washington Post,* Apr. 30, 2019.

333 **He even added:** U.S. Department of Justice, press conference, *Attorney General William P. Barr Delivers Remarks on the Release of the Report on the Investigation into Russian Interference in the 2016 Presidential Campaign,* Apr. 18, 2019, https://www.justice.gov/opa/speech/attorney-general-william-p-barr -delivers-remarks-release-report-investigation-russian.

333 **Even if one leaves aside:** U.S. Department of Justice, *Report on the Investigation into Russian Interference in the 2016 Presidential Election* (2019), appendix C:1–2.

333 **This is also not true:** John Dowd and Jay Sekulow letter to Robert Mueller, Jan. 29, 2018.

333 **Since our investigation:** Oral argument at 47:24, *Trump v. Vance,* 941 F.3d 631 (2d Cir. 2019) (No. 19-3204), https://www.c-span.org/video/?465172-1 /circuit-hears-oral-argument-president-trumps-tax-returns-audio-only &live&start=2833.

334 **Trump, Barr insisted:** U.S. Department of Justice, press conference, *Attorney General William P. Barr Delivers Remarks on the Release of the Report on the Investigation into Russian Interference in the 2016 Presidential Campaign,* Apr. 18, 2019.

334 **Describing our examination:** William Barr letter to U.S. Congress, Mar. 24, 2019.

334 **Barr again repeated:** U.S. Department of Justice, press conference, *Attorney General William P. Barr Delivers Remarks on the Release of the Report on the Investigation into Russian Interference in the 2016 Presidential Campaign,* Apr. 18, 2019.

334 **Our report makes clear:** U.S. Department of Justice, *Report on the Investigation into Russian Interference in the 2016 Presidential Election* (2019), 1:4.

335   **But Barr went further:** Andrew Desiderio and Kyle Cheney, "Barr held in contempt by House Judiciary," *Politico*, May 8, 2019.

335   **That omission is all:** William Barr letter to U.S. Congress, Mar. 24, 2019.

335   **What actually happened:** U.S. Department of Justice, *Report on the Investigation into Russian Interference in the 2016 Presidential Election* (2019), 1:2.

335   **And in his April 17, 2019, press conference:** U.S. Department of Justice, press conference, *Attorney General William P. Barr Delivers Remarks on the Release of the Report on the Investigation into Russian Interference in the 2016 Presidential Campaign,* Apr. 18, 2019.

335   **Barr slyly stated:** William Barr letter to U.S. Congress, Mar. 24, 2019.

335   **Again, nowhere did Barr explain:** U.S. Department of Justice, *Report on the Investigation into Russian Interference in the 2016 Presidential Election* (2019), 1:110, 129–30.

336   **Barr's conclusion was that:** William Barr letter to U.S. Congress, Mar. 24, 2019.

336   **But this ignores:** U.S. Department of Justice, *Report on the Investigation into Russian Interference in the 2016 Presidential Election* (2019), 1:51–65.

336   **He noted that:** William Barr letter to U.S. Congress, Mar. 24, 2019.

337   **Eventually, when our report:** Testimony of William P. Barr, Attorney General, *Hearing on the Department of Justice's Investigation of Russian Interference with the 2016 Presidential Election,* May 1, 2019.

339   **concluded there was no evidence:** Neil A. Lewis, "Whitewater Inquiry Ends; A Lack of Evidence Is Cited in Case Involving Clintons," *The New York Times,* Sept. 21, 2000.

342   **Moreover, the Department's general policy:** U.S. Department of Justice, Justice Manual § 9-27.760 (2018), https://www.justice.gov/jm/jm-9-27000 -principles-federal-prosecution.

342   **Currently, only the attorney general:** 28 C.F.R. § 600.1.

■ INDEX

ABOUT THE AUTHOR

ANDREW WEISSMANN teaches at New York University School of Law, is a legal analyst for NBC and MSNBC, and is a partner at Jenner & Block. Previously, he served as a lead prosecutor in Robert Mueller's Special Counsel's Office and as chief of the Fraud Section in the Department of Justice. From 2011 to 2013, Weissmann served as the general counsel for the FBI. He also directed the Enron Task Force, which prosecuted executives involved in Enron's collapse. As a federal prosecutor for fifteen years in the Eastern District of New York, Weissmann prosecuted bosses of the Colombo, Gambino, and Genovese crime families. He holds degrees from Columbia Law School and Princeton University and attended the University of Geneva on a Fulbright Fellowship.

■ ABOUT THE TYPE

This book was set in Granjon, a modern recutting of a typeface produced under the direction of George W. Jones (1860–1942), who based Granjon's design upon the letterforms of Claude Garamond (1480–1561). The name was given to the typeface as a tribute to the typographic designer Robert Granjon (1513–89).